MW01008849

H. M. Wright Pub. Inc
2100 3rd Ave. #2601
Seattle, WA 98121

MARY BAKER EDDY

HUMANITY'S DIVINITY

Continuing an Examination of
the First Edition of
SCIENCE AND HEALTH

Helen M. Wright

BY THE SAME AUTHOR:

Mary Baker Eddy: A New Look

Mary Baker Eddy's Church Manual & Church Universal & Triumphant

Mary Baker Eddy: God's Great Scientist, Vol. I

Mary Baker Eddy: God's Great Scientist, Vol. II

Mary Baker Eddy: God's Great Scientist, Vol. III

If Mary Baker Eddy's Manual Were Obeyed

America: Cradle for the Second Coming of the Christ

Mary Baker Eddy Reveals Your Divinity

Mary Baker Eddy, Leader Forever (44 page pamphlet) FREE

Dedicated to my beloved husband, Bill, to my good friend, Elizabeth Zwick, and to the reader in gratitude for all we have accomplished together, and will continue to accomplish in our effort to restore Mary Baker Eddy to her rightful status in world consciousness.

"Our Master said, 'The kingdom of heaven is at hand [it is within your consciousness].' Then God and heaven . . . are present. . . . They are now and here; and a change of human consciousness, from sin to holiness would reveal this wonder of being."—Mary Baker Eddy, *Un.* 37:6.

It's time for us to get acquainted with our real Self, Infinite Good made visible.

ABBREVIATIONS

Abbreviations for titles of Mrs. Eddy's writings are those used in the Concordance to *Miscellaneous Writings and Works Other than Science and Health.*

Her Other Writings are often referred to as Prose Works.

The following four books were compiled by Richard Oakes:

Six Days is the abbreviation for *Mary Baker Eddy's Six Days of Revelation,*

EOF is the abbreviation for *Essays and Other Footprints,*

DCC is the abbreviation for *Divinity Course and General Collectanea,*

Seventh Day is the abbreviation for *Lessons of the Seventh Day.*

S & H or *Science and Health* refers to 1910 ed.

Note: *Readers familiar with Christian Science will discern that the truths herein presented all have their origin in the "hopelessly original" writings of Mary Baker Eddy.*

All Jokes are courtesy the *Reader's Digest.*

CONTENTS

Contents

CHAPTER 8

CHAPTER 9

CHAPTER 10

CHAPTER 11

CHAPTER 16

CHAPTER 17

CHAPTER 18

CHAPTER 19

PART II

CHAPTER 20

CHAPTER 21

CHAPTER 26

DEFENDING THE TRUTH ABOUT OUR LEADER

CHAPTER 27

WHY MRS. EDDY HID HER TRUE IDENTITY
A TIME TO KEEP SILENT

CHAPTER 28

BETRAYED BY HER OWN STUDENTS

CHAPTER 29

"WHO WAS SHE?" – WHO WAS THE WOMAN
AT THE FUNERAL?

PART I

HUMANITY'S
DIVINITY

HUMANITY'S DIVINITY
CONTINUING AN EXAMINATION OF THE FIRST EDITION
OF SCIENCE AND HEALTH

"Mary Baker Eddy appeared on earth in accordance with Bible prophecy. Penetrating deeply beneath material surface–appearances she saw man's basic problem was the illusion of being a material personality encased in a matter body. She realized the whole material creation including man himself must be recognized as only a limited and faulty interpretation of reality rather than reality itself. She saw all human experience is just the externalization of conscious and unconscious thought; that even the crucifixion of the flesh, in the case of Jesus, was but the objectification of a mental struggle, the life and death struggle between Jesus' recognition of Spirit as reality and 'the atheism of matter' (S&H 580:27).

"Her timeless God–inspired words 'bluntly and honestly give the text of Truth' and show mankind how to 'solve the problem of being. . . . The works I have written on Christian Science contain the absolute Truth, and my necessity was to tell it. . . . I was a scribe under orders,' she states. Revealed by God, her writing puts on record divine Mind's revelation, the 'final revelation [which will unfold forever] of the absolute divine Principle of scientific mental healing,' and will lead humanity 'into all truth.' Mrs. Eddy had found the open door from the sepulchre of matter.

"Through her written Word, she has shown the world how to come forth from its tomb—come out of the hypnotism that it is encapsulated in matter, subject to discord and death. Thus she fulfilled Jesus' promise of the 'Comforter,' and his prophecy in Revelation: 'there shall be no more death, neither sorrow nor crying, neither shall there be any more pain.' Through her 'the promises will be fulfilled' (S&H 55:21).

"Mrs. Eddy's exposure of evil as totally unreal, as merely hypnotic suggestion, and her founding of this truth in human consciousness, constituted the watershed of human history. Because of her teaching, humanity today faces a giant leap forward as it understands God's decree: 'I will overturn, overturn, overturn it,' until we see ourselves as God–beings, as individual Mind reflecting upon itself as Mind, Spirit, Soul, Principle, Life, Truth, Love. Because Mrs. Eddy revealed that our foundation is at the top, namely, our foundation is the divine Mind that is Love, mankind now faces the greatest creative restructuring since the beginning of time, as we find man to be the offspring of the highest, not the lowest, qualities of Mind.

"Rising out of the raging surface of change, a new, and extraordinary 'foursquare' civilization looms on the horizon as our reconceptualization opens up undreamed of vistas of man's power and dominion transforming the universe into a home of marvelous light." (From my book, *Mary Baker Eddy: A New Look, Advertisement*).

This present book, the fifth in a series exploring Mary Baker Eddy's first edition of Science and Health *which unveiled the Woman prophesied in the Bible,* is concerned with the First Edition's *FIFTH CHAPTER*, entitled *"PRAYER AND ATONEMENT."*

"Prayer and Atonement" is a very special chapter, central to Mary Baker Eddy's revelation. It is also unique in that it is the only section of the original book which she carried forward without substantial revision.

As has been brought out in my previous four books on the first edition of Science and Health, Mrs. Eddy's first statement of the God–given message that came to her in 1866 was **MOMENTOUS**. It is very different from the editions that followed, with the exception of the next thirteen editions. Then a change came. The first edition was based directly on her 1866 great revelation and on her nine years of demonstration, teaching and practicing. It pours forth its God–revealed truth without reservation. In its pages the unveiled revelation, clear and powerful, sounds as a trumpet blast to awaken sleeping human consciousness to our true identity as one with Infinite Good.

But many people in 1875 were not ready for such a forthright summons. It was misinterpreted and rejected. She herself was denounced by pulpit, press, and faithless students. Realizing most people needed to be slowly prodded awake, Mary Baker Eddy restated her revelation in softer terms. Translating divine inspiration into arguments more familiar to her readers, *she brought God's womanhood down to them.* Through the following 418 editions she muted the clarion call. Finally in 1910 she said she had taken this truth and "hidden it, and hidden it, and hidden it, and if I hide it any more they will never find it."

But not Chapter V, *"PRAYER AND ATONEMENT"*—its truth was never hidden! Mary Baker Eddy retained this portion almost word for word, changing it only to make it more prominent. In later editions "PRAYER" became the first chapter. This chapter teaches us true prayer is not rattling at the gate, begging God for something; rather it is acknowledging that the kingdom of God is within our consciousness and is the answer to any problem that would hold us in a prison of fear. Education and prayer is not teaching something to ignorance, it is bringing to light the intelligence that is omnipresent. This allows us to cease crucifying ourselves on the cross of self–deception. We *crown ourselves* when we realize the truth about ourselves, that "All consciousness is Mind," and Mind is God. What is appearing to us has to be God, since "God is All." Jesus and Mrs. Eddy—God's two witnesses, God's two Wayshowers—were true representatives of the individualized Mind (*Mis.* 101:31), because they embraced the universe within their own consciousness.

Our prayer must be: Open my eyes to see the wonders of Infinite Good's kingdom within me—the omnipresence of intelligence that is Love. Once we know our own consciousness is God, then "one with God is a majority," just as being one with 2x2=4 is a majority; and we, like Jesus, can speak with authority, knowing we are consciousness and not body. To discover that there is no power other than our own Mind, our consciousness, is to make our at–one–ment with *all* power. We not only have all power, we actually *are* all power for "God is *individual* Mind (*Mis.* 101:31), as well as universal, *since It is all.*

In the first edition ATONEMENT is discussed together with Prayer. In later editions "ATONEMENT AND EUCHARIST" became the second chapter. "At–one–ment" is an exact Science. To be understood it must be demonstrated individually. We can never demonstrate the Principle of being until we make our at–one–ment with it. An insight into the unity—the at–one–ment—that exists between God and man is the most profound knowledge that can come to the human consciousness.

Here we might ask, "How do I know that Mind is conscious of Itself as me? I am conscious of myself; I am aware that I exist. With what other Mind could I be aware of my existence? My consciousness of myself as existing is Infinite Good being conscious of Itself as existing as me.

We have no place in the At–one–ment unless we understand the real "I" of us is God, as Mrs. Eddy states on page 588:9 of our textbook. "On this statement that 'I' is God and not man, was built the church of Christ" (first ed. p. 210). We must find Principle as our own Mind which expresses itself as what is called man. "Man is not God, and God is not man"—Cause is not effect, and effect is not Cause, but they remain one. A correct view enables us to overcome the world, materiality, since this world is only as material as our belief of it.

Mrs. Eddy's primary commitment was to the sharing of a vision of ultimate reality. As Jesus called Lazarus to come forth from the tomb, so the writings of Mary Baker Eddy call the world to come forth from its tomb, and find that what we are so diligently striving to become, we have forever been and shall forever be. True prayer and at–one–ment means living Mary Baker Eddy's great discovery. It means bursting from the tomb and following our Leader in her teaching that evil is unreal and *that our own right Mind is the only power,* forever in at–one–ment with reality, the infinite good called God. This simple, profound message rings through every edition of Science and Health, too clear to need translating, and too important to be hidden away.

Since Chapter V of the first edition has come down to us so little changed, most readers will already be thoroughly familiar with the words of this chapter. Therefore the author does not think it necessary to take PRAYER AND ATONEMENT apart and examine it phrase by phrase. Instead, the emphasis in this book will be on what is unfolding in *all* of Mrs. Eddy's writings regarding true prayer and at–one–ment.

Since Mrs. Eddy in *Miscellany* p. 136:3 has alerted us that "Atonement and Eucharist" is *her* life story[1] as well as the story of Jesus, we will look in depth at Mary Baker Eddy herself and her fulfillment of prophecy. We will look at her significance, as "the woman" prophesied in Scripture who was unveiled in the first edition of Science and Health; the woman that "shall compass a man [compass Christ Jesus' teaching]" (Jer. 31:22).

It is important to remind ourselves here that **"woman does not mean a person, but refers to conditions of thought, or the revelation of Truth,** as Mrs. Eddy taught. Woman or Christ or Love may be expressed in multitudinous ways as what we call person, but is not *confined* to that person; otherwise when that person dies Woman or Christ or Love would be obliterated. There must be a sharp distinction between the world's sense of a mortal Mrs. Eddy (a being confined to 1821–1910) and the everpresent Revelator of Science with whom Mrs. Eddy is identified, just as there must be a distinction between the human Jesus and the Christ he demonstrated. We shall see how Mrs. Eddy's consciousness represents the motherhood of God, at one with the consciousness of Christ Jesus which represents the fatherhood of God, as in the statement: "The Lamb's

---

[1]"At this period my demonstration of Christian Science cannot be fully understood, theoretically; therefore it is best explained by its fruits, and by the life of our Lord as depicted in the chapter Atonement and Eucharist . . ."

wife presents the unity of male and female as no longer two wedded individuals, but as two individual natures in one. . . ." (S&H 577:4). (Lamb symbolized Love).

Jesus prophesied the coming of the "Comforter," and at the end of "Atonement and Eucharist" Mrs. Eddy says, "This Comforter I understand to be Divine Science." Jesus revealed to St. John, on the Isle of Patmos, that the "Comforter," the Christ, would come in the form of "a little book" brought by a "mighty angel," meaning the spiritual consciousness of Mary Baker Eddy who represented the God–crowned woman. He prophesied that this woman, the woman of the Apocalypse, would bring forth the "man child"—the full and final revelation of God, teaching us our true divine Christ–identity, the kingdom of God within our own consciousness.

Jesus, understanding the oneness of being, said, "Heaven and earth shall pass away, but *my words shall not pass away"* (Matt. 24:35). As century followed century, his words have been heard with awe and reverence, but the vast Science that lay behind his sacred words and deeds remained to be discovered by "God's messenger" to this age. Fulfillment of prophecy can take the fullness of time. Isaiah's prophecy of the Virgin Mary, and of Jesus, came to pass seven hundred years after it was given. Jesus' prophecy of the Comforter, and his revelation to St. John, came to pass nearly two thousand years later. Then the "little book" Jesus spoke of to St. John, the Revelator, was written by a "scribe under orders" whom "God had been graciously preparing . . . during many years for the reception of this *FINAL* revelation of the absolute divine Principle of scientific mental healing [that should come at "the time of the end" (Dan. 12:4, 9)]," and that will unfold forever.

Mrs. Eddy assures us, "God ["the Mind of Man"] wrote the textbook" which teaches that "in divine revelation, material and corporeal selfhood disappear, and the spiritual idea [true identity, the reflection of Truth, or Christ] is understood." (*Mis.* 311:26; S&H 107:3; S&H 561:20).

This has come to pass in **our time**. Mrs. Eddy was made the Wayshower. (See *DCC p. 23.*) "There is too much looking backward two thousand years," she said. "They will find there is a Way here in Concord as well as in Palestine" (MBE *Recollections. p. 81).* Mrs. Eddy is **NOW**. She said (*My.* 318:31), "I do not find my authority for Christian Science in history, but in revelation. If there had never existed such a person as the Galilean Prophet, it would make no difference to me. I should still know that God's spiritual ideal is the only real man in His image and likeness."

In her spiritual evolution, Mrs. Eddy's entire process was to get the spiritual revelation first. When she had that, she searched the Bible for confirmation. Notice that the first edition of *Christ and Christmas* had no Glossary; but the second edition shows scriptural texts as the basis or proof.

Because "woman compasses man," Mrs. Eddy's revelation was entirely independent of anything written, said, or done by Jesus or anyone else, although she grounded it on the Bible, saying, "The Scriptures are very sacred. . . . Christian Science . . . breathes through the sacred pages the spiritual sense of life, substance, and intelligence" (S&H 547:23).

How fortunate we are, and "privileged in having the untranslated revelations of Christian Science." Now it is up to us to live it, knowing that Infinite Good exists as you and me. There is only God. There is not God and something called a mortal. As we learn to read the textbook with the same Mind that wrote the textbook, the healing ministry of Christian Science will be restored. Why? Because as we study and *learn* the truth, this truth will become fact to us just as 2x2=4 is a fact that we can focus on at any time, anywhere. Then we can say, "I am the light of the world," and there is no boundary for the "light" that I AM. You are never separated from your true consciousness which is Mind, God. (See *Un.* 24:12.) Learning what we already *ARE* brings heaven to earth, wiping out the false belief in a little personal "I."

Because, as mentioned, most readers are familiar with Prayer and Atonement, this book will not be so much a commentary on the fifth chapter of the first edition, as an impassioned plea for us, as Christian Scientists, to get our act together and start practicing on a deeper level. Can we do less? The torch has been passed from Mrs. Eddy to us. She looked forward to advancing thought to carry this torch of liberty. She pleaded: "Judge not the future advancement of Christian Science by the steps already taken . . . Let the Word have free course and be glorified. The people clamor to leave cradle and swaddling clothes."

Helen Wright, Autumn, 1994

CHAPTER I

PRAYER LIFTS US OUT OF THE SHADOW OF DEATH

A NEW DAY CALLS

⌐Great horizons stretch before us. For untold ages we have mistakenly lived in a narrow valley. Now, the very cliffs that walled us in are becoming ladders leading to higher ground. With the coming of Christian Science to the world, mankind is being lifted out of the hypnotism imposed by the false viewpoint of the physical senses, lifted out of the mendacious beliefs which have held us in fear, superstition, and ignorance of our oneness with the infinite good we name God—resurrected from belief in organic life. The words (Ps.46:10) *"Be still, and know that I am God,"* resonate within us; if "God is One and All," how can you and I, in reality, be anything but the infinite good we call God?

The rays of spiritual, eternal Truth are breaking through the mist of material ignorance revealing to each one that, indeed, "the kingdom of God is within you." With this dawning, we discover I AM the eternal and fill all space; I am infinite and wholly unconfined. Nothing can now hold back the tide of change that is on its way, ushering in the day when Mind (God) will be the Messiah and "mind will no longer grovel at the feet of matter" (Mary Baker Eddy, *The Christian Science Journal*, Vol. 1). We will know "I Am that I AM" —I am the infinite good we call God, since God is all. "The Lord he is God; there is none else beside him" (Deut. 4:35).

THE CHAPTER "PRAYER" CALLS FOR REFORMATION

Prayer and Atonement, the fifth chapter in the first edition of Science and Health, opens us to our true being. Students of Christian Science have found that Mrs. Eddy's chapter on Prayer is of such searching character that no one who really studies it and abides with it can remain unreformed, untransformed. He cannot stay where its message found him. These pages tell us: that for which we earnestly pray is already an established fact within our own individual consciousness since Infinite Good is the reality and substance of our true individual consciousness.

The 70 pages of this wonderful first edition chapter, "Prayer and Atonement," boldly, unreservedly tell us of our at-one-ment with the infinite good called God. They tell us that Infinite Good or God, our Mind, includes its manifestation, man, and that what is called "man, or image," is our likeness. We should stand in awe before these divine facts. But these 70 pages call for reformation; Mrs. Eddy knew the cross was necessary to obtain the crown. In the business world today the buzzword is "restructuring"—often a euphemism for sad layoffs—but in this chapter restructuring means "laying off the old man with his deeds" and recognizing our present divinity, our Christhood, our oneness with God.

Let's look at a few of the first edition's vital statements on "Prayer":

Page 294: "If we are sensibly with our body we are not Soul, Life, Love and Truth and therefore not in the harmony of being and oneness with the Father [not aware that Infinite Good, our true mind and consciousness, is living its Life as us—not aware that our understanding of Christian Science is God working as us]." Page 287 tells us in effect, "If we are not grateful for Life, Truth, and Love [which constitute our being, and which she has just told us we are] . . . we are insincere."

Page 289: "We cannot reach heaven, the harmony of Life [which is living Its Life as you and me] except we *understand* the Principle of harmonious being that alone destroys personal sense [hypnotism and error]."

Page 291: "It is the practice and *understanding* of our God-being that gains the ear and right hand of omnipotence."

Page 293: "The power of Life, Love and Truth [which you are] will destroy sin, sickness, and death, and enlarge the capacities of man [your reflection], revealing [your] God-given dominion."

Page 294: "After a momentary cessation in the belief and dream of Life in matter, whereby Life, that is God, unfolds itself, comes the understanding and consciousness of dominion over the body that casts out error and heals the sick." Why? Because we have found out that we never had a matter body. The appearance of a matter body was induced by hypnotism, the Adam dream.

Page 303: "The belief that Life originates with the sexes, is strongest in the most material natures; whereas the understanding of the spiritual origin of man cometh only to the pure in heart."

PRAYER IS THE CELESTIAL STAIRWAY

PRAYER is the celestial stairway of Christian Science by which we climb out of the "valley of the shadow of death." As explained in this first edition chapter, "Prayer and Atonement," it is akin to Jacob's Ladder.

In Prayer, the thought-angels ascend and lift hope to at-one-ment with Infinite Good.

The first edition's Chapter V begins on page 283, asking: "Does prayer bring us nearer the divine source of all being and blessedness?"

Yes, the chapter answers, but it is the prayer of works and not just words. Prayer, Mrs. Eddy writes, is the habitual struggle to be always good, the habitual desire to know and do the will of God. It is the yearning in secret and striving for the accomplishment of all we ask. As in mathematics, God, our divine Principle, only works as we work. Habitual goodness is praying without ceasing, in which motives are made manifest by the blessings we bestow. (See S&H p. 4:12). The chapter emphasizes that our progress depends entirely on our own efforts. Without fervent desire and striving, nothing happens. And Love must be the foundation of all action. **Love is Christian Science. The kingdom within us is Love, and is waiting for us to express it.**

A loving attitude, purity, sincerity, self-surrender, are the steps that lead higher. "Desire, expressed in daily watchfulness and assimilation to the divine character, moulds and fashions us in [Infinite Good's] image." Prayer does not change God. It changes us. Being a Christian Scientist involves an inner transformation in order to become a transparency for the divine. The requirement that 'the human' be scientifically translated is the insistent theme of her earthly mission. Over and over we are taught that ours "is the kingdom, and the power and the glory"—the dominion and "sovereign power" (*Pul.* 3:7). The key word is *understanding*.

We find the kingdom of heaven within our consciousness when selfless Love fills our heart, when there is a compelling urge to help others, relieve their suffering, point out the way that will bring them happiness. This is the Principle, Love, within us pressing us toward God-directed purposes. "Have a cell less in the brain, and a fiber more in the heart," our Leader counseled. Her foremost concern was that her Christ-teachings be actually lived.

CHRISTIAN SCIENCE REDEEMS US TO OUR DIVINITY

For thousands of years mankind has been turning to God <u>FOR</u> something—to *GET* something. There is no such God—there is no God that can give us something, any more than the principle of mathematics can give us something. Understanding alone gives us all. Christian Science redeems humanity to its divinity—its true identity. Jesus made it clear that we already have received that for which we are asking. Prayer is knowing that our real consciousness is the Infinite Good, called God. If we did not have consciousness we would not have God.

In the first advent, Jesus exemplified and showed the humanity of divinity. In the second advent Mary Baker Eddy showed and demonstrated the divinity of humanity, brought to light by Science or God's (your own Mind's) Self-knowledge. Thus Christian Science redeems humanity to its divinity, its divine identity.

Mrs. Eddy tells us repeatedly that Infinite Good does not have to be achieved, it is not to be attained—if it had to be attained it would be something outside the kingdom of God within our consciousness. Everything has already been created and is already ours. It only has to be *realized*. Through study and practice we gain the change of viewpoint that alone is necessary. When we turn to God as "out there," we set up a sense of separation that prevents demonstration. The real turning to God is turning to the Truth, and the Truth is "I and the Father [Mind] are one." This is true and is reality, but as long as we are hypnotized to believe there is a selfhood apart from God, "most footprints on the sands of time have been, and will be, left by workshoes." However, to him that hath ears to hear, let him not stuff them with cotton.

From the beginning of time the Adam dream or hypnotism has held us in its cruel clutch, making us believe matter is real. How do Mary Baker Eddy's writings show us the way of escape from the diabolical mental grasp it seems to have on all humanity?

The key is to become aware of our true identity as divine. Then we can no longer be pilloried by the false belief that we live in a matter body. This awareness that nothing can hurt us because we don't have a matter body, is heaven here. Realizing we are God-being, constituted of bodiless bliss, gives us the courage to stand up to error and vehemently refuse to accept mortal mind's (hypnotism's) suggestions, which are always a ticket to nowhere. "The body, or matter, has never yet informed man of disease; a **belief carries the telegram to the body, and the body manifests only the sufferings of mortal mind**," said Mrs. Eddy.

"Our work," she said, "is not to change God's work, for that is finished and perfect. Neither is it to make error nothing, for it is that already; our work is to stand (apparently) in the midst of it, unmoved, knowing its nothingness" (DCC 186).

INSANITY HEALED

As in countless other instances, Mrs. Eddy proved this in a healing recorded by Clara Shannon. One day when Mrs. Eddy had finished her lesson in the September 1888 Primary Class, she asked Clara to wait after the other members had gone.

As Mrs. Eddy was standing in the Classroom at 571 Columbus Avenue, a gentleman called to see her, bringing with him his sister, who greatly needed healing.

Mrs. Eddy met them at the door of the room, and asked him to wait downstairs, while she talked to his sister. The belief was insanity, and the sister looked terrified. Our Leader told me her delusion was that a serpent was coiled around her body and was crushing her.

I stood in amazement, watching Mrs. Eddy's face as she turned and looked at the woman who fell on the floor screaming, "It's crushing me, it's killing me."

Our Leader looked upwards as if she had seen the face of an angel in her communion with God [her own Mind].

In a moment she said to the woman, "Has it gone?" There was no reply. Mrs. Eddy repeated her question but the woman still seemed not to hear. Then Mrs. Eddy spoke with authority and asked, "Has it gone?" The poor woman looked up and her whole body was shaken and quivering as she answered, "Yes!"

I watched the changes that came over the woman's face from fear to peace and joy. And, Oh! the love that was expressed in our Leader's face as she looked down on her, stretched out both arms and lifted her up, saying, "Get up, darling."

Then our dear Teacher took that needy one's head on her shoulder and patted her face, as she lovingly talked the truth to her. Mrs. Eddy then went out of the room and talked to the brother. . . .

During the evening [Mrs. Eddy] turned to me and said, "You saw what happened to that lady today? Well! She will never be insane in this world again." And she has not been.

Mrs. Eddy in this healing was beholding in Science the perfect woman who appeared to her where an insane woman appeared to others, and Mrs. Eddy's *CORRECT VIEW* healed the woman. Since the real man is made in the image of Life, Truth, and Love there is no place for error to operate in. Error comes to us for recognition and we give it the only power it has. Mrs. Eddy refused to give it power, identity, or recognition. She bore witness not to the lie, but to the woman's true identity, which is Soul, the source of all freedom, happiness, and changeless spiritual integrity.

Mrs. Eddy lived the Love that reflects all bliss. "The divinity of the

Christ was made manifest in the humanity of Jesus," while the divinity of humanity was made manifest in the Love reflected by Mary Baker Eddy.

"JUST THE FACTS, MA'AM. JUST THE FACTS"

Long ago there was a television series, in which the "investigator" always demanded: "Just the facts, ma'am. Just the facts." This is what we should hold to: "Just the facts." The spiritual *facts* entertained and realized bring about the boundless "rhythmic round of unfolding bliss." The facts put us in possession of the unburdened sense of Truth and Love that "wipes the tears of time away."

When we stand for the spiritual facts about health, wholeness, harmony, and the argument comes that there is no evidence of health and wholeness, our work must be to stand more firmly in the spiritual facts, the Truth. We must cast out fear, mustering the courage to think and feel: "None of these [errors] move me." We don't have to make ourselves perfect; we already are; we don't have to make error unreal, it already is.

Prayer, as Mrs. Eddy interprets it, is just the revelation of the omnipresence of present perfection, the revelation of the perfection that has always existed. When you experience a healing in Christian Science, it is a revelation of Truth; it proves that heaven is here. Reality must be here or you could not experience it. All that we misinterpret as material substance and form is here, but not as matter. It exists as eternal good, immutable Spirit. We only need to *learn to view it correctly,* as Mrs. Eddy taught a student whom she thanked profusely for a service. The student said, "Don't thank me; thank God." With a smile, Mrs. Eddy replied, "I didn't know there was any difference."

PRAYER MEANS REALIZING OUR PRESENT PERFECTION

It is important to base our practice upon our *present completeness and perfection* rather than thinking we are advancing toward it. Emphatically Mrs. Eddy states: "Unless you fully perceive that you *are* [now] the child of God, hence perfect, you have no Principle to demonstrate, and no rule for its demonstration" (*My.* 242:8). I am complete **now. I lack nothing.**

We must *become aware* of our present perfection. Unless we realize this perfection is already an established fact, we have no Principle to demonstrate. In math we know the multiplication table is already established. Nothing can touch it. Our work is to learn it and abide by the principle and rule, as Mrs. Eddy demonstrated.

CHAPTER 2

PRAYER REQUIRES A CHANGE OF CONSCIOUSNESS

MRS. EDDY IN THE SPIRIT ON THE LORD'S DAY

"It was a fall morning, November 11, 1890. Mrs. Eddy was in the habit of taking a morning stroll before beginning the day's work, and one of Laura Sargent's duties was to have her wraps in readiness. But on this particular morning Mrs. Eddy was on the **mount of revelation** even as St. John on the Isle of Patmos. In after years Laura stated that she had never before been in such a heavenly atmosphere, but at the time it was more than she could bear and she was impelled to leave the room.

"Our Leader was in the Spirit on the Lord's day," which can be glimpsed from what she wrote; but what Laura saw of this spiritual experience is as follows: As Laura entered the room Mrs. Eddy was so absorbed in her writing that she did not notice Laura standing with her wraps. As several minutes went by Laura began to sense the import of the occasion. The heavenly atmosphere was beyond anything she had ever experienced. She could not bear it long; she could not remain in this heavenly light. In like circumstances Peter, James, and John "fell on their face and were sore afraid;" but Laura left the room.

"When she returned a little later Mrs. Eddy was *still* writing, *totally oblivious* to anything else. Laura slipped her overshoes onto her feet, then left the room again, not returning until summoned by the bell a full hour or more later.

"The Leader had Laura summon Calvin Frye and other members of the household, and when they were all seated she said to them, I want to read you what God has given me this morning." Then she read them the closing pages for her chapter, "The Apocalypse," which are relatively unchanged from the fiftieth to her last edition in 1910 [which begin:] "The Revelator had not yet passed the transitional stage in human experience called death, but he already saw a new heaven and a new earth. . . ." (See S&H 572:19 - 577:31.)

"Her beautiful face was radiant as she finished reading and announced that she was ready for her morning walk. "Will you bring my overshoes?" she said to Laura. When told they were already on her feet, she asked in surprise, "When did you do that?"

"On the twelfth of November Mrs. Eddy wrote to Mrs. Nixon: 'My *last words for you all in the Book* Science and Health, were written yesterday and sent off." (*The Founding, p. 59, Doris Grekel*).

"ALL IS A CONSTRUCTION OF CONSCIOUSNESS"

The quote above appeared in the 50th edition, in 1891, matter was no longer on its way out, it was no longer disappearing "under the microscope of Spirit" (S&H 264:21); **IT WAS FINISHED!** Mrs. Eddy had seen "that the heavens and the earth to one human consciousness, that consciousness **which God bestows** are spiritual, while to another, the **unillumined human** mind, the vision is material. This shows unmistakably that what the human mind terms matter and spirit indicates **states and stages of** consciousness" (S&H 573:11). "But, say you, is a stone spiritual? To erring material sense, No! but to unerring spiritual sense it is a small manifestation of Mind, a type of spiritual substance." Viewed with material sense it is material; viewed from spiritual sense it is spiritual. Forty years later, circa 1930, the world's foremost physicists were saying the same thing—that "All is a construction of consciousness."

"I saw a new heaven and a new earth for the first heaven and the first earth **were passed away. . . .**" Here she makes it clear that the new heaven and new earth are not **overcoming** the first heaven and the first [material] earth; they were **PASSED AWAY!** She and the Revelator were "on our plane of existence while yet beholding what the eye cannot see— that which is **invisible to uninspired thought.** This testimony of Holy Writ sustains the fact in Science, that the heavens and the earth to one human consciousness, that **consciousness which God bestows,** are spiritual, while to another, the **unillumined human** mind, the vision is material. This shows unmistakably that what the human mind terms matter and spirit indicates **states and stages of consciousness.**

"St. John's corporeal sense of the heaven and the earth had vanished, and in place of this **false** sense was the **spiritual** sense, the **subjective** state, by which he could see the new heaven and new earth, which involve the spiritual idea and consciousness of reality. This is Scriptural authority for concluding that such a recognition of being is, and has been, possible to men in this present state of existence,—that **we can become conscious, here and now, of a cessation of death, sorrow, and pain. . . .** When you read this, remember Jesus' words, 'The kingdom of God is within you.' This spiritual consciousness is therefore a present possibility [as Mrs. Eddy proved when she wrote these pages]" (S&H 573:3). A right spiritual consciousness brings the cessation of error, of "death, sorrow, and pain."

We must understand that the material universe is our false point of view. Animal magnetism is within us. It is our false consciousness, hypnotism—it is when we are not seeing that all is Infinite Good, "infinite Mind, and its infinite manifestation." What other way is there to handle what looks like animal magnetism?

Mrs. Eddy then shows us that "It exalted him [John, and her too] till [they] became conscious of the spiritual facts of being and the 'New Jerusalem, coming down from God out of heaven,'—the spiritual outpouring of bliss and glory. . . . The beauty of this text is that the **sum total of human misery . . . has full compensation in the law of Love. . . .** " (S&H 574:11).

It is all **a matter of CONSCIOUSNESS.** Exultantly, rapturously, Mrs. Eddy exclaims, "Think of this, dear reader, for it will lift the sackcloth from your eyes. . . . The very circumstance, which your suffering sense deems wrathful and afflictive, Love can make an angel entertained unawares." It is just a matter of consciousness whether you accept the material point of view with its "sum total of human misery," or the spiritual. Mrs. Eddy, like Jesus, perceived that the material sense of "this world" is an illusion. She saw how Jesus overcame "this world" through understanding that it was merely an illusion induced by universal hypnotism. In quiet ecstacy she urges: "Arise from your false consciousness into the true sense of Love, and behold the Lamb's wife [the Lamb is the spiritual idea of Love which we all must wed]."

Nothing can hinder us from having the divine standpoint Mrs. Eddy had that November morning in 1890. If you are the wife of the spiritual idea of Love you are wedded to Love, where all sense of error "has passed away." Mrs. Eddy saw that Love is our very essence, and our only "enemy is ourself" (in belief). (See *Mis.* 10:30). "When the mist shall melt away, you will see clearly the glory of the heaven of love within your own hearts" she confided.

TAKE THE STANDPOINT OF PRESENT PERFECTION

"God is all true consciousness" (*Un.* 4:12). Mrs. Eddy taught her students to practice from the standpoint of their present perfection—their oneness with Infinite Good—from the standpoint that each one now is the Christ, Truth, in reality.

Jesus taught: *"Whatsoever thou shalt bind on earth shall be bound in heaven."* Why does Mrs. Eddy say, "The misinterpretation of such passages has retarded the progress of Christianity and the spiritualization of the race"? (*No.* 32:1). *Not understanding that all progress is made on this side of the grave,* theology teaches that one can finish his work elsewhere or in another way than Jesus did. But Jesus declared he was "the way." He finished his work on earth by *overcoming* death and the grave. After his resurrection his consciousness advanced beyond the concept of a matter form, and the physical Jesus disappeared. "Jesus demonstrated the divine Principle of Christian Science when he presented his *material* body absolved from death and the grave" (*My.* 218:13).

Jesus and Mrs. Eddy proved their divinity right here on earth, and taught others to do so. When you add and subtract, multiply and divide, you demonstrate the principle of mathematics; just so, exercising your spiritual power demonstrates your spiritual Principle. "Ye shall know the truth" about yourself here and now. Know that you are Mind, God, that expresses Itself as the spiritual man. You are both God, AND God **made manifest.** There is only *ONE.* God's own undivided Selfhood is individualized as you and me. (*See Mis.* 101:31). You are not a matter man. There is only infinite Mind, your Mind, manifesting itself as its divine nature.

Because the kingdom within your consciousness is the Principle, you, in reality, are Self-governed. "Now is the accepted time" to know that you, as you presently appear, are, in reality immutably perfect because this *is the real universe peopled with spiritual beings: "The universe of Spirit is peopled with spiritual beings. . . . infinite space is peopled with [Infinite Good's] ideas"* (*S&H* 264:32 & 503:15).

"THE CARDINAL POINT OF DIFFERENCE"

"The cardinal point of difference" in Mrs. Eddy's teaching is "that by **knowing the unreality of disease, sin, and death,** you demonstrate the allness of [Infinite Good]" (*Un.* 9:27)—where "infinite space is peopled with God's ideas." This difference separates her **system** from all others, since her **system** is built wholly on the infinite good called God. Her revelation of the unreality of evil was a scientific fact of such incredible magnitude that after nearly a century and a half even devoted students have scarcely realized the impact it will have. "Scarcely a moity . . . is yet assimilated **spiritually** by [even] the most faithful seekers" (*Mis.* 317:14).

The question is often asked, "Why didn't Mrs. Eddy explain her "system"—the system based on (1) the seven synonyms for God, (2) that operate through the Word, Christ, Christianity and Science; (3) on the four levels: Christian Science, absolute Christian Science, divine Science, and Science itself?

Mrs. Eddy answers: "The Science of physical harmony, as now presented to the people in divine light, is radical enough to promote as forcible collisions of thought as the age has strength to bear" (*Un.* 6:10). When Hanna saw the system in her textbook, Mrs. Eddy said, "Yes, it is all there, and will be explained at the right time." She urged, "'Wait patiently on the Lord;' and in less than another fifty years His name will be magnified in the apprehension of this new subject." Exactly as Mrs. Eddy foresaw, in fifty years, Mr. Doorly of London began to see the "system" in the textbook.

"Not one millionth part of what I have discovered has as yet been seen," Mrs. Eddy wrote—just as we have not seen one millionth part of mathematics. Her Science is **infinite!** And it will unfold forever.

The secret of Christian Science is that infinite good (God), our own Mind, "the creative Principle, Life, Truth, and Love, expresses itself as what looks like you and me and the universe.

There are not two worlds. The world we now live in is the spiritual world. Let's not turn away from it; we need only view it rightly. We need to see through the "mist that watered the whole face of the ground" veiling the true man from our sight. But the real man—and the Infinite Good he coexists with—has never been touched any more than clouds touch the sun, or 2X2=5 touches the principle of arithmetic. Jesus didn't go anywhere when he ascended. He just realized his *spiritual perfection* here and now.

SEEING THE REAL MAN—JESUS AND ZACCHAEUS

The real man is the individual you are looking at or dealing with, when seen correctly. Note how Jesus' correct view changed Zacchaeus. Luke tells us that Zacchaeus was "the chief among the publicans, and he was rich." He was the tax collector. Zacchaeus no doubt had already longed for a better life and no doubt felt Jesus could help him. He wanted very much to see Jesus as he passed through Jericho, but could not because of the great crowds that had gathered, for Zacchaeus was "short of stature." So "he ran ahead and climbed up into a sycamore tree to see Jesus, for he was to pass that way." (Luke 19:1-9).

When Jesus saw Zacchaeus he astonished the crowd—who regarded Zacchaeus as a sinner—by saying: "Zacchaeus, come down; today I must abide at thy house." Jesus had seen this man's good point. Zacchaeus loved to entertain; and Zacchaeus "received him joyfully"! "And Zacchaeus stood [and before the whole crowd confessed his sin]; and said unto the Lord: Behold, Lord, the half of my goods I give to the poor; and if I have taken any thing from any man by false accusation, I restore him fourfold." So completely had Jesus' example of "beholding in Science the real man," impressed Zacchaeus that he too wanted to be a mirror in which the likeness of God could be reflected.

How different was Zacchaeus from the rich young ruler (Luke 18:18-24) who wanted the heavenly treasure but was not willing to make the sacrifice. To give up his earthly treasure *that he could see*, for the heavenly treasure that *could not be seen*, was too great a risk. Jesus loved the rich young man dearly, but said unto him: "One thing thou lackest." Zacchaeus had what the rich young Pharisee lacked. To Zacchaeus, Jesus said, "This day is salvation come to this house [to the consciousness of Zacchaeus]."

PRAYER HELPS US LEARN WHAT OUR TRUE "I" IS

We all need to get the right view, to learn to see as Jesus and Mrs. Eddy did, as Infinite Good sees. A friend told me that she was seeing a relative as crotchety and quarrelsome. Suddenly she said to herself: "I have got to *WANT* to see her that way, and if I *WANTED* as much to see her as she really is, as Infinite Good sees her, it would be a blessing." Changing her view did prove a blessing to my friend. It transformed her relationship. Later this relative bequeathed my friend quite a sum of money with which she was able to do much good in the world.

We will all be blessed when we learn to see beyond the person. In her definition of "I" or "Ego" (S&H 588:9) Mrs. Eddy teaches that the "I" within you is God; and your I, being omnipresent consciousness, goes wherever you go.

From the second edition in 1878 to the fifth edition of 1908, a quotation had appeared on the flyleaf of Science and Health concerning the wrong sense of "I." The April Journal, 1889, informs us this "I, I, I, I itself I," was a rebuke to personal sense. Mrs. Eddy's entire mission was the dissolving of the personal "I" so that the I that is God becomes our only "I," conforming to her definition of "I" (S&H 588:9).

Prayer can lift us beyond the personal sense of I. In the fifth edition of 1908, Mrs. Eddy replaced the quotation with her own prayer of thanksgiving:

> Oh! Thou has heard my prayer;
> And I am blest!
> This is Thy high behest:-
> Thou here and EVERYWHERE.

In such an exultation and affirmation personal sense is vanquished. With rapture unspeakable she had glimpsed a higher realm. Compare this prayer to Jesus' prayer at the tomb of Lazarus, "Father, I thank thee that thou hast heard me. And I know that Thou hearest me always" (John 11:41, 42). Only this type of prayer could have raised Lazarus after he had lain in the grave four days. But even then, Jesus said that he prayed only for the sake of others, "that they may believe that thou has sent me." As Mrs. Eddy tells us:

The mental act of thanksgiving carries one far beyond the realm of doubt into that atmosphere of Truth and faith where all things are possible. Go not back to [the old way of] asking but continue to give thanks that you have received.

THE KEY TO PRAYER

Prayer is not asking for things necessary to human happiness. It is *ADMITTING* that each one's individuality is God (see *Mis.* 101:31; *Un.* 48:8); and the one infinite Mind—which is our Mind when our mind is free from hypnotic suggestion—has supplied man with everything needed. When Jesus said, "Ask, and it shall be given you," he no doubt realized that people in his time were too materially minded to be told they were spiritual beings in full possession of the kingdom of heaven here and now.

The key to prayer lies in: "What things soever ye desire, when ye pray, believe that ye receive them, and ye shall have them" (Mark 11:24)—believe that ye are a spiritual being in heaven and have received all good here on earth. That which you realize within the *invisible* will be *visibly* expressed on earth. All the spiritual energy we need is within ourselves. It is our understanding of this that constitutes "at-one-ment." *This is what Jesus meant when he said, "I came forth from the Father and am come into the world, again I leave the world, and go to the Father."*

"Going to the Father" means going to the kingdom of heaven within our own consciousness. It is not a ticket to nowhere. Mrs. Eddy teaches us that heaven and earth are one entity. Earth, viewed rightly, is the visible evidence of heaven, the phenomenon of heaven. That which constitutes divine consciousness or heaven is manifested as the visible earth, which is simply the outward, revealed expression or effect of thought. Once we discover our health and joy in right thinking we look nowhere else for it.

Going to the Father or heaven means going to our right Mind, God, that which is "incorporeal, divine, supreme, infinite Mind, Spirit, Soul, Principle, Life, Truth, Love" (S&H 465:9). We are one with these seven synonyms for Infinite Good, since, as Mrs. Eddy tells us, "the spiritual monitor *understood* is coincidence of the divine with the human, the acme of Christian Science" (*Mis.* 100:20). Through prayer we find all within ourself.

WE ARE ONE WITH GOD

We begin to climb the celestial stairway of prayer when we open the door of understanding and begin discovering our true identity. On page 285 of the first edition's fifth chapter, "Prayer and Atonement," Mrs. Eddy tells us that *"God is not a separate Wisdom from the Wisdom we possess."* (Note capital W.) In the final edition she gives the above-mentioned seven synonymous terms to define God in what is called the **Word** order, which shows the relationship between Truth and error, or how does Truth destroy error. This **Word** order is the law of divine creativity or the law of divine illumination because we start to learn what *we are* when we learn *what God is:*

(1) As one with Mind, God, we are wisdom, intelligence, power. "Man has no Mind but God. . . ." (S&H 319:20). "All is under the control of the one Mind, even God" (S&H 544:16), assuring right action, direction, and control.

(2) As one with Spirit, meaning good, we learn Mind is the **ONLY,** and is our true substance. Man individually and collectively is one with Spirit or there would be no understanding, no reflection, which are qualities of Spirit. When we read Science and Health that's the Word, the letter; when we live the Truth it is presenting, that's the Spirit, the Christ.

(3) As one with Soul, spiritual understanding, we learn our changeless identity as one with Infinite Good; Soul is the core of oneness, like 2x2=4 it never changes, insuring safety, balance, bliss, beauty, constancy.

(4) Mind, Spirit, and Soul as ONE then constitute our Principle, our true foundation. A Principle has to operate. It operates as Life, expressing itself as true consciousness, Truth, which is Love. Oneness with Principle is at-one-ment with infinite harmony where all ideas are operating in perfect relationship in the divine system of being.

(5) As one with Life, existence or isness, our divine individuality is indivisible from immortality, from infinite inspiration and constant progression—never needing to be created, "never born and never dying."

(6) We are one with Truth, because through Mind, Spirit, Soul, as our Principle, which expresses itself as Life, we find our consciousness to be

Truth. We know our consciousness is the same consciousness as God or we would not be conscious of this truth. We are one with health and wholeness, one with the perfect standard of Truth, dominion. Consciousness never goes anywhere. It is forever omnipresent. That is why there is no death.

(7) As one with Love, we learn we are, in reality, the omnipresence of present perfection, embraced by and encompassing all that Love embraces in its plan, purpose, peace, and glory.

These seven synonyms are what is called the Word of God, showing us how we approach and partake of our true being. (2) Christ shows us the ever-successful operation of this Word. (3) Christianity shows us how these seven are unlimited and operate unconditionally. (4) In Science we learn these seven synonyms for God have always existed in our consciousness as the present fact and never need to be created.

The mortal dies daily and is reborn into the perfection of Being as it reflects the fourfold calculus of Word, Christ, Christianity and Science. As the denominational aspect of Christian Science fades, its vital role as the Science of all sciences is being discerned. The world is clamoring for a change of consciousness. Since "spiritual evolution alone is worthy the exercise of divine power" (S&H 135:9), "material history [will draw] to a close" as thought grasps the divine fact that Christian Science is the universe—meaning "all turned into One—turned into Love, your own divine consciousness that never "loses sight of loveliness." As we begin to spiritually understand this, life will become terrific!

In the first edition Mrs. Eddy states: "At present we know not what we are, but hereafter, we shall be found Love, Life and Truth, because we understand them" (p. 77).

"I AM GOD AND NOT MAN, THE HOLY ONE IN THE MIDST OF THEE" —Hosea 11:9.

GOD AND MAN ARE ONE

Defining God (S&H 465) Mrs. Eddy states (in part): "Principle and its idea IS ONE, and THIS ONE IS GOD." Then she says this One, (the one you are, that I am, in reality) has a reflection. You, the real divine you (not the "you" that is hypnotized to believe the evidence of the physical senses) have the Mind of God which expresses itself: "Man is the expression of [Infinite Good's] being" (S&H 470:23). But God and man remain one; who would think of trying to separate the shadow from that which is the reason for the shadow? "Matter held as shadow," Mrs. Eddy said, "is the idea of God, but matter held as substance is a belief and error."

"This Mind [your Mind] is the divine Principle, Love." It "alone possesses all faculties . . . it is the all-hearing and all-knowing Mind . . . and creates [its] own likeness in ideas" (S&H 488:23; 7:24; 257:12). "God, the Mind of man," *must* express itself. Science and Health makes it clear that the "I" or Ego of you and me and of all, is Mind, God, and not body. It demands that we see the individual mentality as God rather than man. Hosea's tremendous teaching: *"I am God and not man, the Holy One in the midst of thee,"* along with similar statements by Isaiah and other prophets, are a glorious premise on which to establish the understanding that awakens us from the Adam dream we now are so sound asleep in. The Second Coming of the Christ is awakening us—Christ is the activity of Truth in our consciousness.

In Mrs. Eddy's definition of man she tells us, "man is the reflection of God, Mind [your Mind]. . . that which has no separate mind from God [your Mind]." We must begin to evaluate what we see for what is really there when seen spiritually, knowing that Infinite Good's will, operating in or as heaven, is coincidentally operating on earth. What is called "man" is the activity of God, infinite Mind, our own right Mind, which includes a spiritual mental sense of body. This is a fact, like 2x2=4, while the materiality we think we see arises only "from the false testimony of material sense" (S&H 301:25). Science reverses this false testimony, and we realize it is entirely our own fabrication, like seeing a flat earth.

When we, as metaphysicians, think of body correctly, we see it not as material but as conscious thought forms or divine ideas of infinite Mind. Then we find that pain, stiffness, weakness, inflammation, swelling, weariness, are hypnotic suggestion only—"the false testimony of false material sense, of mind in matter" (S&H 108:25)—which can be cast out of our thought. As we rid ourselves of these material suggestions, we attain at-one-ment, in which the body of Infinite Good's creating is found perfect and whole. Nothing can touch us once we find, through Mary Baker Eddy's writings, that we don't have a matter body. All that hinders our realization of present perfection is the reality we make of matter—which makes the body appear as matter.

We must have faith that what Mrs. Eddy teaches—the truths we have been repeating—*are true NOW*. This is the prayer that is the celestial stairway. When Mrs. Eddy writes that "the Christian Scientist is alone with his own being and with the reality of things,"(*Mess. '01.* 20:8) she is telling us that we are *both* the one Mind or divine consciousness, the

Principle, *and* its manifestation; we are *both* Mind *and* the vehicle, the channel, the instrument, the body, the form, the outlet, for its expression.

The divine Mind and divine body or expression constitute individual being. God is appearing as you. God, divine Mind, is manifest as individual being. (See *Mis.* 101:31). Seen correctly, everyone you are aware of is God appearing as individual being. There is only ONE. There is not God and man. Principle—which Mrs. Eddy makes clear (in the first edition) that you **are—always remains *one*** with its expression, namely, that "Principle and its idea is one." The outer is just the expression of the inner consciousness, and there will come a time when, through study and practice, we will climb out of the narrow valley that, through false beliefs, walls us in. Then, having found there is no matter body to experience inharmony, pain, death, sorrow, we will rapturously experience what we already are and have always been.

Remember Mrs. Eddy had seen that your perfection is a *PRESENT FACT, here and now,* and not a goal to be attained. She had seen that "the heavens and earth to one human consciousness, that consciousness which God [your right Mind] bestows, are spiritual, while to another, the unillumined human mind, the vision is material [showing] unmistakably that what the human mind terms matter and spirit indicates states and stages of consciousness" (S&H 573:6).

In the following incident, Joe's experience highlights the contortions of the human mind, and that all is a matter of viewpoint.

Joe had ordered an expensive suit for a banquet, and the tailor finished the alterations just in time. But as Joe left the shop, a sudden rainstorm doused the jacket and shrank one of the sleeves.

"We can't do anything about it today," the tailor told Joe when he returned to the shop. "Just stretch the sleeve over your hand, and no one will notice."

With his arm contorted, Joe left the shop, and again was doused by rain. This time, a pant leg shrank.

"I can't take care of that now!" exclaimed the tailor. "Pull the bottom of the pants over your heel, and nobody will notice."

His body twisted, Joe again left the shop. Two women were passing by.

"That poor man!" said one. "I wonder what's wrong with him?"

"I don't know," said the other. "But he sure is wearing a nice suit!"

CHAPTER 3

AT-ONE-MENT—FINDING OURSELVES ONE WITH GOD

LEARNING OUR TRUE IDENTITY

Material sense disappears as the truth is learned. We learn the Science of our being in the same way we learn the science of mathematics. As the principle of mathematics includes all calculations and withholds nothing from us, so it is with Love, the divine Principle of our being. It also withholds nothing from us.

Nothing is more certain than that the time is coming when all shall recognize and obey their divine Principle as the only governor. But we can never live our at-one-ment until we cease looking upon God as other than an ever-active Principle to be utilized in every walk of life.

We must realize God is not a separate being but is the omnipresent power of Good. We must learn to work out our own salvation. While a principle is always available to us, it can't come and work out a problem for us. We must come into oneness with the Principle of our being step by step, just as we come into oneness with the principle of mathematics. Through study and practice we gradually learn to drop the mortal seeming until reality breaks through to us. Then our prayer becomes like that of Jesus and Mary Baker Eddy, "deep and conscientious protests of Truth" (S&H 12:13) and we find that "the whole earth is transformed by Truth" (S&H:191:14) through the transformation of the material by its fading out in the realization of the spiritual. In this at-one-ment with Infinite Good we find heaven here—heaven on earth.

In metaphysics (as in mathematics) we cannot begin the discovery of our true identity by believing a mistake. The basic error, Mrs. Eddy tells us, is the Adam dream—the belief of mortal birth which causes the body to appear as matter. This is the veil that hides our true identity. We must remember we are not human beings; but "to be immortal, we must forsake the mortal sense of things, turn from the lie of false belief to Truth, and gather the facts of being from the divine Mind" (S&H 370:2). The "I" or Ego of you and me and all is Mind and not body. Only because the delusion that we live in a matter body **seems so real** do we think we are separated from God, infinite good.

We should know better. We should realize our oneness with God. But all down history's slippery slope we have (through ignorance) clung to the cruel belief that God is a Being separate from man instead of realizing our oneness with Infinite Good.

WHAT IS ATONEMENT?

What is Mrs. Eddy teaching when she states: "The *atonement of Christ* reconciles man to God" (S&H 18:13)? This "atonement" can only be accomplished as we *BE and DO* the divinity we actually are, as we cultivate thinking of ourselves as divine. The main emphasis in Atonement is laying down the mortal. Jesus and Mary Baker Eddy are our examples. They show us how to "rise above" the mortal sense of things. They knew everything was within themselves, that their very being was God. Each one's individuality is God. (See Un. 48:8). Error must be healed subjectively within ourselves. Today with the Second Coming we are realizing the individual mentality is "God, the Mind of man," since "man has no Mind but God " (S&H 470:17; & 319:20). When we discover the absolute truth about *Infinite Good and man as one, we will have unified them in our own consciousness.* This frees us from the false sense of a separate self. (See S&H 522:10.) In this knowing that God is our Mind we find the oneness of being taking place.

"I HAVE SET BEFORE THEE AN OPEN DOOR" (Rev. 3:8)

"The description of man as purely physical, or as both material and spiritual," Mrs. Eddy writes, "is the Pandora Box, from which all ills have gone forth" (S&H 170:28).

Through the centuries, as the prophets struggled to free themselves and mankind from this Pandora Box—this encompassing veil—they were promised that in the fullness of time a Virgin would appear whose pure thought would be able to conceive the Christ idea. Centuries passed. Then the prophecy regarding the Virgin was fulfilled; Jesus came and dictated to St. John in the Book of Revelation:

"These things saith he that is holy, he that is true, he that hath the key of David. . . . Behold, I have set before thee an open door" (Rev. 3:7 & 8).

What is this open door? On page 499 of Science and Health Mrs. Eddy indicates that the "open door" is Christian Science with its "Key to the Scriptures."

Its essence is the great Truth which Jesus demonstrated and which Mary Baker Eddy's Science explains: "I and my Father [consciousness or Mind] are one." Note that Jesus put the "I" in that statement before the Fatherhood of God. The "I" here stands for Jesus' womanhood, Love, the Christ. This is the basis of the "miracles" Jesus performed. Jesus was never without his womanhood element. It is the "treasure hid in a field. . . the pearl of great price" by which, through Mary Baker Eddy's teaching, our own real self is recognized as the power and glory, "the only I or Us."

WE ARE SOUL, LIFE, TRUTH AND LOVE

On page 294 of "Prayer and Atonement" in the first edition, Mrs. Eddy tells us that if we regard "omnipotence as a person whose ear we would gain, WE ARE NOT SOUL, LIFE, LOVE AND TRUTH, and therefore not in the harmony of being and oneness with the Father [Mind] in demonstration of the Spirit and power." Here she instructs us our *real* being is "Soul, Life, Love and Truth." She had already informed us in the first edition that "we are Principle," and numerous times that "we are Spirit and Soul," telling us that "we shall be Life, Truth, and Love when we understand them." These are synonyms for God. When we actually reach this understanding, practically, might not looking back on today's world seem like the age of the dinosaurs?

Since our Mind is God, something greater than the human personality is keeping and guiding us in our search to gain the spiritual Life. Thus, when there seems to be no answer to our problems and difficulties, we still know we cannot abandon this spiritual search. Where would I go? "Whither shall I go from thy spirit? or whither shall I flee from thy presence?" (Psalm 139:7).

We know God, infinite good, has to be omnipresent since it is our real Mind, therefore we find that in reality we are right back in the kingdom of heaven; and to acknowledge the presence of Infinite Good right where we are (be it heaven or hell, sickness or health), is a form of prayer. Prayer is knowing that "beneath thy feet life's pearl is cast," and "the place whereon thou standest is holy ground"—we are walking in "the promised land."

True prayer is the acknowledgment that Infinite Good is omniscient, and since Infinite Good is the all-knowing, the little "i" doesn't have to know anything. From the beginning of time we have been hypnotized to think we are this little "i" when all the while we are the "I" that is Mind, that is omniscient, possessing "sovereign power to think and act rightly" (*Pul.* 3:7). Breaking through this hypnotism calls for the listening attitude of prayer. We must look to "the all-hearing and all-knowing Intelligence, to whom every want of man is understood, and by whom it will be supplied" (First ed. 286).

OUR TRUE HERITAGE

Through Mrs. Eddy's teaching of this great truth we are learning that our true heritage is to recognize Infinite Good is our true consciousness here and now. "When the mist shall melt away you will see clearly the glory of peace and the heaven of Love within your own heart." And because the Self of man is God, we have the dominion. Reasoning from Principle we find we already are, always have been, healed, and are joyously triumphant.

When problems come we have the power through right thought and ideas to meet and destroy the claims of evil since evil is just a mistake. The nothingness of evil becomes apparent once we have consciously overcome it, but it can't be clear if we just overlook it. We must proceed with courage, knowing, since God is our Mind, we have dominion over all contingencies.

Looking out from Mind, Jesus could heal Lazarus. He knew Lazarus was one with him in Infinite Good, and that there was no such thing as a dead man. Christian Science redeems us from the false belief that we are separated from Infinite Good. All good is now. There will never be any more good than there is present right here and now. In our consciousness—the kingdom of God within us—dwells boundless energy and ability to conquer and achieve.

"The ultimate of the entire teaching of Christian Science is to restore to man his consciousness of the divine Mind as his only Mind." —Gilbert Carpenter, Sr.

The kingdom of God within our consciousness, our divine Mind, is the endless source of ideas taking form as a boundless supply of happiness, beauty, and intelligence necessary to meet every need. So we don't add to what we already are; rather through prayer, study and practice—as we recognize error as merely hypnotism—*we restore, through realization, more and more what we already are.*

A Christian Science friend told me that one day a rumpled sort of fellow looking like a refugee came into her office. She soon realized his gap-tooth aw-shucks demeanor was hiding a very angry man. He had just been demoted. My friend's convincing explanation that dropping his emotional baggage—his hypnotized state of lingering hurt, anger—and replacing them with the truth of Infinite Good's omnipresence, was all that was needed. Within a week he found a position comparable to the one he had left.

Why don't we demonstrate our infinite capacity more? Why do we "judge by appearances" and fail to recognize error? Because we are deceived by the five physical senses with which hypnotism "pains, fetters, and befools" us (*Mis.* 173:24). The material senses have been "liars from the beginning." But they are only like a bad dream. No matter how scary the dream is, when we wake up we *know* it wasn't real, don't we? It will be the same when we—through the teaching of the Second Coming of the Christ—have learned what we really are as one with God. In reality, we are the consciousness that is God. When through spiritual education we find our body is just ideas, what can touch us? As Mind individualized (see *Mis.* 101:31) we create the world we walk through, and Infinite Good is found to be the source and condition of all we experience or are aware of.

"We possess our own body, and make it harmonious or discordant according to the images that thought reflects upon it. The emancipation of our bodies from sickness will follow the mind's freedom from sin. . . . *the feeblest mind, enlightened and spiritualized, can free its body from disease as well as sin*" (*Peo.* 10:21; & 11:5). It's up to us. We have "sovereign power."

"The foundation of mortal discord is a false sense of man's origin," nothing more. Since "God, the Mind of man, never sins. . . . [and] man has no Mind but God" (S&H 470:17 & 319;20), "when the Science of being is universally understood, every man will be his own physician, and Truth will be the universal panacea" (S&H 144:27).

ARE WE MAN? "CERTAINLY NOT!"—MARY BAKER EDDY

"We are Spirit, Soul, and not body," Mrs. Eddy tells us in the first edition of Science and Health. Over and over she makes it clear "man" is idea, our Mind's idea. "All that is good is Spirit [Infinite Good]; and the idea of [Infinite Good] is real, and nothing else is real." To really understand this is not easy. "Then what am I and what is man?" we again ask.

In *Science of Man* when the question was asked, "Are we man?" Mrs. Eddy answered emphatically: "*Certainly not. You are Spirit, Soul, Principle.*" She had seen that *the mental element is God. She could think. Only consciousness can think. An idea can't think. The reflection in the mirror can't think.)* "*All consciousness is Mind [God],*" Mrs. Eddy declares. *What have you ever known that did not require and involve your thinking?* All that is ever needed to find heaven at hand is a change of thinking. When our thinking is right our experience will be right. Our whole objective universe is a creation of our thinking; it will be as good as our thinking is good.

Mrs. Eddy realized students get into trouble when they think they are "man" rather than Mind that reflects itself as what is called "man" or idea. "All is infinite Mind [your Mind] and its infinite manifestation. . . . man is the reflection of Mind [**your Mind**]" (S&H 468:10 & 475:17). Mind, your Mind, that is God is the only Mind, and its highest idea of Itself is called "man." Thus we are not man other than that our expression is called "man"; man is the expression of our Mind. Our substance is Spirit. Our identity is Soul. Our Principle (Mind, Spirit, Soul) expresses Itself as Life, Truth, and Love. There is only one answer to the question, What is God, and the answer is, I AM. I already am perfect, spiritual, I already am in heaven. "The Christian Scientist is alone with his own being and with the reality of things" (*Mess. '01.* 20:8).

God is the Mind, the Life—the Infinite Good that is living Its Life as you and me. Explaining this truth Jesus said: "He that seeth me seeth Him that sent me." This is our foundation. All flows out from this God consciousness that I am. There is **only** the ONE. Our consciousness is the substance of all form and activity. The divine Mind reveals Itself to Itself. The prophets had become aware, if only for brief intervals, of the Life, the revelation of Love, that Jesus would later acknowledge as the Principle of his being. **Abraham's fidelity to Truth caused the mist of false creation to recede sufficiently so he could see Melchizedek, the man of God's creating, "having neither beginning of days nor end of life."** Enoch and Elijah so entirely lost the disguise of material existence that they disappeared from mortal sight. (See Gen. 5:24; and II Kings 2:14.)

Error—hypnotism, false education—tells us we are mortal man instead of coexistent with Love. As we take the "little book" and "eat it up," we lay down the mortal, and gain heaven, harmony.

"The time cometh," Mrs. Eddy writes, "when the spiritual origin of man, the divine Science which ushered Jesus into human presence, will be understood and demonstrated [by each one of us]" (S&H 325:26. See also 476:4; 543:8; 557:19.)

Mrs. Eddy defines "I" as "Divine Principle; Spirit; Soul; incorporeal, unerring, immortal and eternal Mind" (S&H 588:9). This is what you and I are. What is called "man" is the manifestation of this I that I am, of this Mind that is God and is the Mind of you and me, or individual spiritual consciousness. It could not be otherwise when God's law is: "I AM

ALL." Man is Truth incarnate, that which is *visibly* being all the ideas of Mind—your Mind. God "*is* my individuality and my Life" (*Un.* 48:8). Man is a calculus of ideas; man is the *knowing* that divine Mind is being. But again we ask: Is the "I" that I Am, the same thing as "man"?

THE TERM "MAN" USED IN DIFFERENT WAYS. "I" AM NOT "MAN"

Mrs. Eddy uses the term "man" in different ways, as do also the Bible writers. Sometimes she uses the term "man" to signify the body, and sometimes to signify individuals or mankind, sometimes as the image and likeness of God, *but never does Mrs. Eddy say that you are man* or that you are image. As we have seen, when asked: "Are we man?" Mrs. Eddy answered unequivocally: **"Certainly not!"** You are the thinker. An image can't think. In statements like: "Keep in mind the verity of being,—that man is the image and likeness of God" (S&H 414:26), she is not saying that you are man.

GREAT TRUTHS FROM THE FIRST EDITION

The great truth that you and God [infinite good] are one was openly set forth in the first edition, but because of "the fixedness of mortal illusion, and the human hatred of Truth" Mrs. Eddy gradually, in later editions, hid this trenchant truth. Some of my most spiritually-minded readers still seem concerned regarding Mrs. Eddy's statement to her early classes, "You, my students, are God." To make her teaching on this point clear, I will quote a few statements found in her first edition of Science and Health. These are the scientific facts, before which we should stand in awe. But, of course, they are only attainable through **growth in Christian character** as her many references to "grow" and "growth" teach us:

"The belief that God has a separate being leads to multitudinous errors. . . . Man is the phenomenon of Soul. . . The final understanding that we are Spirit, must come, . . . At present we know not what we are, but hereafter [through study and growth] we shall be found Love, Life, and Truth, because we understand them. . . . Jesus, who demonstrated this over eighteen centuries ago, said, 'The works I do ye shall do'" (p. 77).

"You the Soul [a synonym for God] and circumference of being (for the body is but the idea of 'you'), [you] are a law to your members, and the law-giver that makes your body discordant or harmonious" (159). "All formations are shadows of being, and **WE** their Soul and substance" (280). "Soul [your true identity] exists not without man and the universe, for it is never separated from the complex and reflex shadow of itself" (233). "Science reveals to spiritual understanding the body without sensation, and man the reflex shadow of Soul; and Soul embracing all the faculties of being, having no lack of emotion, speech, sight or sound" (355).

"The ultimatum of being corroborates the statement that man is shadow and not substance; [you are not in the shadow of yourself]; we are daily hastening to this proof" (57). "I" signifies God and not man" (*ibid.* 149 and S&H 588:9). "Jesus . . . understood he was Spirit" . . . We learn we are Spirit alone . . . . That we are Spirit, and Spirit is God, is undeniably true" (p. 155). "We are Spirit that mixes not with matter (156). "We are Spirit, Soul" (169). Jesus "built his church on: . . . I am God, and man is the offspring of Soul and not sense. . . . I is God and not man" (210).

"To be out of an imaginary existence in matter, and realize one's self not body, but Soul [God], is the ultimatum of being" (218). "All should recognize themselves Soul [a synonym for God]" (222). "When realizing Life as it is, namely, Soul . . . we shall expand into Truth and self-completeness that embraces all things, and need communion with nothing more than itself to find them all" (223). "Joint heirs with God are the partakers of an inheritance where there is no division of estate, we are Spirit, . . ." (225). "This is not losing man nor robbing God, but finding yourself more blessed AS PRINCIPLE than person, AS GOD THAN MAN, AS SOUL THAN SENSE" (227).

There are many more such statements setting forth the great revelation that came to her in 1866, namely, that you are Spirit, Soul, Principle, Life, Truth, Love, reflecting Itself as "man."

WHAT AM I?

Man, your Mind's expression, is *image*. "The compound idea named man is unintelligent; it is a lifeless image and reflection of Principle or Soul" (First ed. 222). Of itself, an image has no power. What can your image in the mirror do? You can think, can't you? Can your image in the mirror think? Can it be conscious? Can your image in the mirror plan something? Can it reason? Can it say: "All power is given unto me?" Does it have intelligence? Jesus never thought of himself as different from those around him. Then note what he did! Could an image do that ?

Neither Jesus nor Mrs. Eddy taught that we are an image. When Jesus weighed in with his important statement: "He that hath seen me hath seen the Father," he was saying that all right mentality is the Father or primal Cause. "I and my Father are one," means that your right mentality and "the Father [Mind]" are one in quality. It doesn't mean they are the same in quantity—"All are but parts of one stupendous whole [but the whole is in every part as we learn from holography]" (My. 269:12; also S&H 361:15). He saw that his Mind and God were one intelligence. "Father and son" means Cause and effect, or "Principle and idea is one"—at-one-ment.

We must see that it is not man conscious of God; man doesn't include God. Rather it is Mind, God, our Mind, conscious of itself, of its ideas. What have we ever known that did not require consciousness, Mind, thinking?

Each individual consciousness (being Mind, God) is the consciousness of God AND MAN, Principle AND IDEA. Isn't it always God, our right Mind, that does the unfolding, the knowing, the thinking? This is "the spirit . . . the flesh profiteth nothing." Everything is a creation of our thinking and will be as good as our thinking is good; therefore "Hold thought steadfastly to the enduring, the good, and the true."

In the first edition Mrs. Eddy tells us explicitly, emphatically, that we are Principle. She repeats that we are Spirit, we are Soul, and that while at present we know not fully what we are, yet it is certain that *"WE SHALL BE Love, Life and Truth, when we understand them"* then all the barriers that error huffs and puffs about will have passed away.

If we want to understand Love, Life, and Truth, we must dig a little deeper into Mrs. Eddy's teachings. We don't progress in math by devoting thought only to the part we like. Neither do we progress in Science by clinging only to what is easiest for us.

OUR MIND, OUR CONSCIOUSNESS, OUR LIFE, IS GOD!

Mary Baker Eddy writes "All consciousness is Mind; and Mind is God,—an infinite, and not a finite consciousness. This consciousness is reflected in individual consciousness, or man, whose source is infinite Mind" (*Un.* 24:12). She is talking about our Mind, the Mind we now have when it is free of hypnotic suggestion. Even humanly, can you think about your mind? No. You think as it; and Mrs. Eddy's discovery is based on the fact that we think, or know, as Mind itself. Mind, your Mind, is the source, she says. It is its own cause and effect. This must be so since "the Christian Scientist is alone with his own being and with the reality of things" (*Mess. '01.* 20:8). The grandeur and vastness of her discovery that "all consciousness is Mind and Mind is God" is that she saw our actual Mind, *here and now,* as the Mind or "I" that is God. This reveals our present capacity to discern and experience generic man, meaning all that reflects God, infinite good.

From our textbook we learn, "Principle and its idea is one, . . . and this one is God." If God is All and in all, then what are we? Remember, "God wrote the textbook," said Mrs. Eddy. "I only held the pen;" and God's "scribe under orders" (*Mis.* 311:26) tells us three times that "God is the only Life" (S&H 289:4; 324:14; & 472:1). This "Life is Mind, the creator reflected in His creations" (S&H 331:5). You and I know we express life. If God is the *only* Life, then the life we now have has to be God, doesn't it? And that Life which is Mind in all its radiance has no age. It is coursing through us endlessly, faultlessly, agelessly. Like the six-year old, who was asked, "How old are you?" we can all get rid of this albatross, by answering as he did, "I don't have any old."

We only need to awaken out of the deep sleep, mesmerism, of the Adam dream to see that actually we live in eternity **now**, even though error would have us believe in a past, present, and future. But there is only the one Life, Infinite Good. Can we see the infinite power in Mrs. Eddy's statement, "God is my Life"? You, the expression of Life triumphant, are sound and whole, full of the vigor of Life. No longer will there be the three ages: youth, middle age, and "You're looking good!" Real living is determined by the degree of our loving. Man lives to express Good. The quality of our thought determines the quality of our life.

The real mind we now have is the one Mind with no connection to the bogus tyranny of death-dealing mortal mind, alias hypnotism, that would lash and pillory us with fear and disease. The Soul (identity) we now have is the one Soul, the one identity that assures us we are "the temple of the living God!"—a fact we are all destined to learn as we overcome the material sense of things. Our Leader exultantly reminds us, "God is the sum total of the universe. Then what and where are sin, sickness and death?"

THERE IS NO MATERIAL MAN

Consider carefully: God is Mind, God is Spirit. God is not matter. If God is the sum total of the universe, what and where is man? In reality, there is no material man. The truth of what we call "man" is spiritual qualities that express Infinite Good, qualities that express Mind, Spirit, Soul, Principle, Life, Truth, Love. This is what Jesus proved on the mount of transfiguration and in the ascension.

"Spirit is not materially tangible, [but] . . . the individuality of man is no less tangible because it is spiritual and because his life is not at the mercy of matter." The true thoughts that make up our *spiritual* body "are perfectly real and tangible to spiritual consciousness" (S&H 78:21; 317:16; & 269;17).

In the final edition, Mrs. Eddy refers to: "Man, as the offspring of God, as the idea of Spirit . . ." (S&H 29:30), and tells us "Man is the expression of God's being [of your being]" (S&H 470:23); "that which has no separate Mind from God; . . . that which possesses no life, intelligence, nor creative power of his own, but reflects spiritually all that belongs to his Maker" (S&H 475:19).

IDEAS THE GREAT MOVING FORCE

To say that man is the idea of Spirit with no separate Mind from God is not to belittle man. Ideas are the great moving force of history. "Man is idea . . . the compound idea of God including all right ideas. . . . Ideas are emanations of the divine Mind [your Mind] . . . . [While ideas can't think or reason, they] are tangible and real to immortal consciousness" (S&H 475:13; 88:10; 279:11). What a power and transformation will be ours when we understand this! Ideas, thoughts, have no boundaries, no limits. In their transcendent dimensionless realm dwells all you will ever need for joy, happiness, spiritual being.

Ideas are the moving force of the world, and "man," we are told, "is the idea[1], the image of Love" (S&H 475:13). What is called man is the reflection of your real Mind, your real Mind's expression. There is nothing greater or more powerful than the power of thought, the Word made flesh, made practical.

Man is not a point in space or a limited thing. He is the intelligence, the knowing of Mind—Mind's knowing—the knowing with the Mind you now already, in reality, have. Therefore man lives through all space, just as 2x2=4 exists through all space.

Your perfection is omnipresent, and the *personal sense* of yourself is just hypnotism. There is no more connection between your real self, which is always at hand, and the personal sense of yourself, than there is between 2x2=4 and 2x2=5. We are each individual creative intelligence, letting the light of truth, our Christ understanding, dissipate the false personal sense.

THE ONLY REAL "I" IS GOD

The entire being is found in Mind. Everytime you use "I" correctly, it

---

[1]Our ignorance of the power of ideas reminds me of the traffic cop who pulled over a speeding motorist and asked, "Do you have an ID?" The motorist replied, "About what?"

means God. Man is the evidence of the Principle which Mrs. Eddy in the first edition tells us plainly you are, saying: "Jesus regarded himself Principle." She urges us to do the same, saying WE WOULD FIND OURSELF "MORE BLESSED AS PRINCIPLE THAN AS PERSON." How can it be otherwise when "the kingdom of God is within you—and your "I" is defined as "Divine Principle; Spirit; Soul; incorporeal, unerring, immortal, and eternal Mind" (S&H 588:9)?

Isn't this what Jesus meant with his (Matt. 13) parables? (1) "The kingdom of heaven is like treasure hidden in a field [in your consciousness]"; (2) "Like leaven which a woman took and hid [in science, theology, and medicine]"; (3) "Like a mustard seed [which grows to infinite KNOWING];" (4) "Like a pearl of great price [when we discover our true consciousness is Love, God]." The parables all tell us that as we awaken from the Adam dream our vision expands, and we discover ourselves. Our at-one-ment with God is impelled by Love.

"Man originates in God," in Mind (your Mind), and it is "God [your Mind that] expresses in man [note "in man," not **for** him but **in** him] the infinite idea forever developing itself, broadening and rising higher and higher from a boundless basis" (S&H 258:13). Note that it is God ("God the Mind of man") that does the expressing. Expression, manifestation, reflection bring out the ideas of Mind and constitute the body of God. It is always God (Mind, your Mind) that does the reflecting. *What I as Spirit and Soul am conscious of, is called man.*

Mrs. Eddy explained that when one stands in front of a mirror, one's "image and likeness" in the mirror isn't something that has to grow up to the original that is standing in front of the mirror. It is spontaneously the full reflection of the original. The real you is all that Mind, Spirit, Soul, Principle, Life, Truth and Love are—all that Infinite Good is—expressed individually, since "Thou art ever with me and all that I have is thine" (Luke 15:31).

THE GLORIOUS TRUTH:
WE ARE SPIRITUAL AND PERFECT HERE AND NOW

The glorious truth is that we don't have to *become* spiritual and perfect, we only have to accept the fact that we are so, here and now. How could we "let Truth uncover and destroy error," (S&H 542:19) if this Truth wasn't our own Mind?—our own right thinking? How could pain "be ruled out by the might of Mind" (*ibid.* 391:11) if this Mind wasn't our Mind here and now? How could we "rise in the strength of Spirit" (*ibid.* 393:12) if we weren't Spirit? How could we "rise to the true consciousness of Life as Love" (*ibid.*391:30) if we were not already this Life that is Love? Through spiritual education "we can, and ultimately shall, so rise as to avail ourselves in every direction of the supremacy of Truth over error" (S&H 406:20).

As we end this chapter and launch into the next, let us remind ourselves of Jesus' glorious instruction, remembering, "Through the magnitude of his <u>human</u> life, he demonstrated the divine Life" (S&H 54:1).

In John 4 we read of the Samaritan woman at the well. She had accepted the prophetic Scripture, and said to Jesus, "I know that Messias cometh, <u>which is called the Christ</u> . . ."

<u>"Jesus saith unto her, I that speak unto thee am he . . ."</u>

Again, (John 9) to the man born blind, Jesus said, "Dost thou believe on the Son of God? He answered and said, Who is he, Lord, that I might believe on him? And Jesus said unto him: **Thou has both seen him, and it is he that talketh with thee."** Jesus was *divinely human.*

When Peter saw the ***coincidence of the human and divine***, Jesus was happy, and quickly answered, "Blessed art thou, Simon Barjona: for flesh and blood hath not revealed it unto thee, but my Father which is in heaven" (Matt. 16, 17).

CHAPTER 4

WE MUST FACE THE TASK BEFORE US
THE POWER IS IN OUR HANDS

In Mrs. Eddy's sermon, *Christian Healing (p. 10:13),* she with divine authority, states emphatically : "God is All, and in all: that finishes the question of a good and a bad side to existence." Then she makes it clear that we are the arbiter of our own fate; we are the attorney for the case, we are the judge:

"If you wish to be happy, argue with yourself on the side of happiness; take the side you wish to carry, and be careful not to talk on both sides, or to argue stronger for sorrow than for joy. You are the attorney for the case, and will win or lose according to your plea."

The Bible admonishes us to watch our thoughts—[see Matt. 24:42-44]—lest they become words and lest, as Science teaches us, they become "matter" in belief. We should notice that matter has **"I AM NOTHING"** stamped on its hindquarters. We are each a sentinel, charged with keeping watch over our thoughts, challenging, arresting, and destroying at once every "enemy" thought, and replacing the material sense of things with the facts of being.

"Know, then, that you possess sovereign power to think and act rightly" (*Pul.* 3:7). We can always replace negative with positive thoughts. If we understood the awesome power of our thoughts we would be better sentinels, carefully guarding our words, remembering that often "silence is golden." The power and the responsibility is in our hands.

If there was something called "God" that was going to work out our salvation, Jesus' example and Mrs. Eddy's life work on our behalf would not have been necessary. They, as God's "two witnesses," came only to show us **HOW** to do our work, not to do it for us. Christian Science teaches that we must look neither ahead, behind, right or left, up or down for salvation. Knowing we are one with God would give us access to power beyond comprehension to "work out our salvation," which lies in learning the truth regarding our *present* divinity. Christian Science comes forth from God to resurrect man from organic life and lift him back into oneness with God which he never left in reality. Salvation must be sought within for it is consciousness rather than circumstances that must be changed. Prayer and Atonement, as Mary Baker Eddy shows us, is the process by which we do this.

THE "CROSS": YOU ARE YOUR OWN PHYSICIAN

There is a cross to be taken up. "If we are not secretly yearning and openly striving for the accomplishment of all we ask, our prayers are 'vain repetitions'" (S&H 13:6).

We must win our way to heaven, making our one ambition a holy desire *to know God in order to know what we are.* In our struggle for victory over "the beast," we must patiently persist even when "on the ropes." We cannot command success, we can only deserve it. In this quest, industry is a better horse to ride than genius, and Mrs. Eddy counseled, "Work, work, work, watch and pray." As we continue to declare the truth concerning everything error is lying about—*knowing* that the declaration of Truth breaks the claim—we make progress spiritward.

Mrs. Eddy makes it clear that there is nothing greater or more powerful than God's thoughts passing to man, and "thought [accepting] the divine infinite calculus." If we realized how powerful our thought is we would never think a negative thought. We hurt no one but ourselves when we indulge bitterness or unforgiving thoughts. Again, we must "be careful of our thoughts; they may become words at any minute."

Be vigilant. "Beloved, believe not every spirit, but try the spirits whether they are of God" warns St. John. (I John 4:1). The beloved disciple is telling you to be alert and ready to clobber those aggressive mental suggestions that are not of Infinite Good. Error with its fancy footwork and mixed signals would exploit a weakness wherever it finds one, and mire us in iniquity, as it vainly pushes "against the current running heavenward." Let's be spiritual Lancelots and grenadiers, crossing swords with every hypnotic suggestion. Tell error bluntly defeat is not an option. Keep this up until success reigns. Then our mind having reached a higher level will not return to its former dimension. "In Christian Science there is . . . never a return to positions outgrown " (S&H 74:29).

INTELLIGENCE NOT AT THE MERCY OF FLESH

Mrs. Eddy urged us: "Discard all your sense of selfhood—all that is involved in the belief of birth, heredity, association, time, decay, death" (Letter to Judge Hanna). Take time each day to know nothing can govern your actions or come to your thought that is not from the divine Mind. Intelligence is always the divine Mind in evidence and is never at the mercy of flesh. (See *Mis.* 181:15). Replace the *material sense* of things with the facts of being.

In the first edition Mrs. Eddy states: "You possess your own body and make it harmonious and immortal, or discordant and mortal. You, the Intelligence, embrace the body in comprehension and completeness; put away, then, the error of belief that matter embraces you in mystery and disease; *'you,'* the Soul and circumference of being, (for the body is but the idea of 'you,') are a law to your members, and the law-giver that makes your body discordant or harmonious, according to the ignorance or understanding, the error or Truth that governs it."

So, when error beckons us to follow in lockstep with it, we should head for the exit, determined to think "holy thoughts and heavenly strain that make men one in Love remain," and so bring these into our experience.

CASTING OUT ERROR THROUGH OUR GOD-BEING

Regarding *"being,"* the first edition states:

"Jesus cast out error . . . through his God-being." (p. 384). "Looking away from sense to Soul . . . we regain the understanding of our God-being" (p. 226); "had we the understanding of our God-being . . . we should have no fear of matter" (p.275); "your God-being . . . destroys all error, sin and death" (p 392); "Jesus held all that he was, God, and wrought from the standpoint of his God-being" (305).

What was possible to Jesus is possible to us, as we gain the understanding of **our** God-being. Didn't Jesus promise: "greater works than these shall he do"? (John 14:12). Your real Mind, being both cause and effect, is intelligence, the only substance. Your expression, manifestation, called man, is the being of all ideas, the evidence of divine Being—your God-being.

Belief in disease is ignorance of reality. It is hypnotism. Once seeing what Mary Baker Eddy discovered about us, we will enter our God-being. Our real Mind knows no more about disease, sorrow or pain than the principle of math knows about all the mistakes made in mathematics. As our thought is filled with divine Science, we are able to nullify medical beliefs in the only place they can be nullified, that is, at the point of our *belief in them.*

THE ULTIMATE OF MRS. EDDY'S TEACHING

We all seem to be a conglomeration of beliefs, both good and bad. As we, through the study of the "Comforter," the Second Coming of the

Christ, begin to exchange these beliefs for right ideas, God's ideas, we put on the "new man"—the *understanding* of the infinite good we call God.

Mrs. Eddy writes:

What a faith-lighted thought is this! that mortals can lay off the "old man," until man is found to be the image of the infinite good named God, and the fullness of the stature of man in Christ appears.

In mortal and material man [which we think we are at the moment], goodness seems in embryo. By suffering for sin, and the gradual fading out of the mortal and material sense of man, thought is developed into an infant Christianity; and feeding at first on the milk of the Word, it drinks in the sweet revealings of a more spiritual Life and Love. These nourish the hungry hope, satisfy more the cravings for immortality, and so comfort, cheer, and bless one, that he saith: In mine infancy, this is enough of heaven to come down to earth. (Mis. 15:22)

The textbook teaches us how to *BE* the revelation. Mrs. Eddy urges us to "rid ourselves of the belief that man is separated from God [from the kingdom of God within our consciousness], and obey only the divine Principle, Life and Love. Here is the great point of departure for all true spiritual growth" (S&H 91:5). "To be out of an imaginary existence in matter, and realize one's self not body but Soul [a synonym for God], is the ultimatum of being" (First ed. p. 218).

PERSISTENCE WINS

We must continue the struggle with unceasing prayer—not the old orthodox, or childhood, prayer, "Now I lay me down to sleep, and pray the Lord my soul to keep,"—but rather "the habitual fervent desire to do the will of [Infinite Good]." We must cling to our oneness with infinite good. This alone helps us in the irresistible conflict between the flesh and the Spirit. Unceasing prayer is knowing our present Christ-expressing selfhood. Training our thought steadfastly in the acknowledgement of God's presence, "judging righteous judgment," is true prayer.

In a certain way Harvey proved that "sincerity and *persistence* alone win the prize."

"How do you account for your longevity?" asked the reporter on Harvey's 110th birthday.

"Well," Harvey replied. "I never smoked. I never drank. I was always in bed and sound asleep by ten o'clock. And I've always walked three miles a day, rain or shine."

"But," said the reporter, "I had an uncle who followed that exact routine and died when he was 62. How come it didn't work for him?"

"All I can say," replied Harvey, "is that he didn't keep it up long enough."

We need to persist in our study.

Persist in study to "show thyself approved unto God, a workman that needeth not to be ashamed, rightly dividing the Word of God," as St. Paul admonishes. This alone awakens us from the hypnotism that veils the Truth. It awakens us from the dream of life in matter to see the great *fact* that Infinite Good is our real and only Life.

True prayer brings to light our "primitive, sinless, spiritual existence. . . . Through the [sore] travail of mortal mind, hope deferred, the perishing pleasure and accumulating pains of sense, [we lose ourselves as matter, and gain a truer sense of real being as Spirit that expresses itself as the spiritual man we have always been in reality]" (*Mis.* 17:27). True prayer—our work and study— awakens us to an awareness of our oneness with God.

THE GREATEST JOB ON EARTH

We are engaged in the greatest job on earth, namely, to become aware of our true selfhood, our Godhood. To accomplish this: (1) we must love and cherish the idea Mind gives us. All ideas are within our own right Mind. Reviewing Mrs. Eddy's definition of God, we learned that Mind, the all-knowing, is characterized by wisdom, revelation, control, basis, origin, power, cause. (2) Spirit shows us how to keep pure what Mind is, to see its glory unclouded by error. It shows us reality, true substance. Spirit is living the Word we have studied. (3) Soul enables us to abide in it, be sincere and persevere in it. Soul, Mrs. Eddy tells us, is spiritual understanding, our true identity. (4) In Principle we see the oneness and impersonality of Mind, Spirit and Soul which constitute our Principle; honesty, consistency, harmony and spiritual power characterize God as Principle. (5) As a result of seeing we are Mind, Spirit, Soul, Principle, our divinity becomes a living attitude. (6) It then becomes Truth to us; it becomes our consciousness. (7) We experience the fulfillment of Love. Heaven, Mrs. Eddy once explained, is finding the answer to a problem. It is a state of consciousness that can be experienced here and now in proportion to our grasp of reality.

These seven steps constitute prayer in action. Practicing them—our God-being—all things become possible to us.

THE PRIMAL SLAVERY

Our Holy Grail is "take the land and occupy it," for Infinite Good "hath made us all kings and priests unto God" (Rev. 1:6; 5:10; & 20:6). The primal slavery is accepting human life as defined by the physical senses. As Christian Scientists we must be vigilant, and not succumb to negative thoughts or let them cast a pall of fear over us. Begin today to see correctly. Unsee the lie about man as a material being. Let us rejoice at the present uncovering of evil; it indicates growth in the right direction, for "evil uncovered is self destroyed" (*Mis.* 210:2; see S&H 96:7).

Mortal mind with its primal slavery sometimes uncovers evil in unique ways as when the hospital patient was worried. "Are you sure it's pneumonia, doctor?" he asked. "I've heard of cases where a doctor treated a patient for pneumonia, and he ended up dying of something else."

"Don't worry," said the doctor. "When I treat a patient for pneumonia, he dies of pneumonia."

As we press ahead with spiritual education aimed at a realization of all Mrs. Eddy has written, we can make the end of the twentieth century an historic turning point for our Cause and for Christian Scientists' healing ability, the lack of which (since the late 1940's) has been the Achilles heel in our movement. But Infinite Good's design will not be thwarted. We can forge ahead with confidence, each saying, "I am the individual appearing of Mind, God," and each knowing that behind all our work is Love's plan to draw all back to Her.

CHAPTER 5

LOVE IS THE FIRST STEP
WE MUST LOVE THE IDEA
MIND GIVES US

"Keep awake by loving more; love the idea of God and you will love God; you can only love God [incorporeal, divine, supreme, infinite Mind, Spirit, Soul, Principle, Life, Truth, Love] as far as you love [Infinite Good's] idea, and love will be EXPRESSED. . . . Love does express itself; it HEALS . . . Prove your love. Love is God and expresses itself" (DCC 9). "Love alone is Life," wrote Mrs. Eddy. All must accomplish Love. It is the only corrective and conquers every discord.

"Love the idea of God," we are instructed. "Man is the idea of God . . . the compound idea including all right ideas." We are told that Love expresses itself, it HEALS, and we are given the assignment: "Prove your love." We can't escape this task. We must love man, and we must express this love through healing. But how is this possible?

Mrs. Eddy taught us that ever-present Love is the very nearest thing to us at all times, and that it is the nature of infinite good (God) to bless us. Why? Because this infinite good or Mind that is our Mind, is Love. Love is our divine Principle. It is what, in reality, we are. We would relax, "let go and let God" if we could just become aware that we are living in Love, NOW. As we have already seen, Love is Christian Science. The kingdom within you is Love and is waiting for you to express it.

"YOU, MY STUDENTS, ARE GOD"—MARY BAKER EDDY

Mrs. Eddy told the pupils in her first class, "You, my students, are God." Why could she tell the class this? Because the divine revelation had shown her there is nothing beside Infinite Good; "that all real being is in God, the divine Mind [your real Mind]; that Life, Truth, and Love [which she tells us we are], are all-powerful and ever-present."

She saw also what the error is that shuts out the true sense of Spirit, of reality. To Laura Lathrop Mrs. Eddy explained, "The body and you are not one. You are not in the body, talking to it, and it cannot talk of itself. [It is delusion. A flesh, blood and bones body is just a hypnotic picture.]

You are spiritual, not material; you are my good, faithful, follower of Christ—the image of [Infinite Good]. Indeed, you are this idea and have no strife with the flesh. You reflect God, and His image is like unto Spirit, not matter. The flesh [being just hypnotic suggestion] is not you. Realize this, and you are master of the situation."

As we have an honest fervent desire to know the truth about ourselves—which is the essence of true prayer—the way will open up to learn it.

Guided step by step in the understanding and demonstration of our true nature, we lovingly follow the example of our Leader, who taught us the one thing needful was learning to love, to love under all circumstances, even when we are tempted oppositely. Love has to be our starting point. Love is the core, the substance, of our true being. Only Love can clear our sight and enable us to see correctly. No one since Jesus ever so exemplified divine Love as did our Leader. Cherishing her example, we will open ourselves to see that man lives by Love, lives for Love, lives in Love, ordained to be conscious only of Love.

Through "prayer and at-one-ment" with God, Mrs. Eddy, like Jesus, "beheld in Science the perfect man, who appeared to [her] where sinning mortal man appears to mortals" (S&H 476:32). She saw clearly because of her Christ-like love. Clear correct seeing is the essence of true prayer. Mrs. Eddy saw man "through the lens of Spirit . . . never severed from Spirit," as she writes in *Miscellany*: "How is man, seen through the lens of Spirit, enlarged, and how counterpoised his origin from dust, and how he presses to his original, never severed from Spirit" (p. 129:15). We should be outraged at what animal magnetism (hypnotism) does to us to make us believe we are "severed from Spirit," and are not one with God.

GOVERNED BY REVELATIONS OF LOVE

Mary Baker Eddy was governed by the revelations that came to her, particularly the revelations of Love—of man's being as Love. James Gilman in his *Recollections of Mary Baker Eddy*, writes that on a certain visit with Mrs. Eddy he said:

"You look like an entirely new personage today." It seemed a droll remark to make, but it was a spontaneous expression. She thought so, for an instant perhaps, and then she began to say that last night she had come to revelations that had exceeded anything she had had before, in which she saw plainly that all things were put under her feet and the Love of God was so manifest, it exceeded anything she could

describe. All things were dissolved in it; all sense of evil, all antagonism; nothing was left but the sea of God's immeasurable Love. I felt
awed and as if a word in response from me would be a sacrilege. (p.
64).

The power of this Love through which Mrs. Eddy was continually
removing ignorance and hypnotism can be learned from her many spontaneous healings. Mrs. Emily Hulin wrote to Mrs. Eddy:

> At the conclusion of your address [in Central Music Hall in
> Chicago in 1888] I noticed a poor woman who had entered the audito-
> rium on crutches, and who was evidently badly crippled, stretch out
> her arms toward you in a beseeching manner. You looked at her with
> eyes full of compassion and love, as it seemed to me, and immediately
> she laid down her crutches and walked out as anyone in a normal con-
> dition would do!
>
> I cannot tell you of the awe that fell on me or the impression I
> received, and I then determined to learn more of this wonderful truth
> at the fountainhead. — The Overwhelming Evidence.

MISS JONES' EXPERIENCE AT PLEASANT VIEW

Elizabeth Earl Jones tells of the love she felt in each of her contacts
with Mrs. Eddy:

> Only those who have come in contact with our dear Leader can
> realize the quality and magnitude of her love. It was a love so pure
> and spiritual, so exhilarating, so all-embracing, that it lifted one clean
> above the earth, and one felt like walking on air for days. I just cannot
> describe it. It was not a vague, impersonal love;—SHE LOVED
> YOU. It was your individual share of her heart's great love. It was like
> the way [Infinite Good] loves us.
>
> [In June, 1903, when Miss Jones heard Mrs. Eddy's Balcony
> Address at Pleasant View she states:] It seemed to me that I never
> heard anything that went straight to the heart like the closing words of
> that address: "TRUST IN TRUTH, AND HAVE NO OTHER
> TRUSTS."

Miss Jones tells of a young girl at this Pleasant View meeting who had
come hoping to see and hear Mrs. Eddy but found herself at the end of a
long line of people and so had to stand in front of the house while Mrs.
Eddy spoke from the balcony in the back.

The girl said she "was almost overcome with disappointment when she realized she was not going to see Mrs. Eddy, and very likely would not hear what she said," so keenly had she set her heart upon seeing and hearing our Leader. She felt like weeping, but overcame it by thinking, "If anyone has to be in this position I am glad it's me, and not another." Then she began to thank God that there were others who could see and hear, and to be grateful that she was privileged to be there at all. She did hear every word that Mrs. Eddy spoke.

Mrs. Eddy left the house by the front door to get in her carriage to go on her daily drive. She saw this dear young girl standing at the end of the column of students where she could not see the balcony. Mrs. Eddy went to the young girl, put her hand on her shoulder, looked lovingly into her face, and tenderly said, "Dear, parting only makes the heart grow stronger." The young girl said she felt Mrs. Eddy's love so strongly as our Leader put her arm around her and looked into her eyes—that the young lady was almost in tears. She said, "Oh, her love, her love! I did not know there was such a love." She seemed almost overcome.

Miss Jones sums up the young girl's beautiful reward:

This shows that if our thought is right we can never lose anything. This girl was thanking God that others could see our dear Leader even if she could not, but her heart was almost broken with disappointment. . . . We gain immensely when we silence self and sense through unselfish love for others, and for all mankind.

As we left the place I looked back where the thousands had stood. One would never have guessed that even one person had trod upon the grass, for not one blade seemed to have been trampled on, and the flowers and everything were as fresh and unharmed as possible. This made a great impression on me.

The young girl's experience of feeling loved was shared by many. Mr. Kimball's deep feeling when he first talked with Mrs. Eddy, he expressed as, "I never felt so loved in all my life!" Sibyl Wilbur also was deeply touched by the love she felt during her first conversation with Mrs. Eddy. She held her hand over her heart, and said, "Why didn't someone tell me!" The love that the young girl, Kimball, Sibyl Wilbur and others felt, emanated from the Christ-mentality of Mrs. Eddy. It seems not unlike the enfolding love and warmth, the utterly indescribable unconditioned love people who have had near-death experiences sometimes speak of.

A SUBLIME CHRIST-LIKE LOVE

The following two healings show the atmosphere of Love surrounding Mary Baker Eddy. I include them for newcomers, in case the Tomlinson book recording them has not been returned to the Christian Science Reading Rooms. They, again, demonstrate that Mrs. Eddy "saw the Love of God encircling the universe and man," causing her to love everything with a Christ-like love.

Among those who visited Pleasant View in the year 1897 was a mother with two small children. The little girl had a very sore spot on the top of her head which protruded and was much inflamed. On their way from the Middle West to Pleasant View, she cried bitterly when any attempt was made to comb her curly hair. In telling this mother's experience, Mr. Tomlinson states that "the whole thing was a most trying ordeal and it was only through showers of tears that the little one was finally made ready to go. A light straw hat, with a wreath of daisies could not be worn.

"After the speaking was over at Pleasant View, Mrs. Eddy sat on the porch and greeted the people as they passed through the porte-cochere. The mother was preceded in the line by her children. When these two little ones, a boy of nine, and the girl of seven, arrived in front of Mrs. Eddy, they stopped the whole procession and stood looking up into her face smiling joyously. Mrs. Eddy looked at them and then looked at the mother, and smiled back at the children, as someone told them to pass along.

This is the mother's account of her illuminating experience:

I wish I could make the world know what I saw when Mrs. Eddy looked at those children. It was a revelation to me. I saw for the first time the REAL Mother-Love, and I knew that I did not have it. I had a strange, agonized sense of being absolutely cut off from the children. It is impossible to put into words what the uncovering of my own lack of real Mother-Love meant to me.

As I turned in the procession and walked toward the line of trees in the front of the yard, there was a bird sitting on the limb of a tree, and I saw the same love, poured out on that bird that I had seen flow from Mrs. Eddy to my children. I looked down at the grass and the flowers and there was the same Love resting on them. It is difficult for me to put into words what I saw. This Love was everywhere, like the light, but it was divine, not mere human affection.

I looked at the people milling around on the lawn and I saw this

Love poured out on them. I thought of the various discords in this field, and I saw for the first time, the absolute unreality of everything but this infinite Love. It was not only everywhere present, like the light, but it was an intelligent presence that spoke to me, and I found myself weeping as I walked back and forth under the trees and saying out loud, "Why did I never know you before? Why have I not known you always?"

I don't know how long it was until my boy came to me and said, "Come, mother, they are going home." I got into the carriage and drove back to the hotel, but that same conscious intelligence and Love was everywhere. It rested upon everything my thought rested on.

When we got back to the hotel, there was no boil on my child's head. It was just as flat as the back of her hand. . . . For weeks this experience had a strange effect on me. I could not bear to hear anyone speak in a cross, ill-tempered tone, or do anything that would cause pain. . . .   Each time I saw Mrs. Eddy I had a wonderful revelation of God. I know she was no ordinary woman. God had anointed her with the oil of gladness above her fellows, for she "loved righteousness, and hated iniquity" (Heb. 1:9). —Tomlinson: Twelve Years With Mary Baker Eddy.

LOVE FOR HER ENEMIES HEALED CANCER

Even Mrs. Eddy's enemies experienced the healing power of her love. During the "Next Friends Suit" a group of the press came to vilify, "to hold Mrs. Eddy up to scorn and ridicule, expose and denounce her."

The chief man among this group, representing a big New York newspaper, was known as a particularly hard-boiled reporter and a steady drinker. He had been afflicted for some years with a cancerous growth of the throat, which was extremely painful and at times overwhelmed him completely.

One evening as they were all sitting in his room at the Eagle Hotel, drinking and smoking, bored with their stay, this man was suffering with his throat; he had lost his voice entirely and was unable to speak a word. Mrs. Eddy had asked me [Tomlinson] to call these men by telephone [Alexander Graham Bell had just recently invented the telephone, and Mrs. Eddy always availed herself of whatever was new and helpful. She may have been sitting next to Mr. Tomlinson when he phoned to inform the newsmen that it was impossible for her to see them.] She cautioned me at the same time, "Be sure to ask for the leading man and speak directly to him."

The telephone rang and one of the younger reporters answered. According to instructions, I asked to speak to the head man, whose name he mentioned, but was told that this man was too ill to come, and could not speak if he did come to the telephone, and could not speak <u>anyway</u>. Remembering Mrs. Eddy's instruction I said, "Tell him to come to the telephone; he can hear what I say even if he can't talk."

Accordingly, the suffering newspaper man came to the telephone, showing decided anger (as I was later informed). He listened for a few moments. Those in the room, of course, could not hear what was being said, but when this man turned away from the telephone, he not only could speak perfectly, but he was healed.

The healing stirred these men. They sat around, looking at each other, unable to comprehend what had happened and more startled by it than anything else. They had of course heard that Christian Scientists claimed to heal the sick, and they knew that their comrade had been healed. . . . Their whole position was overthrown by this proof offered before their very eyes. They packed their bags and left.

Some years later a relative of this man called at my office in Boston, and gave me the following message: "My uncle requested me to see you and to tell you that in his last days he turned to Christian Science, and he knew that he owed a debt of gratitude to Mrs. Eddy for his healing in Concord" (ibid. pp. 62-65).

The wonderful thing concerning these healings was that because of our Leader's daily work for all mankind, thousands of her students were doing instantaneous healings with no relapses; and millions of healings were taking place the world over. This same healing ability, that continued until the late 1940's, will return when Mrs. Eddy is restored to her rightful status in world consciousness.

She healed the cases her students failed to heal. Pondering and communing with her heavenly Father [her own divine Mind], she meekly broke the bread of Truth with her fellow creatures. In the face of opposition greater than the world had known since the advent of Christianity, she could not be swayed from her God-appointed task. In the secret recesses of her heart Mary Baker Eddy guarded the truth that God had revealed to her.

PROGRAMMED FOR LOVE

"Mrs. Eddy's demonstration of the Love that filled her heart would not permit her to harbor anything but a forgiving thought.

"On January 29, 1904, she said to her household, 'Wrongs are done to me, and yet I turn right around and do them a kindness; not because I intend to do so, but I cannot help it; I do it without thinking."

Here we have our Leader revealing a great metaphysical point about herself in a way that to the thoughtless might seem merely a declaration of sentiment, or of an inherently sweet nature. In reality it was her declaration that SHE FUNCTIONED UNDER GOD, so that whatever she said, or did, by treating people in a kindly way, was not because she was a good woman, moral, unselfish and sweet tempered, but because she had demonstrated God's government to the extent that it had become second nature. [She was love incarnate.] Whatever God required her to do, she did.—Gilbert Carpenter, Sr.

One Sunday morning (August 15, 1909) Mrs. Eddy told her household students that the way to destroy animal magnetism, error, is to *love* your enemies. "Turn your thought to the operator [the one expressing error and hate] with a sense of love, and that will destroy the belief in hate." Then she read from I John 4:20: 'If a man say I love God, and hateth his brother, he is a liar; for he that loveth not his brother whom he hath seen, how can he love God whom he hath not seen?'" She urged her followers to be delivered from hating, from all evil, and to lift this load of offal off all mankind, because the more we understand and express divine Love, the more we truly live. To really live, we must love divinely.

THE REAL CHRISTIAN COMPACT IS LOVE

Mrs. Eddy knew that "the real Christian compact is love for one another. This bond is wholly spiritual and inviolate" (*Mis.* 91:10). Her realization of divine Love called into expression the beauty of holiness, the perfection of being which healed, regenerated and saved all who turned to her for help. It healed and regenerated even those who came to harm her. She prayed for her enemies—prayed "that the light that is never dim may so encompass them that no night is there." It was the Love Mrs. Eddy lived and *WAS* that healed the newspaper man. The divine Love that filled her heart enabled God to use her to fulfill Bible prophecy and bring humanity the Second Coming of the Christ.

By her example Mrs. Eddy showed us that the Principle, Love, is within our consciousness. It doesn't need to be proved, but only learned, and demonstrated. In this way we demonstrate generic man—alias the image and likeness of God—as she did.

Trouble cannot stay when divine Love is realized, for Love assures us no one is outside of all-embracing divine Love. Mrs. Eddy's discovery brought the radiance of divine Love to everything she beheld. As we learn our true identity it will bring the radiance of divine Love to all we behold. Having learned that God is Love we are now called to prove it. How? By *BEING LOVING.* Millions of copies have been sold of Drummond's *The Greatest Thing in the World,* which contains Stephen Grellet's immortal paragraph: "I shall pass through this world but once. Any good that I can do, or any kindness I can show any human being, let me do it now and not defer it. For I shall not pass this way again."

TAKING ACTION IN LOVE WE FREE OURSELVES AT LAST

Study and practice of what Mrs. Eddy has given us, paying prayerful attention to her words, faithfully cultivating spiritual mindedness, enables us to put on the full panoply of sovereignty and loving kindness. Spiritual mindedness becomes our armor, our protection from the wiles of the devil, and pushes us "nearer the grooves of omnipotence" (*My.* 107:20).

"Resist not evil" means that as we translate evil's appearance into Mind, we see the unreality of evil. Today the doomsday clock is ticking on for what looks like evil. We are beginning to see that it isn't ten feet tall; it isn't even one inch tall, so we don't ask, "Where is the cavalry?" Instead, we dismiss it with an abiding sense of its nothingness.

Resist not evil means forgive as we would be forgiven. Obeying Luke 6:27-38, returning good for evil, love for hate, has since day one been our sure defense against hypnotism's evil whispers. Of course, evil, hypnotism, doesn't care how much it is found out, if we continue to bow down to it, allow it to remain and do its work; but heeding every statement in the textbook, we tune out the wavelengths of evil or hypnotism, and cut our apron strings to wrong points of view. Thus we finally free ourselves. Having learned from our mistakes, we forget them and move on, entertaining positive thoughts only.

CHAPTER 6

LOVE'S HEALING DEMONSTRATION
WE ARE CHALLENGED TO
TAKE ACTION

Mrs. Eddy urged her students to cultivate the spirit more than the letter. She never wanted us to maroon ourselves in metaphysical abstractions. What was needed, she saw, was "an outpouring of love, of the Spirit that bore witness, fervor in speaking the Word, tenderness in searching into their needs, feeling the spirit of Christian Science together with its letter." In Science and Health she wrote: *"THE WAY TO EXTRACT ERROR FROM MORTAL MIND IS TO POUR IN TRUTH THROUGH FLOOD-TIDES OF LOVE"* (201:17). This teaching caused the *Denver (Colorado) News* to comment: "The growth of this form of religious faith . . . is the greatest religious phenomenon of all history. The world is enormously richer for this reincarnation of the old, old gospel."

Spiritual mindedness is not something we achieve passively. In the first edition (p. 301) Mrs. Eddy urges us to "'work out our own salvation' [for this] is the demand of Life and Love; and to this end God worketh with you." We are challenged to take action. *"The highest prayer is not one of faith merely; it is demonstration."* (S&H 16:2).

When a student in the class of 1883 said she didn't know what she was supposed to do with what she was learning, Mrs. Eddy smilingly confided, "You are going to heal with it" *(Historical Sketches, p. 136).*

Mrs. Eddy was always direct, resolute, calm, authoritative. With unflinching firmness she concluded the third day of the 1885 class with, "Now go home and take your first patient" *(We Knew Mary Baker Eddy, Second Series, p. 9).*

The stress in Mrs. Eddy's classes was always on healing, on practice and proof in demonstration. She never left the students abandoned in metaphysical abstractions. To her, **every healing was evidence of our divine Principle at work, and of the kingdom of heaven within, and all around us.** Mrs. Eddy recorded:

Healing is demonstration; nothing else is. . . . I lectured one time where the spiritualists tried to break up the meeting; they would jump up and contradict without being asked. A lady in the audience . . . was taken with one of her attacks of gall stones; fell on the floor in excru- ciating pain; I said to the spiritualists, "Now is your time to prove what your God will do for you; heal this woman." They jumped about and did what they could, but she grew worse and worse. I stepped down from the platform, stood beside her for a moment and the pain left; she rose and sat in her chair and was HEALED. This went broad- cast, and through the healing [such as this] the Science was brought to notice. (DCC 3).

Christian Science was ushered in with healing. Its healing power reached every corner of the earth. This is why when we think of Christian Science, we think of healing. To William P. McKenzie Mrs Eddy said: *"Unless there is less teaching, less church making, and better HEALING, and more of it, our denomination will sink into the slough of past sects in having a religion of the letter without the spirit—a doctrine without demonstration."*

Mrs. Eddy's whole mission was to establish the Science of the Christ in human thought in a way that would transform thought so as to bring the understanding and realization that humanity is whole, healthy, because it has its origin in divinity rather than in human evolution. To do this Mrs. Eddy "quietly put aside profession and the noise of much speaking, and reduced a man's church membership to the acid test of his ability to heal the sick." This ability is necessarily dependent on the extent to which we reflect Love. As we find ourselves to be Love, we will demonstrate it.

At present our movement seems overwhelmingly beleaguered, by (gasp!) personality-rule at the helm, whose hocus pocus bibble-babble has a virtual death grip on the sheep in the field. This is in accordance with scriptural prophesy (Rev. 12:12 & 17): "Woe to the inhabiters of the earth . . . for the devil is come down unto you, having great wrath." But Christian Scientists' healing power will again come to pass. That is why the devil's wrath is now so great—"because he knoweth he hath but a short time" (Rev. 12:12) as earnest Christian Scientists are working to restore their healing power.

But before we further explore the subject of healing, we must voice a caution. There is real danger in an authoritarian, absolutist approach to healing.

COMPASSION MUST TEMPER OUR ZEAL

Today we have seen how the inharmony ingrained in the human pas- sions—ecclesiastical domination with its craving for power, and other

"First Degree" mortal mind indulgences—have brought the once mighty Christian Science movement almost to ruin. Its healing mission has all but ground to a halt. Mrs. Eddy at one time called her church's Board of Directors, "stuffed shirts and trained monkeys." The trained monkey is in evidence today when suffering fellow Christian Scientists who, getting no help from other Christian Scientists, are put out of the church if they are caught seeking help from the medical profession.

Love must always be the basis of our healing work. It must include compassion for people in all their limitations, and a readiness, like Mrs. Eddy's, to meet them where they are. There is no place in Love for the arrogance shown by those in power and authority, who penalize desperate Christian Scientists for seeking "temporary" help. It is particularly deplorable when seriously ill children are involved, depending on Christian Science practitioners who clearly do not have the understanding necessary to meet the case. Christian Science, understood, meets every case, but who today understands sufficiently to meet every case? A lapse of judgment can leave in its wake serious, even fatal, consequences. Whether or not to seek temporary help should not be the cliffhanger it appears to be, since our Leader explicitly states:

> Christian Scientists are harmless citizens that do not kill people either by their practice or by preventing the early employment of an M.D. (*Mess.* '01. 33:29).

This, of course, should not be construed as an excuse to go tootin' off to the doctor for every minor ailment, but rather that we should heed Mrs. Eddy's recommendation (*Manual, p. 92)* that:

> Each member of this Church shall strive to demonstrate, by his or her practice, that Christian Science heals the sick quickly and wholly, thus proving this Science to be all that we claim for it.

A PLACE FOR TEMPORARY MEANS

Mrs. Eddy also lovingly counseled in the textbook:

> If Christian Scientists ever fail to receive aid from other Scientists, . . . God will still guide them into the right use of **temporary** and eternal means. (S&H 444:7).

In Christian Healing (p. 14:10), we read:

> If you employ a medical practitioner, be sure he is a learned man and skilful; . . . In proportion as a physician is enlightened and liberal is he equipped with Truth, and his efforts are salutary.

In the face of this wonderful advice and admonition from our Leader, those in the "seat of great authority" are committing a mental crime in falling back on fire and brimstone, and ostracizing those who take Mrs. Eddy's advice and seek temporary help in cases where a practitioner does not have the understanding needed.

The recent spate of misguided parents—often terrified of what their practitioner or Boston will say—hauled into court for their injudicious conduct in failing to call for "temporary" help, has done incalculable damage to the reputation of Christian Science. Sadly, when a hundred teachers and the ecclesiastical Board of Directors all bray in unison, a funny thing happens. Nearly everyone believes them, further paralyzing the healing movement. But Mrs. Eddy's counsel is clear:

> Until the advancing age admits the efficacy and supremacy of Mind, it is better for Christian Scientists to leave surgery . . . to the fingers of a surgeon while the mental healer confines himself chiefly to mental reconstruction. (S&H 401:27)

She certainly indicates here that the practitioner should remain with the patient. If necessary, the loving practitioner gets right in the ambulance with the patient.

On page 464:13-20 of the textbook Mrs. Eddy states that if "a Christian Scientist were seized with a pain so violent that he could not treat himself mentally . . ." he could have a hypodermic injection. This was added to the textbook because Mrs. Eddy sometimes suffered intensely before knowing exactly how to lead the Christian Science movement forward. In **one** case the suffering was so intense that a hypodermic injection was administered. But Mrs. Eddy didn't just say, "Everything is peachy!" She looked for the cause of the suffering, and took the steps God was demanding. The next day she included in the *Manual*: "**No more Communion.** The Mother Church of Christ, Scientists, shall observe no more Communion seasons" (p. 61). The violent pain had made her aware the people were coming to Boston, *looking to her instead of to God.*

PHYSICIAN REFORM THYSELF

Clearly respecting the compassion, dedication, and skill of the medical profession in its own sphere, Mrs. Eddy urges them to open their eyes to a larger sphere, saying, "*We further recommend that Materia Medica adopt Christian Science.*" (S&H 441:20).

Material medicine is beginning to make a change of base. We see this happening on all sides. Titanic forces are being unleashed on the medical fraternity to clean up their act, reinvent themselves, and get with the mental and spiritual. Doctors see fundamental change is coming and they had better respond to it or go the way of the buffalo, carrier pigeons, and dinosaurs. They are seeing how drearily wrong it is to deal only with what looks like a matter body. Disenchanted, they are seeing it is time to make the emperor put his clothes back on.

Enlightened M.D.s are leading the exodus from outmoded ways, recommending alternatives to present methods. Many are saying: "People have no idea how much they are influenced by their minds." Mailboxes today are stuffed with: "How to unclog your arteries WITHOUT surgery, WITHOUT drugs"; "How to live to 120 and still have a full head of hair." "Discover the 'miracle' of healing yourself through the power of your mind. . . . Turn on the spigot of Love and let it flow freely," they are advising.

A *Seattle Times* full-page article: **"MIND/BODY MEDICINE; WHAT'S AILING YOU MAY BE IN THE HEAD,"** reveals Depak Chopra's *Ageless Mind, Timeless Body* has sold more than one million copies. Doubleday has printed 450,000 copies of Moyer's *Healing and the Mind.* Dr. Siegal's *Love, Medicine & Miracles* has sold more than a million copies. Dr. Benson's Book, involving transcendental meditation has passed 3 1/2 million copies. Dr. Norman Cousin's book on the benefits of laughter has been a best seller. Physicians are saying 90 percent of doctor visits are due to stress. In the life after life category, Eadie's "Embraced by Light" has sold over two million copies, and been translated into many languages.

M.D.s agree a laugh a day keeps the doctor away. "Laughter is one of the most effective ways to interrupt the stress building up in you during the day," writes a famous surgeon. "No living creature except man can laugh." When we are heavy with heartache we can laugh and console ourself with: "This too shall pass." Writes another, "Smile, it increases your face value." In a basic shift of emphasis physicians are recognizing that the mind is the most important element in healing.

Advanced M.D.s are still in the minority, however. And today, as America is racing toward socialized medicine, it is well to remember Mrs. Eddy's warning to Annie M. Knott: "Medical thought might become so organized that the practice of Christian Science would be almost impossible. When that time comes I want my students to take every means possible to make Science and Health available to the whole world" (*Six Days, P. 321, Oakes*).[1]

---

[1] The Mary Baker Eddy Institute has Science and Healths available for distribution. 2100 3rd Ave, suite 2601, Seattle, WA 98121.

HUMANITY AT THE CROSSROADS

The whole earth is making a change of base as we break away from a material universe. In the midst of the chaos we see, the Christ is at work. In the "overturning" materiality is being scuttled, and "through great tribulation something is being painfully born. We are at one of those watersheds in human history, at a crucial crossroad—invisible at the time—that is changing the way we think. While not many discern it, it is also a process which mortal mind and body undergo in the change of belief from a material to a spiritual basis. "We are in the midst of a revolution; physics are yielding slowly to metaphysics [leading the way to Science]; mortal mind rebels at its own boundaries; weary of matter, it would catch the meaning of Spirit [the only substance and reality]" (*Hea.* 11:6).

We are at the beginning of our journey toward realization of our present oneness with infinite Love, not at the end. In years to come everyone will know *"THERE IS NO DISEASE"* (S&H 421:18), and to think there is, will be recognized as dealing in erroneous beliefs. Then seeking help from another source than our own divine Mind will move into the shadows and will become as obsolete as other human institutions such as slavery, dueling, flogging, eunuchism, and human sacrifice.

In the meantime, let us not judge one another, but offer each other the full measure of our understanding of Love, remembering not by judging others but by *inspiring others to judge themselves* has anything worthwhile been accomplished.

"LOVE IS THE WAY"

"Our salvation is through Love," Mrs. Eddy wrote. "Call God Love always and bend all your efforts toward achieving perfect love in thought, word and deed. This is the way. All is won through it. Its presence gives me all. Its absence takes away from me. . .Our only way to heaven is through Love" (*DCC p.181*). All right effort will bear fruit, whether we see it or not. "The secret of being victorious lies within ourselves" Mrs. Eddy said. "A state of perfect honesty is a fortress impregnable to evil influence."

CHAPTER 7

CHRISTIAN SCIENCE HEALING

WHAT IS A CHRISTIAN SCIENCE TREATMENT?

Divine Love is at the core of every Christian Science healing. As early as 406 B.C., Sophocles wrote: "One word frees us from all the weight and pain of life: that word is love."

A Christian Science treatment begins and ends with Love. The minute I really **KNOW** God is Love, error ceases. A heartfelt feeling of love for the patient—a feeling of love that is beyond what can be expressed in words, negates any sense of error trying to flood the practitioner's mind. A practitioner, knowing "Thou [Infinite Good] art ever present," must get the deep inner conviction that if he can rid himself of negative thoughts, cleanse himself of all sin, then God's power can work through him to heal the patient. He becomes aware that healing is just the revelation of the perfection that has always existed.

When a patient calls you, assure him you will help him. Then immediately go to God in fervent prayer. Don't think of the patient or the condition he mentioned. Keep your Mind stayed on Infinite Good. Ask: What do I know about God as Mind, as Spirit, as Soul, as Principle, Life, Truth, Love? In the body of infinite Good's creating there can be no disease, no inharmony, etc. A good treatment always leads back to the realization of God as individual being. (See *Mis.* 101:31).

The patient is a victim of universal hypnotism. At the moment he doesn't know how to free himself. We grease the skids for error's exit when we look right at the false picture and know, "You are a lie. I do not believe you"; and walk away. We must see the patient, or any one, is God made manifest. This removes the "veil." If he complains of skin disease or broken bones, remind him that he is God-qualities: intelligence, good, joy, harmony, gratitude, honesty, peace and patience, and none of these have skin or bones.

A treatment is the recognition of the nothingness of the "claim"; it deals only with God. The truth is that the kingdom of God is already within the patient's consciousness, so it doesn't have to be achieved.

Infinite Good and its individualization are one. Our work is to become aware of this divine fact, and die to material sense in order to see what is **really there.** "Death is not the real stepping-stone to Life and happiness. They are now and here; and a change in human consciousness, from sin to holiness, would reveal this wonder of being" (*Un.* 37:8).

How often do we read the textbook seeking a healing when, in reality there is nothing to heal. Perfection IS here and now. The healing comes as we read and obey: "Seek ye first the kingdom of God." Then the healing will be added.

In Revelation XII, St. John presents the birth of understanding by the symbol of a woman giving birth to a child. The birth begins with Prayer that shows us the inward attitude necessary, and "Atonement" shows the requirements the student must meet in order to be one with God—namely the constant turning away from material sense, etc. Thus we arrive at heaven which is not a place but symbolizes the point in our warfare when we actually realize for the first time that the "dragon," the great crowned power, alias evil, error, that has always been honored as reality, is seen as unreal, as hypnotism only. Then "the dragon is cast out of heaven." (See Rev. 20: 1-3, 10, 15; also I Cor. 15:24, 28.)

The Bible warns against judging by appearances. No matter what the patient's problem is never upbraid or censure him. "Neither do I condemn thee." The patient wants you to know that such conditions *do not exist in reality,* and the practitioner must be convinced of the unreal nature of that which is troubling the patient.

A practitioner's work is a life of prayer. The demonstration takes place in the consciousness of the practitioner. He knows he is not going to restore a sick body to its normal function, purpose and harmony because the body always is whole, complete, perfect. He has nothing to do to make it so but to **realize that truth,** and **stand fast in spiritual identity.** Behind every externalized form is the man of Infinite Good's creating. To have "the crown of rejoicing," he must "grapple with sin in [himself] and in others" (S&H 29:2). Longfellow wrote, "If we could read the secret history of our enemies we should find in each man's life sorrow enough to disarm all hostility"—and replace it with Love.

Our only motive in treatment is to prove our oneness with our Principle, Love. The Truth in my consciousness is the Christ, the healing agent. A Christian Science treatment, therefore, is "the acknowledgment of present perfection." It is the conscious operation of the divine Mind on the part of the practitioner, who knows that the only effective prayer is the realization of the allness of the one Mind, Infinite Good. We must understand ourself to be the functioning of that Mind, and must struggle with error until we rise above it. As we do, "even the pangs of death disappear, accordingly as the understanding that we are spiritual beings here *REAPPEARS*" (*Peo.* 1:16).

The operation of the divine Mind includes within itself all good. As "ambassadors for Christ" we are entrusted with the authority of God. "Christian religions have always taught that God is omnipotent, omnipresent and omniscient," states Stanford Viera in *Awake Thou That Sleepest,* "but in the next breath they teach that evil in the form of sin, disease, discord, disaster, death is very powerful and present everywhere. Now if evil is real and has presence, then this completely contradicts the truth of God's all-power and all-presence."

Mrs. Eddy showed how illogical these theological teachings are. She told her students "You are accepting only one percent of the good that belongs to you." Since we are one with God we cannot be less than the allness of harmony, the allness of strength and health, the allness of good in all its aspects. Our real Mind knows no evil just as sunshine knows no fog, or darkness. There is no incurable disease; our oneness with Infinite Good gives us an abiding sense of Life. There is no such thing as too late. "If everything else fails, try blessing the situation." We find freedom and are liberated from the haunting memory of past mistakes when our compassionate love forgives a wrong, and we see that evil is never part of us. When everything seems to be going wrong, laugh! Our spirit of gratitude will add to our smiles and laughter.

ENTERTAIN THE SPIRIT OF TRUTH AND LOVE

A Christian Science treatment has to do with thought. Every thought we think is contributing its share to the ultimate of our life. We are the custodian of our own mentality; we must choose each moment what to think. "God requires that which is past." Don't look back except to remember the good. Learn to forgive. "He that cannot forgive should be careful not to sin." We have to give up the error we thought even one second ago! Turn from it by the law of substitution, i.e., substitute a right thought. When error argues lack of time, discouragement, failure, defeat, etc., substitute eternity, gratitude, victory, triumph!

Christian Science practice needs the greatest self-discipline. Seek the understanding and wisdom to rebuke error. Have courage to speak the Truth, and the grace to remain silent when words are not needed. Moments come in life no words can explain. Their meaning can be articulated only by the inaudible language of the heart. (See *Mis.* 262:10;

100:19.) Practitioners talking on the telephone, know they are talking to themselves at the other end since *there is only ONE*. The awareness of Infinite Good does the healing.

Heaven or hell is determined by what goes on in our consciousness. Heaven and healing come as we entertain "the spirit of Truth and Love"; "the truthful arguments you employ" (S&H 418:22) will conquer the error. The only Mind there is, is our Mind. We must claim it, knowing now is the patient the Son of God. Now is the kingdom of God within him. The patient, every person, is God in disguise, God appearing as the person. NOW is the kingdom of God within the practitioner. Treatment blesses all concerned.

In reality the patient doesn't need healing, but the painful human sense cries out for help. It is the spiritual understanding of the practitioner that the patient is reaching for. The practitioner realizes that he must reduce a claim of any kind to a false belief; appearing where? Appearing at the door of the practitioner's own thought. He is never handling the patient's thought; he is handling false beliefs, over which he has dominion; he can refuse to give error reality. "With [our] stripes—the rejection of error—the [patient] is healed" (S&H 20:15) since "I, if I be lifted up from the earth will draw all men unto me."

The true idea of the universe and man enabled Jesus and Mrs. Eddy to embrace the universe in their consciousness, so they automatically governed it instead of letting it govern them. They "held fast that which is good." This is the sum total of demonstration. Infinite Good is All; there is nothing besides it.

Mrs. Eddy, speaking of Jesus' healing of the man born blind, made it clear that "neither hath this man sinned nor his parents" because *THEY WERE BOTH THE DIVINE MAN.* So illuminating was Mrs. Eddy's explanation, that Mrs. Wilcox says for a long time she saw clearly that there was no such thing as a "sinning mortal man." Instead there was only the perfect man. Hypnotic suggestion alone makes it look material and in need of healing. She saw that her so-called matter man was the divine in reversion, or "seen through a glass darkly."

What we see as a disturbing factor (a sick body or lame hand or foot) is but the mental misperception of the perfection that is here and now. So we are not going to restore a body, a hand, or foot, to its normal harmony, function and purpose, but we are going to know that it is always whole, complete and perfect. We are going to realize there is nothing we have to do to make it so except realize this Truth, and then stand fast in *spiritual identity.*

To Mrs. Eddy sin, sickness, death were unreal. Once when a student asked Mrs. Eddy what she was doing, Mrs. Eddy said she was "reversing past experiences one by one." This insistence upon seeing only **good as real** is what made the world beautiful to Mrs. Eddy. She saw through the delusion of matter. Once she said, "I wish I could tell you what I see when I look at a rose."

"In Science, Mind [your Mind] is *one,* including noumenon and phenomena, God and His thoughts" (S&H 114:10). Why? Because infinite good, God, your real Mind, speaks, sees, knows, *as* man. When we become aware that "Soul [our true identity] and its attributes [are] forever manifested through man"—through that which expresses our Mind—we can heal the sick and give sight to the blind. (See S&H 210:11.) Isn't Mrs. Eddy here saying that we cannot separate cause from effect?—cannot separate God and man? Isn't effect where cause is? Doesn't this tell us we all must give up the belief that we are human beings, living a life separate from Infinite Good? Jesus and Mary Baker Eddy by their life and works presented to the world the Life that is God. They were the "light of the world," showing us how we too can be the light of the world.

Just think, if we really knew the truth that there is nothing "out there" to battle with—that we are only dealing with the belief of a supposititious mind at the door of our own thought— what joyous relief would be ours, knowing there is no sick man to be made well. Cast out the belief of dealing with persons, places, things, that we have to demonstrate over them. Do we demonstrate over 2x2=5? Shall we sleep as did the disciples, or stay awake, seeing the allness of Infinite Good? "Awake, thou that sleepest!"

Since "God [is] the Mind of man," and "man has no Mind but God," must not the individual mentality be God? Christian Science teaches us how to speak as one having authority—to accept the convictions of our own Mind as the facts of existence. We do not depend upon the words of others. We state the absolute truth about Infinite Good and its reflection, man, as it actually is in reality, in oneness. We know we are God in action; and we see the forms about us as the manifestations of living Spirit, as Mrs. Eddy did when she touched Adam Dickey's arm and said: "Adam, this is Spirit," and repeated several times, "You are Spirit." Her spiritual perception gave her the transparency of consciousness through which she could see all is Spirit.

Because "desire is prayer," when you find yourself desiring, know the desire is already fulfilled in Mind or you could not desire it. Know you have already received it. Demonstration is only becoming conscious of the thing we desire, since all good is always at hand, just as 2x2=4 is always at hand. All good has existed eternally in reality—in our own right Mind; and realization or demonstration means reaching a point of conviction.

This is why as we "rise to the consciousness of Life as Love" and realize "Love alone is Life" (S&H 391:30 & (*Mis.* 388:10) we can drop the term Life as the creator, since all has always existed, just as 2x2=4 has always existed. It was never created. It just is. In the textbook's last chapter, "The Apocalypse," Mrs. Eddy uses Truth and Love almost exclusively.

Mind is the power that forms the image, and gives that image form, outline, color. God, our Mind, is the only cause, and "God will heal [that is, reveal perfection] . . . through man whenever man is governed by God," just as the mathematical principle will solve a problem when the pupil adheres to the principle. Man is the means by which Mind reflects its ideas in tangible form.

The basis of every Christian Science treatment is Jesus' statement: " 'The kingdom of God is within you'—is within reach of man's consciousness here, and the spiritual idea reveals it" (S&H 576:21). Therefore healing is nothing more than changing our consciousness to see that what is called man is always within Infinite Good's allness. When we begin to comprehend the real man, the imperfect man disappears.

THOUGHT REVEALS IT ALL

Matter is the supposititious opposite of thought, of the ideas of Mind. Matter cannot think, act, speak. A leg cannot walk, an arm cannot lift itself. The eyes do not see, nor do the ears hear. It takes consciousness to see, hear, feel. Your present body is not matter. Correctly seen, it is a state of true consciousness; there is one spiritual body, constituted of right ideas, and that body is your body, here and now.

On body, Mrs. Eddy wrote: "There is no error or sin that can mesmerize me into seeing a body. . . . Know what God is, and that is what body is. Heaven is here or we would not be here. . . man is the body of God [of Mind, your Mind]. . . . **There is no matter substance.** *Your matter body is a belief only. . . . In the belief that the body is substance is embraced the whole error of sickness and death. All is Mind and Mind's idea.* In reality there is no corporeal man" (A Carpenter item). "God's [your Mind's] thoughts are perfect and eternal, are substance and Life" (S&H 286:21. See also p. 513:19 and 114:10). These show what God's "family" is.

Thought reveals it all. Through thought we can advance ourselves spiritually or keep ourselves prisoners of the flesh. **There is no matter to be cured. Only a belief needs to be changed.** As we search intently to learn our true being, forgetting the body, healing takes place. Jesus said, "It is the spirit [right thinking] that quickeneth; the flesh [the physical] profiteth nothing. Physical and mental healing is like the shadow that follows us when we walk in the sunshine.

A suggestion comes: "You're getting a cold." It is only a suggestion, but if you don't stop it there, you may say, "I have a cold," which then becomes belief, and you will suffer from it if you do not detect it. But if you instantly refute that anyone could have a cold, it stops the supposition dead in its tracks. When a Christian Scientist is asked for help with some error, he quickly says to himself, "He hasn't got it; he is one with God, and God doesn't have a cold, or any error!"

FORM THE HABIT OF RIGHT THINKING

Thought is self-sufficient. We call upon our divine Mind for support in learning what we need to learn. The present fact is Infinite Good and man are one. *Unity of Good, p. 8,* teaches that everything we are aware of is a construction of consciousness.

As we form right mental conclusions, our body will reflect this right thinking in health and wholeness, since body is the embodiment, idea, image, likeness, of the thoughts that are being entertained. At a time of grief and great need in a friend's life the following lines on right thinking were helpful to her:

> Think smiles, and smiles shall be.
> Think love, and love will grow.
> Think good, and good is here.
> Think joy, and joy ne'er ends.
> Think faith, and faith's at hand.
> Think peace, sublime and sweet,
> And that peace you will meet.
> Think this: "I'm going to win!
> Think victory, think "I can!" —Anonymous

Realizing the immense value and importance of our thoughts, knowing that in all the universe there is nothing more powerful, we should form the habit of thinking thoughts of health and harmony, thoughts of Love, knowing that no one needs anything but Love. "Love alone is Life," wrote Mrs. Eddy. Think how Jesus loved:

When "they brought young children to him that he should touch them. . . . His disciples rebuked those who brought them. But when Jesus saw it, he was much displeased and said to them, Suffer the little children to come unto me and forbid them not for of such is the kingdom of God [because little children have no sex urge—at least they didn't in Jesus' time.]. **AND HE PUT HIS HANDS UPON THEM AND BLESSED THEM**. (Mark 10:12-16).

Jesus knew we all need to be hugged occasionally. He was giving the gathered crowd a spiritual lesson—the lesson we all are "children" needing to be loved by those who have the understanding of Love. He knew we were not yet where we could do without the "second degree" human touch, which is grounded in the divine.

"And there came a leper to him, beseeching him. . . . And Jesus, moved with compassion put forth his hand, AND TOUCHED HIM." Note, *Jesus touched him even before he spoke to him.* To touch a leper was unthinkable! People threw stones at lepers if they came too close. Think how that man must have longed for someone to *touch* him. That longing—to be loved, to be *touched*—was his deepest need, so Jesus touched him, and **then** healed him.

RIGHT THINKING BRINGS HEALTH, WHOLENESS

That same healing Love is always with us. When almost unendurable sorrow or sense of loss strikes, one can gain great comfort and strength from Mrs. Eddy''s words:

> *Are earth's pleasures, its ties and its treasures, taken away from you? It is divine Love that doeth it, and sayeth, "Ye have need of these things." A danger besets thy path?—a spiritual behest, in reversion, awaits you.* (Mess. '02.19:21). *The very circumstance which your suffering sense deems wrathful and afflictive, Love can make an angel entertained unawares* (S&H 574:27). *"God's plans are going on as best for you and me, whether we know it or not; but in the knowing and in the glad supposition of that fact, there is rest and peace" (DCC 94. See also Hea. 10:13-25).*

If the "treasure, taken away from you" was a spouse or other loved one, remember Mrs. Eddy's words, "the avenger of Truth stabs us through those we love most, as much as to say, 'You have no moral authority for loving aught but God and His likeness.' Our remedy is to watch, work, and pray to make first one's self and then all others into that likeness, patient, meek, loving....(*DCC* 276). We can know he or she was never in the matter-body delusion. That matter body was just a disguise. Say, like Jesus, "Loose him [from the belief he ever lived in a matter body] and let him go."

Since "man is the expression of God's being" it is the body of right ideas—that does not get sick and die—that is rightly called man. Watch your beliefs rather than your body," Mrs. Eddy urged.

> *We can see that the body is controlled by mind, when we realize the powerlessness of the body as matter. This is demonstrated by smiles, tears, a blush, action of the body in coming and going to different localities. The eyes have no power to weep, the face no power to smile, the arm no power to lift itself, the limbs no power to walk. [We know] the condition of the body in sickness, paralysis and death to be its response to the fear which is produced in consequence of the ignorance of the fact that mind governs instead of the body. Show [your patients] that this discordant action is unconscious to them until they are awakened to it. . . . Body and mind are one in action, or the visible manifestation of an invisible power. (DCC 187)*

Hatred or any un-Godlike quality or indulgence has a lethal effect on the organs of the body. Mrs. Eddy explained that the organs of the human body are not self-controlled. Can the organs of a corpse act by themselves? No. Again, neither are the bodily organs under the control of the **conscious** mind. We know this because the beating of the heart, the digestion of food, etc. go on without our thinking about them. A **sub-conscious** mind governs them. But we have learned that this subconscious mind is greatly influenced by the *conscious* mind. As we form habits of either good or bad, loving or unloving thought, and this is fed to the unconscious mind, we have a constructive or destructive effect on the bodily organs.

WATCH WHAT YOUR THOUGHTS ARE. LABOR THERE

Boldly, and with staunch confidence, Mrs. Eddy instructed:

> *You can make your house—the body—just what the mind is. The discouragement brought to you, you are able to expel as an unwelcome guest. This is the ground on which all must work. Watch just what your thoughts are, and labor there until success greets your efforts. If you think you haven't time to attend to it, say: I have; or if you think you need help, prove it otherwise. There is no one who can help you like yourself. There are no conditions hindering. They are*

only what you admit. ["Error comes to you for life and you give it all the life it has."] Whenever you take this position you go up higher. . . . Students are morally responsible to meet any error in themselves [this is the crux] then it will disappear from the patient [as Jesus and Mrs. Eddy and thousands of dedicated practitioners proved]; it is not the patient; it is some moral wrong in the student. (From William Johnson's History of the Christian Science Movement.)

Speak vehemently to error. In overcoming hypnotism we can't use a butter knife on what requires a chain saw. But don't be discouraged by occasional setbacks. Failure is not always the fault of the practitioner. We can get solace from Jesus' not healing of Judas. Some so-called patients are unteachable.

MAINTAIN YOUR ONENESS WITH DIVINE LOVE

The Christian Scientist has learned that God is the only cause and effect; hence the only power. Anything that is not loving and God-like cannot then be real or true. Our business—even when everything seems to have gone wrong—is to maintain the facts, maintain our oneness with divine Love. "When trouble overwhelms," Mrs. Eddy said, "sing a hymn . . ." Many have found they were helped immeasurably by belting out "Onward Christian soldiers," or "Shepherd, show me how to go," and the more dramatic they waxed in their singing the freer they became. When error comes to us for life we should give it the shaft instead of giving it the only life it has. Nothing is more powerful in healing disease and discord than the realization that Love is omnipresent and omniactive.

"What is it to love?" asked Mrs. Eddy.

To always see the man of God's creation, and nothing else, and to separate from our thought of man any belief of fear, sin or disease. This is Love. Let us strive more earnestly to reflect this Love in our homes, where little errors so often tempt us to lose sight of the real child of God. (DCC 216).

First get the healing for yourself, "Physician, heal thyself"! Why? So that you may be full of understanding, love, patience. We help others by what we say, what we do, by what we are when we are full of patience, love, understanding.

To silently maintain that *perfection is the fact (Truth), and only perfection has Life, makes it live.* But once we accept a false belief we animate it with the power of our own mind; therefore we are responsible for the only power it seems to have.

In the Carpenter book, *Fragments,* Mrs. Eddy encourages, cheers, comforts, emboldens us with these words:

Relax your thought. [Outer peace can be gained through law; but inner peace only by Love.] Your body is held tense, rigid by your tense thought of self. Let go; you are living in Love; you govern your body through Mind, and you know that man's true selfhood is not slave, but master. [Because God is All as everyone—the whole is in every part. God gives all of Itself to everyone]" (p. 161).

Let go, then, of the albatross chaining you to fear and misery. There really is no problem that needs to be solved. A so-called "problem" is always hypnotism, from which we need to awaken, just as we awaken from a dream in sleep.

One needs to protect himself from his own false beliefs alone; therefore the only wrong thinker, or mental malpractitioner there is or can be is one's self. The beam in one's own eye is the whole of evil. Of what does our human concept consist, and who created it? All our warfare is located within the confines of our thought. . .

Declare yourself into heaven in every treatment, and out of error. . . . When the suggestion comes to you that you can not do any one thing, declare positively, persistently, that you can [Mary Baker Eddy, in the Second Coming of the Christ, has assured you that you too are the Christ.] God, good, works through you; [and] the good you do and embody gives you the only power obtainable" (*ibid.* 161; 166; 163; 170).

Laura Sargent, who lived in Mrs. Eddy's household, reports:

Mrs. Eddy said to us many times, "We must get out of these senses and we must love more. Meet every temptation with more love until you feel Love's restoring power

TO HEAL, HOLD FAST TO LOVE

Giving a treatment means holding fast to Love, our Principle. In this life, what everyone wants is love. We want to receive it, we want to give it, *be* it. Love is of God. We look for it in and of God, and whatever of Love we express is Infinite Good expressing Itself. Seeing this, we enter an entire new consciousness of life. Mrs. Eddy counseled: "Love fulfills the law of Christian Science, and nothing short of this divine Principle [Love], understood and demonstrated, can ever furnish the vision of the Apocalypse, open the seven seals of error with Truth, or uncover the myriad illusions of sin, sickness, and death" (S&H 572:12). The seven seals are God's opposites, which Mrs. Eddy **opened when she showed the opposites of her seven synonyms for God**. Again, she counseled:

> *Love is the only and all of attainments in spiritual growth. Without Love, healing is not done and cannot be, either morally or physically. Every advanced step will show you this until the victory is won and you possess no other consciousness but Love divine.* (A Carpenter reminiscence.)

This explains why she ends Science and Health—ends the chapter Apocalypse—with LOVE. "[DIVINE LOVE] is my shepherd. Four times LOVE is in all capital letters. Evolution in its seven stages always had a telefinalistic point of view, and spiritual growth will continue until we possess no other consciousness but this DIVINE LOVE.

Even physical scientists are beginning to see that Love is the central and final point. This "Truth of being—this LOVE, coming to our consciousness—opens the prison doors to the sick and affects the body as nothing else can." It eliminates fear—the hardest of all taskmasters—because the presence and power of Infinite Good are always right with us just as the round world was always with the people 500 years ago while everyone was believing it was flat.

DOES GOD HEAL?

We often hear: God heals, or God will heal the sick. But Mrs. Eddy says, "God will heal the sick *through man, whenever man is governed by God*" (S&H 495:1). This is analogous to the way mathematical principles solve a problem when the pupil is governed by them. Does God know anything about sickness? Does the principle of mathematics know anything about all the errors made? Can the principle come and correct $2\times2=7$? No. The principle is merely available to us; it doesn't know error. The principle only works through the mathematician's *understanding*. Similarly, since our own Mind is God, God only works as we work.

What is going to heal sickness, sin, discord of every nature? *Our understanding.* Our understanding that our Principle is Love and knows nothing about sin, sickness, discord, is what heals. We have to correct our thought. We never have to "heal" a person or thing. The help is never to heal a disease; the help is only to reveal the patient's spiritual identity. Our work is to become conscious of what we already are as one with Infinite Good. "There is no disease." Disease and discord are illusion only, hypnotism.

The principle of mathematics is within our consciousness, but seriously, folks, did it ever work out a problem for us? We had to go to school and learn it—*learn* the multiplication table, etc., and in this way become one with the principle of mathematics. It is the same with the divine Principle of our being, the Principle that is Love; it has been there from everlasting, but has it ever come down and healed a case of measles? No. "God will heal the [measles] *through man* whenever man is governed by God [has learned the truth about himself, and has the understanding of God], in the same way that the principle of numbers will solve a problem in arithmetic **whenever the student is in line with the principle**, as Mrs. Eddy explains on page 3 of Science and Health.

LOOKING WITH GOD'S EYES HEALS THE SICK

What makes healing difficult is that the evidence of the five physical senses seems so real, hence the tenacity of belief in sickness and discord. We believe what the eyes see. But Jesus said, "Having eyes, ye see not." We don't see what is already really here. In the presence of Omnipresence is there anything to be healed, changed, overcome, reformed, or destroyed?. No. What you are looking at is the incarnation of God—God in disguise. We need to see as Mrs. Eddy saw. When she touched Adam Dickey's arm and said, "Adam, this is Spirit," she was viewing rightly. She saw all the qualities of God right there—saw Infinite Good made manifest as what looked like Adam Dickey. Mrs. Eddy demonstrated spiritual consciousness; she saw beyond what the eyes see, to that which is real. Like Jesus, she was awake, and not sound asleep in the Adam dream. If God is All, and God is Spirit, what could "Adam" be, but Spirit, when **rightly** viewed? Everyone we see if viewed correctly is God, appearing as individual being. (See *Mis.* 101:31.) This is our foundation stone for healing. (See S&H 357:19.)

What renders both sin and sickness difficult of cure is, that the human mind is the sinner, disinclined to self-correction. . . . The human thought must free itself from self-imposed materiality and bondage. . . . As a material, theoretical life-basis is found to be a misapprehension of existence, the spiritual and divine Principle of man dawns upon human thought. (S&H 218:12; 191:16; 191:8).

"The human mind will sometime rise above all material and physical sense, exchanging it for spiritual perception, and exchanging human concepts for the divine consciousness" (S&H 531:10).

"Matter is not the vestibule of Spirit" (S&H 356:8). The divine and human coincidence does not involve the human mind, which must disappear as Truth is learned, since "the human mind and body are myths" (*ibid.* 150:32). Healing will become easier as we better learn the deep truth Mrs. Eddy has hidden in her books, namely, that we have all the power God has, since we are one with God.

Learning that our own right Mind is the power, we realize there is no power, called "divine Love"—that does the healing— outside of our own consciousness, our own right Mind. The divine Love the practitioner entertains, *or is,* does the healing. We do not correct a discord; we correct *our thought* about it. Since in reality there is no error, a treatment is the action of Truth eliminating the *belief* of error.

The right thinking of the practitioner—knowing that the patient is the individual appearing or manifesting of God—heals the problem. Healing is the increasing awareness of perfection rather than the casting out of disease or want. "Healing is like sculpturing" said an early student of Christian Science. "The true model is in the thought before it becomes phenomenally expressed."

To heal the sick, the discordant, we need only get the correct view. Since "man has no Mind but God;" and since "God, the Mind of man, never sins" (S&H 319:20 & 470:17) there can, in reality, be nothing that needs healing. We need only remove hypnotism, the false beliefs we are entertaining. We have the power to exchange false beliefs for the Truth once we learn to look with God's eyes.

MRS. EDDY QUICKLY HEALED CHILDREN

In the Second Coming, nowhere was the healing power of Love better demonstrated than in Mrs. Eddy's own life. She had a great love for children, and often healed them of some dire affliction, or raised them from death. Typical of such healing was that of the janitor's thirteen-year-old daughter who was consumptive and extremely weak. One day he left her at Chickering Hall where he worked, and where Mrs. Eddy preached. Mrs. Eddy saw the child and talked briefly with her. When the father came for the girl he found her well, healed.

Another time Mrs. Eddy called at the home of a child she had not seen for several days. The child's mother, crying bitterly, said the child had just died. Asked to see the child, the mother consented but said nothing could be done; it was too late. Taking the lifeless body in her arms, Mrs. Eddy became conscious only of Life, Truth, and Love. She remained *oblivious of the material* until the child sat up and asked for her mother.

There were many such cases of healing and of restoration to life of persons who according to the medical belief had passed on. In an unpublished article, "The Kingdom of God Within You," Mrs. Eddy explains how such healings are possible:

"As a metaphysician you are never dealing with person, place or thing. You are dealing with a suppositional mind, which includes within itself all there is to material sense, to the sick, sinning, or dying mortal. . . . No discord is outside of that which comes to you as your own consciousness. Because of this very fact, and because you are alone with your own being in your closet, you have supreme power to handle all that presents itself to you."

Mrs. Eddy saw demonstrably: "The notion that both evil and good are real is a delusion of material sense, which Science annihilates. Evil is nothing, no thing, mind, nor power." Spirit, being all, can have no opposite.

WE MUST LAY OFF THE MORTAL SEEMING. Our capacity for self-delusion has made the ride to the realization of the kingdom within long and bumpy, as the prophets and Jesus envisioned it would be.

"From beginning to end, whatever is mortal is composed of material human beliefs and of nothing else" (S&H 478:24). Every trouble is only human belief. In any discord, we are dealing with mental beliefs. "The whole, of that which constitutes being to me, must rise as I rise, and must be drawn into that altitude of Mind that I accept as mind [note small m]" (Early Carpenter Foundation *Collectanea,* p.142) "Fear not, for I [the I that is your own Mind] am with thee. I [this kingdom of God that is within thee] will never leave thee, nor forsake thee." It goes where "I" go. The crucial statement by Hosea (11:9): "**I am God and not man,**" is of sublime and glorious import to us. Who or what is the "I" that is "God and not man"? It is your real Mind, as Mrs. Eddy reveals in her definition of "I" (S&H 588:9).

The Science Mrs. Eddy discovered is something we have to *know* just as we learn to know the science of math or music. Because our real Mind is God, we can lay off the mortal seeming and know. "*All that hinders your [realization of perfect health and wholeness],*" she said, "*is the reality you make of matter. . . . Establish in the back of your mind that there is no matter. See this and you heal all cases of belief since all are founded on matter.*"

Mrs. Eddy assured us that "to affirm anything is to assert its possibility even in the face of all contrary evidence. By affirming that to be true which to all human reasoning or sight seems not to be true at all, you can bring it to pass." Continue to affirm it, knowing that:

Every time you declare you are perfect in God, there goes through your body a health-giving power. . . . There is no incurable disease; there is no such thing as too late." "Faith is the substance of things hoped for." Have faith in the allness of Infinite Good.

BLIND BARTIMAEUS

Isn't this what guided blind Bartimaeus when as the Bible (Matt. 10:46-52) says: *"casting away his garment, he rose, and came to Jesus."* What was this "garment" he "cast away"? Blind people wore a special garment just as a white cane is used today. For blind Bartimaeus that "garment" was his insurance policy, without it he might starve if someone did not give him food as he sat by the roadside begging. The more the crowd tried to stop Bartimaeus from crying, "Jesus, thou son of David, have mercy on me," the louder blind Bartimaeus cried out! Jesus sensing his faith said, "Bring him here." Then blind Bartimaeus did something crucial. He took off his special garment, his insurance policy, his security, and threw it behind him, showing his great faith. Jesus— although it was obvious that Bartimaeus was blind—asked: "What do you want?"

"Lord, that I might receive my sight." To which Jesus responded, "Go thy way. Thy *faith* hath made thee whole."

We need to follow the example of Bartimaeus in faith and persistence. Cultivate spiritual mindedness. Persistently declare the Truth about everything error is lying about, and know that the declaration of the Truth breaks the claim. Seeing spiritually, we recognize error's nothingness. We see sickness, sin, death, as merely a lie about something true—a lie which could not appear unless there was something true and real to lie about. Everyone we meet, or are conscious of, when correctly seen, is the Christ—is God in disguise. Can it be otherwise when *"GOD IS ALL"*?

The activity of Truth in your consciousness is the Christ. The main point, often forgotten, is that Infinite Good is **individual being.** "God is individual Mind" (*Mis.* 101:31). God is the consciousness of individual being. God's Selfhood is individualized as you and me. Every truth we know about God is the truth about individual man. Wouldn't it follow that since God is my individual being, my individual being must embrace infinity? Need anything be added to me? Can anything be taken from my true being?

BODY - CORRECTLY VIEWED

In treatment we must remember Mrs. Eddy's instruction to her workers that the body we now have, **when seen correctly,** *IS* the divine and spiritual body. We must establish in consciousness the spiritual ideas which are the facts about our so-called material body and its functions. Every idea of Mind, of Spirit, of Soul, of Principle, Life, Truth, and Love constitutes our body when our body is rightly viewed, because our present body is embraced in our Mind. Man is the body of the one Mind.

Mrs. Eddy saw there were not two creations: a spiritual body AND a material body. She proved absolutely that **what appears as a matter body—when correctly viewed—is the spiritual body at hand.** "Creation consists of the unfolding of spiritual ideas and their identities, which are *embraced in the infinite Mind [your Mind]* and forever reflected" (S&H 502:29). If a thing exists humanly to us, it is because it exists divinely as fact. The divine fact or idea is all there is to the human concept.

Because error is nothing other than hypnotism, a treatment consists of dousing the whisperings of aggressive mental suggestion with Truth before it explodes into a scandal of disease and fear. The material sense of things has been a liar from the beginning, and **"if [Infinite Good, your real Mind] were understood instead of being merely believed, this understanding would establish health"** (S&H 203:7).

Mrs. Eddy makes clear we must "realize the ability of mental might to offset human misconceptions and replace them with the Life which is spiritual. . . . Mentally insist that harmony is the fact, and that sickness is a temporal dream. Realize the presence of health and the fact of harmonious being, until the body corresponds with the normal conditions of health and harmony. . . **As material knowledge diminishes and spiritual understanding increases, real objects will be apprehended MENTALLY instead of materially"** (S&H 428:19; 412:23; 96:27). We win as we squeeze error out and hold our ground "with the unshaken understanding of Truth and Love."

A treatment is the utterance of spiritual truth about Life as Love, its substance, presence, power, and action. It has nothing to do with the mirage, the hypnotic suggestion, seen as mortal man.

A treatment is simply the activity of truth in consciousness, in your God-consciousness. Your consciousness is God, the one Mind. Every harmonious bodily activity, whether of walking, running, and the like, proceeds from Mind—your right Mind. This must be so since God, Mind, is ALL. The important thing to see is that perfection *IS ALREADY SO*. But we must come into the realization of it through understanding WHY it is true.

She urges, "Know, then, that you possess sovereign power to think and act rightly." When Jesus demonstrated this power, "the people were astonished . . . for he taught them as one having authority." Mary Baker Eddy has taught us to do the same. She knew each one's individuality is God, and that there is nothing we desire—from the infinitesimal to infinity—that is not to be found within ourselves—the only place where any right thing can be found. Our Mind includes it all. Jesus said to the man with the withered hand, "Stretch forth thine hand." All we ever have to do is stretch forth our hand—open our thought—and accept, because everything we could ever need and wish for, divinely, is at hand.

INDULGENCE IN MATERIAL SENSE STOPS HEALING

Why do we so often fail in our treatments? It is not always because we anticipate a second cup of coffee with greater excitement than we do the Second Coming; it is more likely because the *material sense* of things seems so real, and we indulge it, wallowing in the gloom it brings.

To cure bodily disorders, Mr. Eustace, in *Clear, Correct Teaching,* gives this hint on healing: "Remember . . . the only thing that stops you from making Mind All-in-all is your indulgence in the human concept of things—in the finite personal sense of things. That indulgence stops perfect trust in God as All-in-all" (page 800). Mrs. Eddy defines your "I" on page 588:9 of the textbook. This "I" is your divine Self which is leading your human mind out of these indulgences, out of the belief of being a separate personality, apart from Infinite Good. The human mind is so occupied with the wrong teaching of the ages and its selfish indulgence of matter objects—the anti-Christ—that it has not become aware of the real omnipresent divine Self. But through the divine authority brought by Mrs. Eddy's teaching, the spurious authority of the personality is being undermined and destroyed.

"PHYSICIAN HEAL THYSELF"

All a treatment can do is destroy the *belief* in disease and in evil. Whose belief is it? It is mortal mind's belief. Where is it expressed? In the mind of the healer, until the healer has a clear, demonstrable realization that "entirely separate from the belief and dream of material living, is the Life divine" (S&H 14:25). What practitioners have to do in every case, as they struggle in the pre-dawn hours to heal a patient, is to meet their own sense that there could be a matter man, a material body, that can become discordant, as Blanche Hersy Hogue once told me.

This is surely what Jesus and Mrs. Eddy did, and taught their followers to do. What was Jesus doing in his forty days and nights in the wilderness? He was resisting evil, seeing its unreality. The present structure of human consciousness is convinced that matter is real. Therefore dehypnotizing our consciousness is the work facing us. "The whole conflict, the mighty struggle," said Mrs. Hogue, "is going on right in your own consciousness." We must resist evil, see its nothingness, until it dissolves the Adam dream. We all have our "wilderness" experience. For Christian Scientists the "wilderness" is 40 years or a lifetime of study of Mrs. Eddy's writings and the Bible to learn our true identity.

Healing is the effect of our knowing *subjectively* that the oneness of the "patient" with Infinite Good is the present fact. It is because there is only one "I,"—and thus the "I" of the practitioner is also the I of the patient—that healing can take place in Christian Science. "He [Infinite Good] **is** my individuality and my Life" insisted Mrs. Eddy, (*Un.* 48:8; S&H 336:6).

HOW MRS. WILCOX RESTORED A DYING WOMAN

Mrs. Wilcox tells of a time in her early practice when she had a case that was passing on. Her teacher could not help her:

I was so overwhelmed with fear and grief that I went up into my attic, and the words on page 444:7-12 [S&H] came to me and I "turned from the lie of false belief to the truth of being" (ibid. 370:2) as never before, and that dying woman was released in my thought, as such, and she lived. She lived abundantly for thirteen years, and never needed another treatment. . . .

Mrs. Eddy showed us that we must come to the place where we did not even desire to heal the sick, because if we desire to heal the sick we first have to believe there are sick mortals to be healed. We shall heal the so-called sick, instantly, when we <u>understand man to be God's presence, never mortal</u>, never sick. As we gain that understanding, that understanding is the Christ or the real Self of us, and it could no more recognize sick mortals, as entities, than light can recognize darkness.

It is surely right to "heal the sick . . ." but we can only do this as we "cast the beam out of our own eye," that is, we are to become the consciousness that we have ever been, namely, so entire that there is no false sense in us. [Again, "physician, heal thyself.]

To restore the sick and sinning, Jesus—by the realization of what man actually is—*healed himself* of the belief there was a material man that could experience these maladies. You are Mind, Spirit, Soul—the nature of God—which constitutes the Principle that you are; and this Principle expresses itself as the Love that alone is Life and that forever embraces the Truth about all things.

When we, through an intense yearning for the guidance of Spirit, have destroyed *our false sense of evil,* we have done all that can be done, and all that is necessary. In mathematics, we would not attempt to thrust in our personal beliefs and opinions. We are content to observe the facts of the subject proving themselves as our consciousness enlarges. When we learned 2x2=4 and not 5, we did all we needed to do to correct the error. If we just knew the truth about ourselves as surely and fully as we know 2x2=4, nothing could harm us.

We must learn what our temptations and errors are, and seize the moment to battle down fear, impatience, frustration, anger, hurt feelings, and any other hypnotic shadow. Focus on the small stuff as well as the big. With ax in hand, challenge practices locked in decades of die-hard habits. To heal we must prevent evil suggestions from entering our thinking and face the snags of dimly discernible, deeply-rooted beliefs that are the obstacles to reform. "The warfare with one's self is grand" (*Mis.* 118:25); through it we mentally join ourselves to Infinite Good. When we are conscious of our true Self as the divine Principle, Love, it will speak through us words of wisdom. And Love, the essence of this Infinite Good, will direct our lives.

To Frank Walter Gale, Mrs. Eddy wrote:

> "The healing will grow easier and be more immediate as you realize that God, good, **is all,** and good is Love. You must gain Love, and lose the false sense called love. You must *feel* the Love that *never* faileth,—that perfect sense of divine power that makes healing no longer power but grace. Then you will have the Love that casts out fear. When fear is gone doubt is gone and your work is done. Why? because it was never undone. (We Knew Mary Baker Eddy, Second Series. p. 28).

Mrs. Eddy taught us the life of Love. "If you love, you can raise the dead. Love will heal death; that is the way I have raised the dead, by Love—by Love that is above the human." Her love included the whole universe, and when everyone in the universe was included in this Love, there was no one to resist the omnipresence of present perfection.

Mrs. Mimms reports that in Mrs Eddy's last class she asked the students: "What is the best way to do instantaneous healing?" There were many answers. But when the students had given their answers, Mrs. Eddy said, "I will tell you the way to do it. It is to love! Just live Love—be it— Love, Love, Love. Do not know anything but Love. Be all Love. There is nothing else. That will do the work. It will heal everything; it will raise the dead. Be nothing but Love" (*We Knew Mary Baker Eddy,* Second Series).

"BE NOTHING BUT LOVE." Mrs. Eddy knew it would not be easy. In my visits with Mr. Eustace he told me that one of Mrs. Eddy's secretaries had on several occasions informed him of Mrs. Eddy's distress, almost despair, when she thought of what would become of the Christian Scientists when she was no longer here to continually rouse them to wake up and be active in Truth. I heard the same report from Mr. Carpenter, Sr., and from Mr. Tomlinson in my visits with them.

Mrs. Eddy wanted us *to be the voice of God,* not just "listen" for God's voice. If we are, then never doubt that Isaiah's "small and feeble remnant" will prevail; never doubt that a small group of thoughtful, wise, committed truth-knowing citizens can change the world; it is the only thing that ever has.

CHAPTER 8

SPIRIT SHOWS US HOW TO KEEP MIND'S IDEA PURE

GROWING AWAY FROM ERROR WE BECOME PURE IN SPIRIT

What did Mrs. Eddy mean with, we must "gain Love and lose the false sense called Love"? How do we achieve the "Love that is above the human" by which we can heal even death? The answer lies in knowing ourselves as Spirit, at one with Infinite Good, and rejecting the original sin, the illusion of human birth which clouds our sight and separates us from our true being as Spirit.

Mrs. Eddy tells us the time is coming when "the spiritual origin of man, the divine Science which ushered Jesus into human presence, will **be understood and demonstrated [by each one]**" (S&H 325:26).

Isn't this what Jesus meant when he explained to the woman of Samaria that the "well of water" was <u>within</u> her consciousness—that everything ALREADY IS, so it can constantly spring up into everlasting Life. (See John 4:10,13,14) "Water" is a symbol for purity; also for newness and renewal. "The real man is not of the dust, nor is he ever created through the flesh; for his father and mother are the one Spirit, and his brethren are all the children of one parent, the eternal good" (*Ret.* 22:18). Each one, in reality, is the Christ, the full understanding of God.

To see through the nothingness of error, we must keep our thought pure. We have seen that in order to work out any problem, we need to turn completely away from the mistaken human sense, and keep thought on the infinitude of good as an infinitude of divine ideas. Man is "the expression of God's being" (S&H p. 470) means "man is idea, the compound idea of Infinite Good." Man is not matter. In teaching us this, Mrs. Eddy tells us **what man is, and what man is not.** And it is up to us to keep our thinking pure.

In her Chapter 5, "Prayer and Atonement," Mrs. Eddy says, "The belief that life originates in the sexes, is strongest in the most material natures; whereas the understanding of the spiritual origin of man cometh only to the pure in heart," who have learned to have no further use for the physical, "the flesh [that] profiteth nothing"; and who will henceforth create and express only with Mind-substance, the only medium needed in the realm of Infinite Good. "To know there is no personality is more important than to know there is no disease"—Mary Baker Eddy.

On page 59 of the first edition (regarding lessons of Spirit) Mrs. Eddy instructs: "We must recognize ourselves Soul [God], and not body, and outside the body [alias the Adam-dream]. . . . But in order to do this we must grow away from all that is error and become pure in Spirit to receive or impart the lessons of Spirit." Only then does the realization come that you are now walking in the kingdom of God. It is right here, and is manifesting Itself all around us, but being sound asleep in the Adam dream we are totally unaware of it. Only through Mrs. Eddy's great revelation, are we learning that all outward material seeming is but the shadow of divine reality. These "shadows" are created by our misconceptions, our belief of being separated from the kingdom of God within us.

THOUGHT MUST BE PURIFIED

Our thought must be purified. Mrs. Eddy has many pertinent references to purity. For example, explaining the conception of Jesus she says, "Mary's conception of him was spiritual, for only *purity* could reflect Truth and Love which were plainly incarnate in the good and *pure* Christ Jesus. He expressed the highest type of divinity which a fleshly form could express in that age. Into the real and ideal man the fleshly element cannot enter. Thus it is that Christ illustrates the coincidence or spiritual agreement, between God and man in His image" (S&H 332:31).

Again, she writes: "The time cometh . . . [when] white-robed purity will unite in one person masculine wisdom and feminine love, spiritual understanding and perpetual peace" (*ibid.* 64:18-25).

TRACING ERROR TO ITS BEGINNING REVEALS TRUTH

It was Mrs. Eddy's *understanding* of Truth that enabled her, in this age, to be the mediator between Spirit and the belief of flesh which mortals have struggled with since time began. She knew that error had a beginning: "As both mortal man and sin have a beginning, they must have an end" (S&H 538:27). But tracing error to its beginning she found only Truth present. The error was always a lie about the truth. *Unless a truth is there first, no lie can be told about it. So the lie always points to the Truth.*

St. John, knowing there is nothing besides Infinite Good and its idea or man, and knowing also that it is the spiritual man who has been hypnotized to believe in a matter man, emphasized:

"Beloved, *now are we the sons of God [notice "NOW"]*, and it doth not yet appear what we shall be: but we know that when He [the true knowledge, your oneness with infinite good] shall appear, we [you and I, the spiritual man] shall be like Him [like infinite good] And every man that hath this hope in him *purifieth* himself even as He [Infinite Good] is *pure.*"

Therefore man must purify his thoughts in order to overcome the illusions he entertains of matter. Our whole job is to overcome the hypnotism that makes matter look and feel real. *"Belief in a material basis, from which may be deduced all rationality, is slowly yielding to the idea of a metaphysical basis, looking away from matter to Mind as the cause of every effect"* (S&H 268:6).

Consciousness, Mrs. Eddy tells us, is the essence of all existence. Perfection is the universal *fact.* As we become aware— become conscious of this fact of present perfection—error exits.

Everything is already ours. Why is it so hard for us to accept this teaching that there is nothing to be attained, nothing to be achieved? If true consciousness were *"attainable,"* it would be apart from our own consciousness, something other than the divinely real consciousness we already have and *are.* Why do we set ourselves up as material entities, separate from the infinite good, God, our own Mind? (See Philippians 2:5, 6.)

NO CORPOREAL CREATION

The answer lies in the reluctance to give up original sin.When Laura Sargent asked Mrs. Eddy, "Mother, what do you mean by 'sin, sin, sin'?" Mrs. Eddy answered, "I mean the connubial relation." She explained, "Infinite Good being All-in-all, and being masculine, feminine and neuter, what need is there for sex? God or infinite good made all quite unconsciously of sex or gender." (Preserved by Carpenter Foundation).

Mrs. Eddy once explained: "God is Father AND Mother—one; the Christ reflects the male and female Principle—one—not two. And the end of the belief in male and female as two, will be when woman stops child-bearing. . . . Sexuality and sensuality of any kind are not of God" *(DCC.* p. 14).

"DEATH WILL NEVER CEASE UNTIL YE WOMEN CEASE YOUR CHILD-BEARING"

The prophets were aware of this great truth. In Job, "who sinned not in all he said," we read (Job 3:1-3): "After this opened Job his mouth, and cursed his day. And Job spake and said, Let the day perish wherein I was born, and the night in which it was said, There is a man child conceived."

The great prophet Jeremiah lamented and said:

"Cursed be the day wherein I was born: let not the day wherein my mother bare me be the blessed. Cursed be the man who brought tidings to my father saying, A man child is born unto thee. . . . Wherefore came I forth out of the womb to see labour and sorrow, that my days should be consumed with shame?" (Jer. 20:14, 15, 18).

This theme runs from Genesis through Revelation. Jesus' knowledge of original sin made it possible for him to overcome all evil, and he carries this theme throughout the New Testament. Remember he said: *"Death will never cease until ye women cease your child-bearing,"* showing his knowledge of original sin. To this Mrs. Eddy on Dec. 7, 1903, added: "The end of the belief in male and female will be when woman stops child-bearing? In Luke 17:27 and 21:23, Christ Jesus warns: *"They did eat, they drank, and married wives, they were given in marriage, until the day that Noah entered into the ark, and the flood came, and destroyed them all. . . . Woe unto them that are with child, and to them that give suck . . .for there shall be great distress in the land, and wrath upon his people."*

As Jesus was being led away to be crucified, Luke reports Jesus' last instruction and warning to the throng that followed: *"Blessed are the barren, and the wombs that never bare, and the paps which never gave suck"* (Luke 23:29).

Matthew 24:19 reiterates: *"And woe unto them that are with child, and to them that give suck . . ."* Mark 13:17 repeats this statement by Christ Jesus.

In Matthew 23:9: Jesus instructed: *"Call no man your father upon the earth: for one is your Father [Mind], which is in heaven."*

Again, speaking of error, Jesus said: *"Ye are of your father the devil [mortal mind, hypnotism] and the lusts of your father ye will do. He was a murderer from the beginning [we see here that Jesus knew the error the spiritual man had made. If it wasn't the spiritual man who made the error, then there are two causes, which Christian Science denies]. . . . When he [the result of the spiritual man's mistake, alias the mortal seeming] speaketh a lie, he speaketh of his own: for he is a liar, and the father of it" (John 8:44).*

Materiality has, since time began, been deeply ingrained; and while it is never too late for people to grow up, never too late for people to give up their prejudices, few are willing to do so, and many vigorously resist it. Jesus and the prophets had real courage when they exposed original sin—they knew they were licked (outnumbered) before they began, but they began anyway and saw it through, even when they knew it would cost them their lives. Tradition has it that Jeremiah whose work descended like the great rays of the setting sun, "was sawn asunder."

But it was Christ Jesus' complete knowledge of original sin—which, remember, Mrs. Eddy told Laura Sargent was the connubial relation—that made it possible for him to overcome all evil. This understanding of original sin made it possible for the entire mortal Jesus to disappear in the ascension.

HOW THE DEPARTURE FROM TRUTH BEGAN

In her copyrighted article: "Man and Woman," Mrs. Eddy states: "In the divine Mind there is no sex, no sexuality, and no procreation. . . . The departure from Truth commenced with the words sex, sexuality, sensuousness, matter; and these are the objective state of what is called mind separated from God, the one Mind." The Bible writers' inspired vision led them to realize that creating corporeally was the error that must be cast out.

This theme runs throughout Mary Baker Eddy's writings. For a long time I saw her thrust at "original sin" in nearly every paragraph of Science and Health and her Prose Works. I brought out much on this subject in *Mary Baker Eddy: A New Look.* And from whom do you think I got the most favorable comments? The men. One man wrote: "The theme of original sin runs through the whole book." Many said they were glad to see it exposed, instead of, as usual, swept under the rug.

Most people *don't want* to see it. Like the Cardinal whom Galileo urged: "Come and look through my telescope, and see for yourself!" they reply: **"But I don't want to see!"** They would hide behind what Mrs. Eddy was forced, by the total ignorance of her times, to write, namely: "Marriage should improve the human species." Triumphantly and with exaggerated innocence they insist: "You see! Mrs. Eddy wasn't against bringing children into the world." They have no idea what Mrs. Eddy was up against when "[her] discovery undermined the favorite inclinations of a sensuous philosophy" (S&H 121:2) or what an incredible work lay before her to awaken mankind from the belief that man is a creator, and what an astounding achievement her fulfillment of scriptural prophecy was. To the materiality of her time her teaching was like a lead balloon. The ignorance she had to meet was enough to drive any thinking person around the bend. Her chapter "Marriage," she tells us, saved the cause. It came where people were. Her teaching that in reality "there are no sexual organs, only in false belief, for all is created, and man or woman are not creators" (DCC 132) was not understood. Students were like a fish not perceiving water, or like a man who is starving with a loaf of bread in each hand.

People don't want to give up what they falsely think is pleasure in matter. When I first saw this great overriding truth in the textbook, every Christian Scientist I knew got an earful as I started explaining the sacred truth I had gleamed from our Leader's writings; but I soon learned my explanation was about as welcome as a skunk at a garden party. Most, it seems, are content to just scamper about a bit in "the letter." Mrs. Eddy said, "I dread the ordeal through which marriage must past and we with it."

Today, however, with the dawning of "Woman's Hour" many men and women **are** seeing the light, and there is a far more ready ear for the central theme of the Bible and Mary Baker Eddy's revelations which reveal that creation is intact and will be so seen when human generation ceases. "The multiplication of a human and mortal sense of persons . . . is not creation. [It is] dense blindness" (S&H 263:27). To James Gilman Mrs. Eddy confidently asserted: "Heaven is not a breeding ground for mortals," and she would be proud of our country today as it toughs it out with the Vatican on freedom of choice for women **world-wide**, easing the burdens of motherhood by improving women's status as they escape the treadmill of constant pregnancies.

TWO NATURES IN ONE INDIVIDUALITY

It is only the Adam dream that separates Infinite Good's likeness into male and female. This is what Mrs. Eddy found when she traced the lie of gender to its beginning. In the only, in reality, man and woman are one spiritual individuality, one divine consciousness, the "two witnesses" as one. "Look long enough, and you see male and female one—sex and gender eliminated; you see the designation *man* meaning woman as well, and you see the whole universe included in one infinite Mind and reflected in the intelligent compound idea, image or likeness, called man, wedded to the Lamb, pledged to innocence, purity, perfection. Then shall humanity have learned that 'they which shall be accounted worthy to obtain that world, and the resurrection from the dead, neither marry, nor are given in marriage: neither can they die any more: for they are equal unto the angels; and are the children of God" (Luke 20:35, 36, and *My.* 268:29).

Just think how unburdened we would feel if we even glimpsed what we really are! (Note: Since God is just a shortened term for infinite good—and is the infinite whole—the personal pronoun, "He" seems very inappropriate. That's why in my writings I seldom use it.)

⤳LUST AND SENSUALITY ARE NOT OF GOD

Mr. Calvin C. Hill tells how Mrs. Eddy healed him of lust and sensuality. Calvin Hill became a student of Christian Science after being healed of various maladies, the most severe of which was a case of indigestion that doctors could not help him with.

Describing this particular visit with Mrs. Eddy (as recorded in *We Knew Mary Baker Eddy,* Third Series) he states:

> *Mrs. Eddy looked at me searchingly as I put my question:*
>
> *"I wish you would point me to some place in your book that will enable me to overcome the thought of lust and sensuality."*
>
> *She replied most emphatically, "I will!"*
>
> *I remember she lifted her head with that far-off look, as though she saw into the very heart of heaven. She talked for some time denouncing the Adam-dream and thoroughly exposing its falsity. She spoke over and over again of the nothingness of mortality and of the reality of the spiritual creation. She supplanted the garment of the flesh with the robe of Spirit.*
>
> *The light that dawned upon me that day has dwelt with me in greater or lesser degree ever since and has enabled me to understand her revelation better as the years pass.*
>
> *She talked as long as I could follow her; but when she saw that her statements were beyond what I was capable of understanding, extending her hand, she said quietly, "That will be all today, dear."*
>
> *This characteristic gesture, concluding our interview when I had ceased to follow her explanation, was to become very familiar in the future.*
>
> *As I left Pleasant View to return to the depot, after this memorable and uplifting experience, I felt as if I were walking on air. Nothing seemed real except the truth which Mrs. Eddy had affirmed and which was inscribed on the disc of my consciousness. People were passing in different directions, both on foot and in carriages, but I was scarcely aware of them—they seemed to be moving in a mist.*
>
> *I boarded the train for Boston, and as I rode along, my thought was completely occupied with the great illumination of the reality of Spirit and the nothingness of matter. I felt that I had been lifted to the*

mount of transfiguration. For a number of days all I could think of, all I could hear, was what Mrs. Eddy had said to me in answer to my question, and the spiritual light which I received during that interview remained with me in all its glory.

From that time I was a different man; hence I feel warranted in saying that I experienced a measure of spiritual "new birth" on that wonderful day. However, later I had to learn that being lifted up by another, even by our Leader, is not working out one's own salvation; which is to say that there is no vicarious [at-one-ment]. I saw that I had to work my own way up the hill of Science, that I had to prove in my own experience the truth she had affirmed to me—I had to work it out in demonstration.

A month later I received a letter from Mr. Frye in which he said that he did not know why Mother requested it, but that she asked me to look on page 95, second paragraph, of Science and Health. In the fifty-fifth edition 1891, then current, this read as follows:

"The devotion of mortal mind to some achievement makes its accomplishment possible. Exceptions only confirm this rule, proving that failure is occasioned by a too feeble sense of power." In the final edition of the textbook, page 199, these lines were changed to read:

"The devotion of thought to an honest achievement makes the achievement possible. Exceptions only confirm this rule, proving that failure is occasioned by a too feeble faith. [As we work and do our very best, we might here add her urgent plea: "TRUST IN TRUTH AND HAVE NO OTHER TRUSTS" (My. 171:1)].

The following letter from Mrs. Eddy shows that she remembered my first interview with her and that she was eager to give me further light on a problem which everyone must meet and master:

"Goodness such as yours is a sure pre-text of success in all struggles to be better. If a single sin remains—and who is destitute of all sin—be of good cheer for the victory over it is a foregone conclusion. If a supposed sensation exists that God, Good, is displeased with, it must yield and neither fear nor abnormal conditions can hold it. Your good heart is the victor over it NOW, and for ever you know this is the Truth that has made you FREE. You are liberated by divine Love from every false claim of the flesh. The law of Spirit is supreme, it dominates the flesh and you are God's own child. NEVER born of the flesh nor subject to it.

Here you plant your understanding and having done your part, STAND, and God will provide for the temptation [the] strength to overcome it.

On a subsequent visit with Mrs. Eddy which Mr. Hill states was again an "exalting experience" (causing him to become a fine worker in the Cause of Christian Science), Mrs. Eddy asked him:

> *"How are you getting along with that problem you asked me about when you were here last?"*
>
> *"Mother," I replied, "I am not sure I understand just what you meant in your letter."*
>
> *"What don't you understand, dear?"*
>
> *"Well," I said, "You reminded me of your statement that 'the devotion of mortal mind to some achievement makes its accomplishment possible.' By this I understand that if one devotes his thought to any particular line of work he will accomplish something. But the second part of the citation, 'Exceptions only confirm this rule, proving that failure is occasioned by a too feeble sense of power,' I don't know that I understand this. Does it mean my too feeble sense of power in Christian Science?"*
>
> *"You DO understand! That is exactly what it means," Mrs. Eddy replied emphatically.*
>
> **At that moment I awakened as I had not before to a realization of the spiritual power of the statements of scientific truth in Christian Science.**

We all must awaken to the spiritual power of the statements of scientific truth in Christian Science.

WHAT AWAKENS OUR DEEPER REALIZATION?

Could Mrs. Eddy have explained to him that she, like Jesus, had been predestined from "before Abraham was" to be incarnated for "the second appearing in the flesh of the Christ, Truth, hidden in sacred secrecy from the visible world?" (S&H 118:7). (See I John 4:2 which states, "Every spirit that confesseth that Jesus Christ is come *in the flesh,* is of God.")

In Mr. Hill's first visit she had gotten him to glimpse the truth that he had never been separated from his womanhood, so didn't need to seek it outside his own God-being; he forever embodied every male and female quality in his own consciousness which was always one with God. Perhaps now he glimpsed the Fatherhood and Motherhood of God were exemplified by Jesus and Mary Baker Eddy as one, since as Jeremiah prophesied, "A woman shall compass a man [compass Jesus' teaching]."

In *Miscellaneous Writings,* p. 161, "A Christmas Sermon," Mrs. Eddy gives further light on the masculine and feminine representative and shows their *fadeless footsteps throughout the ages. Pulpit and Press* tells us that the window in "Mother's Room" "is designed to be wholly of the work of Mrs. Eddy." This window with its three panels, refers to the *advancement of her consciousness alone,* showing *her fadeless footsteps throughout the ages.* Only through the advancement of her thought will the general thought understand how to advance. The consciousness of Mrs. Eddy succeeds itself. In the words of the prophet (Num. 12: 15), "And Miriam [Mary] was shut out from the camp seven days: and the people journeyed not till Miriam [Mary] was brought in again."

Calvin Hill was amazed at the simple yet profound spiritual idea he received and its far-reaching implications. Statements in Science and Health came into self-evident, clear meaning, higher than the surface meaning. Something wonderful was communicated to him in those visits which forever changed, uplifted and purified his thought. The world was no longer too much with him.

Could it have been Mrs. Eddy's explanation that both she and Jesus were "the root and offspring of David, and the bright and morning star"—the instruction which opens the "Glossary" to *Christ and Christmas?* And that this is why her words have power—in accordance with Revelation 5:5: "the root of David hath prevailed to open the book and to loose the seven seals [the opposites of the seven synonyms for God] thereof." Mrs. Eddy "loosed the seven seals [exposed evil as unreal, as hypnotism only] and opened the book," Science and Health, at "the time of the end."

Rev. 11:3 states: "I will give power unto my two witnesses." Here we are made aware that our true being is not only "root" but also "offspring," not only cause, but also effect; not only Principle, but also idea. (See also Ezek. 2:9 & 10; also 3:1-5. Dan. 12:4 & 9.) Could it be that this explanation of oneness and divine prophecy brought the great light Calvin Hill speaks of?

Could she have explained to him that the "Comforter, Divine Science, was Jesus' womanhood aspect coming to humanity with the incarnation of Mary Baker Eddy? That she "got Mary out of the way" so the Christ could speak through her and spiritually educate us to realize all being is divine? We could then overcome the belief we are corporeal beings as Jesus had overcome and given example.

MRS. EDDY WAS INCARNATED TO OVERTURN
BIRTH AND DEATH

Mrs. Eddy could explain all things because her womanhood included her manhood. This is why she could tell Mr. Wiggin in a class, "I do not find my authority for Christian Science in history, but in revelation. If there had never existed such a person as the Galilean Prophet, it would make no difference to me" (*My.* 318:30-2). Mrs. Eddy knew that she, like Jesus, was "the root and offspring of David, and the bright and morning star" (Rev. 22:16), and from all eternity included every manhood quality. Note that the star appears in most of the pictures in *Christ and Christmas,* her last book, which reveals her as Christ Mary.)

She, like Jesus, was incarnated to fulfill prophecy "in the end time." She fulfilled her mission as one divinely guided. "And the Lord spake unto [Mary Baker Eddy] face to face, as a man speaketh unto his friend" (Exodus 33:11). Up until Mrs. Eddy came no one else on earth had ever found and proven <u>our</u> God-given ability to understand and demonstrate the healing might of Mind to be the same as Jesus had proved it to be.

WE MUST BE RESURRECTED

Mrs. Eddy's writings guide us in our resurrection from the dead—our resurrection from false beliefs, resurrection from the belief of life in the body, of life, substance and intelligence in matter. What we are looking at is always Spirit, misconceived, since God, infinite good, is all.

Mrs. Eddy explained to Mrs. Wilcox that every visible manifestation is actually the form or identity bearing witness to the omnipresence of Infinite Good's idea. What looks like a matter man is really God in disguise. Mrs. Eddy, like Jesus, beheld in reality, THE PERFECT MAN RIGHT WHERE MORTAL MIND SAW MATTER AND ERROR. We must resurrect the true idea of every form in our own consciousness. In this way we gain dominion over all the earth. What looks like a matter man is a temporary misconception as 500 years ago the flat earth was a universal misconception.

EXPLAINING THE SECOND RECORD OF CREATION

To free us from the tyranny of birth, procreation and death—to awaken us from the Adam dream—Mary Baker Eddy had to go back to the beginning and explain the two contradictory versions of creation recorded in Genesis. Consider: In the first record of creation we have the male and female that *God, infinite good, created in Its image and likeness.* Here

God is Father-Mother, two compounded natures in ONE Being; so the man that Infinite Good made in Its image and likeness is two compounded natures in one being, namely, the "man" that is both male and female, ONE—"both son and daughter, the compound idea of all that resembles God. . . His name is Christ Science" (*Mis.* 167:7). Mrs. Eddy explained that the perfection that is Love, God, requires the blending of the masculine and feminine qualities in one consciousness—in your consciousness and in mine. And after our consciousness is renewed and perfect, the true image must appear.

But in the second version of creation in Genesis, after **"there went up a mist,"** what do we have? We have the Adam-dream creation, We have a man AND a woman. We have a man, Adam, from whose rib a woman was taken. Now, can both the first and second records be true? No. Mrs. Eddy had to explain the true and false accounts in the first two chapters of Genesis, because once we see error as error, it can be destroyed. (*S&H 502:9-17 & 403:14-16; Hea. 17:14-18;* Mis. 60:23-10).

Before the "mist" (or mystification), man was entirely mental, a formation of both the manhood and womanhood **qualities** of God. But man, not being satisfied with his degree of expression, formed a false concept of the All, of the infinite good we call God. Thus he became a prodigal from his Father's house. This false concept changed his true concept of the spiritual universe and himself, namely, that "Spirit is the real and eternal" (S&H 468:12). The false concept brought, in belief, a physical universe and a physical man—a mortal that creates other mortals.

Quoting again from her copyrighted article, "Man and Woman," Mrs. Eddy states: "God is All-in-all. [Infinite Good] is masculine, feminine, neuter. [Infinite Good] is the Father and Mother of the universe. What need, then, of procreation or sex, since God is the only creator, and all is made that can be made quite unconsciously of sex or gender?" She saw that the departure from Truth had commenced with the words sex, sexuality, sensuousness, matter; and that these are the objective state of what is called mind separated from God, the one Mind.

Jesus had seen this, and Mary Baker Eddy came to explain and complete his work on earth. Jesus, the masculine representative of God, left the elements of Truth *he* expressed in *her* consciousness. When the human sense of personality gives place to the spiritual image, the new man, the ascended Christ Jesus, the Lamb of God, will stand side by side with the new woman, Christ Mary, the Lamb's wife. The Lamb's wife refers to the wedding of the Christ consciousness of Jesus and the Christ consciousness of Mary Baker Eddy, as one, as our Wayshower. (See S&H 577:4, & *Pul.* 83:29.)

The Lamb is the idea of Love. If we are the wife of that spiritual idea of Love, we are one with it—wedded to it—as Mrs. Eddy was. Again, Mrs. Eddy writes that "evil has [always] tried to slay the Lamb;" but "divine Science shows how the Lamb slays the wolf. Innocence and Truth ["trust in Truth and have no other trusts"] overcome guilt and error" (S&H 567:31). Revelation 5:12-13 then tells us: "Worthy is the Lamb that was slain [by the world's misunderstanding and unrelenting cruelty] to receive power, and riches, and wisdom, and strength, and honour, and glory and blessing. . . . forever and ever."

STARTING WITH MANHOOD WE RISE TO WOMANHOOD

In Science and Health we learn that "the demonstration of being starts with the manhood of being and rises to womanhood as the Christ idea and the Revelator's vision thereof, wherein the Spirit and the bride say come" (*Essays and Other Footprints,* "The Second Coming"). The "woman clothed with the sun" is being revealed as compassing Christ Jesus, fulfilling Jeremiah 31:22: "A woman shall compass a man." Revelation 11:3,4 states: "I will give power to my two witnesses . . . These are the two olive trees, and the two candlesticks standing before the God of the earth." Zechariah 4:11 reads: "Then answered I and said unto him, What are these two olive trees upon the right side of the candlestick, and upon the left side thereof? And I answered again, and said unto him, What be these two olive branches which through the two golden pipes empty the golden oil out of themselves? And he answered me and said, Knowest thou not what these be? And I said, No, my lord. Then said he, These are the two anointed ones [Christ Jesus and Christ Mary, God's 'two witnesses' (Rev. 11:3)], that stand by the Lord of the whole earth." Just as we today recognize Jesus as Christ Jesus, the time is coming when all will also recognize Mary Baker Eddy as Christ Mary. Not the human corporeal Jesus or the human corporeal Mary Baker Eddy, is the Christ, but what they stand for spiritually, and what Scripture prophesied of them.

Mrs. Eddy, in bringing the promised Comforter, the Second Coming of the Christ, will therefore represent the *whole man,* who is today represented on earth by *two witnesses*, the manhood of Jesus, and the womanhood of Mary Baker Eddy. **What awaits us?**

The redemption of sin!

Mrs. Eddy, when asked, "What is sin?" replied, *"The connubial relation."* In *Rudimental Divine Science* she states, "The **emphatic purpose** of Christian Science is the healing of sin" (p.2). It is fundamental in C.S. treatment.

In the first edition, page 240:2 Mrs. Eddy makes the all-important statement: "Error claiming Life in matter . . . was the original sin." This defining statement on the necessity of handling entrenched sin, runs through all of Science and Health, and can be found in her *Other Writings,* such as:

"Sickness and death appeared through [sin], the false supposition of life and intelligence in matter." (*Chr. Heal.* 17:24). See also, *C.S. vs. Pan.* p. 6, "Evil As Personified by the Serpent." In *UN. of Good*, Mrs. Eddy asks: "Which was right, God who condemned the knowledge of sin . . . or the serpent . . . (p. 54). "The serpent claimed to originate in the name of the Lord."

Her words, "The universe of Spirit is *peopled* with spiritual beings" (S&H 264:32), gives us a glimpse of what awaits us. Jesus and Mrs. Eddy, while they were still in mortal form, were in communication with these immortals. "Mortals will disappear," she said, "and immortals . . . will appear as the only and eternal verities of man" (*ibid.* 476:11). In *Christ and Christmas,* discerning her realization of her own I AM, she writes: "For Christian Science brings to view the great I Am, gleaming through Mind, mother [Mary Baker Eddy, the one who is writing the page], man."

CHAPTER 9

THE CONTINUITY OF LIFE
EVIL AND ERROR DO NOT EXIST
IN REALITY

Overcoming corporeal creation we overcome death. If "all things were made by [Infinite Good], and without [Infinite Good] was not anything made that was made," then evil and error simply do not exist. Their seeming existence is aggressive mental suggestion only, hypnotic suggestion. When Martha of Bethany voiced the standard belief that she would see her brother Lazarus again at the "last day," Jesus instantly repudiated that prevailing notion, knowing that wholeness and health were the ever-present fact. "I am the resurrection, and the life!" he boldly announced. "He that believeth in me [notice "in *me*"; he did not say he that believeth in God, but "in me," and in what I tell you], though he were dead, [asleep, and not aware of the facts of Life] yet shall he live," (John 11:1-46) and be aware of himself as he really is.

In reality you now are perfect and immortal. Age is a self-imposed cruel taskmaster. It is but the educated BELIEF that man or existence had a beginning; therefore it is pure illusion. The continuity of life is the most important question in the world today, which even the medical profession is beginning to see. When will mankind wake to the great scientific fact that in heaven Mind-substance is the only medium needed for all the heart yearns for?

"God, the Mind of man," contemplates itself. Where? Within *your* consciousness. When the crucified Jesus lay in the rock-ribbed tomb wasn't it his own Mind—the Mind he called "the Father"—that resurrected him? Jesus held to the true idea. He saw reality, the Christ. His constant acknowledgment of but one power exalted him, and he "overcame the world." His perfect state of Mind lifted him into heaven. He retained his body, his individuality, that reflected eternal life. His Christ Mind had divested him of all the errors that are the opposite of the seven synonyms in Mrs. Eddy's definition of God. In his ascension the physical man, Jesus, disappeared; his consciousness was no longer fettered with a physical body. He furnished conclusive proof that matter is unreal. With spiritual growth we all will experience the same.

After quoting "If a man keep my saying, he shall never see death" (John 8:51), Mrs. Eddy tells us: "That statement is not confined to spiritual life, but includes all the phenomena of existence. . . . **Belief in** sickness and death as certainly as belief in sin tends to shut out the true sense of Life and health." But "advancing spiritual steps in the teeming universe of Mind lead on to spiritual spheres and exalted beings [which we will become aware of as the veil is lifted]" (S&H 429:31 and 513:6). Mrs. Eddy's writings are continually lifting the veil. In the "spiritual spheres" we create and express only with Mind substance.

Mrs. Eddy tells of an experience where: "Immediately I could see those who had passed on, in belief, and they were not dead, but were right here about us; but I had not gained their point so as to be conscious to them, but as it were looked ahead to it; neither did I seem to be in an abnormal state of mind at the time I saw this and yet it seemed as real and tangible as anything ever was" (Preserved by Carpenter, Sr.) On the Mount of Transfiguration Jesus actually had "gained their point so as to be conscious to them." Moses and Elias spoke to Jesus and strengthened him for the coming crucifixion.

Ira Knapp while suffering "the greatest of all earthy bereavements," following the death of his wife, visited Mrs. Eddy at Pleasant View. In the midst of their business interview Mrs. Eddy suddenly turned to him and said: "Ira Knapp, are you still babying that lie about your wife?" She then gave an audible treatment that completely healed Mr. Knapp of all sense of grief and separation. At the conclusion Mr. Knapp somewhat apologetically said he was glad to know there was no more than a wall of partition between him and his wife. At that, Mrs. Eddy leaned forward and said very forcibly, "But there is *no wall!* I see through that 'wall'; *SHE IS RIGHT HERE!"* Then Mrs. Eddy proceeded to tell Ira what Mrs. Knapp was doing. But seeing Ira was not following her explanation, she changed the subject.

"The spiritual idea must have its visible expression, its incarnation, or else Christian Science is only abstraction," Mrs Eddy said. Jesus proved this when he talked with Moses and Elias on the Mount of Transfiguration, when he brought Lazarus back from the tomb, and when he raised himself.

Referring to the death of Edward Kimball's body, Mrs. Eddy said if we looked rightly, "we should see him *here, and realize he never died. As* "*'I AM,'* he existed *"before Abraham was,"* and will always be. In the dimensionless world of thought everything will always be. **Our physical**

bodies are things or objects we are aware of. *They are not things or objects that are aware.*

Our totally false belief that life is in the form we see, in what we are aware of, is like looking at a calculation on the blackboard and believing it is mathematics. What a loss we would feel if someone erased it and we continued to believe that part of mathematics is gone. Mrs. Eddy states that birth and death arise only from the *material sense of things, not from the spiritual.* *"Matter cannot change the eternal fact that man exists because God exists" (S&H 544:7-11),* and "the transition from our lower sense of Life to a new and higher sense thereof, even though it be through the door of death, yields a clearer and nearer sense of Life to those who have utilized the present . . ." (*Mis.* 84:28).

"Death and finiteness are unknown to Life. . . . Mortals waken from the dream of death with bodies unseen by those who think they bury the body" (S&H 469:5; & 429:17). "Death can never alarm or even appear to him who fully understands Life" (*Un.* 40:20).

> *Our Master said, "The kingdom of heaven is at hand.' Then God and heaven, or Life, are present, and death is not the real stepping-stone to Life and happiness. They are now and here; and a change in human consciousness, from sin to holiness, would reveal this wonder of being"* (*Un.* 37:6).

Both Jesus and Mrs. Eddy were ardent crusaders for this needed change in human consciousness that would reveal present perfection.

DEATH MUST BE OVERCOME

Regarding the ascension of Jesus, and what is required of every individual, Mrs. Eddy wrote:

> *On our Master's individual demonstrations over sin, sickness and death, rested the anathema of priesthood and the senses; yet this demonstration is the foundation of Christian Science. His physical sufferings, which came from the testimony of the senses, were over when he resumed his individual spiritual being, after showing us the way to escape from the material body."* (Mis. 105:5).

Adam Dickey recorded another of Mrs. Eddy's explanation of death, as follows:

> *When we can awaken ourselves out of the belief that all must die, we will then have reached a point where death means nothing to us,*

and we will then be able to bring back all that death claimed to have taken away from us. In other words, we will be able to reproduce the presence of those who thought they died, whether it was ten minutes ago or ten years ago. [Jesus on the Mount of Transfiguration reproduced the presence of Moses and Elias who had died many centuries before].

However, when that time comes, death will not appear to us as what it now seems to be, and it is hard to predict even in the light of Science just how things will appear under changed conditions.

Some things we do know.   On page 72 of Science and Health, Mrs. Eddy explains the impossibility of evil being communicated from the departed to mortals, but incidentally remarks that **good** may come to us in this way. She assures us: "Thought on the other side of the grave is not different from thought on this side."

People who have returned after being declared clinically dead tell of their feeling of "indescribable comfort and of being truly loved."

The thousands of "life after life" accounts of people returning after being declared clinically dead, resonate from somewhere within ourselves. We know they are true. Those who have gone on, awaken from the dream of life in matter to know the disease they thought was killing them was never there.

"SHE COULD NOT HAVE SPOKEN"
—Jeanne M. Dams

The chaplain sat by the dying woman's bed in the hospice ward. He knew little about her except that the end was near. Now she was unconscious. The chaplain felt tired and closed his eyes for a moment.

Suddenly he was startled by a loud cry from the bed. The woman was sitting bolt upright. "My God!" she cried out. Then sank back against the pillows, her eyes closed, a look of radiance on her face.

A nurse rushed in. "Did you call out?" she asked the chaplain as she took the woman's pulse, and said: "I'm afraid she's gone."

"No, I didn't speak," the chaplain said in wonderment, still thinking of the woman's ecstatic exclamation. "She did. She cried out, 'My God!'"

The nurse turned to him puzzled. "But she couldn't have. She had cancer of the larynx. Her voice box was destroyed weeks ago. She couldn't have said a word."

Mrs. Eddy wouldn't have been surprised. She states: *If you take away this erring mind, the mortal material body loses all appearance of life or action, and this so-called mind then calls itself dead; but the human mind still holds in belief a body, through which it acts, and which appears to the human mind to live,—a body like the one it had before death. This body [this mental, subjective body] is put off only as the mortal erring mind yields to God, immortal Mind, and [the spiritual] man is found in [the image of Infinite Good]"* (S&H 187:27-2).

ETERNAL LIFE NOT FOUND BY DYING

Mrs. Eddy tells us: *"One theory about this mortal mind is, that its sensations can reproduce man, can form blood, flesh, and bones"* (ibid. 372:6). Notice that "blood, flesh, and bones" are a product of mortal mind and therefore illusion.

Regarding the action of mortal mind, illusion, after it has brought forth the body of flesh and bones (the first death) and passed through the experience of the second death, Mrs. Eddy writes:

"Mortal belief dies to live again in renewed forms, only to go out at last forever; for life everlasting is not to be gained by dying" (S&H 556:10)

However, there never was a time that man could not break the so-called law of death and birth, if only he would awaken from this Adam dream, and grasp the reality of Life in and of Spirit. Jesus, the Messiah, "the last Adam," born of a virgin, was the first to awaken from the Adam dream. His knowledge of God and Christ overcame all error, and dissolved the elements of thought that produced the *human* Jesus. Thus it brought the light which started humanity turning away from darkness and looking for the truth of their Christ selfhood within their own consciousness.

JESUS PRESENTED HIS BODY ABSOLVED FROM DEATH

Mrs. Eddy writes: "Jesus demonstrated the divine Principle of Christian Science when he presented his *material* body absolved from death and the grave.

"[However] neither the Old nor the New Testament furnishes reasons or examples for the destruction of the human body, but for its restoration to life and health as the scientific proof of 'God with us.' The power and prerogative of Truth are to destroy all disease and to raise the dead—even the self-same Lazarus. The *spiritual* body, the incorporeal idea, came with the ascension" (*My.* 218:11, & 5). (Here see Mrs. Eddy's interesting references to "temporal," "temporary," and "temporarily.")

In the following quote notice *probation is on earth while we are still in our flesh and bones body.* Mrs. Eddy speaks of Jesus' probation in the flesh after he raised his body from the grave as an exemplification of human probation: "*Christian Scientists . . . celebrate their Lord's victory over death, his probation in the flesh after death, its exemplification of human probation, and his final ascension above matter, or the flesh, . . .*" *(S&H 35:11),* hence Jesus' saying: *"Whatsoever thou shalt bind on earth shall be bound in heaven."*

Jesus finished his work on earth by *overcoming* death and the grave. He was our example. He said he was "the way." After his resurrection his consciousness advanced beyond the concept of a physical form, and the physical Jesus disappeared. In order to show that he, Christ Jesus, had mastered all belief, he presented the same body that was buried in the tomb, thus preserving his human personality until the ascension.

Resurrection was not exclusive to Jesus. When he said, "I am the resurrection," he was telling us that if we can perceive the "I" (S&H 588:9) within ourselves, we too will resurrect and demonstrate that the Son of God in us cannot die. Knowing this we cannot be crucified by discord, fear, lack, loneliness, or disease.

Mrs. Eddy brought the good news that "the ascension comes because each higher manifestation of Truth uncovers its supposititious opposite to be met and destroyed. Thus we rise step by step until we finally reach a condition which has no erroneous expression. This moment—when the material senses no longer cognize us because we have overcome their claims, have overcome the hypnotism that has held us captive—this moment must be the ascension. To subjective sense, ascension is only expansion from earth to heaven.

One young man who heard Mrs. Eddy's sermons at Hawthorne Hall wrote that Mrs. Eddy carried her listeners "right to the sepulchre where Jesus stepped forth in spiritual triumph. Resurrection, as she presented it," he said, "was more than history or symbol; it was present fact." It was to him, the student, like awakening from a hypnotic trance—from the Adam dream. The starting point in divine Science is that heaven is *here*; there is no error to ascend out of, since good is ALL and ever-present.

In *Essays and Other Footprints, p. 11,* **Mrs. Eddy explains:**

"The spiritual origin and support of the universe and man is their only real origin, subsistence and ultimate. Therefore, the entity or ego of man is Spirit *and man is but the idea of himself AND HIMSELF IS GOD OF WHICH MAN IS THE REFLEX SHADOW.* **["The kingdom of God is within you"—is your true consciousness.] . . . The spiritual origin and existence of man and**

the universe are the truth of man and the universe. A material origin and existence of the universe and man are mythology. The notion that matter is supposed to include Spirit is a misstatement of being. One of the proofs that man is idea and not matter is that man must disappear materially to reappear spiritually or as idea— [reappear as] that spiritual representative of eternal Life or God. Every hour is a partial fulfillment of this statement of being and final spiritualization of all things. For every material hour is mortal and hasteth to its end, even eternity, the final dissolution of all material computation of hours, and the destruction of all organic structure. . . .

[Here let me interject from *Miscellaneous Writings;* p. 286:21. Concerning the death process, Mrs. Eddy explains: "Human procreation, birth, life and death, are subjective states of the human mind; they are the phenomena of mortality, nothingness, that illustrate mortal mind and body as *one*, and neither real nor eternal."

"The false belief that spirit is now submerged in matter, at some future time to be emancipated from it,—this belief alone is mortal." . . . This is why "the true sense of being and its eternal perfection should appear <u>NOW</u>, even as it will hereafter" (S&H 546:1 & 550:12. See also 75:16). Since "the Christian Scientist is alone with his own being and with the reality of things," my real Mind, the only I or Ego, is forever saying: "If I am All, I can have no consciousness of anything unlike Myself, and since I am omni-present, there can be nothing outside of myself." (See Un. 3:24.)]

Continuing her article in EOF, p. 11, she concludes: "A picture in mind cannot be marred or blotted out so long as the mind that contains it is symmetrical and eternal. Now I mean that man is one of the pictures of God's Mind [our Mind] and this picture is a product and not a producer; it is an image, and reflection, the intelligence whereof is the Mind that produced it, and not that man is a separate mind from God, for then man would be a sinner and sin would render man mortal. The only possible way for man to be immortal is to have no separate mind from God, for then man is governed by an unerring Mind and this produces an undying body forever undisturbed by matter" (*ibid.* p. 11, 12).

CHAPTER 10

SPIRITUAL EDUCATION UNCOVERS, DESTROYS ERROR

GOOD BEING REAL, ITS OPPOSITE IS UNREAL

"The origin of evil is the problem of the ages, and confronts each generation anew. It confronts Christian Science. The question is often asked, if God created only the good whence cometh the evil? To this question Christian Science replies evil never did exist as an entity; it is but a belief that there is an opposite intelligence to Infinite Good. This belief is a species of idolatry. The admission of the reality of evil perpetuates faith in evil, and the Scriptures declare that to whom ye yield yourselves servants to obey, his servants ye are. This leading self-evident proposition of Christian Science *that good being real, its opposite is necessarily unreal, needs to be grasped in all its divine requirements" (DCC* p. 219).

Spiritual education is necessary since one cannot correct a mistake until one knows one has made a mistake. Evil and error had a beginning only as hypnotism has a beginning with no past and no future. It is imperative that Christian Scientists understand the origin of evil, and thus rely on their own individual Christ selfhood, as the savior of the body.

Blind belief can never take the place of reason. "There is nothing so detrimental to Christian Science as blind belief." Regarding the healing practice she states, "It is the healer's *understanding* of the operation of divine Principle, and his application thereof, which heals the sick, just as it is one's understanding of the principle of mathematics which enables him to demonstrate its rules" (Mary Baker Eddy, *Principle and Practice*).

It is *understanding* that heals—either your understanding, or the understanding of the practitioner you call on. It was Mrs. Eddy's understanding that healed, and that was able to teach her students to heal just as Jesus taught his disciples to heal. She *KNEW* "matter and evil, including all inharmony, sin, disease, death) are *unreal" (Mis* 27:11); and that God was actually the consciousness of every individual.

Mrs. Eddy teaches: "A false belief is both the tempter and the tempted [that which tempts the spiritual man (you and me)], the sin and the sinner, the disease and its cause" (S&H 393:30). If we think the illusion originates with something *other than spiritual man*, we have two causes, don't we? But Jesus and Mrs. Eddy firmly teach one cause only. This is the point Jesus makes in his parable of the prodigal who was the Son of God. Also after asking: "Whom do **men** say that I am?" he asked, "Whom say **ye** that I am?" implying that humanity's divinity—its oneness with God must be understood. It is also the point Mrs. Eddy is making throughout Science and Health and her *Prose Works.* There is not a second creator that could cause matter to be something other than an illusion.

Since we are the spiritual man right now, and error is the outcome of this spiritual man's wrong thinking, evil and error cannot be overcome until its origin is explained and understood. As someone has wisely said, "Preconceived notions [such as error's pretense of life passing as our thought] are the locks on the door to wisdom." Since we are the "thinker" and are the spiritual man, it is necessary for us to know that believing in matter is *our* mistake. Then we can correct it. If it was someone else's mistake how could we correct it? "Physician, heal thyself." How? "Hold thought steadfastly to the enduring, the good and the true, and you will bring these into your experience proportionably to their occupancy of your thought" (S&H 261:4). Jesus said we must change our way of thinking.

THE PRODIGAL LEFT "THE BROAD BEAM OF LIGHT"

Through universal hypnotism we have been blinded to the understanding of the "Father" for so long we have entirely forgotten it. But in this age through Mary Baker Eddy's teaching, the secret of secrets, our true identity as one with God, is being revealed so that we can return to our true estate as did the son in Jesus' parable of the prodigal, the spiritual man who left the fourth dimension of Spirit, the Father's house. This parable is our story (see S&H 325:26) which recounts our experience as a prodigal, and our awakening to our oneness with God, "the Father," enabling us to find the kingdom of God within our consciousness:

And [Jesus] said, A certain man had two sons: and the younger of them said to his Father, Father, give me the portion of goods that falleth to me. And he divided unto them his living. And not many days after, the younger son gathered all together, and took his journey into a far country [away from the broad beam of light, the fourth dimension of Spirit], and there wasted his substance with riotous living. And when he had spent all, there arose a mighty famine in that land; and he began to be in want. And he went and joined himself to a citizen of that country; and he sent him into his fields to feed swine. And he would fain have filled his belly with the husks that the swine did eat: and no man gave unto him. And when he came to himself, he said, How many hired servants of my Father's have bread enough and to spare, and I perish with hunger? I will arise and go to my Father, and I will say unto him, Father, I have sinned against heaven, and before Thee, And am no more worthy to be thy son: make me as one of thy hired servants. And he arose, and came to his Father [the divine Mind]. But when he was yet a great way off, his Father saw him, and had compassion, and ran and fell on his neck, and kissed him. And the son said unto him, Father, I have sinned against heaven, and in thy sight, and am no more worthy to be called thy son. But the Father said to his servants, Bring forth the best robe, and put it on him; and put a ring on his hand, and shoes on his feet: For this my son was DEAD [not understood, as Mrs. Eddy explained] and is alive again; he was lost, and is found. (Luke 15:11-22, 24).

FOOLED BY A LIE, WE MUST RETURN TO
THE FATHER'S HOUSE

The son (meaning our real self) was fooled by the supposition, the lie, that pleasure could be found in material things and that the material world had more to offer him than his Father's house, alias divine Mind. This lie is the foundation of the material world. It makes the Son (you and me) a prodigal.

The human, the mortal, we have learned, was the outcome of listening to the serpent, the lie about our origin. "In Romans (ii. 15) we read . . . [human] thoughts are 'the mean while accusing or else excusing one another' [criss-crossing each other like freeway traffic on a cow path, as the good in human nature maneuvers for control—"] weary of matter it would catch the meaning of Spirit" (*Hea.* 11:8)] (*Un.* 21:l).

The record starts from the foundation of the world—from the time that error first declared itself as a power, and usurped the throne of our spiritual consciousness, slaying the Lamb. The Lamb spoken of is Jesus, the last human link in the male side of this spiritual individuality where each individual has ALL the God-qualities both male and female. "The marriage supper of the Lamb" means becoming aware of the male and female qualities united in one consciousness—in your consciousness and in mine.

Jesus, the child of the prophets (Matt. 13:16-17; Luke 10:23-24) and the subject of the whole New Testament, is the male representative of the spiritual idea. Of him, Mrs. Eddy states, "This was the Lamb slain from the foundation of the world,—slain, that is, according to the testimony of the corporeal senses [corporeal sense is the "murderer from the beginning"], but undying in the deific Mind." In *DCC* p. 101 we read: "Mother explained the difference between a material sense of love and a spiritual sense. A material sense of love dishonors the one it professes to love through lust. . . . Mother said this is the 'Lamb slain from the foundation of the world.' that is the spiritual sense of Love that is slain from the foundation of a material sense of sexuality." The Revelator represents the Son of man as saying (Rev. 1:17, 18): 'I am the first and the last: I am he that liveth, and was *DEAD* (not understood); [as in the parable of the prodigal son, when the Father says, "This my son was dead..."] and behold, I am alive for evermore (Science has explained me)'" (S&H 334:21). This account of the male representative "leaving the Father's house" at the time of his human birth, and returning in the ascension, is an account not only of Jesus' experience but the experience of every mortal.

How is the "return" accomplished?

"One's first lesson is to learn ones' self" (*Mis.* 129:5). This "human self must be **EVANGELIZED** [by abandoning so fast as practical the material]" (S&H 254:19). In her first three chapters: Prayer, Atonement and Eucharist, and Marriage, Mrs. Eddy dwells like a one-string fiddle on this **evangelization.** These chapters teach that the seed must be sown in the good human qualities. They constitute the bridge to the spiritual, and lead to the realm of the real.

"Ignorance of self is the most stubborn belief to overcome, for apathy, dishonesty, sin, follow in its train" (*My.* 233:19). Do we spend most of our lives thinking and studying about external things, when next to God, the most important knowledge we possess is about ourselves? The most inexcusable ignorance concerns the hidden enemies sheltered in our own mental household. Christian Science "is telling mankind of the foe in ambush." Our constant prayer must be: "Cleanse thou me from secret faults" (Ps. 19:12) The only thing evil asks of us is to be let alone. Wouldn't we call the police if we thought a thief or assassin was in the house? Shouldn't we eliminate that which—so long as it remains in our thought—brings forth sin, sickness, death? (See Matt. 24:43.)

And shouldn't we do this house-cleaning *NOW*? "Error never had a real beginning. There is no past, no future. There is only the ever-present NOW. Mrs. Eddy once chided Clara Choate for singing "In the sweet bye and bye," because she had taught Clara to realize the NOW of every good thing, just as we have the nowness of 2x2=4. Since Mind, Spirit Soul, Principle, Life, Truth and Love are the same today as they were a million years ago, or will be a million years hence, the change must come about *in us.* And it can, since we "possess sovereign power to think and act rightly."

We alone are the "attorney and judge" in each case. "The Christian Scientist is alone with his own being and with the reality of things," ('01. 20:8), so what are we waiting for? Nothing but a change in ourselves! It is not a question of whether the conquest of our false nature can be accomplished, but rather, *ARE WE GOING TO DO IT?* Our divinity must be lived. Said our Wayshower: "To this end was I born, and for this cause came I into the world, that I should bear witness unto the truth." Again, "I have overcome the world"—I have overcome material thinking. "To know Him [our higher consciousness] aright is Life eternal."

Mrs Eddy maintained emphatically that only through our consciousness can something happen to us. Infinite Good is omnipresent but unless we open our consciousness to receive it, nothing of God can touch our life. Sadly, she agreed that "the birthplace of civilization is not Athens, but Calvary." (*Mess. '02.* 10:10). Infinite Good can only come into our experience by a conscious act of our consciousness.

To make the transit from matter to Spirit there is a price to be paid. We must consciously negate the laws of the world, and by an activity of consciousness become aware of the law of Infinite Good operating in our experience, until finally the "I" that is God so permeates human consciousness that we, like Jesus, can say, "He that seeth me seeth him that sent me." (John 12:45). We must reach the place where there is only the Father—our true Mind—revealing itself as the Son, as what looks like you and me. Never forget, what we are looking at is God in disguise. The nature of Infinite Good is ours for the taking. Think of it! We are in possession of the nature of God, freely bestowed upon us if we will but come out of the mesmerism of a **material** selfhood.

Does evil or good work by itself? No. Each requires a medium through which to act. Are we agents for evil? or are we "fellow worker[s] in the gospel of Christ"? (I Thes. 3:2). We all know there is much in our thinking that should come to an end—tares which have for a long time been growing with the wheat. Let them be garnered into bundles and burned. Problems exist only in the universal human mind. They find outlet through us; but the problem is dead if we refuse to let it flow out from us. A problem is the universal belief in two powers. If we know Infinite Good is omnipotent, we destroy the problem in the only place where it existed, namely, in the universal human mind. Evil will disappear from our experience only as Good is recognized and takes evil's place. The consciousness of our true self is on the high road of unselfed love, self-denial, self-discipline, self-forgetfulness.

Let's work diligently to be the self which is identified with God. To this end our textbook reminds us, "The vital part, the heart and soul of Christian Science, is Love. Without this, the letter is but the dead body of Science, pulseless, cold, inanimate" (p.113:5). We can reach our true selves only through Love. Love is the Principle that we are, as Mrs. Eddy tells us, in the first edition.

Hypnotism tells us we are sinful mortals, born of the flesh, but through the First and Second Coming of the Christ we are awakening from this hypnotic Adam-dream. Jesus and Mrs. Eddy came to show us the road human beings must traverse—to emerge from the *sense* of life as physical, with its pleasures and pains—in order to gain the heavenly realm of consciousness. Wherever heaven is, is where one's true identity must be found. That road is the denial of false selfhood. It is up to each one of us to *uproot* "every plant, which my heavenly Father hath not planted" (Matt. 15:13). Only if we do this uprooting are we able to accept Infinite Good's offer of its divine nature, our true identity, that has been laid at our feet. If we don't do this uprooting, are we Christian Scientists?

It is up to us to defend ourselves against our own false sense of ourselves. "[We must know ourselves] before we can know others and minister to human needs . . . You uncover sin, not in order to injure, but in order to bless the corporeal man" (S&H 453:14). We should be grateful and happy to have our sins uncovered. (See S&H 8:30). "The conceptions of mortal, erring thought must give way to the ideal of all that is perfect and eternal. . . . [Good's] creation will finally be seen as the only true conception of being [but only as **we are cleansed** 'from secret faults']" (S&H 260:7).

When I pray, "Let the reign of divine Truth, Life, and Love be established in me and rule out of me all sin," do I see that I have to do the letting? What hinders me, other than "faith in things material"? Am I sincere, when the next minute I forget it and let something unlike God rule my thoughts?

A Christian Scientist's goal should be to glorify Infinite Good, rather than seeking only physical harmony and healing.

It is your individual right to see and acknowledge to yourself that your identity is exactly what Infinite Good made it to be. If humanity's true consciousness wasn't spiritual, Science and Health and the Bible would have no meaning for mankind. These books show us how to "stand porter" until we reach the understanding of our God-being. Isn't "standing porter" what Jesus meant when he said, "If the good man of the house had known in what watch the thief would come, he would have watched, and would not have suffered his house (consciousness) to be broken into"? (Matt. 24:43).

Jesus, our divine Exemplar, finding that error was nothing, could work his way back to "his Father's house." So can we. Indulging fear, worry, disappointment, unhappiness, selfishness, means we are not actively reflecting Infinite Good during that time. And further, these indulgences have a poisonous effect upon the body's physical functions. We pay a terrible price because of them. But they are only mistakes, aren't they? And mistakes are always open to correction (when we know enough of the truth).

DISEASE IS BUT THE IMAGE OF A LIE

"What is disease?" Mrs. Eddy asked a student, who answered correctly. Then she said, "Yes, disease is but the image of a lie. It is not matter or a part of matter. It is but the result of a falsehood [of hypnotism]. As Jesus said, it is but 'a liar and the father of lies.' There is no truth in it. Disease, sickness and sin are to be recognized as the image of wrong thought, and seeing it thus, it is destroyed." What does it mean that disease is the image of wrong thought? It means, to avoid it we have to reform ourselves. If for a moment we could completely look away from our human personality—with all its pettiness, selfishness, weakness, foolish pride, appetites and passions, and see as Jesus and Mrs. Eddy saw—at that moment we would consciously be one with our true being, Infinite Good.

Let's totally reverse these errors, remembering that "the body improves under the same regimen which spiritualizes the thought" (S&H 370:5). If God is All, there can be no reality in error, and we shouldn't bow down to it. Our work is to keep our thoughts of self on the highest plane we know. We must line up with our divine Principle, from which we may draw all that is necessary to take us to the pinnacle of accomplishment.

LET'S WAKE UP! Shake off the lethargy that says, **"Tomorrow** I'll start." This material imposition that wants to stick to you and me doesn't abandon its hold upon us until we divest ourselves of "secret faults" and grow into a realization of our divine origin. The matter body is just a mortal mind picture we carry around with us. But Infinite Good's relation to you and me has not changed just because of the illusions of the Adam dream. The scientific fact is we do not live in or of matter—we never did.

"The divine Mind, not matter, creates all identities, and they are forms of Mind, the ideas of Spirit apparent only as Mind, never as mindless matter" (S&H 505:11). A practitioner, in treating a case, does not acknowledge reality in the picture the patient presents, but keeps in mind the spiritual perfection. Infinite Good forms the individuality of men and women; and that form is the only real form of the patient, and of you and me. When we correct material belief we will become aware of this new spiritual form. But we don't become aware of it if we go blithely on believing in matter-forms. "Consciousness constructs a better body when faith in matter has been conquered" (S&H 425:23).

"The fundamental error [is] faith in things material; for this trust is the unseen sin, the unknown foe" (*Ret.* 31:16). This faith in things material is the great obstruction that stands in our way of being aware of our true identity. It holds our thought to an identity that Infinite Good did not give us, and which we must grow out of before realizing what we truly are. More and more we must think of ourselves as the kind of man that is born of Spirit.

> My world has sprung from Spirit,
> In everlasting day;
> Whereof, I've more to glory,
> Wherefor, have much to pay.
>
> MARK BAKER EDDY

Then we will become aware of "the eternal wonder,—that infinite space is peopled with [Infinite Good's] ideas, reflecting [Infinite Good] in countless spiritual forms [it is here among those 'countless spiritual forms' that our own forms are]" (S&H 503:15; see also 264:32). In reality, can we be anywhere else?

As Christian Scientists, how far have we gone in showing ourselves or the world that this way of life is "within reach of man's consciousness here"? (S&H 576:22)

Our task is to become Love by learning error's unreality. This means casting out fear, and every negative thought. Divine Love unmasks evil, animal magnetism. When spiritual understanding removes the mask, we find nothing is present but **DIVINE LOVE**, the note on which Mrs. Eddy "closes" Science and Health, p. 578:5.

CHAPTER 11

TO DESTROY SEEMING ERROR
WE MUST UNDERSTAND IT

In 1902 Mrs. Eddy told the Board of Education: "The only excuse for teaching is to teach quietly how error is to be destroyed."

> *"To teach students in a class without teaching them how to handle animal magnetism [hypnotism] is like sending soldiers into battle with brass buttons and braid but with no ammunition for their muskets.*
> *"This is a mental age. Malpractice would dominate [and around the world today Satan seems to be in the saddle] therefore unless Christian Scientists are awake to it [and alert to hold error in check] it would hold back Christian Science for centuries"* (DCC 225).

To prevent false thoughts from coming to mind, I must remember that I am a spiritual being in the world of reality. I am now in possession of the kingdom of heaven. Spiritual understanding reveals the truth that I always have been free. Mrs. Eddy demonstrated this when she "got Mary out of the way," and for the first time in human history—through her life and her writings—showed evil to be unreal. Finding out that evil is not real enables us to be one with Infinite Good. Mrs. Eddy's work was twofold, including both the revelation of Truth and the uncovering of error. This meant explaining what reality is **not,** as well as what it is.

Growing away from error involves an understanding of animal magnetism, hypnotism, aggressive mental suggestion, which use the evidence of the physical senses to enslave man. To handle error we have to first face it and understand it. Mrs. Eddy instructs us: *"A knowledge of error and of its operations must precede that understanding of Truth which destroys error, until the entire mortal, material error finally disappears, and the eternal verity, man created by and of Spirit, is understood and recognized as the true likeness of his Maker"* (S&H 252:8-14).

"SIN CONSTITUTES . . . THE PHYSICAL CONCEPTS"

Ret. 67;1 states, "Sin existed as a false claim before the human concept of sin was formed; hence one's concept of error is not the whole of error. The human thought does not constitute sin, but *vice versa, sin constitutes the human or physical concept.*

Where did this false claim come from? When Mrs. Eddy teaches that matter cannot create but that it has a *mental cause,* what does she mean?

What gave matter a mental cause? "A sense of evil is supposed to have spoken," Mrs. Eddy tells us, "been listened to, and afterwards to have formed an evil sense that blinded the eyes of reason, masked with deformity the glories of revelation, and shamed the face of mortals.

"What was this sense? Error versus Truth: first a supposition; second, a false belief; third, suffering; fourth, death" (*Mis. 332:18*). **Where did this false sense come from?** Certainly not from God! But Mrs. Eddy has told us that God, Mind, is the *only generative* power. If the original sin, which originated in matter, was *self-created,* then according to logic and reason there must be *two* powers, one good, one evil. But since the Infinite Good is the only generative and regenerative power there cannot be another power.

Then what looks like matter has to be an illusion, but it seems very, very real. Consider: if matter created itself there would be *TWO* creators. Since there are not two creators, how else could evil and error come into seeming existence? Mrs. Eddy asks:

> *Was there original self-creative sin? Then there must have been more than one creator, more than one God . . . Who dares to say either that God is in matter or that matter exists without God?* (S&H 356:31-32 & 531;21-22)

What is she saying here?

Certainly not that God is the creator of matter. She is forcing us to the only rational conclusion, namely, that God, Mind, is the creator of man. "Man is never God, but spiritual man, made in God's likeness, reflects God" (S&H 70:7).

We have learned it is God, Mind, the only power, that gives the spiritual man consciousness. Mrs. Eddy — unlike the theologians — teaches that Infinite Good never made a physical man called Adam, but that Infinite Good, Mind, Spirit, made man in the image of Mind, Spirit. Therefore the man God made is mental and spiritual. (See S&H 465:17-1.)

It must be the human or physical concept of this spiritual man who is guilty of giving matter a mental cause. Adam, the physical corporeal man, is the manifestation of a mistaken concept of God.

There could not be any other source from which evil and matter could start except from the suppositions entertained by the corporeal man. Why? Because apart from God, who does not know evil or matter, there did not exist (before the beginning of evil and matter) any other thought force than that of the spiritual creation. See Mrs. Eddy's explanation, S&H 301:24.

Isn't it evident that if evil and matter are not self-existent, and if they have a mental cause, it must start from an entity that *was* self-existent? And since there is not a second creator, and Infinite Good could not conceive error, error can only be traced to the misconception of spiritual man.

But how does corporeal man give matter a mental cause? Mrs. Eddy teaches: *"Truth perverted, in belief, becomes the creator of the claim of error"* (Mis. 293:22). The corporeal man perverts the Truth, in belief. This becomes the creator of the claim of error.

How was corporeal man able to pervert the Truth and bring about the seeming appearance of evil? Mrs. Eddy states:

God has endowed man with inalienable rights, among which are self-government, reason and conscience. Man is properly self-governed only when he is guided rightly and governed by his Maker, divine Truth and Love. Man's rights are invaded when the divine order is interfered with, and the mental trespasser incurs the divine penalty due his crime. (S&H 106:7-14).

If man should say of the power to be perfect which he possesses, "I am the power," he would trespass upon divine Science, yield to material sense, and lose his power. (Mis. 184:14-16).

Again, she says, "Man is in a degree as perfect as the Mind that forms him" (S&H 337:10). "The Mind that forms him" is your divine Mind, since "man has no Mind but God." Did **manifestation claim to be a cause**? Did man, possessing the power to be perfect, trespass by saying "I am that power," thinking he could increase in knowledge without the aid of Infinite Good? Again, see Mrs. Eddy's explanation, S&H 301:24.

Mrs. Eddy makes it clear that sin started with man's wrong beliefs about God. These beliefs include evil and error of every kind, which were lies from the beginning. The "talking serpent" symbolizes the transgression by which a lie appears to interfere with the divine order, suggesting that man could increase in knowledge without the aid of Infinite Good, and thus he became a prodigal from his Father's house.

"Truth perverted, in belief, becomes the claim of evil." Wrong notions about God originated in a false supposition that has been accepted as fact, and began our wrong view of the universe and man. (See S&H 357:19.) This wrong view launched every physical thing into temporal existence. "Temporal life is a false existence." (See S&H 122:27 and Mrs. Eddy's other references to "temporal".)

"By man's first disobedience came 'death into the world, and all our woe' " (*Un. 15:1*). By a false concept man changed his true concept of the spiritual universe and himself, and brought into existence a physical universe and a physical man. So we see this wrong VIEW of the universe and man started through a supposition that was accepted as fact. And because of this he became a prodigal and temporarily lost his power.

This explains why Mrs. Eddy says: "*Sin existed as a false claim BE-FORE the human concept of sin [Adam] was formed; hence one's concept of error is not the whole of the error*" (Ret. 67:1-2). The whole of the error is the original sin or false supposition, just mentioned, plus the human concept, namely, Adam.

THE FALSE SUPPOSITION

The original false supposition was about God. Before "the supposition" began, there existed only God, Mind, and Mind's spiritual creation, as one, which was mental; therefore the supposition (hypnotism) must have been mental, and about God.

As Infinite Good is Father-Mother, each of Infinite Good's ideas expresses both the male and female elements. All of God's reflections must express these two natures in one individuality. When men believed a false supposition about the infinite good called God, man changed his dual nature into two physical expressions. This dual nature is counterfeited on the physical plane by the male and female human concepts.

Why can't we say that mortal mind made the flesh and bones body? Answer: We can't say this because that would be saying there is another power besides Infinite Good. Why can't we say, as some are prone to do, that matter does not exist? Because Mrs. Eddy says, "*The material body and mind are temporal.*" Science and Health has about twenty references to "temporal." In Science we know matter is only an illusion. But as illusion it does seem to exist and must be confronted. There is only one Creator, Infinite Good and its creation. There is not something else that can be the creator of error. We are the immortal Son of God, but in belief we are the prodigal son who has made a mistake. We must find our way back through learning what we really are and have always been, here, now, forever.

The "prodigal son" was the Son of God, the only cause and creator, but he had to discover this fact. "[Ours] is an individual kingdom" *(Pul 4:21)*; when we look out from God, our experience begins to be a kingdom of heaven in the midst of what looks like lack, evil, error. Jesus and Mrs. Eddy "unfolded God to man." They illustrated life and Truth in themselves, knowing that it takes God to unfold God to man. They always began with God to find the correct solution. Like Jesus and Mrs. Eddy, once we have learned what we really **are**, we must accept, as the divine facts, the convictions of our true Mind. We have to see that matter is a temporal dream — that "matter is the unreal and temporal," just a misconception.

This correction is happening even now. And who is it that is overcoming this belief of sin and matter? You and I. Science and Health shows us there is only one man, the spiritual man. The prodigal is overcoming error as he returns to his Father. The spiritual man, to whom everything was given, is not a deflection. When rightly viewed, a deflection will be seen as spiritual man. (See Mrs. Eddy's enlightening statements, S&H 502:9-17; and Mess.'00, p. 15:12-18.) Matter did not exist until man believed a "false supposition" about God. But man is destined to find out his mistake and correct it as did the prodigal. Then error will disappear.

THERE IS NO OVER THERE

Mrs. Eddy tells us in many different ways that we must faithfully and persistently train our thoughts in the acknowledgment of the truth of Infinite Good's presence — to see the omnipresent Mind, Spirit, Soul, Principal, Life, Truth, and Love. We must see these seven synonyms for God as reality, as that which constitutes our true Christ selfhood, no matter what error tries to tell us. Nothing is ever really present but Infinite Good and its expression.

There is no "over there." All is here. I am "alone with my own being and with the reality of things." Do we realize this when the claim of Infinite Good's opposite seems to confront us? There is only one "I," namely, God. Mrs. Eddy comes through loud and clear that this "I," or God, is our "I" too; it is our Mind, our Principle, as she tells us; "All is infinite Mind [our Mind] and its infinite manifestation." Lies, hypnotic suggestions about us, have no real Mind to emanate from.

Declare the truth **vehemently** if necessary. And if the healing isn't instantaneous, "go not back to error," but every time the suggestion of something the opposite of Infinite Good tries to enter, stand porter, and declare the truth again. Keep this up, and the error fades out. This is true in countless battles—when the arguments of evil are challenged head on, their ability to hold sway diminishes.

When Jesus was "tempted of the devil" (Matt. 4:1) he challenged the tempter head on, and won an everlasting victory. He saw that he had all power within his own God-Mind.

How complete was this power?

At his last joyful breakfast on the shore of the Galilean Sea, Jesus proved once more to his disciples that all was within their consciousness. They did not need to go fishing for food in the sea. When the disciples arrived on shore "they saw a fire of coals there, and fish laid thereon, and bread" (John 21:9). We only need to "cast the net on the right side"— know that the kingdom of God is within our consciousness. Becoming aware of this, we find all good at hand.

CHAPTER 12

FALSE BELIEF IS IGNORANT
OF ITSELF

THE DREAM STATE AND FALSE BELIEF

In reality, you—the "I" of conscious being—are infinite good (God) itself in individual manifestation. We are all destined to become aware of this God-being that we are. In our sleeping dream our thinking creates all the circumstance—the whole world—we are aware of, but we are *not aware that it is a dream*. Everything in the dream seems real to the sleeping sense. It does, doesn't it? Nothing could be more **real** to the dreamer, until we wake up. We are not aware of the cause of the terror, or what we were laughing at, or any other action we may be experiencing in the dream—not aware it is a mode of consciousness having no other reality than the sense we entertain of it.

It is the same in our waking dream: "Unwittingly [we] sentence [our-self] to suffer" (S&H 378:4). "It is our ignorance of God that produces apparent discord" (S&H 390:7). Compare this dream sense with what Mrs. Eddy writes: "The body seems to be self-acting, only because mortal mind [false belief] is ignorant of itself, of its own action, and of their results,—ignorant that the predisposing, remote, and exciting cause of all bad effects is a law of so-called mortal mind, not of matter." This ignorance is the cause of all our sin, sickness, misery, and death. "It seems to the material senses that pain etc. are in the lungs or elsewhere **in matter** but the fact is that pain or suffering is no more in the body or in matter in our waking states than it is in our night dream, for **both** states are **dreams** and not the reality of being."

This is what the prodigal son found out. He learned that "belief is both the tempter and the tempted, the sin and the sinner, the disease and its cause.]" (S&H 393:30; also 408:31-1. The sin is believing we live in a matter body. The dream analogy tells us it is exactly the same with all of us in our awake experience.

At present we seem to be in a state of amnesia, not being sure who and what we are. We only know **we are.** Jesus and Mrs. Eddy came to awaken us from this amnesic trauma, teaching that there is no more objective reality to a person we see when we are awake than there is to a person we see in our dream, since "the Christian Scientist is [always] alone with his own being and with the reality of things" (*Mess. '01.* 20:8).

We experience the bad dream sensations *until we wake up.* Then the dream creations vanish, for the dream sense is all that constitutes the creations. You saw solid objects in your dream, but there was no objectification of them. Mrs. Eddy makes it clear that "mortals are no more material in their waking hours than when they act, walk, see, hear, enjoy, or suffer in dreams." That which is termed *materiality* is no more solid or concrete than the objects you see in your dream. Once we become aware that we don't have a matter body, but are just constituted of God qualities, what can hurt or touch us? When the amnesia is gone you will <u>know</u> who you are! You will never again depend on an outside source, and will know your <u>real</u> self cannot be improved, since it is now and forever perfect. The warfare is only between "the spirit of Truth and the spirit of deceit" (I John 4:6).

When Mrs. Eddy wrote, "The Christian Scientist is alone [all one with the infinitude of ideas] with his own being and with the reality of things," we can see it is like experiences in dreams. All the life we are aware of, that seems to be out there, is really our own life, in the dream, isn't it? I am one alone. When I dream, don't I live the life of all persons or animals in my dream? I and all the other people in my dream are simply different aspects of my thinking. The hypnotic suggestion of the birth, life, and death of billions of people, separate individuals, is the lie. There is always only <u>ONE</u> in multi-various disguises. "I AM ALL" (*No.* 30:11). Mine "is an individual kingdom," it is the kingdom of God within me. All the while we are in this mortal dream, the Christ beckons: "Behold I stand at the door and knock: if any man hear my voice, and open the door, I will come in to him, and will sup with him and he with me." The **"door"** out of the mortal dream is everywhere. Everywhere you are, is the **door** to Infinite Good's holy creation. It calls to us: "Open the door to Me, to the divine 'I' within you, and experience the end of your prodigal journey."

(We spend a lifetime looking for happiness on the outside when all the while it is within us. No one is going to do for us what we must do for ourselves. We are in paradise now. Only hypnotism makes us believe otherwise. But through the last edition of the textbook we can grasp our true being in its structure, thus making the textbook our impersonal and only teacher.)

Jesus knew this. Of him, Mrs. Eddy says his "true and conscious being never left heaven for earth *even while mortals believed it was here*. He once spoke of himself (John iii. 13) as 'the Son of man which is in heaven,'—remarkable words, as wholly opposed to the popular view of Jesus' nature" (*No.* 36:6). You and I never left heaven for earth. Only in the dream-state do we indulge the *material SENSE* of things. "[Jesus'] physical sufferings, which came from the testimony of the senses, were over when he resumed his individual spiritual being, after showing us the way to escape from the material body [from the dream of life in matter]" (*Mis.* 105:8).

"Life in matter is but a dream that must be exchanged for reality by awaking to the Science of Life, wherein Spirit is found the only real being [Spirit, divine Mind, understanding, is the only substance and reality]" (First ed.). "When the mechanism of the human mind gives place to the divine Mind, selfishness and sin, disease and death will lose their foothold" (S&H 176:13). Then as we, through the Second Coming of the Christ, find we don't have a matter body, disease, discord, death cannot touch us.

Regarding the statement that "life in matter is but a dream," Mrs. Eddy, in answering the question: "Is anything real of which the *physical senses* are cognizant?" tells us that "everything is as real as you make it, and no more so. What you see, hear, feel, is a mode of consciousness, and can have no other reality than the sense you entertain of it" (*Un.* 8:4). Then she adds that it is dangerous to rest upon the evidence of the senses. She says the day-dream is no more real than the night dream. "Mortals are no more material in their waking hours than when they act, walk, see, hear, enjoy or suffer in dreams. We can never treat mortal mind and matter separately, because they combine as one" (S&H 397:24), and are as unreal as the dream we have in sleep.

Suppose you are asleep and dream you are sick and in need of help. Just to illustrate, let's say the person safely asleep in the bed is your real self, and the person in the dream is your personality, or corresponds to it. If the one in the dream was able to see the nothingness of his pain and sickness and his need for help, he would wake up, that is, "lose his life", but he wouldn't be losing anything since it is not real, it is all suppositional. Nothing would be lost because all the time the real man is safe and healthy in a warm bed.

Similarly when we, as seeming mortals, "lose our life" we aren't losing anything, we are only giving up our belief in a matter man, a material man, who is the unlikeness of the Infinite Good that is All and ever-present. When we wake up from the night dream we find we didn't really have a matter body in that dream.

When the dreamer awakens and finds himself safe, he has slid off the hook and entered the sublime category where he *knows* the nothingness of the fear or pain he felt in the dream. In the same way, learning we are God's presence now, we become conscious of our true divine being, and wake up from the day-dream to find that a matter body was nothing other than hypnotic suggestion.

Again, everything in your night dream seemed very real, but it was only as real as the sense you entertained of it, wasn't it? And when you woke up you realized, didn't you, that it was "a mode of consciousness and [could] have no other reality than the sense you entertain[ed] of it." This is what we will realize when we awaken from the Adam-dream of life in matter that we presently entertain. Could anything really touch the body you had in the dream? No, because it wasn't a matter body. In the same way, in the waking dream, when through spiritual education we find we don't have a matter body, we cannot be touched because we are just God-qualities, diseaseless, ageless, endless, and ever harmonious. Once we understand we don't have a matter body, we will find ourselves in a state of boundless bliss. In Christian Science we learn:

> *All must give place to the spiritual fact by the translation of man and the universe back into Spirit. In proportion as this is done, man and the universe will be found harmonious and eternal.* (S&H 209:21).

"The identity or idea of all reality continues forever; but Spirit, or the divine Principle of all, is not *in* Spirit's formations." "The artist is not in his painting. The picture is   the artist's thought objectified. . . . Life is never structural nor organic, and is never absorbed nor limited by its own formations." (See S&H 309:29-2). Mrs. Eddy's explanation regarding dreams (S&H 71:5-20) ends with the statement: "From dreams also you learn that neither mortal mind nor matter is the image or likeness of God, and that immortal Mind is not in matter."

Under the marginal heading, "Mind is substance," she tells us, "Divest yourself of the THOUGHT that there can be substance in matter, and the movements and transitions now possible for mortal mind will be found equally possible for the body" (S&H 90:8).

OUR MISTAKES MUST BE CORRECTED

Unless we look beneath the Adam dream and see *WHO WE ARE,* it is not possible to know why we are here, where we came from, or where we are going. But becoming aware of *who we are*, one with God—"Principle [our Mind] and its idea [being] one"—we, like the prodigal son, will say: "I have sinned against heaven, and before Thee . . . Then shall we know:

"I came forth from the Father, and am come into the world: again I leave the world, and go to the Father" (John 16:28). Jesus knew of the glory he had with Infinite Good before the dream of life in matter overtook him. (John 17:5).

"Only by losing the false sense of Soul [true identity; self-sameness with God] can we gain the eternal unfolding of Life as immortality brought to light" (S&H 335:22).

Jesus said, "Ye shall know the truth and the truth shall make you free," meaning that the conceiver of the beginning of mortal mind would be free from this false conception. Mortal mind had a beginning; it did not exist prior to its beginning. The spiritual man antedated his false conception, therefore he will still exist after the error, the mist, is cleared away.

We are all spiritual (mental) beings and have had preexistence with the whole of Infinite Good, Spirit, Mind—as Jesus maintained when he prayed: "Glorify thou me *with thine own self,* with the glory I had with Thee before the world was [before this dream overtook me]" (John 17:5). Wordsworth wrote, "Our birth is but a sleep and a forgetting. . . . Not in entire forgetfulness, and not in utter nakedness, but trailing clouds of glory do we come from God, who is our home."

Men in all ages have glimpsed this preexistence. Socrates (as Plato described it) taught that "it is a *failure to remember, an amnesia, that allows men and women to get 'lost' in the manifest world as if it weren't the very Divine itself. Thus lost in the shadows of the cave—lost in a fragmented space and time—men and women suffer the fate of all lost souls, of all fragments, because they do not 'remember the Whole.'"*

Our single greatest need and want is to experience our radical and prior **wholeness.** But, do we, through ignorance, unconsciously resist it? Are we unwilling to risk losing our own little ego that we cling to for personal identity? As one with the Mind that is Love, each one contains the information of the whole. By correcting our mental errors, seeing through the hypnotism enslaving us, we can regain our spiritual perfect state of being. How do we do this? By learning the Science of our being. Mrs. Eddy tells us, **"Hold thought steadfastly to the enduring, the good, and the true, and you will bring these into your experience propor-**

tionably to their occupancy of your thought." The marginal heading here is: **"Thoughts are things"** (S&H 261:4).

SPIRITUAL EDUCATION MUST TEACH US TO SEE WHAT IS TRULY THERE

Evil never existed as an entity. Therefore, because evil does not exist as an entity acting independently of man's thinking, but is the false belief of the spiritual man—the man you are here and now—it is possible to erase every vestige of error, in proportion as man overcomes belief in evil. Our work is learning to disbelieve what our eyes see. To every human being who sees the sun rise, it appears the sun is rising. Who sees the earth turning, and the sun stationary? But we know the sun is not rising though to all appearance we see it rising.

Now, since we vividly see the sun rising why, today, don't we believe the sun is rising? We disregard it because we have *learned* better. If we can disregard what our eyes tell us in this instance, why do we believe our eyes when we see sickness and other discords? How can we say that what the eyes see one minute must be the truth when what they see the next minute is a lie, an illusion, hypnotic suggestion? We say this error is true because "I see it." Truly, "having eyes [we] see not," as Jesus said.

This, and countless other instances, show us we cannot rely on the five physical senses. They see and know only what they have been educated to see and know. What the eyes see has nothing to do with what is really there. You can see 2x2=5 on the blackboard, but since you have learned that 2x2=4 it does not fool you.

Like Jacob, we need to wrestle with false beliefs, until we find we are, here and now, the spiritual man that is overcoming evil. Only by uncovering the original sin through spiritual education can we finally wake from the Adam dream to truthfully say there is one God, infinite good.

CHAPTER 13

"YOU ARE PRINCIPLE, MIND"

FIRST EDITION CONTAINS ELEMENTAL COMPLETENESS

In sermons preached BEFORE Mrs. Eddy's time, Jesus' most powerful sayings (such as his instruction to Philip, "he that hath seen me hath seen the Father"; and, again, "I and the Father are one") were seldom, if ever, mentioned. A reader quickly notices in the first edition of Science and Health that Mrs. Eddy often quotes, "I and the Father are one," and builds her arguments around the oneness. On p. 210 we read: "On this statement that . . . 'I' is God, and not man, was built the church of Christ . . ." Boldly, unequivocally, she states: "The belief that God has a separate being [from you and me] leads to multitudinous errors." Mrs. Eddy's first edition of Science and Health flooded the world with the light of revelation. The individual rays of light cannot be detached from their source nor from their harmony with each other. The standpoint of the first edition is that we **are** the God-crowned woman; we are the Principle that is one with its idea.

When we examine her deepest teaching we find there are not God AND man; there are not two; there is only One, namely, "Principle and its idea *is one*." There is only the infinite good we call God—the kingdom of God within our consciousness—expressing itself as what we call man.

This is why in the first edition of Science and Health Mrs. Eddy says: "Jesus regarded himself Principle," and tells us we would be greatly benefited if we too regarded ourself Principle. This Principle is constituted of Mind, Spirit, Soul, and expresses itself as Life, Truth, and Love, which you are.

In Christian Science we learn that the Principle which we are (namely, the kingdom of God within our consciousness) has to have an expression, and "man is the expression of God's [your Mind's] being" (S&H 470:23). There isn't God AND man. There is only the infinite good we call God (your own divine Mind, the Principle) expressing itself AS man, as what looks like you and me. This is why Mrs. Eddy could teach her students that "healing is like sculpturing. The true model is in the thought, before it becomes phenomenally expressed."

Because the goodness that is one with Infinite Good is an animating vitalizing dynamic presence, there is no power that can destroy it. In the first edition of Science and Health we read: "Let go the belief you live in matter, and . . . personality will be swallowed up in the boundless Love that shadows forth man; and beauty, immortality, and blessedness, be the glorious proof of existence you recognize. This is not losing man nor robbing God, but *finding yourself more blessed as Principle than person, as God than man, as Soul than sense, and yourself and neighbor one."*

OTHER SALIENT TRUTHS FROM THE FIRST EDITION

Mrs. Eddy's first edition is very clear concerning our true nature: "That we are Spirit and Spirit is God is undeniably true" (p. 155). Again, regarding body, she writes (p. 225) "We are Spirit, but knowing this not, we go on to vainly suppose ourself body and not Soul." On page 77 we read: "The final understanding that we are Spirit [a synonym for God] must come." On page 65 she writes: "When we are Spirit we shall have gained the high import of this Scripture, 'I and the Father are one,' and shall find . . . that 'I' signifies . . . Soul [a synonym for God] and not body." Speaking of Jesus, she says (p. 137), **"He who was God,** and not in man . . . taught us Principle is God, and God is Love."

Note: *"He who was God."* Isn't that an amazingly frank and unequivocal statement? Is it any wonder that Mrs. Eddy had to hide this blunt truth? Of course, some religions do teach that Jesus was God, but Mrs. Eddy did not mean that the corporeal Jesus was God. By this statement Mrs. Eddy meant that your true being, if you were as aware of it as Jesus was, would also be God. And the term "man" would mean your Mind's manifestation or expression.

On page 274 we read: "Knowing we are Intelligence and not intelligent matter; Soul and not sense, is the Truth that destroys all sickness, sin and death."

Again, regarding body, we read: (p. 362), "To understand their God-given dominion over the body would reassure and encourage the sick, and impart healthy action to the body. Knowing their mental power, they would meet sickness fearlessly . . ." (Page 294): "Sorrow is turned into joy when we become conscious Soul (i.e., realize our true identity), able to govern the body with Life, Truth and Love." (Remember, she has told us "we shall be Love, Life, and Truth when we understand them.")

On page 454 we read: "We have told you before all is mind; therefore what you term physical effects are purely mental ones."

Mrs. Eddy's first fourteen editions of Science and Health contained these celestial statements that tell us we are Spirit, Soul, Principle, Life, Truth, and Love when we understand them; but she early learned these clear, forthright, unadorned, God-impelled statements of Truth were misunderstood.

In Mrs. Eddy's time people were steeped in old theology. You prayed to God, as though God was something up in the sky that could come down and help you. Because of this gross ignorance Mrs. Eddy had no alternative except to patiently lead humanity out of this mental darkness step by step like a mother leads a child in gradual stages of understanding. This necessitated veiling or hiding some of her revelation until people were ready to receive it.

Bible scholars speak of three levels of spiritual attainment, each fuller and richer than the last. (1) In the Old Testament men knew only a God in heaven; (2) then came the incarnation when the Father came near to men in Christ Jesus; (3) then the third level, the Spirit, Truth, came with Christian Science, the "woman compassing a man, compassing Christ Jesus' teaching. Christ Jesus stands for divinity coming to man, while Christian Science stands for the restoration of humanity to its original divinity. Mrs. Eddy breathed every symbol of the Bible into a living idea.

Today, in the third dispensation, "ignorance is no longer the stepping stone to faith"; and buried in the textbook and her other writings are the divine teachings that invite you to take the grand leap. They reveal that you, yourself, are the Principle—your own right Mind is the Principle. Here and now, you are divine, since "God is All," and you and I are not something besides this Allness.

If God is ALL, there can't be God AND something else, can there? Mrs. Eddy teaches us that God is both cause AND effect. But because cause is not effect, and effect is not cause, God's aspect as Principle is not the same as God's aspect as idea. Mrs. Eddy makes this clear in her statement, "man is not God and God is not man" (S&H 480:19). Still they are one. There is only *ONE*. "Principle and its idea is one." What is called man can't be anything but the expression of God, Mind, your Mind, the Mind you now have when free from hypnotic suggestion, since "All is infinite Mind [expressed, manifested]" and "man is the expression of God's [of Mind's, your Mind's] being" (S&H 470:23).

"Christ expresses God's spiritual eternal *NATURE*" (S&H 333:9). Since God is Mind, your Mind, wouldn't this mean—when viewed correctly—that Christ expresses your spiritual eternal nature? Mrs. Eddy uses Mind, Spirit, Soul, Principle, Life, Truth, Love, as synonyms of both

God and Christ, but she never uses these terms as synonyms of spiritual man, reflection, idea, which can't think.

"The Science of being inevitably lifts us higher in the scale of harmony, and will ultimately shake off all shackles that fetter the mind ripe for advancement" (First Edition). Our constant transformation by the ideal, shows that our divinity is in evidence as concrete human expressions. Our consistent desire to do right will bring us into a fitness for holiness without which we cannot receive holiness, as Mrs. Eddy reminds us in her chapter, "Prayer."

CORRECT IDENTIFICATION SEES PRESENT PERFECTION

Mrs. Eddy instructs we must realize our <u>present</u> completeness. We must insist on "the omnipresence of <u>present</u> perfection" rather than feeling we are advancing *toward* perfection. This is the significance of Jesus' teaching: "Son, thou art ever with me and all that I have is thine," in his prodigal parable. It is also the meaning of Mrs. Eddy's stirring question: "When will mankind awake to know their <u>present</u> ownership of all good?" (*My.* 356:1).

Correct identification is all that is ever needed. Since Infinite Good is All, reason tells us evil of any nature cannot be real. We do not live in a universe, but realize the universe is in us. We live *AS* a universe and as "man, including the universe" (S&H 502:26).

In both the first and final edition of Science and Health Mrs. Eddy makes it clear there is only one, and that one is you, having the Mind of God. This divine Mind that is your Mind expresses itself. "Man is the expression of God's [your Mind's] being" (S&H 470:23). Since "the Christian Scientist is alone with his own being and with the reality of things" (*Mess. '01.* 20:8) we can know we "possess sovereign power to think and act rightly."

Jesus and Mary Baker Eddy, God's two witnesses represented the perfect unity between God and man. When we discover that there is no power other than our own Mind or consciousness, we make our "at-one-ment" with all power and all intelligence. "God is individual Mind," Mrs. Eddy tells us; and "this one Mind and His individuality comprise the elements of all form and individualities, and prophesy the nature and stature of Christ, the ideal man" (*Mis.* 101:31). <u>We are the real man, the ideal man, the Christ. Let us start to act as though we knew we were the Christ.</u> "Principle and its idea is one," and this one is you.

Let us claim the "wisdom, knowledge, and power of God." We not only have all power, but actually we *ARE all power.* Jesus said, "Ye are gods [ye are God], and the Scripture can not be broken." (See John 10:34, 35, & Ps. 82:6.) All color, form, and substance are *within* us. (*S&H 512:21). Everything truly good that we could ever wish or hope for is already within our God-Mind.*

LEARN TO SEE WHAT IS REALLY THERE

Mrs. Eddy's great mission on earth was to teach us that evil and matter are not real, but are illusion, hypnotism, and that matter must be translated into Mind. (See *Mis.* 25:12). We find the kingdom of heaven on earth when we begin to realize that every visible manifestation is actually a form or identity bearing evidence to the omnipresence and omnipotence of an eternal, spiritual idea. The true idea, the Christ, of every form in our consciousness, must first be resurrected in order to gain dominion over the earth. We must not look away from the forms. The forms identify Mind's ideas. *We only need to see what is really there.*

We should never look for apparent causes for inharmony since this is an admission to oneself that there is a power besides Infinite Good. Since God is All, and there is no error, if we are ever to experience healing it is because we are *healed and perfect NOW* in reality. This is why we should not strive to make ourselves perfect, but to __KNOW__ ourselves perfect.

Christian Science teaches us to mentally destroy any error on the body by correcting our thought. The illusion of a material body has to be the outcome of the corporeal man's wrong thinking. That is why we declare for spiritual perfection in order to heal the body.

Through Mrs. Eddy's teaching man's conception of God has evolved from a finite sense of a man-like God, to a practical understanding of our oneness with Infinite Good, namely to "I and my Father [Mind] are one" which forever dissolves the personal "I." We can't conceive of Infinite Good being any closer than Mrs. Eddy's great discovery that Infinite Good is our own consciousness —that our own Mind is the only "I," the divine Principle which proclaims itself by Its consciousness, man.

Infinite Good has to be our own real Mind or we would have no Principle to demonstrate. Science and Health affirms: "Man has no Mind but God. . . . [this] Mind is the divine Principle, Love" (S&H 319:20. See also 325:26). "Divine Mind [*your Mind*] is the only cause or Principle of existence" (*ibid.* 262:30). This Principle that is Love expresses itself as what looks like you and me and the universe. There is no God up in the sky. We learn Truth just as we learned that the earth is round and not flat. Our Leader's writings will educate us out of the dream state that at present keeps us in ignorance, and "pains, fetters and befools us." As we step by step lose the conviction in matter's and evil's reality we awaken to an entirely new concept of man and the universe, and go to Infinite Good not through death but through Life, through Truth.

When "Jesus said, 'I and my Father are one'. . . he taught no selfhood as existent in matter. In his identity there is no evil. Individuality and Life were real to him only as spiritual and good. . . . You would be none other than this [spiritual] man if you would subordinate the fleshly perceptions to the spiritual sense and source of being." (See *Un.* 46:13, & line 10.)

To perceive that Infinite Good and our consciousness are one, is to "let that Mind be in [us] which was also in Christ Jesus [and in Mary Baker Eddy]." Then we will demonstrate our real consciousness, our divine Principle, Love. This is true prayer and the only way to make our "at-one-ment" with the infinite good we name God. Ask yourself: "How can I live this Principle unless I discover it is within my own consciousness here and now?"

MANKIND IS AWAKENING

The ordinary views of atonement (at-one-ment) are undergoing a great change. Salvation does not come by proxy—each has to work out his own salvation. Salvation comes by daily sacrifice of false beliefs. Man must awaken to the fact that evil originated with the spiritual man's thought, *like the prodigal who left his Father's house, thinking he could do better on his own.*

Man can no longer lay the blame on a supposed power other than himself. *"Ignorance of the error to be eradicated . . . subjects you to its abuse. . . . The law of the divine Mind must end human bondage, or mortals will continue unaware of man's inalienable rights, and in subjection to hopeless slavery"* (S&H 446:31; 227:7).

Therefore, "know thyself," know what you really are as one with Infinite Good. It was for our sake that Jesus assumed the form of a man. He knew that he was God, perfect being, "Who, being in the form of God, thought it not robbery to be equal with God: But . . . took upon him the form of a servant, and was made in the likeness of men" (Phil. 2:6,7). It was not the human corporeal Jesus that was God, but his Mind, his *understanding,* on which everything hinges.

When Jesus, our Wayshower, declared that he was the light of the world, the way, the Life, the Truth, the response from the Pharisees was: "We stone thee . . . for blasphemy; because that thou, being a man, makest thyself God" (John 10:33).

They were right, in a way: Jesus did this very thing. He made himself one with God and furthermore he said, "Follow me!" For "The works that I do shall ye do also, and greater works." . . . Come unto me"—come unto the Christ reality of yourself; discover your true Christ identity. Christ is another way of saying that God has appeared as you. You are God revealed; all revelation must take place within your own consciousness.

Mrs. Eddy states: "God is His own infinite Mind, and expresses all" (S&H *310:10*). *This is the Mind Jesus claimed as his Mind* and which Mrs. Eddy teaches us is our real Mind.

You and I are the consciousness with "whom all things are possible and in whom all things exist." This consciousness and its expression is all there is. With this holy consciousness "thou shalt decree a thing, and it shall be established unto thee" (Job 22:28). Let us then be done with the belief of separateness from Infinite Good, done with personalities, with a personal "I," limitation, bondage. Let's BE that which understanding shows us we eternally are. Here and now our only need is to accept the **"seamless robe"**—meaning "Principle and its idea is one." This is the **"wedding garment**," namely, "I and the Father [Mind] are one."

In the Second Coming of the Christ, Mrs. Eddy shows us how we can think as Jesus thought, speak with confidence as Jesus spoke, make ourself one with God as he did, for we are all "one stupendous whole" where each includes all.

OUR OWN RIGHT MIND IS THE "ALMIGHTY POWER"

At-one-ment with God is not to wipe out evil or banish it as though it were something, but is the awareness of our present perfection—the awareness that our own right Mind and consciousness is the Almighty power. At-one-ment is Mind embracing all as the one infinite Selfhood and its perfect spiritual identities. At-one-ment is Mind in its true state as the infinite indivisible whole. We must tell ourselves the truth about ourselves. I am the power, as Mrs. Eddy tells us: **"Know then that you possess sovereign power to think and act rightly,** and nothing can dispossess you of this heritage and trespass on Love" (*Pul.* 3:7).

We must find that WE ARE that which we are seeking, namely, God; leave the "far country" where we are imprisoned in a mortal, erring mind or human intellect, where we, like the prodigal, walk in darkness, toiling with sweat and tears. This ignorance must be totally renounced as we trace our origin back to Infinite Good, and find, "Son, thou art ever with me, and all that I have is thine."

OUR ONENESS WITH INDIVISIBLE LOVE

Because Jesus was fully aware of his (and our) inherent God-being or God-state, he alone was called "the only begotten of the Father." He revealed to us that he was God and not man, and that what he was, we are too. In our ignorant state, this is very hard to accept. But it is the central point boldly set forth in Mrs. Eddy's first edition which unveiled the scripturally-prophesied Woman. The truth Mrs. Eddy told her pupils in her first class: "You, my students, are God" is the point she hid in later editions. She had "learned . . . the fixedness of mortal illusions and the human hatred of Truth" (S&H 330:4).

In the first edition Mrs. Eddy speaks of Jesus, as "He who was God." She shows us we are all entitled to the indivisible divine Love, perfection, power, and intelligence, in the same way we are all entitled to the sunlight, or to all of mathematics. It is only a matter of *understanding*, of claiming our oneness with infinite Love. In this oneness with God, Mrs. Eddy said, you find that "all the truth and beauty of God's creation is **YOURS** *AND YOU"*; for yours is the "kingdom, and the power, and the glory, forever." This is so because your true consciousness is the one Mind, God. Christ, divine self-revelation, is always at hand. You stand at the confluence of two mighty rivers: the allness of Infinite Good, and your acceptance of this Infinite Good, as your own Mind.

Therefore rejoice not over a demonstration, but rather rejoice because you have learned the truth, and found yourself and everyone to be the Truth and the Life that is God. This Life is the great and glorious reality to be experienced here and now. Remember, there is only *ONE*. You are not two because your Mind has an expression, an image, a reflection.

MRS. EDDY'S DEFINITION OF "I"—PRINCIPLE NOT PERSON

Mary Baker Eddy's definition of "I" (S&H 588) tells you what you are as "Divine Principle; Spirit; Soul; incorporeal, unerring, immortal, and eternal Mind."   It is important to realize that Mrs. Eddy did not hesitate to go beyond all preconceptions of the "I." She said: "'I' [your real "I"] signifies God, not man; Principle, not person," and counseled that it was "more important to know there is no personality than to know there is no disease."

Today many Christian Scientists have been lulled to sleep by the constant incorrect teaching that we are man rather than divine Principle. How few are aware that the very Christ we proclaim, is none other than our true Selfhood—that our real "I" is God. How few are today steadfastly renouncing all that has to do with the flesh, mortal mind, and mortal man. "When will mankind awake to know their present ownership of all good?" (*My.* 356:1). When will we awaken from the deep sleep to become aware that "I AM that for which I searched. . . I am that I Am." Only in our true state as the one "I" can we experience the perfection and power of our present real being.

The "promised land" is beneath our feet. We always stand on holy ground. But only as we become disillusioned with a material sense of life are we ready to lay down our life as a personality or seeker for Truth. And only then do we actually *accept* the truth that I have never left heaven for earth. "Only those men and women gain greatness who gain themselves in a complete subordination of self" (*My.* 194:10). Mrs. Eddy got Mary out of the way "in a complete subordination of self."

Through struggling to be what we have always been (and to function as the one true Selfhood), we approach the time "when mortal mind [which is hypnotism] will forsake its corporeal, structural, and material basis, when immortal Mind and its formations will be apprehended in Science, and material beliefs will not interfere with spiritual facts. . . . Sometime it will be learned that mortal mind [hypnotism] constructs the mortal body with this mind's [the hypnotized mind's] own mortal materials. [Hypnotism alone makes us see and feel a mortal body.] . . . In divine revelation, material and corporeal selfhood disappear, and the spiritual idea is understood" (S&H 402:8; & 561:20).

THE BODY IS AS SPIRITUAL AS THE MIND
LIKE PRODUCES LIKE

When we realize that our real body is as spiritual as our Mind, then our form or identity will appear as spontaneously as the figure four or seven accompanies the idea of four or seven. This spiritual body comes with the "ascension" in consciousness. The Principle of being was demonstrated when Jesus presented his body absolved from death and the grave "in his mighty, crowning, unparalleled, and triumphant exit from the flesh [from illusion,from hypnotism]" (S&H 117:21).

"All is infinite Mind," and this Mind can not express itself as a corporeal being, since like produces like. Mind must express itself as idea. So what we are looking at is always idea, or God in disguise, since there is only one. Hypnotism alone makes us think it is a mortal corporeal body that we see instead of "bodiless bliss" which has tangibility, form, outline, and color just as the forms in our night dreams have. Once we, through Mrs. Eddy's teaching, learn we don't have a matter body, we will experience this "bodiless bliss" that is heaven here.

NOTE TO READER

Volumes I, II, and III of my books *Mary Baker Eddy, God's Great Scientist,* and *Mary Baker Eddy Reveals Your Divinity* go deeply into the salient points of Chapters I to IV of Mrs. Eddy's first edition of Science and Health. (Available from Rare Book Co. and from Bookmark.)

CHAPTER 14

STAND UP FOR TRUTH

NEHEMIAH'S WALL AGAINST HYPNOTISM

In order to establish our perfect at-one-ment with Infinite Good, we must gather the facts of existence as far as our consciousness is able to understand them, and bring these FACTS to bear mentally on our false beliefs. When we, as the Son of God, have accounted for the original sin, we will find it originated in our own thought, and that it exists only as a supposition. A supposition about what? About Infinite Good and our at-one-ment with it. Evil is a temporal sense of existence that must be overcome.

Our remedy for sickness and discord is to stand up for the truth about ourselves, entertain the "facts," instead of letting error push us around with all those lies about deficiencies, pain, weariness, loss of memory, stiffness, hurt feelings, etc. None of these aches and pains or loss of peace or faculties, etc. is real. We must keep declaring that since these hypnotic suggestions are not coming from our Principle, Love, they are not real; therefore there is no problem. A lie about God, infinite Love, is never a reality. Just because the whole world at one time believed the earth was flat, that didn't make it flat.

Like Nehemiah, we must build a wall against mortal mind's aggressive suggestions. Through Mrs. Eddy's great Discovery—her **dis-**covering or **uncovering** of sin, sickness, discord, death and every error as nothing other than hypnotic suggestion—we are beginning to see why we have to build a "great wall" against the evidence of the five physical senses. This wall shields us against the hypnotism, the Adam dream, that makes us believe we live in a corporeal body, subject to discord, sin, sickness, death.

How did Nehemiah proceed to build his "wall"?

He states (Neh. 2:12), "And I arose in the night . . . neither told I any man what my God had put in my heart to do." It is very important not to noise abroad one's plans. If we do, the devil is sure to put stumbling blocks in our path.

ALL MUST BUILD THE SYMBOLIC WALL

Nehemiah's determination to build the one great wall that needs to be built—the wall against the hypnotism that makes us believe the evidence of the five physical senses—is a thrilling story. Nehemiah defended himself against Sanballat and Tobiah (who represent the physical senses) when they heaped scorn and ridicule upon him and the builders.

"Nevertheless," states Nehemiah, "we made our prayer [silently, fervently]." They rehearsed their "at-one-ment" with God and "set a watch against them day and night"—against the evidence and testimony of the five physical senses. They stood "porter at the door of thought."

"For the builders, every one, had his sword [the "sword of Spirit," spiritual strength, understanding] girded by his side, and so builded. And he that sounded the trumpet [that warned of the aggressive mental suggestion of the enemy] was by me."

Nehemiah's teaching seems to be in a capsule what Mrs. Eddy explains so carefully in her chapter "Christian Science Practice": how to build the wall to separate us from erroneous beliefs—how to "stand porter at the door of thought." The "sword of Spirit"—the instant realization of "the omnipresence of present perfection"—must be "girded by our side." Mrs. Eddy always had the sword of Spirit at her side, and wielded it with great authority.

THE HUMAN MIND MUST BE TRANSLATED OUT OF ITSELF

Since "the entire being is found in Mind," Nehemiah was on firm footing when he built the wall against the hypnotism that makes us believe there could be such a thing as error of any kind.

"Error, having neither Principle nor identity is not a person, place, or thing, and being without substance, life or intelligence, we learn it is illusion" wrote Mrs. Eddy. (See also S&H 71:2) She asks Christian Scientists to open their eyes, their spiritual discernment, and awaken to the true nature of evil as simply an illusion of material sense, awaken to its false claims, methods, subtlety, etc., and then to realize its nothingness, its utter powerlessness to control or to harm.

Our conceptions of God must change, must become more enlightened in order to lift us out of the Adam-dream we have so long been mired in. We must accept new, better, higher ideas of God, our true Mind. The *human sense* must be lifted higher and higher until it catches the vision Christ Jesus and Mrs. Eddy had. Then, lifted out of the Adam-dream, we joyfully realize, "Why, I don't have a matter body. I am Mind that never expresses itself as the illusion called matter, but always as Mind's manifestation.

Science and Health, p. 573:8, tells us that to "the unillumined human mind, the **vision** is material." Note it is the vision that is material not the heavens and the earth. It is all a matter of consciousness. Therefore Mary Baker Eddy exemplifying pure Mind, and knowing the human mind was a sinner, "disinclined to self correction," was able to translate matter out of existence.

> *The human mind, will sometime [through spiritual education] rise above all material and physical sense, exchanging it for spiritual perception, and exchanging human concepts for the divine consciousness. Then man will recognize his God-given dominion and being"* (*S&H* 531:10).

Mrs. Eddy disabuses and stirs the human mind—which "has been an idolater from the beginning" robbing and enslaving us—to a change of base. "The human mind does not increase in wisdom, **wisdom decreases the human mind.**"

> *The real man being linked by Science to his Maker, mortals need only turn from sin and lose sight of mortal selfhood to find Christ, the real man and his relationship to God, and to recognize the divine sonship. [She knows there is no greased-lightening approach to this realization, that it will take time: "the ages must slowly work up to perfection, even though] Christ, Truth, was demonstrated through Jesus to prove the power of Spirit over the flesh,—to show Truth is made manifest by its effects upon the human mind and body, healing sickness and destroying sin. (S&H 316:3)*

The vastness, the magnitude, the grandeur of Mrs. Eddy's discovery that all consciousness is Mind, God, is that we are learning our very own Mind (when awakened from the Adam dream and freed of hypnotism) is God, here and now. The compounding of the male and female natures constitutes the generic spiritual man, the man that the Father-Mother Mind [your God-Mind here and now] made in its image and likeness. (See S&H 319:20 & 470:17.)

Mrs. Eddy writes (S&H 476:11), "Mortals will disappear, and immortals, or the children of God (the thoughts of our divine Mind), will appear as the only and eternal verities of man." These thoughts, called "children of God" will appear in your individual being; they constitute your universe since you, the Christian Scientist are "alone with [your] own being and with the reality of things," having "sovereign power to think and act rightly."

> *The term Mind and body literally means God and man, for man is the expression of God [of Mind, your Mind], and the manifestation of Mind is the embodiment of Mind. Therefore man is God's [Mind's] body. . . . Body is therefore the aggregation of spiritual ideas [ideas that are always universal, eternal, no more open to question than is 2x2=4, never confined to location or time] forever controlled by the law of Life, harmonious and eternal. This understanding of perfect body is the savior to the belief of body, and is the law of recovery to any and every claim of error. (Copyrighted statement by Mary Baker Eddy, Jan. 19, 1886).*

THE CLAIMS OF EVIL MUST BE OVERCOME

When error rattles at the gate we must remember the entire kingdom of God is within our consciousness. In Christian Science we know each claim of evil that comes to us must be made a stepping stone to go higher. We should not keep tramping over old territory again and again, but realize the more claims we conquer the faster we are climbing out of the hypnotism walling us in. Intelligence, Mind—the Mind we now have when instructed in Truth—is meeting it all for us. Love destines us to finally see there are no conditions of matter, no sorrow, sickness, lameness, or pains, no discord of any nature, because there is no such thing as matter.

Each victory won over self and sickness strengthens us for the next contest until we can say with St. Paul, "I have fought a good fight." The presence and power of Infinite Good always has been and always will be present to dispose of the illusions of evil.

In the first edition Mrs. Eddy speaks of Jesus as "he who was God." It is interesting to note that Jesus promised: "He that believeth on *me [note he did not say on God]* the works that I do shall he do also." Man, or manifestation, is the visible evidence that there is the infinite good, called God, which Mrs. Eddy shows us is our own right Mind.

"Science understood," she writes, "translates matter into Mind" (Mis. 25:12). "Metaphysics resolves things into thoughts, and exchanges the objects of sense [that which we see in our day-dream] for the ideas of Soul. . . These ideas are perfectly real and tangible to spiritual sense. . . . The individuality of man is no less tangible because it is spiritual, and because his life is not at the mercy of matter" (S&H 269:14; and 317:16). This is why nothing will be able to harm or alarm us once we realize we are Life, Truth, and Love, and are no longer fooled into believing we have a matter body.

When Mrs. Eddy asked the class: "Which was lost: the spirit or the letter?" the class answered, "The spirit." But Mrs. Eddy said, "No. The spirit was maintained; it was the letter that was lost." The "letter" *explains* "the omnipresence of present perfection" and the unreality of error. The letter *explains* why Jesus' awareness of error's unreality enabled him to heal every manner of sickness and raise the dead. The letter explains why we too, through learning the truth about ourselves as one with God, having the Mind of God, can also do what Jesus and Mary Baker Eddy did.

The earthly mission of both Jesus and Mrs. Eddy was to "translate substance into its original meaning, Mind" *(Mis.* 74:16). In Science and Health, under the marginal heading, "Spiritual translation," we read that ". . . all must give place to the spiritual fact by the translation of man and the universe back into Spirit. In proportion as this is done, man and the universe will be found harmonious and eternal" (S&H 209:21).

Once we have learned that our Principle is Love, and expresses itself in health, holiness, harmony, we can look at disease and discord and know their nothingness. This is why we study the definition of God. Only by studying what Mind, Spirit, Soul, Principle, Life, Truth, and Love are, can we learn what *we really are*, what our true nature is. Mrs. Eddy teaches us that "I" and the seven synonyms for God are one thing—but, of course, to us they are one thing only to the degree that we understand them. Then our lives reflect them.

WHAT DOMINATES SCIENCE AND HEALTH?

What, from start to finish, dominates Science and Health, the prophesied "little book"? It is the answer to the question: "What is God?" Mrs. Eddy worked 40 years to bring humanity the answer to that question. Why is the answer to that question so important? Because it tells you and me what we are, since "I and the Father [Mind, God] are one."

In the first edition of Science and Health, Mrs. Eddy, speaking from a mountain-top vision makes it plain that you, the individual mentality, are Mind, Spirit, Soul, Principle, which are terms for God, and which express themselves in Life, Truth, and Love. "God, the Mind of man," is self-existent and self-expressed. Mrs. Eddy never repudiated anything she wrote in the first edition. But seeing mankind was not ready for this divine revelation she, in later editions, hid it in such a way as to require spiritual growth for readers to discern the deeper spiritual truth about themselves.

Mrs. Eddy tells us (*Ret.* 37:1) that her first edition of Science and Health contained the complete statement of Christian Science. Today we know it contained the *elemental* completeness; that it is by no means the finished product of her forty-four years' labor with the textbook, during which time she wove its vertical and horizontal strands into "the bride's vesture"—into one consistency "without seam or rent," to constitute the divine Science of man.

Just think what power, what authority we would have if we actually realized that "incorporeal, unerring, immortal and eternal Mind" is our Mind now, and that OUR OWN MIND IS THE PRINCIPLE, CONSTI-TUTED OF MIND, SPIRIT, SOUL, that expresses itself in Life, Truth, and Love! This is the power that is ours when we purify our thought and turn away from sin—from the illusion of human birth and a matter body that ends in death.

THE TRUTH SHINING THROUGH ALL HER WRITINGS
"WHAT I WROTE TWENTY-FIVE YEARS AGO"

We need to hold firmly to the divine Truth which shines through all Mary Baker Eddy's writings, but particularly blazes forth in the first edition. That has not always been easy.

When the Boston Board of Directors posthumously published Mrs. Eddy's *Miscellany,* they really laid an egg when they included a 1908 notice NOT in Mrs. Eddy's sealed manuscript. This notice states in part: "What I wrote on Christian Science some twenty-five years ago [in 1883] I do not consider a precedent for a present student of this Science [because how to teach the nothingness of error evolved slowly and was not yet finalized in 1883.]"

Why did the Directors include this notice by which many students have been purposely misled to believe it referred to the early editions, thus making the notice emerge as an ominous saboteur of the first and other early editions? Was it because the early editions contained Mrs. Eddy's **strong disapproval and denunciation of material church organization?** (She had foreseen that her great discovery would become nothing but lifeless words if material organization continued.)

While persecution and "the human hatred of Truth" forced her in the beginning to organize her little band of followers, her "dread" (*Ret.* 47:3) of material church organization with its "peril" (*ibid.* 45:6) never changed. But God showed Mrs. Eddy how to protect her life work from the peril of organization—which had nullified every other great spiritual movement—by writing the *Church Manual.* And when the Directors repeatedly asked her to change the *Manual* so they could continue, she always replied: **"I have not the right or desire to change what God directed me to do, and it remains for the church to obey it"** (*Permanency of the Mother Church and its Manual*, p. 8). She knew "eternity awaits our Church Manual," and mortals must leave their swaddling-clothes...for the form and comeliness of the divine ideal" (*My.* 230:2 & 257:8)

Because her early editions were vocal in expressing disapproval of material organization, and because this did not augur well for vested interests bent on continuing the material organization, they obviously seized the opportunity this 1908 notice offered, to attempt to discredit those early editions.

What did this notice actually mean? Written in 1908, the words "twenty-five years ago" refer to circa 1883, the period in which Mrs. Eddy was leading the field in exposing animal magnetism and all that pertains to evil. When the field became fearful of what animal magnetism would do to them, she realized they needed to stop focusing on error and return instead to the sublime Truth expressed in her earlier writings, as well as in her latest work. Thus the true message of this note was to caution about what she "wrote 25 years ago" in <u>1883.</u>

In 1899, Mrs. Eddy urged: "Beloved Christian Scientists, keep your minds so filled with Truth and Love, that sin, disease, and death cannot enter them" (*My.* 210:2) To do this we need to turn not only to her last edition, but also to her first edition, the importance of which she affirmed when, sixteen years after she wrote it, she called it "The Precious Volume." She states (*Ret. 37:1):* "The first edition of my most important work, Science and Health, containing the complete statement of Christian Science . . . was published in 1875." The plainly, correctly stated facts that were divinely revealed to Mrs. Eddy during the great revelation that came to her in 1866, were presented to the world in her first edition of Science and Health. They cannot be overthrown by pen or tongue. "The Precious Volume" stands to reveal our true identity.

MRS. EDDY CHANGED THE WORLD'S THINKING
THE EXAMPLE OF JESUS AND MARY BAKER EDDY

Jesus and Mary Baker Eddy were Self-governed, meaning God-governed. Why did St. John call Jesus "the only begotten Son"? Jesus *lived* the life of "Prayer and At-one-ment," and until Mrs. Eddy brought the Second Coming of the Christ, no one except Jesus was ever found willing and able to disbelieve the evidence of his eyes and the voice of his training; no one but Jesus was ever found capable of accepting Life lived only in relation to, or in at-one-with, God. (See definition of Jesus, S&H 589:16.)

Until Mrs. Eddy came, no one but Jesus had ever consecrated himself wholly to his relationship with God. It was this consecration that gave Jesus the right to be called the Messiah, the "anointed one," or the Christ.

Mrs. Eddy, in the Second Coming of the Christ, shows us how we all can do what Jesus did, and what she too demonstrated. She brings to humanity the "Holy Ghost" which she defines as: "Divine Science; the development of eternal Life, Truth and Love" (S&H 588:7). With the Second Coming of the Christ, we learn evil is unreal, and that we are all "the Christ" when rightly viewed. Christian Science teaches us to see the face of God in even what looks like the most hardened sinner.

We are indeed privileged to live in an era where our consciousness can understand the language of Spirit. Two thousand years ago men could not comprehend Truth, and Jesus wisely did not utter it to dull ears. Today, through Mary Baker Eddy's revelations we can hear, understand, and demonstrate the Mind that was in Christ Jesus.

ARE WE UP TO THE CHALLENGE?

Jesus said, ". . . let the dead [i.e. personality thoughts] bury their dead." Those who are not thinking spiritually scientific thoughts are dead. They should wake up, and bury their dead (mortal) thoughts until the mortal disappears. Mrs. Eddy said, "The time for thinkers has come. . . . Contentment with the past and the cold conventionality of materialism are crumbling away." She stormed the very threshold of personal thinking, personal domination, priestcraft, and opened a super-highway into the kingdom of heaven, where we see what we really *are* and *have always been.* She could do this because, like Jesus, she had been predestined "before Abraham was" to bring the Christ, Truth, to the world, to fulfill Jeremiah's prophecy that "A woman shall compass a man," by compassing all that Jesus taught and was.

Through the teachings of Jesus and of Mary Baker Eddy all are destined to learn the Truth—to become conscious of the changeless perfection constituting you, me, and everyone. Only when we know Truth as certainly as we know 2x2=4 do we really know it. Through spiritual education we come to realize we are the very same Truth that Jesus knew he was, and can say with him: "I am the Truth."

CHAPTER 15

MANIFESTING OUR DIVINITY

HOW TO INDIVIDUALIZE INFINITE POWER

The conviction that being is entirely good came to Mrs. Eddy with a power that transformed the whole human experience. It came as Infinite Good's view, or a God's-eye view, that showed everything in the universe to be an expression of the divine Principle, Love. This led her to see:

> To live so as to keep human consciousness in constant relation with the divine, the spiritual and the eternal, is to individualize infinite power; [to be in coincidence with the divine] and this is Christian Science. . . . Divine Love, impartial and universal, as understood in divine Science, forms the coincidence of the human and divine, which fulfills the saying of our great Master, 'The kingdom of God is within you' (My. 160:5 & 265:20).

> The atmosphere of the human mind, when cleansed of self and permeated with divine Love as was the Mind of Christ Jesus and of Mary Baker Eddy, is the coincidence of God and man that brings heaven to earth.

This is our true state of being here and now. The study and practice in which "evil is destroyed by the sense of good" (S&H 311:13), brings to view and makes practical the kingdom of God within us. Repeatedly Mrs. Eddy tells us "God is All." *No & Yes, p. 30:11*, states: "God's law is in three words, 'I am All'; and this perfect law is ever present to rebuke any claim of another law." Why is it ever present? Why can it rebuke any other law? *Because the kingdom of God is within you,* and so can rebuke any other law. Your real being is the Principle of all good. So, of course, this law is present to rebuke any claim of another law, just as the multiplication table, once learned, is present to rebuke any miscalculation. All that is required is that we learn what the Second Coming of the Christ reveals, and *practice* it. When we build this understanding into our consciousness, we usher in the Church Universal and Triumphant, the **isness** of all good.

WHAT IS CHRIST'S CHURCH?
What Created 2x2=4?

The only Church that will stand the storms of time is the cultivated spiritual understanding of Truth in the thinking of the individual. Everything true IS. IT HAS NO CAUSE. "He, [Mind] hangeth the earth upon nothing" (Job 26:7). All is a construction of consciousness—an awareness of ISNESS.

Mary Baker Eddy built the Church of Christ, the superstructure of Truth, when she founded the Christ Science in human consciousness. This made Christian Science practical. The Church Universal and Triumphant is the Church we build in our consciousness, making it the indwelling temple of Infinite Good. It is "the structure of Truth and Love" we build through an understanding of the Second Coming of the Christ.

In the Church of Christ, the Mind of man (the only Ego) destroys the belief that man can ever be separated from complete understanding. It shows us that all error, inharmony and discord are belief and illusion. Consider the hypnotic suggestion that we have to struggle to reach heaven. In contrast, Christian Science teaches that when a demonstration occurs it shows we have become aware of the harmony that already exists—heaven here, now, and all around us. It is only the carnal mind's ignorance, hypnotism, the Adam-dream, that waits for perfection.

TUNE INTO THE DIVINE

The demand upon us is that we must break the claims of inertia and stagnation, which are malpractice.   Because Mary Baker Eddy brought the Second Coming of the Christ, the panacea for every ill is to put the booster rockets under whatever she tells us, and **whatever tells the truth about her.** Then the lift-off will bless all mankind. She has taught us Infinite Good is All. Its infinite ideas are everywhere present as **isness.** Therefore we can tune into this Good at any moment. It is just a matter of "Choose ye!"

Helping his listeners defend themselves against the workings of evil, a Christian Science lecturer said: "We who are in this auditorium are aware that there is right now passing through this audience, a continuous current of thought, expressed in words or in music. If we had a radio receiving set, we could adjust it so it would make these sounds audible; it would reproduce whatever is being sent forth from the broadcasting station.

"It is well known to us all," he said, "that we can, at will, tune in anything we wish to hear and, likewise, we can tune out that which we do not wish to hear. This is analogous to our thought world, in that we have the capacity to think divine thoughts which are everywhere present. We can think infinite ideas emanating from the infinite good called God, or we can listen to the beliefs and suggestions termed "mortal mind." How grateful we are that Mary Baker Eddy tuned in and listened to what Infinite Good was broadcasting and thus alerted us to our divinity.

The oneness and allness of infinite good means this infinite good is actually manifesting itself as what looks like you and me. It is Infinite Good's perfect nature manifested as man's nature. <u>All there is to the material universe is actually the spiritual universe dimly seen, misconceived, incorrectly interpreted.</u>

LAY ASIDE PERSONALITY

We can only succeed in "the warfare with one's self"—which Mrs. Eddy says "is grand" (*Mis.* 118:25)—by laying aside our sense of material personality with its want and woe, for the great impersonality of Love. Since error of any kind is nothing more than aggressive mental suggestion, she tells us (*DCC 29*) "There are no personalities, for God is impersonal, and to personalize ourselves, to say 'I,' etc. is to selfishize ourselves. To personalize others is to selfishize others. This is not Christian Science." When we impersonalize husband, family, friends, we get to keep all the lovely things about them. Ideas don't die and disappear, don't change and deteriorate. Again, "To know there is no personality is more important than to know there is no disease." In doing her wonderful healing work, Mrs. Eddy said, "I got Mary [the personality] out of the way." Then there was only"incorporeal, divine, supreme, infinite Mind, Spirit, Soul, Principle, Life, Truth, Love" to deal with, as her real Self—and as the real self of the patient. *KNOWING* this, she had sovereignty, and could release the patient from the prison of agony his body had become.

Our work is to impersonalize, de-personalize friends, relatives, everyone. When Jesus washed his disciples' feet, he was washing away the belief that they were human beings rather than divine. To Philip, Jesus said, "He that hath seen me, hath seen the Father"—the real Mind of Jesus, expressed as what is called "man." Animal magnetism tries to "pain, fetter, and befool" us with the belief of personality, when there is no matter-personality except in belief, which is hypnotism. We free ourselves to pursue our mission when we detach evil from the individual.

We don't think of God as being sick, discordant, sinful, lacking, or dying. If man is God's image, how can man be lured into believing he has these dire debilities? The Oscar for angst goes to those who "believe that God has a separate being." Here again we see it is vain to plead for divine intervention when we know Infinite Good has already given us everything. The remedy is to blot out the sense of personality, the "murderer" (John 8:44). Putting off the mortal by realizing the Science of man is the only way to practice Infinite Good's presence, since "this is life eternal"—*is,* not shall be. All education is correction of thought. This is as true in metaphysics as in mathematics. At this moment you are— always have been—God's presence.

"He that loseth his life for my sake shall find it," said Jesus (Matt. 10:39) We lose our life in matter just as we lose it in a dream when we wake up. We find real Life as we lay down (lose) the mortal sense of life by seeing the nothingness of this material personality. We do this by turning away from self, and toward others with an outpouring of the same great impersonal Love Mrs. Eddy demonstrated.

RIDDING ONESELF OF THE FIRST DEGREE TRAITS

Love, we have seen, is not sensual affection, but is expressed in a renunciation of sensual affection, in an understanding of the nothingness of matter. It is impossible for a man to love truly while governed by material instincts. Those material instincts are themselves the very disruption of any spiritual understanding of Principle. They contain all the elements of inharmony ingrained in human passions. Paraphrasing Browning: "How do I con thee—how do I 'pain, fetter, and befool' thee? Let me count the ways": through the anti-Christ characteristics that Mrs. Eddy warns us against, (S&H 115:20-24), the "First Degree: Depravity [traits], namely, "evil beliefs, passions and appetites, fear, depraved will, self-justification, pride ["the death's head at the feast of Love"], envy, deceit, hatred, revenge," etc.

The "First Degree" traits which include such negative qualities as impatience, being easily hurt, taking offense, being critical or fearful, make us servants of error. Who is free of all of these? A little boy proudly boasted: "My grandfather is a very important public serpent." Who isn't, at times, an "important serpent"?

We need to be more alive, awake, aware, alert concerning these "First Degree" traits. And when we have put them out, we must fill our thoughts with love and goodwill. This is a mental law. We can drop a knife, fork, or spoon, and rid ourselves of it; but when it comes to a wrong thought, we can only rid ourselves of it by filling our thoughts with positive thoughts—love, goodwill, joy, faith in good. This is called the **law of substitution.** When negative thoughts come, obey Jesus admonition, "resist not evil," just as we don't resist 2x2=5; we substitute the right answer.

Having renounced sensual affection, and other evil traits, be quick to fill the mind with good qualities, and avoid the tragedy that happens when the void is not filled, as Luke 11:24-26 teaches:

> *When the unclean spirit is gone out of a man, he walketh through dry places, seeking rest; and finding none, he saith, I will return unto my house whence I came out. And when he cometh he findeth it swept and garnished. Then goeth he, and taketh to him seven other spirits more wicked than himself; and they enter in, and dwell there: and the last state of that man is worse than the first.*

It reminds me of a little incident:

> *"We have a skunk in the basement," shrieked the caller to the police dispatcher. "How can we get it out?"*
>
> *"Take some bread crumbs," said the dispatcher, "and put down a trail from the basement to the back yard. Then leave the cellar door open."*
>
> *Sometime later the resident called back. "Did you get rid of it?" asked the dispatcher.*
>
> *"No," replied the caller. "Now I have two skunks in there!"*

Mrs. Eddy—knowing that all you behold, though it appears without, is really within—urged: "Keep your minds so filled with Truth and Love, that sin, disease, and death cannot enter them" (*My.* 210:1).

THE GRAND HUMAN QUALITIES

Frederick Dixon writes: "In order to love spiritually, it is necessary to learn to banish any picture of a universe evolved from matter. Instead of the material thoughts which flood the human carnal consciousness—[from the news media, and more especially from television, much of which is just a radio-active desert of filth leading people into a mental sewer]—there must come, aware or unaware, those angel thoughts which constitute a true understanding of Principle." Jesus was the Christ because "he hated iniquity and loved righteousness." It was said of him that "His rebuke is fearful." He knew that it is the consciousness of what we already *are* that does the work of removing what we are not.

What were the human qualities that made Mary Baker Eddy equal to her mission, and brought her into coincidence with the divine?

She lists these human qualities which she called the "Second Degree" on page 115 of Science and Health, as: "Moral. Humanity, honesty, affection, compassion, hope, faith ["trust in Truth and have no other trusts"], meekness, temperance."

This includes being steady and dependable, able to stick with a job until it is the best you can do, and to keep your word. These qualities, persisted in, will cause people to think you are a genius. More than that, they will bring you closer to your divine self. They will bring about St. James' assurance that "the Lord shall raise him up," that is, will make us to be what we can be.

"Humanity" is defined as "Kindness, benevolence, benignity, philanthropy, tenderness, sympathy, charity, humaneness, kindheartedness." Other than Christ Jesus no one ever lived who expressed more of these qualities than did our Leader.

Mrs. Eddy prayed continuously, "Divine Love, give me grace, meekness, understanding and wisdom for each hour of this day." She was praying to her own Mind—which she knew was also the Mind of all. We would do well to take her prayer as our model, adding, as the *Joyful News Letter* quotes, "Dear God, help me to be the person my dog thinks I am."

"The human self must be evangelized" (S&H 254:19).

Our work is to develop those "Second Degree" qualities, listed above, that lead up to the spiritual high ground.

In proportion as we live these "Second Degree" qualities we are cultivating and experiencing the spiritual, which Mrs. Eddy designates as the "Third Degree," namely: "understanding." This enables us to become aware of our true being as "Mind, Spirit, Soul, Principle, Life, Truth, Love." The more the wonderful "moral" qualities constitute our consciousness, the more we learn to express the spiritual qualities of "wisdom, purity, spiritual understanding, spiritual power, love, health, holiness."

Of course in Science we know these spiritual qualities constitute the fabric of our being here and now, but it is only through spiritual teaching and learning that we become **aware** we are endowed with every God-quality. Cultivating the "Second Degree" qualities we reach spiritual understanding and spiritual power.

MANIFESTING OUR DIVINITY
HUMAN KINDNESSES ARE DIVINE LOVE IN ACTION

By putting divine Love into action in daily life we align ourselves with the Principle, Infinite Good. Mrs. Eddy discerned the presence of the Christ, and lifted a world sunken in sin to see the ideal man. This begins with "seeking not so much our own as another's good." To Augusta Stetson she wrote: *"Oh, how good it is to do good!! There is no bliss but in loving others."*

Most failures come from people who have the habit of making excuses instead of vehemently, if necessary, declaring one cannot be mesmerized. No form of error can prevent us from doing good infinitely. It is important to show human affection. The "letter" without the Spirit, Love, can be extremely cruel. In Christian Science practice it is most important to always do the kindly thing. Loving mankind, we find countless opportunities for giving service. Helping others we help ourselves. A Christian Scientist's life is full of the little human kindnesses—small acts of sacrifice, a word of encouragement. How often has the smile of a right thinker warmed a whole room or a situation. A smile costs nothing in money, time, or effort, but it can be of supreme importance in someone's life. A smile disarms suspicion, fear, anger, and brings forth the best in the other person—which is immediately reflected back to us. These human kindnesses are divine Love in action. As our gifts and talents are used to help others, we grow spiritually.

"A TIME TO LOVE...." (Ecclesiastes 3:8)

In Mrs. Eddy's article, "Fidelity" (*Mis.* 339), she admonishes: "In the battle of life, good is made more industrious and persistent because of the supposed activity of evil. . . . In the mental collisions of mortals and the strain of intellectual wrestling, moral tension is tested, and if it yields not, grows stronger. The past admonishes us: with finger grim and cold it points to every mortal mistake; or smiling saith, "Thou hast been faithful over a few things.

". . . Art thou a husband, and hast pierced the heart venturing its all of happiness to thy keeping? Art thou a wife, and hast bowed the o'erburdened head of thy husband? Hast thou a friend, and forgettest to be grateful? Remember, for all this thou alone canst and must atone. Carelessly or remorselessly thou mayest have sent along the ocean of events a wave that will some time flood thy memory, surge dolefully at the door of conscience, and pour forth the unavailing tear."

A gifted minister preaching on Ecclesiastes 3:8, "A time to love . . ." spoke of Thomas Carlyle, the famous Scot essayist and historian who married his secretary, Jane Welsh. Then, being human, made a mistake. Carlyle and Jane loved each other dearly. After their marriage Jane continued to serve as his secretary. After several years she became ill. Carlyle, a hard worker, became so absorbed in his writing that he let Jane continue working for some time after she became ill. Finally she was confined to her bed. Although Carlyle loved her dearly, he seldom found time to stay with her long. He was busy with his work.

"When Jane died they carried her to the cemetery for the service. The day was miserable—raining hard and the mud was deep. Following the funeral Carlyle went back to his home. He was taking it pretty hard. He went up the stairs to Jane's room and sat down in the chair next to her bed. He sat there thinking how little time he had spent with her and wishing so much he had a chance to do it differently. Noticing her diary on a table beside the bed, he picked it up and began to read in it.

"Suddenly he seemed shocked. He saw it. There, on one page, she had written a single line. "Yesterday he spent an hour with me and it was like heaven; I love him so." Something dawned on him that he had not noticed before. He had been too busy to notice that he meant so much to her. He thought of all the times he had gone about his work without thinking about or noticing her.

"Then Carlyle turned the page in the diary. There he noticed some words that broke his heart. 'I have listened all day to hear his steps in the hall, but now it is late and I guess he won't come today.' Carlyle read a little more in the book. Then he threw it down and ran out of the house. Friends found him at the grave, his face buried in the mud. His eyes were red from weeping, and tears continued to roll down his cheeks. He kept repeating over and over, 'If I had only known.' But it was too late for Carlyle.

"[As humans, we all make mistakes that send] along the ocean of events a wave that will some time flood [our] memory, surge dolefully at the door of conscience, and pour forth the unavailing tear. . . The wisdom that might have blessed the past may come too late]" (*Mis.* 339:26). While our loved ones must have the money we make to live," concluded the minister, "it is the love we have that they really want. Give it now before it is too late."

William Ward counsels: **DO IT NOW.** "Your good is here. Accept it! Your joy is near. Embrace it! Your power is within. Harness it! Your victory is now. Claim it! Your freedom is real. Declare it! Your abundance is overflowing. Share it! Your problem is purposeful. Bless it! Your Spirit is divine. Free it! Your love is great. Give it! Your faith is mighty. Use it!"

CHAPTER 16

PRAYER MUST BE PRACTICAL— FAMILIAR PRECEPTS

Now is the time to give encouragement, loving sympathy for all that is right, and to perform kind deeds. Prayer—the celestial stairway—is right practice expressed in the simple, daily practice of loving. Of what good would the understanding of our present holiness and perfection be if it wasn't translated into human experience or daily living?

Prayer must be practical. How practical was Mrs. Eddy? In her early classes, if a couple had no place to leave their child, Mrs. Eddy would tell them to bring the child along. In at least one case she taught an entire class with a little girl sitting on her lap. Mrs. Eddy could do this because of what *she was*, namely, the embodiment of divine Love. As we practice the small expressions of love made tangible, experiences will cause us to progress until we too become the embodiment of Love divine.

Mrs. Eddy's example and teaching can help us manifest divine Love in our daily life. "Wise sayings . . . may fall to the ground rather than on the ear or heart of the hearer; but a tender sentiment felt, or a kind word spoken, at the right moment, is never wasted" (*Mis.* 127:27).

Mrs. Eddy urges: "'Ask God to give thee skill in comfort's art'" (Ret. 95:4). Today we seem surrounded by people who are hurting. Be available, approachable. Don't be too busy to just <u>care</u>. Often a dog's sympathetic lick gives more of the transfusion of Love that is needed than cliches and platitudes. Loneliness is a disease of our time. It strikes the divorced wife and husband, the poor, the elderly, the sick. Peer through the mask that may be hiding a scarred soul, and remember that a tangible way to be a comforter is listening and caring even when you are hurting too.

"Write kindness in marble, injuries in sand, remembering the essence of genius lies in knowing what to overlook." We can all recall the pleasure we experience in the feeling that comes over us when we have genuinely forgiven an enemy. "The greatest of all arts is the art of living together." Love is the only power in the universe, and you are loving and therefore strong.

The result of living Christian Science must be a better and purer **humanhood**, expressed in honesty, meekness, gentleness, loving kindness, sympathy of the right sort. We reach a spiritual state ONLY through improved human conditions. Happier, more harmonious earthly environments must be the precursor of the heavenly. "Be ye therefore perfect" is, of course, the grand *finale,* not the first step, nor the intermediate steps. It is attained only by treading the "thorn-road," which the Master and our Leader trod.

Coincident with true humanhood must be uniform kindliness and consideration of the rights and prerogatives of others; St. Paul's "brotherly love, *in honor preferring one another,*" is important, as we "grow from the infinitesimal to the Infinite" (S&H 336:7).

"Speak gently, it is better far to rule by love than fear;
Speak gently: let no harsh word mar the good we may do here.
Speak gently: 'tis a little thing, dropped in the heart's deep well;
The good, the joy that it may bring, eternity shall tell" (*Christian Science Journal*).

THE BLESSING OF HUMOR

Humor is a form of love; it is the affectionate communication of insight; at the root of much humor lies the love of Truth. It has been said that humor is a spontaneous, wonderful bit of an outburst that just comes—unbridled, unplanned, full of surprises. It is also an affirmation of dignity—a declaration of man's superiority to all that befalls him.

"Humor," a professor said, can also "show you are not overwhelmed or flustered by mean or unkind remarks." A young lady (arguing with a man about a parking space) interrupted him when he began directing foul language at her. She asked: "Does your mother know you talk like that?" He cracked a smile. She got the space. Humor can be the art of gracefully avoiding conflict without compromising either your dignity or your opponent. By introducing a humorist twist, you can change a situation from abusing to amusing. Casual good humor will see you through most sticky situations because humor rings with the magnificent conviction that there is something hidden in the spirit of man that, if called forth, can enable him to surmount trouble and suffering, and sing "Glory, hallelujah," even though "nobody knows the trouble I've seen."

PUT RESOLVE INTO ACTION

Take action when disaster strikes. The "prodigal" didn't lie in the gutter when trouble came; he made his way home. He reached out; he acted. "Be in thy place. Stand, not sit!" Mrs. Eddy wrote. The only thing that ever sat its way to success was a hen, states Sarah Brown. "The smallest deed is better than the grandest intention."

People who believe in discipline exude a kind of assurance, but they don't hesitate to ask others for help. We all need help sometimes, even as we all have the power to be great since greatness is determined by service to others and to ourselves.

Regarding honesty, for those who are so cooperative they can never say "No," for fear of hurting someone's feelings, or for wanting to be all things to all men, there is no greater time-saver than "honesty." It is super-important to have priorities that we regard as sacred. Other time-savers are overlooking one another's little lapses, and always acting as though nothing had happened no matter what has happened.

Regarding speech, Mrs. Eddy said it is loving and courteous to speak clearly, distinctly, making sure your listener hears. It may also save you some embarrassment. The check-in clerk in Maine registered a young man who confessed to being new at camping. After assigning him a site she told him not to remove all his clothes because this was a family park. "Pardon me?" he asked. She repeated her comment.

"Why are you telling me this?" he demanded.

"Didn't you just tell me you were a nudist? she inquired.

"Madam," came his frosty reply, "I said I was 'new at this.'"

Similarly, when writing, it is a kindness to check spelling. A church bulletin read: "Ushers will eat late comers."

MAKE PEOPLE FEEL GOOD ABOUT THEMSELVES

A few words can make a big difference and may bring someone closer to realizing his own true perfection.

Coming home from a movie, Betty thought the leading man was attractive; George didn't.

"But it wasn't just his physical appearance," Betty said. "He was strong, but kind and sensitive. That's what I find attractive in a man. Though you don't always act that way, you're really strong and self-confident, too, George," she continued. "I love you for that."

Strong? Self-confident? A surprised George had never thought of himself in those terms. He usually sat back and let others make decisions for him, even push him around. "Then I thought, I do have those qualities in me," George recalls, "And I decided from that moment on, no matter how I felt in a situation, I would try to appear strong and self-confident." From that moment he was a changed man.

Yes, words have power to bless or to harm. Words spoken— especially those charged with strong feeling or emotion—produce events in our life that conform with the spoken word. This is why it is vital to speak positive words. Mrs. Eddy taught that it is extremely important to affirm constantly words that are in keeping with your goal, and to continue these affirmations of good.

Yes, words have power. I remember as a child (when teased) I would, with an air of aloof martyrdom, retaliate with the taunt:"Sticks and stones break my bones, but words can never hurt me, ha! ha!" But this is *not* true. **Words can inflict a lifetime of emotional misery**—hurt, resentment—especially when they come from those who should love us.

A parent's criticism and lack of moral support can cause lifelong heartache for a child. As a child, didn't you yearn for love and acceptance? Have you ever stopped longing for love and acceptance? However, it's never too late to learn the awesome power of the spoken word, and ask wisdom—our own God-Mind—to help us give and accept unconditional love. We have the power to give our children, our marriage partner, and all we meet, the love they long for. All yearn to know someone loves and accepts them unconditionally, that they are first with someone. In marriage most look for a way to face the world without feeling alone— finding someone that cares for you more than anyone else. Basicly men and women want the same thing: honesty, loyalty— someone that's self-assured and has their act together.

In Christian Science our prayer is an intense yearning for the guidance of Spirit that teaches us to love—to gain that Christ-like love that causes tired eyes to lighten up with confidence and joy when they meet ours: "Teach me to love that weary backs may straighten from the touch of sympathy." The Infinite Good we are one with has built into us the unlimited potential of extending love to others—to do great things. Know enthusiastically that you have infinite possibilities for good as you insistently claim what you already **are**. But this means **getting rid of all that's negative and evil in one's thought.** It is done by pouring in floodtides of Love. (See S&H 201:18.) And like Isaiah, saying to the Lord, "Here am I; send me."

THE POWER OF GOOD-WILL AND ENCOURAGEMENT

One of the most precious things anyone—man or business—can have, is the goodwill of others. In explaining Proverbs 18:24, "A man that hath friends must shew himself friendly," a minister told of a man in the Old West who was tried for stealing a horse, for which he could be hanged.

No one liked the man whose horse had been stolen. He did not have the good will of the people in his town, having always gotten the best in dealings with the town's people; but the evidence against the accused was very strong.

When the Jury returned to the courtroom, the judge asked: "Gentlemen of the jury, have you reached a verdict?" The chairman of the jury stood up. "Yes, we have, your honor." "What is your verdict?" inquired the judge. A few moments of silence. Then the chairman spoke. "We find the defendant not guilty if he will return the horse."

After silencing the laughter in the court room the judge admonished the jury to reach another verdict. An hour passed. Then the jury re-entered the courtroom, took their place in the jury box, and the courtroom grew silent.

"Gentlemen of the jury, have you reached a verdict?" began the judge. The courtroom was totally silent. Everyone eagerly awaited the verdict. The chairman read the decision reached by the twelve good men, tried and true: "We find the defendant not guilty, and he can keep the horse!" The courtroom burst into laughter!

The old Biblical admonition is true. "We reap what we sow," concluded the minister. Will Rogers advised, "So live that you wouldn't be ashamed to sell the family parrot to the town gossip."

ALL NEED ENCOURAGEMENT

We never forget those who have encouraged us. I remember many years ago, after finishing high school, I was working for an insurance company, when the Assistant Manager called me in one day. I had made many mistakes. Heart pounding with apprehension, I wondered if he was calling me in to dismiss me. Instead, "Helen," he said kindly, with a smile that lighted up the whole office, "Have you thought of going to College?" Go to College? Nothing was further from my mind as I had no money. "Get yourself a part-time job, and go." I spent the next 6 years at the local University, and have never ceased being grateful to that dear Assistant Manager for his encouragement that day so long ago.

As we look back over our life we see that every truly wonderful thing or experience came by grace. We didn't plan it. It wasn't our doing. "Which of you by taking thought can add one cubit unto his stature?" (Matt. 6:27). We personally didn't bring it to pass. It came from Love. As you sit thinking, you realize that all you are **truly** grateful for, came by grace. Grace may appear as any really good thing. Every good thing we have accomplished has been grace accomplishing it as us. Grace is the ultimate simplicity, the Holy Grail. To drink from the Holy Grail is to drink from a life lived by grace, a life that *"trusts in Truth and has no other trusts."*

In this life of Love, family members should encourage each other. Don't hesitate or be afraid to say, "I love you. I appreciate you. I'm proud of you." Each one of us needs to feel loved, needed, appreciated. If you see people **as God made visible** you immediately confer upon them a higher level of self-esteem. You transmit, without words, a greater sense of security and belonging. These feelings, more than material possessions, are what all people crave at this state of their growth.

Nor should we underestimate the value of patience and persistence. I had been working diligently, persistently, on a book. Suddenly it became too long. As I prayed, it came to me to divide it into three books: Vols. I and II became *Mary Baker Eddy, God's Great Scientist,* and the middle of the book became *If Mary Baker Eddy's Manual Were Obeyed.* Finally came the day to fly the three manuscripts to the Printer in Salt Lake City, Utah. As I stood, with manuscripts in my briefcase, and looked one last time at my empty desk, I shall never forget, as long as I live, the holy feeling of gratitude, of release, of accomplishment. It was a moment of awe, of happiness, rapture, bliss. It was like feeling God's presence.

When there's good news that can help humanity, there's only one thing to do: Get the word out to as many people as possible. Even if you feel you are the most ungifted person in the world (as I did), if you try hard and do what you can, an unseen power helps you, if you persevere. "Unto Him that is able to do exceeding abundantly above all that we ask or think, according to the power that worketh in us" (Eph.3:20). Yes, "above all that we ask or think"! This was my experience. I mention it only as a testimony which "More than a mere rehearsal of blessings . . . scales the pinnacle of praise and illustrates the demonstration of Christ" *(Manual 47:14).* "To reach the port of heaven," said Oliver Wendell Holmes, "we must sail, sometimes with the wind and sometimes against—but we must sail, not drift or lie at anchor." Then God helps us.

Let's not be afraid to open our Bible for inspiration—as a certain woman now is. She said she opened her Bible at random for guidance. It opened to Matt. 27:5: "Judas . . . went and hanged himself." That was not the advice she wanted so she quickly opened it again. This time to Luke 10:37, which read, "Go, and do thou likewise"!

Let us not be so easily discouraged. God only works when we work, just as in mathematics nothing works unless we work. And remember: "exceeding abundantly above all we ask . . . *according to the power that worketh in us."* Let's buy that! Keep in thought: *"The Lord shall raise him up"* (James 5:15).

THE ONE MIND WILL TELL YOU

When you perceive that the one Mind, God, is your Mind, you will know what to say and think whether it's handling cases of emergency, or just comforting a friend. "Ye shall receive power" (Acts 1:8). Infinite Good is nearer and more available than any human sense of persons or things. In dealing with others, see what <u>they need and want</u>. Give **that** before you focus on your own needs. Practice paying attention even when you don't feel like it. An M.D. said, "Sainthood emerges when you can listen to someone's tale of woe and not respond with a description of your own."

Avoid any remark which might promote fear. Remember, a smile can lighten up the whole world for a friend, a neighbor, or even a passerby, and is often remembered a lifetime. When simply visiting with each other, we should keep our conversation on the high side. We never know when something we say can be almost life-saving for a friend. Suggestions with the spark of truth are worth a hundred repetitions of sound platitudes. We are in the business of helping people into heaven, and Love is a game that all can play, and all win. When asked for help or advice, utter only absolute Christian Science, having confidence in Infinite Good as All. Confidence is contagious, as is lack of confidence; therefore remember <u>"I AM ALL."</u> Our own divine Mind, our real Mind, is this Allness individually expressed. (See *Mis.* 101:31). "What is it to love? To always see the man of God's creation and nothing else. And to separate from our thought of man any belief of fear, sin, or disease. This is love" *(DCC 216)*.

I sought after nothing but how to become wholly God's. This made me resolve to give the all for the All. I renounced all for the love of Him, everything that was not He; and I began to live as if there was not but He and I in the world. —Brother Lawrence.

Infinite Good is living its Life as you and me this holy day. We have "sovereign power" to choose. So, choose ye, to love, to laugh, to persevere in good, to give, to heal, to praise.

Someone has injured you? betrayed a trust? Don't let it give you fits! Get rid of any bitterness toward that person, whatever their motive may have been—self-seeking or the wish for self-glorification, animosity or just forgetfulness. Said the Psalmist: "It is God that avengeth me."

Our work demands we refrain from recrimination which won't heal the situation. In the moment's mortification (at our own lack of wisdom, perhaps, in trusting someone unworthy of our trust) we must strive to return good for evil, and not mire ourselves in frustration. We are cutting our spiritual teeth when we overcome indulgence in recrimination or self-pity; and for each such demonstration we kneel at the foot of the bed and give profound thanks. "Never mourn over an experience. It is a thing of the past, but not so the manifest power of God resulting therefrom."

No one had more adversity to meet than did Jesus and Mrs. Eddy, whose every forward step was met with the revilement and persecution of a scoffing world. The cup they drank, every honest, generous student will also at least taste. As Mrs. Eddy told Ira Knapp, "When you have tasted gall and wormwood you are ready for manna." Instead of harboring a wrong thought, immediately turn around and use that energy to say or do a loving, kind thing. No Christian can understand Christian Science and not love it. Attacks afford opportunity to explain Christian Science. And when the attacks "cease to bless they will cease to occur" (My. 143:23). "Resist not evil," means we should quickly substitute a positive thought—a thought of forgiveness. (See *Mis.* 12:1). In Christian Science we learn how powerful a thought is for either good or evil —thoughts can keep us well or make us sick.

Problems are opportunities for spiritual growth. Let's not let them harm us by indulging in self-pity, resentment, etc. We must learn how to leave *lovingly* every seeming wrong done us. In this way we give, and then "it shall be given unto thee." *It is only when we inspire others to judge themselves that something has been accomplished* since we can never change anyone but ourselves.

"The Father in secret is unseen to the physical senses, but He knows all things and rewards according to motives" (S&H 15:7). A wrong motive is apparent in the case when the divorce lawyer happily explained: "I have succeeded in making a settlement with your husband that's completely fair to both of you."

Client: "Fair to both of us! I could have done that myself. What do you think I hired a lawyer for?"

HATRED A REMINDER TO TURN TO LOVE

Knowing that a sense of hatred is the opposite of Love, Mrs. Eddy taught that if anyone is the victim of hatred or injustice, the remedy would be to see that hatred, being the opposite of Love, is nothing other than hypnotic suggestion. Since Love is real and is the Principle, it exists everywhere, is generic. Hatred is God's opposite. It does not exist except in illusion; and this illusion is just a *reminder, a signal,* calling our attention to the Love that does exist. Therefore, should you ever seem to be the victim of hate, tell yourself, vehemently if necessary, to stop indulging the belief of being a victim of hate and injustice. Do not resist evil, see it only as a call to keep your thought on that which DOES exist, namely, Love. Whenever the error comes, instantly reject the lie, and contemplate the infinite ways in which Love is appearing everywhere.

How often have we seen that "the very circumstance, which [our] suffering sense [deemed] wrathful and afflictive, Love [has made] an angel entertained unawares" (S&H 574:27). How grateful we are when we have withheld the sharp retort, returned good for evil, and obeyed: "Always act as though nothing has happened, no matter what has happened"; then thankfully observed how it blessed both us and the seeming culprit! How often has: "Least said, soonest mended," helped us. Mrs. Eddy knew our only "enemy" is ourself. Jesus knew he had no enemies. He even asked forgiveness for those responsible for nailing him to the cross. In forgiveness, let us follow the example of Jesus and Mrs. Eddy. When we have done something incredibly stupid, like losing our temper or holding a grudge, and the boom is about to be lowered on us, aren't we grateful if when pleading, "Give me another chance!" it is given?

"Let us meekly meet, mercifully forgive, wisely ponder, and lovingly scan the convulsions of mortal mind, that its sudden sallies may help us, not to a start, but to a tenure of unprecarious joy" (*My.* 201:16). Listen again to Mrs. Eddy's immortal words: "How good and pleasant a thing it is to seek not so much thine own as another's good, to sow by the wayside for the way-weary, and trust Love's recompense of love" (*No.* 3:21).

MARY BAKER EDDY MADE JESUS' TEACHING PRACTICAL

Mary Baker Eddy knew we are not inspired unless we are practical. She made Jesus' teaching practical in all the little things of daily living. It was because of this practical application of the Master's teaching that Mrs. Eddy could write: "Through the magnitude of his human life, he demonstrated the divine Life" (S&H 54:1). What Mrs. Eddy said of Jesus, the world can today also say of her.

"All I have ever accomplished," she said, "has been done by getting Mary out of the way, and letting God be reflected." This is true prayer; remembering "the atonement of Christ reconciles man to God" (S&H 18:13).

A student who cherished her inspiring interviews with Mrs. Eddy as the most exalted moments of her life, reports that Mrs. Eddy spoke of spiritual things with an intimacy that revealed her vision vividly to one's consciousness, leaving a deep and lasting impression that could have been not unlike what the disciples must have felt on the Mount of Transfiguration.

The pure and holy consciousness of Mary Baker Eddy revealed the new heaven and the new earth. *Her divine consciousness beheld this celestial universe while she was still on this plane of existence.* We also will behold the universe of Infinite Good when we understand <u>practically</u> the Second Coming of the Christ as set forth in Mary Baker Eddy's writings.

HOW DO WE "WIN THE PRIZE"?

Mrs. Eddy says that in Christian Science, as in every department of life, "self-denial, sincerity, Christianity, and persistence alone win the prize."[1] We have to *want* to gain understanding, and then somehow a way opens up. I remember when I was a young student, my husband's first job after graduating took us to one of those small towns where there wasn't much to see or do, but what you *heard* sure made up for it. I, however, heard something good. Often "in a wooden house a golden room we find." I found this golden room in a live and seasoned Bicknell Young student who invited me to visit.

Almost every weekday for a month I pedaled my bike two miles to her door for an hour's talk. That I learned a lot was evidenced when the local Christian Science Society decided to give a lecture, I was asked to introduce the lecturer.

Sometimes our strength lies solely in our tenacity. "Seek ye first the kingdom of God . . ." Then slowly the shackles of false belief are broken because we find that the kingdom of God which we are seeking is our own Mind. Every conception is found to be under the dominion of our Mind, and the struggle to become that which we already are, will finally be over. But while the race is on, as St. Paul admonished, we should be running instead of still lacing up our track shoes.

---

[1] How <u>not</u> to "win the prize": A business man finding he couldn't open his safe phoned the prison Warden who quickly sent over an inmate. The prisoner dialed carefully, listened intently, and the safe opened.

"Thank you," said the owner. "How much do you figure it's worth?" "Well," said the inmate, "last time I opened the safe I got thirty thousand."

CHAPTER 17

INFINITE GOOD MUST BECOME OUR CONSCIOUSNESS

THE TRUTH WILL SET US FREE

What did Jesus mean with, "I can of mine own self do nothing"?—followed immediately by: "When you see me, you see the Father [God]"? Or when he said, "It is the Father [Mind] in me that doeth the works." It must mean that *without understanding*—without the Mind that is God—he could do nothing. He proved that it is our own right Mind, conscious of itself—the "Mind [that] is its own great cause and effect" (*Mis.* 173:12)—that "doeth the works." In mathematics it is our understanding that solves the problem.

In this saying: "Of mine own self I can do nothing," Jesus tells us his work had nothing to do with a mortal personality. The power was from the kingdom of God within his consciousness. It is also always from within our consciousness. "All power is given to me in heaven and in earth." All power is given to us when we gain an *understanding* of our true identity.

The spiritual consciousness which enabled Mrs. Eddy to fulfill her God-sent mission is our only real consciousness too. We will become aware of it through spiritual education because it already is our divine consciousness. Of this consciousness ("the holy city"), St. John writes: **"I saw no temple [no matter body, no material structure, no corporeality] therein; for the Lord God Almighty [our own right Mind, our own divine consciousness] and the Lamb are the temple of it."**

The accumulated error of the ages dies slowly, and usually with severe struggles, but we are all destined, through Mrs. Eddy's spiritual instruction, to arrive in consciousness where we experience heaven on earth here and now, as she did, and with no matter body. "In divine Science," Mrs. Eddy says, "man possesses this recognition of harmony [heaven on earth] **consciously** in proportion to his understanding of God" (S&H 576:23). I can be consciously conscious of present perfection in proportion as corporeal sense yields to the incorporeal sense of God and man. Then "mortals [material and corporeal selfhood] will disappear, and immortals . . . will appear" (S&H 476:11) as understanding enables us to "dwell in the [consciousness] of **LOVE** forever."

JESUS AND MARY BAKER EDDY HAD FAITH
IN THEIR UNDERSTANDING

Of this ability to heal, Mrs. Eddy states: "God will heal the sick *THROUGH MAN WHENEVER MAN IS GOVERNED BY GOD [by Truth]*"—just as the mathematical principle will solve a problem whenever the student follows the principle. Does the principle of mathematics do anything other than just be itself? (See S&H 3:4.) Notice here how quickly Mrs. Eddy adds that it is Truth that casts out error. (S&H 495:2). True thought alone is required, and there is nothing more powerful than thought. It is "[**KNOWING**] the truth [that] shall make you free," said Jesus. (John 8:32) Realizing there had to be a grain of receptivity, Jesus asked patients: "Believe ye that I am able to do this?"

Jesus and Mrs. Eddy had absolute faith in their understanding of Life and Mind. To the centurion who had a sick servant, Jesus said, "I will come and heal him." Again, "All power in heaven and on earth is given unto me."

When Mrs. Eddy raised the dead, she spoke with authority. She knew her Mind was God, and that God was all there was to the one called a patient. Calvin Hill writes: "In my remembrance of Mrs. Eddy there is no one thing that impressed me more than the faith she had in her own words. . . . Mrs. Eddy's faith in the correctness of her interpretation of divine Science, when all the world doubted, transcended human belief. . . . This faith on her part left a deep impression on me. It seemed to stand back of every word she spoke. . . ." (*We Knew Mary Baker Eddy, p. 18*). There is far more to Mrs. Eddy's great Discovery than the world has yet realized. "Scarcely a moiety. . . is yet assimilated spiritually by [even] the most faithful seekers" (*Mis.* 317:15). In a letter to Mrs. Stetson she indicated that we have seen only one millionth part of it.

THE HARD PART—REALIZATION OF TRUTH

It is easy to *intellectually* see the truth of our "at-one-ment" with Infinite Good, to talk and write about it. It is not so easy to get the absolute *realization* Jesus and Mrs. Eddy had. Spiritual truth becomes a law of God in our experience only in proportion to our **realization of it.** First we acknowledge it; then comes the realization. Eventually we all will make the transition from law to grace.

To aid the learning process Mrs. Eddy established the C. S.Publishing

Society. "The education of the future will be instruction in spiritual Science. . . ." (*Mis.* 61:4). The Publishing Society was established to teach, to instruct in spiritual Science. (See *Mess. '01.* 30:4.) How much more advanced we all would be had her Deed of Trust to the Publishing Trustees not been jettisoned by the *Manual*-terminated Board of Directors with the acquiescence of a totally non-comprehending field.

Fortunately the efforts of the "small and very feeble remnant," have today stirred the ecclesiastical cauldron. Now a dozen swords of Damocles dangle over the heads of the would be usurpers of Mrs. Eddy's place. Pushed to the wall, the hierarchy's ship of state is listing badly as fewer career Scientist board its sinking vessel. Having had it up to their ears with ecclesiasticism's anti-freedom crusade, more and more freedom seekers are jumping ship and turning on their own to a deeper study of Mrs. Eddy's writings.

Such "**learning**" is necessary because mankind is so blinded by the physical sense testimony that when it tries to step into "the pool of Bethesda" [meaning "house of mercy"], another [hypnotic suggestion, like a sheet of steel] steppeth down before it" and veils from mankind the truth that humanity is spiritual and perfect now—veils from us that "the place whereon we stand *IS* the "promised land," and is "holy ground."

RECOGNIZE MANIFEST FORMS AS SPIRITUAL

If we fail to recognize the manifest forms—the forms we now see before us—as spiritual and perfect when *RIGHTLY VIEWED*, we make Spirit a non-entity and veil the spiritual man. This world is no more material than our belief of it. Once we realize that "all is Spirit," the MATERIAL SENSE of everything will disappear. We have to learn to resurrect the true idea of every form in our consciousness. Then we gain dominion over the earth. "Science understood, translates matter into Mind" (*Mis.* 25:12). What we see before us, when rightly viewed can't be anything but God, since *"God is ALL."* (See *Mis.* 60:28; S&H 310:6; & 269:17).

Today we believe our body is matter, but as Mrs. Eddy's discovery continues to take us on a beautiful ride up the spiritual information superhighway, the time is coming when we will realize our body is spiritual; then it can appear anywhere as spontaneously as the figure 4 accompanies the idea of 4.

WHO TOLD US WE WERE "MAN"?

Mrs. Eddy's divine logic, in the Second Coming of the Christ, dissolves the false, material sense of man and of "this world," as Jesus called the false concept of the world he overcame. Her logic brings to an end thousands of years of human reasoning which has always had two values, right and wrong, Spirit and matter, good and evil. Who told us we were only "man"? Mrs. Eddy sets this right when in the first edition of Science and Health she tells us plainly, <u>openly, that we are Principle (Mind), and what is called "man" is our likeness.</u>

Principle is the kingdom of God within our consciousness. Zephaniah shouts, "The Lord thy God <u>in the midst of thee</u> is mighty" (3:17). Isaiah too, exuberantly sings: "Cry out and shout . . .for great is the Holy One of Israel in the midst of thee" (12:6). With stubborn daring Hosea gloriously proclaims, **"I am God, and not man, the holy one in the midst of thee"** (11:9). Who pays attention to that? Mrs. Eddy once said "the reason Christian Scientists don't demonstrate supply is because they believe they are man rather than God." (Carpenter Foundation).   Our forgetfulness of these divine facts reminds me of the absent-minded professor whose wife asked him as he came in, "Did you see this? There's a report in the paper of your death."

"Dear me," said the professor, "We must remember to send a wreath."

RENDING THE VEIL OF BELIEF IN A MATTER BODY

Jesus said, "Having eyes see ye not" (Mark 8:18) Sir Arthur Eddington agreed that existence cannot be seen *as it really is* when the vision seems to be filtered through the veil called the eye of man. Looking through mortal eyes, and the material *sense* of things, constitutes the *veil.* "The side of nature which seems to the senses as matter, is but the veil that hides the reality of being. The visible universe is but the picture of the mind's ideas, the expression of thoughts, the hieroglyphic record of the art and meditation of Deity. . . . This world is the veil obscuring the brighter glory that lies beyond it."—Mary Baker Eddy. Through all her writings Mrs. Eddy is removing the veils.

St. John, the divine Scientist, because of his spiritual vision, saw a woman clothed with light" who realized her Mind was God, a woman who would bring the Second Coming of the Christ. She lights the path— the path we all must travel—which teaches mortals that "in divine revelation, material and corporeal selfhood disappear, and the spiritual idea is understood" (S&H 561:20).

The "veil" will be lifted once we spiritually realize it is nothing other than hypnotism and aggressive mental suggestion which drag us down a road we don't care to travel. Hypnotism makes us believe we are corporeal beings with a mind of our own which inhabits a matter body that can become sick. Understanding lifts the veil and gives us a new conscious-ness, an illumined consciousness, which sees that nothing from the external world can be reflected in the body anymore than a rose can get into the mirror. *The picture of illness is always thrown from within. Our thoughts have tremendous power; they create happiness or misery.* Peace is an inside job. We will be at peace when we know we are spiritual beings rather than material bodies. With understanding, all discordant conditions leave, since "the heavens and earth . . . [to] that consciousness which God bestows, are spiritual" (S&H 573:6). There we find we are Love in action.

The Bible has many references to the veil (and vail), which descends on us with the belief of mortal birth—birth into a matter body. There is no doubt that both Jesus and Mrs. Eddy had revelations from long before their incarnation and life on earth began. But for most of us revelations are blocked by the veil which descends at mortal birth. Isaiah (25:7) writes: "And he will destroy in this mountain the face of the covering cast over all people, and the vail that is spread over all nations." Note his perception that all people and all NATIONS (all states of thought) are victimized by this veil (the hypnotism) that obscures true existence. Mrs. Eddy brought the Truth about us out of obscurity, fulfilling Isaiah's prophecy that the veil would be lifted.

Isaiah's illumined consciousness saw things as they are. He knew that an understanding of Infinite Good "will swallow up death in victory; and the Lord God [our own Mind when free from hypnotic suggestion] will wipe away tears from off all faces; and the rebuke of his people shall he take away from off all the earth; for the Lord hath spoken it" (*ibid.* verse 8). Prophetic words! This has already come to pass, and will be com-pletely fulfilled as Mrs. Eddy's teaching is more widely accepted and demonstrated.

Isaiah was aware that the veil only SEEMED to cast a shadow over that which is genuine. He realized that this "covering" would be elimi-nated—as is being done today through an understanding of our Leader's writings. World thought is being transformed by the "Comforter" Jesus promised—by the "little book open in the hand of the angel" which he prophesied in Revelation 10:2.

ST. PAUL AND THE VEIL

St. Paul has a vital message concerning the veil in Chapter 3 of II Corinthians, verses 13-16: Moses covered his face with a veil, for the mind of the children of Israel was blinded. He concludes: "When [we] shall turn to the Lord, the "veil shall be taken away." The veil is being "taken away" by the Second Coming of the Christ.

A "veil" is something interposed between the vision and that which is seen, separating the seer from that which can be seen. So we have dualism, which is the cause of all our difficulties. Webster defines dualism as a "twofold division. Any theory which considers the ultimate nature of the universe to be twofold, or to be constituted by two mutually irreducible elements. . . ."

This division, this illusory picture of separateness between the one who sees and that which is seen is called the "veil" in the Bible. Vision is perception, an activity of consciousness. **We know that if we were unconscious we would see nothing even if our eyes were open. This is proof that the eyes do not see.**

Jesus showed contempt for the belief of material eyes having power to see, saying: "Having eyes, see ye not? and having ears, hear ye not?" (Mark 8:18).

Answering a question regarding insanity, sent by the editor of *The New York World*, Mrs. Eddy closed with: "Neither life nor death, health nor disease, can be produced on a corpse whence mind has departed. This self-evident fact is proof that mind is the cause of all effect made manifest through so-called matter. The general craze is that matter masters mind; the specific insanity is that brain, matter, is insane." (*My.* 302:6).

PUTTING ON THE WHOLE ARMOR OF GOD

Mrs. Eddy urged us frequently to ask ourselves, "What am I entertaining in thought?" and to reconcile ourselves only with good. Why? Because the more we realize Infinite Good is all, and that what seems to be going on which is unlike Infinite Good is only hypnotic suggestion, the more we are putting on "the whole armor of God." (See Eph. 6:13-17).

Living Christian Science means expecting good, and giving good. "When we give someone a thought of Truth," said Mrs. Eddy, "we are giving him something he can give again to someone else, and still have and keep throughout eternity." She discovered that every human being can alter his life by altering his attitude of mind, his thinking. What a world of beauty and wonder we could view if all the divine thoughts Mrs. Eddy entertained could have been recorded. She knew that the smallest truth is mightier than the greatest lie the world has ever known; that the one is as enduring as eternity, the other as transient as a shadow.

Only hypnotic suggestion makes sin and sickness seem to appear.

Error didn't fool Jesus or Mrs. Eddy. They knew that as Truth progresses, error grows more subtle and aggressive, but it never becomes something; it always remains an illusion (hypnotism); and is met and destroyed with the understanding that divine Love is the only power. The good thoughts we have externalize, outpicture themselves, just as what the artist has in mind outpictures itself on the canvas. Error may seem great and powerful in its apparent magnitude, but continue to speak the truth to it and it collapses.

The biblical "wilderness" is where we press on until a material sense of existence is "Christianly and scientifically reduced to its native nothingness" (S&H 572:5). Mrs. Eddy defines "wilderness" as "Loneliness; doubt; darkness. Spontaneity of thought and idea; the vestibule in which a *material sense* of things disappears, and spiritual sense unfolds the great facts of existence" (S&H 597).

As we stumble through this "wilderness," how grateful we are for that which throws light on what we really are as divine beings, one with Infinite Good. Purged finally of our reliance on the illusory material world, we turn from doubt and darkness to Truth and light. The material sense of existence is dissolved as we realize the truth revealed by the "God-crowned woman."

In Mrs. Eddy's *Christ and Christmas* the first picture shows the head of a woman in the upper right-hand corner, symbolizing the woman of the Apocalypse prayerfully bowed over a dark mass, "the long night of human beliefs." The chaotic mass in the picture suggests St. John's heavenly dragon (old theology), which Mrs. Eddy defines as the sum total of error (the belief that man is separated from God). Its tail is divided to represent hypocrisy, while the snarling serpentine beast symbolizes the lust and hate that stalked God's two witnesses. In a lesser degree it stalks all who walk in the spiritual path.

But unto him "that overcometh, and keepeth my works unto the end, to him will I give . . . the Morning Star" (Rev. 2:26)—unto him will I give the kingdom of heaven *he never left.* "Do not I fill heaven and earth? saith the Lord" (Jeremiah 23:24). Only the veil of human birth ("the last enemy to be destroyed")—that ushered in the belief in matter—makes us think we left this oneness with Infinite Good.

ALL MUST YIELD TO REASON AND REVELATION

To overcome the veil it is not enough to merely accept Mrs.Eddy's teachings. We must apply the full resources of intellect to understand them. "Reason is the most active human faculty . . . . The dream that matter and error are something must yield to reason and revelation. . . . Reason, rightly directed, serves to correct the errors of corporeal sense; but sin, sickness and death will seem real (even as the experiences of the sleeping dream seem real) until the Science of man's eternal harmony breaks their illusion with the unbroken reality of scientific being" (S&H 327:29; 347:26; & 494:19). The matter body we have in the waking dream is no more real than the body we have in the sleeping dream.

Mrs. Eddy emphasized the all-importance of reason. She states *"that God is BOTH noumenon AND phenomena,"* and insists that both *"reason and revelation declare that God [Mind] is the first and ONLY cause."* Any *effect without a CAUSE [Mind] is inconceivable. "According to reason and revelation, evil and matter are negation:* for evil signifies the absence of good, God, though God is ever present; and matter claims something besides God, when God is really *ALL"* (Mis. 23:18; & 27:20). "Science and Health has effected a revolution in the minds of thinkers . . . and given impulse to reason and revelation, goodness and virtue" (*No.* 13:22).

"THINKING MAKES IT SO"

The activity of Mind must be to think, and this is why Mrs. Eddy tells us, "the time for thinkers has come" (S&H vii:13). Only by *thinking* can we reach the stage where we *know.* Mrs. Eddy has about 120 references to "learn" and "learning." You learn with the mind you now have, until you reach the stage where you *know. The nature of Mind is to think. Understanding is arrived at through thought.*

Mrs. Eddy placed Shakespeare's quote: "There is nothing either good or bad but thinking makes it so," on the fly-leaf of Science and Health along with her "prayer," and St. John's "Ye shall know the truth, and the truth shall make you free."   "Thinking makes it so" brings to mind the account of the "Light and the Cross" by Arthur Gordon:

The patient in room 78 was very frightened. The doctors had little hope for the surgery scheduled in the morning. When the nurse suggested that she pray for strength, the patient said she didn't believe that prayers were answered. "During the night," said the nurse, "I went into her darkened room with my flashlight. Rather suddenly I was called away. In the morning a most extraordinary change had come over her. She no longer seemed frightened. 'I'm going to be all right,' she told me. 'I know, because I prayed, and my prayers were answered. I asked for a sign, and I was given one.'"

"A sign?"

"I saw a light," she said in a whisper. "And in the center of the light, a cross. It was on the wall at the foot of my bed. I'm going to be all right."

"After attendants had wheeled her away, I looked in her bed and found what I was looking for—my flashlight. A week earlier I had dropped it and cracked the glass, and had mended it with a tiny cross of adhesive tape. Obviously, when I came in during the night, I had left it by mistake. Half buried in the blankets, it must have projected a circle of light, just as the patient said . . . with a cross in the center."

"Did the patient recover?"

"Of course! She THOUGHT her prayers were answered."

THE POWER OF RIGHT THOUGHT

We *know* that "thinking [made] it so," and that Mind controls the body completely. If thinking makes a thing, then thinking must be a cause. Since Mind is the only cause, then thinking must be this Mind, this creator in the act of creating.

Mrs. Eddy states: "Christian Science explains all cause and effect as mental, not physical . . . . *Through this action of thought* and its results upon the body, the student will prove to himself by small beginnings, the grand verities of Christian Science" (S&H 114:23 & 384:12).

In the 500 or more times Mrs. Eddy uses "thought," "thoughts," and "thinking" in Science and Health she tells us what right thinking will do and what wrong thinking will do. In a hundred different ways she tells us right thinking lifts disease off the patient whereas wrong thinking fastens disease on the patient.

Mrs. Eddy shows us that we must learn to depend on our own right thinking as the panacea for all ills. Within our right thought lies the power to bring forth harmony and heaven. Heaven isn't something up in the sky. Heaven is right accomplishment, having needs and desires we are gratefully able to fulfil; knowing we have dominion to conquer challenges; having goals and joyfully reaching them; constant divine progress. It is only through our right *understanding* that "divine Love [which, in reality, "I AM"] will meet every human need"—through *our* true, right reasoning.

We have to learn what God *is* before we can judge if something is Godlike or not. Mary Baker Eddy's definition of God is destined to change the world's thinking and usher in the millennium. This is where the study comes in. It is only through learning what we *really are,* as divine, that our at-one-ment with Infinite Good manifests itself. Only through study and practice can we actually begin to *KNOW* it. A parrot can say 2x2=4, or God is Love, but those utterances would not be based on the understanding of mathematics or on the understanding of divine metaphysics.

Giving birth to right understanding involves labor pains, alias *learning*. This is why Science and Health has about 120 references to learn, learning and learned. When we step by step <u>learn</u> what God is, through what the Second Coming of the Christ has revealed, we become one with the Principle that has always been latent within our consciousness. When I actually realize that I and the Principle of being are one, the healing will be spontaneous, as healings were in the case of Jesus and of Mrs. Eddy, God's two witnesses, and of all who have followed and practiced what they were taught. Why? Because "the Principle of all cure is God [the Mind of man]" (*Mis.* 3:18). The Principle *KNOWS* the Truth; the Principle is the Truth; it knows nothing of error, and neither will we when we have learned the Principle, and are as at one with it as were Jesus and Mrs. Eddy.

THE SECRET THAT FREES

The conviction of Infinite Good's presence dispels material sense. It opens human consciousness to receive the Truth that frees. Getting the consciousness of Infinite Good's **OMNIPRESENCE** is the secret that frees. The creative Principle has always been within us, but has been veiled by the belief that we were born into matter. As Mrs. Eddy explained, "human birth—to be born into the belief of matter—is the last enemy to be overcome." Christian Science teaches us how to overcome the belief in physical life that ends in death.

How do we overcome it? Just as we overcome ignorance in mathematics. The mathematical principle is within us. We are one with this principle. But did we always know that *5 + 5 = 10?* No. We had to *LEARN* it, didn't we? The more we learn in mathematics, the more we become one with the mathematical principle. The link to understanding is *learning*.

It is the same with learning our divine Principle, Love. Here the hard part is that "the human self must be evangelized" (S&H 254:19). But we continue to learn our divine Principle, Love, fact by fact, until the complete realization dawns: "I and the Father [Mind, divine consciousness] are one." Every universal fact is already within our true Mind, our divine consciousness. Science and Health, p. 502:27, tells us "the creative

Principle—Life, Truth, and Love—is God." This creative Principle is within our consciousness. It expresses itself in Life, Truth, and Love, which we are destined to understand. **When a healer gets the consciousness of God's presence, the patient is healed.** Christian Science is the divine revelation disclosing the world of Spirit, of reality. It proves practically that the ideal is the real.

In the first edition of Science and Health, Mrs. Eddy wrote:

> *A student said to us, "I understand your explanation of Truth, but I cannot understand error;" and why? because he made it something, and we, nothing; he gave to error a local habitation and a name, making it what it is not, even an entity and a power" (p. 266:15).*

When the chains of educated belief, hypnotic suggestions, that now fetter us, are broken, we shall behold the "new heaven and the new earth," for the belief that we live in a matter body will have passed away. Infinite Good has become our practical life.

> *"Science speaks when the senses are silent, and then the evermore of Truth is triumphant. The spiritual monitor understood is coincidence of the divine with the human, the acme of Christian Science. Pure humanity, friendship, home, the interchange of love, bring to earth a foretaste of heaven" (Mis. 100:19).*

In the triumph of Truth we come face to face with the spiritual idea. Who or what is the spiritual idea? You are, since Mind and its idea cannot be separated, can it?—and you now understand that your own Mind is God when it is free from the hypnotic spell that seems to have overtaken us with human birth. Eventually it must dawn on us that "heaven is not a breeding ground for mortals." Then we will see, as Mrs. Eddy saw, that this Mind that is your Mind expresses itself as the spiritual idea, as what looks like you and me. In divine revelation (Thought will finally be understood and seen in all form, substance, and color, but without material accompaniments") (S&H 310:6), similar to a night dream, where there is no matter as we find out when we wake up. The "material accompaniments" are the disguise that we, as God-qualities, are wearing. (See Mrs. Eddy's references to disguise, disguised and disguises in Science and Health and Prose Works.) What a glorious sense of existence awaits us when we actually realize we are made of God-qualities!

"WHAT THOU SEEST, THAT THOU BEEST"

Why did Mrs. Eddy quote Plato's immortal words: "What thou seest, that thou beest"? (*Hea.* 8:15). Because there is no "over there." It is all *here* in our consciousness. Seeing correctly we will see only perfection. If we remember that a lie is always a lie about the Truth, we won't come unglued and taken to the cleaners by the lie's cruel, false and tenacious suggestions. The lie is always about something divinely real; we must stand up to it immediately, before we get caught in mortal mind's vortex. Tell the lie to go back to the nothingness from which it came. Our real identity can't see what the lie is saying about the omnipresence of present perfection, anymore than the principle of mathematics can see all the errors made in mathematics. Having learned that "the Christian Scientist is alone with his own being and with the reality of things," we know we have the power to instantly unsee error whenever it tries to come to us to give it life.

If we entertain a false claim (an illusion), say of sickness, it becomes as tangible as any reality. "Everything is as real as you make it, and no more so" is Mrs. Eddy's answer to the question: "Is anything real of which the *physical senses* are cognizant?" (*Un.* 8:4-5). When error presents itself we have to know it is a lie about the perfect Principle which is the only cause and creator.

WE NOW ARE ONE WITH GOD

Science works from the premise that we are already and forever *there.* Getting this straight is the most important thing to remember. Nothing can make us what we **are** not already in reality. It can only bring to light our oneness with our present perfection. This is why "we understand best that which begins in ourselves, and by education brightens into birth" (*My.* 253:26).

Mrs. Eddy saw the only need was a successive removing of that which veils Truth. The universal belief in matter is the veil. To take away this veil, Mary Baker Eddy, representing the woman of the Apocalypse, brought from heaven the truth about matter's unreality. She brought this Truth from heaven to benighted human understanding, through four descending levels of consciousness:

(1) On the Science itself level (where Mrs. Eddy's thought was, and with which she is identified) she writes: "In the universe of Truth, matter is unknown" (S&H 503:10-11).

(2) On the divine Science level she writes: "Divine Science, rising above physical theories, excludes matter." (S&H 123:12-13).

(3) On the absolute Christian Science level we read: "The creations of matter arise from a mist or false claim, or from mystification, . . ."

(S&H 523:7-9). In Latin, "absolute" means "to set free, to loose, not confined." We live in the absolute, and by grace, when we experience oneness with God. When we know *all is God, then we know that what looks like a human is just God wearing a disguise.* Our true consciousness is the divine power, expressed individually. (*Mis.* 101:31). There is only Oneness. Realizing this oneness sets us free. The One includes everything real and true.

(4) On the Christian Science level we read: "Matter . . . the opposite of Spirit; . . . (S&H 591:8-13). "Spirit is the real . . . matter is the unreal " (S&H 468:12-13).

WE MUST BECOME AWARE OF WHAT WE ARE

In reality, we don't have to "seek" God. We only have to awake to realize the only "I" already is God. The "I" that I AM cannot "achieve," in reality, since "I" cannot grow into understanding any more than an image in the mirror has to grow up to what is standing before the mirror. I can only become **aware** of that which I already am, that is, awaken to it. But *awakening* and becoming *aware* means "work, work, work, watch and pray"! Each has a God-given talent that must not be wasted, reminding me of the dog who went into the employment office seeking help finding a job. "With your rare talent," says the clerk, "I'm sure we can get you something at the circus."

"The circus?" echoes the dog. "What would the circus want with a plumber?"

"We lose . . . when doing the work that belongs to another" (*'00.* 8:18). Let us each pursue the work God points out, and so find our place in infinite Good's great Love.

CHAPTER 18

PRAYER BRINGS US INTO
AT–ONE–MENT

REJECTING NEGATIVE THOUGHTS IS PRAYER

The aim of the chapter on Prayer is to bring us into oneness with Infinite Good, **our real self.** Here, as we have seen, **thought is all-important. A negative thought must instantly be rejected. Give it the ax and turn thought to Infinite Good's omnipresence.** Daniel speaks of the "abomination of desolation standing in the holy place." The holy place is your consciousness, and the "abomination of desolation," means any negative thought or belief that Infinite Good is not present where it is needed. **Prayer means working earnestly to see the presence of infinite good right where error confronts us.**

The "I" and the body are one. The "I" must be changed in order to change the body. . . We must see all false claims as conditions of mortal mind [alias hypnotism] entirely distinct from the person. . . . Ignorance is the one great error, and this is only another name for unconscious mind [hypnotism]. When this is removed, harmony or the conscious Mind governs. When teaching music or mathematics we remove the ignorance on the subject" (DCC p. 187-188).

All things which are termed material are actually mental. *MATTER IS MERELY THOUGHT OBJECTIFIED.* Disease held in thought may project itself on to the body. Divest thought of it by knowing: "I and God are one." I can't think anything Infinite Good could not think, I cannot see anything God does not see or I would be bigger than God. Can God see a sick man or a sick animal? See as God sees. When looking at a man or an animal, see intelligence, companionship, joy, love, movement, action, faithfulness. None of these are material. As we go higher we see there is no *material* man or animal—there is no flesh, blood and bones man, since all is Mind manifested; and Mind does not manifest itself as matter to be healed. Hypnotism, alone, makes the body look and feel material.

When the Dr. Kildaire series was on television, and a disease with its symptoms was minutely described, doctors all over the country were inundated with calls from patients reporting they had all these symptoms. "A minutely described disease costs many a man his earthly days of comfort" (S&H 197:5). We can vehemently drive out thoughts of fear, heartache, loss, and build into consciousness what Infinite Good, what Love, knows about us. We never deal with anything except our own thoughts, and we have the power to select and control our thoughts. Our destiny is never in the hands of other people or circumstances. Victory is ours when we work spiritually, because we are applying infinite power to the situation. What we sow in thought we reap in experience. We can switch immediately to what we know to be the Truth of being. Let's start now to select carefully all day the kind of thoughts that are constructive, remembering any mental activity that enables us to rise to the spiritual standard of Soul—of our true identity—is a form of prayer.

TELL ERROR, "GET LOST!"

When error steps up its assaults, just give it the cold shoulder, derail it and "take no prisoners." It's time to storm the beaches. Get the subterranean stuff out on the table and deal with it. Any error trying to gain entrance should be sacked immediately. The first five seconds are most important. We instantly know 2+2=5 is incorrect; just so, we should *immediately* know the error coming to us for life is nothing but hypnotic suggestion. Too often we shoot ourself in the foot with negative thoughts that don't put us on the fast tract to health and wholeness. In today's vernacular tell error: "Scram! Beat it! Bug off! Shut up! Get lost!" Or, in Jesus' words, "Get thee behind me Satan . . . Ye are of your father, the devil . . . he was a murderer from the beginning and abode not in the truth, because there is no truth in him." Such instant slamming error to the mat, is honoring God, and is *de rigueur* now and forever.

Reminding ourselves constantly that Infinite Good is omnipresent, and that our real self is the presence of God here and now, is true prayer. It will make sweeping cutbacks in the nonsense we so often entertain— we entertain it because of the thousands of years of traditional thinking which is the great hindrance to accepting our divinity. But when Christian Science is better understood, "doing unto others as you would have them do unto you," will become a cosmic law and work like the law of gravity. Claiming constantly that Love is working through us, is prayer. The type of thought we allow to become habitual will find expression on the plane of action.

While in reality we are perfect now, we don't understand it; so, "the ages must slowly work up to perfection." The spiritual facts about ourselves are gained step by painful step. "Though the mills of reform grind slowly," we **do finally** become "good stewards" concerning the mess we inherited with human birth. Our task is "to begin aright and continue the strife," dropping the indulgence in a material sense of things. This assures us that when the roll is called up yonder we will wear the crown of the faithful.

With wisdom—the perfect blend of intelligence and love—there is no limit to the conquests that divine intelligence working in mankind can achieve. Jesus, in reference to our divine destiny, quoted the Scripture, saying: "Is it not written in your law, I said, Ye are gods? If he called them gods [God] unto whom the word of God came, and the scripture cannot be broken . . ." (John 10:34-35), then what are we as we understand our oneness with God? Having the Mind of God are we not God incarnate? God made visible? God in disguise?

As human nature is exchanged for the *divine,* then patience combined with a gentle unhurried expectation of success will bring about the necessary healing. Patience and persistence are indispensable elements in successful work. Patience, as it abides through the long watches (untinged by resignation) is a steadfast spiritual quality that crowns us with the joy of demonstration.

THE PRICE OF ONENESS

The question is, "Where is your heart?" The story of the rich young man "[who] . . . went away sorrowful: for he had great possessions" (Matt. 19:22), is really mankind's sad story. Because we have great possessions of preconceived ideas—pride born of academic distinction, material or sentimental attachments, habits we have no intention of renouncing—these mortal traits keep us chained to the rock of suffering, chained to that which keeps us exiled from oneness with Infinite Good, and its revelations.

In her chapter "Atonement and Eucharist," the Eucharist part tells us that the price we must pay to experience oneness with God is the evangelization of the human self—the development of the transitional qualities: "Humanity, honesty, affection, compassion, hope, faith, meekness, temperance." Studying these qualities with the Concordances we find each is rooted in God. They constitute the passover from the dream state to reality. They rid us of the leeches keeping us from seeing: "entirely separate from the belief and dream of material living, is the Life divine" (S&H 14:25; **see also** *Un.* 49:8).

The transitional qualities constitute true human identity, **true human-hood,** that is coincident with Infinite Good. They are required to meet error head on, working, watching, praying. Mrs. Eddy warned us that she could not continue to do the work for us. We must do it for ourselves, and "if it is not done the Cause will perish and we will go along another 1900 years with the world sunk into the blackest night" *(DCC* 251).

Will the world enter a new dark age, or will there be a brave new world full of understanding and promise? Mrs. Eddy assures us of "the divine influence ever present in **human** consciousness" (S&H xi). "Human" here is very significant: On the shoulders of the 20th Century Christian Scientist is placed the task of averting a second downfall of **genuine** Christianity. Read Mrs. Eddy's warning in her *Message for 1902.18:25.* The cardinal, vitalizing element in this demonstration is our "noble" conduct toward Mary Baker Eddy.

"God demands a more Christian, zealous and persistent effort to resist evil and overcome it," she admonished, "or our Cause will again be covered by the rubbish of centuries" *(DCC* 50). It is foolish to think we don't have to make a conscious effort to learn this great Truth that was revealed to Mrs. Eddy. Just as in mathematics, God only works as we work. *The only thing error asks is to be let alone.*

When we frequently forget this, we are like the absent-minded professor, of whom the manager complained:

"Professor Schmaltz has left his umbrella again."

"He'd leave his head if it was loose," observed the waiter.

"That's true," replied the manager, "I just heard him say he was going to Switzerland for his lungs."

HOW DO WE REACH GOD?

How do we reach God? We become aware of the infinite good called God—that we already are one with—through exercising the qualities of God. Spiritual growth comes from putting into practice the knowledge we already possess. We must remind ourselves constantly that the infinite good called God is omnipresent and that *our real self is the actual presence of God here and now*. To this end our Leader stressed the importance (as she wrote Judge Hanna) to *"keep a time for meditation every day to ponder in thought your infinite, harmonious, Christ-expressing self-hood, and claim it as you. Drink in its perfection, its moral beauty, its integrity, worth, its unspeakable safety [it is as safe as 2x2=4]; all the truth and beauty of God's creation is yours and you. . ."*

Mind, *our own right Mind,* is the divine Principle, Love, and can produce nothing unlike Itself. Christian Science is based on the Principle that "God is All-in-all." This is its <u>entire</u> basis. Everything else is a deduction from this Principle, and "to keep consciousness in constant relation with the divine, the spiritual, and the eternal is to individualize infinite power."

Mrs. Eddy makes it clear that Christ is making the atonement. Her definition of an individual spiritual man is, that he is Christ, the Son of God. "The atonement of Christ reconciles man to God, not God to man; for the divine Principle of Christ is God, and how can God propitiate Himself?" (S&H 18:13-15 & *Mis. 96:17-23. See also S&H 24:15-19*).

THE KINGDOM, THE POWER AND THE GLORY

Prayer is the affirmation that brings us closer to the understanding that ushers in the millennium. The last line of the Lord's Prayer, "Thine is the kingdom, and the power, and the glory," which has mistakenly been thought to be the truth about a God apart from our own true Mind, is actually a declaration about our real selfhood, which is always at one with God, the kingdom of God within.

Shouldn't prayer then be a hymn of gratitude for this kingdom of infinite good that is now and forever established within our real being, our God-consciousness, and needs only spiritual education to gain the realization, the awareness of it?

As we live a life of prayer—that is, *as we take to heart Mrs. Eddy's statements of the divine truth about ourselves* and experience their power—the realization comes to us that the infinite good we name God is the solution to every problem. We turn away from the problem that appears, and go within, convinced that this is a spiritual universe. It must therefore have a spiritual solution to what appears to the lying material senses as inharmony of any kind.

Reading our textbook with expectancy, the kingdom of God within us is able to receive. We begin by knowing we already have, for the kingdom of power is within us. An unselfed love within us yields up the mortal sense in order that demonstration may be the outcome of divine law.

VITAL INSTRUCTION FROM OUR LEADER

Nearing the end of her long sojourn on earth with us, Mrs. Eddy gave us this cardinal instruction on how to go within: "Unless you fully perceive that you <u>are</u> the child of God, <u>hence perfect</u>, you have no Principle to demonstrate, and no rule for its demonstration. . . . You can never demonstrate spirituality until you declare yourself to be immortal and understand that you are so" (*My.* 242:8 & 3). *This is the truth about our-selves as it was openly, unreservedly set forth in her first edition, and it should be taken seriously.*

Remembering Jesus' answer to Pilate: "My kingdom is not of this world" (John 18:36), takes us out of this world and lifts us into "My kingdom," where we are in "at-one-ment" with the infinite good called God. Then Mrs. Eddy states, "the marvelous unity of man with God [is] shadowed forth in scientific thought." Remember there is nothing more powerful than thought. She adds, "Sooner or later the whole human race will learn that in proportion as the spotless selfhood of God is under-stood, human nature will be renovated [the human race will understand its true identity] and man will receive a higher selfhood derived from [Infinite Good], and the redemption from sin, sickness and death will be established on everlasting foundations" (***Un.* 6:4 & 5:24**).

THE LORD'S PRAYER IN THE FIRST EDITION—REVISITED

Mary Baker Eddy clearly shows us the way in her explanation of the Lord's Prayer. But before we look at "The Lord's Prayer" let's say a few words about its author, Jesus.

St. John knew he could not begin his Gospel with the birth of Jesus, as Matthew, Mark, and Luke had done. Why? Because Jesus denied human birth. He claimed God (infinite good) as his Father and knew that when he had finished his ministry Infinite Good would "glorify" him "with the glory I had with Thee before the world was"—before this dream of human birth overtook him.

St. John knew also that he could not begin his Gospel as Mark had done, when he opened his Gospel with the ministry of Jesus. Why? Because John couldn't record what Jesus taught without making clear who Jesus *was*.

Thus, St. John starts out: "In the beginning was the Word [the logos which means communication]. And the Word [the communication] was with God, and the Word [the communication] was God." All this was later explained as "I and the Father [infinite good, Mind] are one [thing]." Jesus was the communication between God and man. He was the only way whereby Infinite Good or God could be known, in that age.

"As many as received him, to them gave he power to become the sons of God . . . born not of blood, nor of the will of the flesh, nor of the will of man, but of God" (John 1:12-13). Jesus was called the "only begotten son," because until Mary Baker Eddy came, no one was ever found who fully shared Jesus' conviction that man is not born of the flesh.

THE LORD'S PRAYER

We now come to the Lord's Prayer in the first edition. In Mrs. Eddy's first edition of Science and Health, the "Prayer" part of her chapter "Prayer and Atonement," ends with her interpretation and spiritual significance of the Lord's Prayer, as follows:

(**Note:** Many readers will not need the bracketed explanations. I put them in because as Shakespeare says, "the good is oft interred with their bones," that is, many of us are so buried in materiality that, as Mrs. Eddy once said, the word "God" fails to influence us as it should. Nevertheless in her day she <u>had</u> to use it. Hopefully our continuous explanations will not offend the spiritually brilliant who have no need of explanations).

> *Harmonious and eternal Principle of man,*
> *Nameless and adorable Intelligence,*
> *Spiritualize man;*
> *Control the discords of matter with the harmony of Spirit.*
> *Give us the understanding of God [our true Mind],*
> *And Truth will destroy sickness, sin, and death, as it destroys the belief of intelligent matter,*
> *And lead man into Soul, and deliver him from personal sense [hypnotism, the belief in a personality apart from God],*
> *For God is Truth, Life, and Love [which on the preceding page she has stated we in reality <u>are</u> since we are God's presence] forever."*

Notice her characterization of God as Principle, which in the first edition she has stated we are. Notice also that here in her interpretation of the Lord's Prayer she defines evil as "personal sense," alias hypnotism, the belief we have a personality, apart from God. What a heavenly light these illuminations bring us!

This celestial light is in accord with Jesus' prophecy to St. John regarding the "little book": "And I saw another mighty angel come down from heaven, clothed with a cloud: and a rainbow was upon his head, and *his face was as it were the sun*, and his feet as pillars of fire; and he had in his hand a little book open . . ."

Regarding the appearance on earth of the "little book" clothed with a *cloud*, Mrs. Eddy explains: "To mortal sense Science seems at first obscure, abstract, and dark." Then she interprets the prophecy "and his face was as it were the sun," saying: "When you look it fairly in the face, you can heal by its means . . . for God is the light thereof" (S&H 558:10).

What is this heavenly light leading to? What is its ultimate goal?

Answer: It is leading us to the spiritual *understanding* that in reality we never left the Father's house—that we are forever one with Infinite Good, namely, that "Principle and its idea is one" (S&H 465:17). Mrs. Eddy has taught us we are the Principle when free of hypnotic suggestion—when we are awakened from the Adam dream. Again, she has taught us that we, the spiritual man, made a mistake that must now be corrected. The heart of the Lord's Prayer is: "Give us the understanding of God" so we become aware of our true identity, since "metaphysical Science teaches us there is no other Life, substance, and intelligence but God" (*Hea.* 16:4).

PRAYER GIVES US THE UNDERSTANDING OF INFINITE GOOD

True prayer shows us more clearly than we saw before what *we already have and are, and most of all, shows us what the infinite good, called God, is.* Mrs. Eddy did not just pick up her pen and romp briefly into the subject of prayer. Rather, she saw the Lord's Prayer as a statement of the perfection of being.

Her spiritual interpretation of the Lord's prayer in the first edition pleads for God's spiritualization of man; it pleads for God's control of the "discords of matter"; for God's leading "man" into Soul," and for deliverance from "personal sense" alias mortal mind, alias hypnotism. The vital sentence in the prayer is: *"Give us the understanding of God."* Every thought in this interpretation leads man to God, and we have the rainbow of promise upon the head of the angel that is bringing its message to the-human consciousness.

The import of this message is to unite Life with Love, "for Love alone is Life." Whose life is to be united with Love? Our Life. This is why Jesus, our great Exemplar, could say: "All power is given unto me in heaven and in earth." He knew his Mind was the Principle, Love. Thought which is in accord with Principle is allied to omnipotence. Both Jesus and Mrs. Eddy make it clear we can't just think about Mind; we must think *as* Mind. If, or when we accept the Infinite Good as our Mind, wouldn't thoughts then have their source in Infinite Good? Wouldn't thoughts then be Mind's utterances—the utterances of this infinite good we call God?

From this interpretation of the Lord's Prayer in the First Edition to the final changes in Science and Health we can see how Mrs. Eddy lifted the Lord's Prayer beyond the point of Jesus' first announcement of his mission as "the kingdom of heaven is at hand," to her declaration of "the new birth, HEAVEN HERE, THE STRUGGLE OVER" (*My.* 158:12).

Sibyl Wilbur, in her book, *The Life of Mary Baker Eddy,* tells that

Mrs. Eddy stated "she had a mission from God to complete the work of Jesus Christ on earth" (See her chapter entitled, "The First Edition of Science and Health".)

What has Mrs. Eddy accomplished by her progressive changes in the Lord's Prayer?

For nearly 2000 years, the Lord's Prayer had remained static. Mrs. Eddy, forbidding formulas, showed that prayer must be progressive and active, meeting the needs of the time, the need of the moment, or it will be like yesterday's manna.

Prayer is here and now. The "I" that I am is God, as Mrs. Eddy defines your "I or Ego" (S&H 588:9). She declares this "I," that is your "I," as "Divine Principle; Spirit; Soul; incorporeal, unerring, immortal, and eternal Mind."

As we persistently maintain the truth about our oneness with Infinite Good, this, to human sense, externalizes itself as our experience and we find heaven right where we stand. This is what is meant by "prayer and at-one-ment."

CHAPTER 19

HEAVEN HERE
AND NOW

EXCEPT THE LORD BUILD THE HOUSE

The Second Coming of the Christ is teaching you and me that we, the "I" of conscious being, are actually the infinite good we call God in individual manifestation (*Mis.* 101:31). Cause and effect are not the same ("man is not God, and God is not man") but are still one—as you and your thoughts are one. "I and my Father [Mind] are one," not two, since "God's law is in three words, 'I am All'" (*No.* 30:11). This is why "whatever is possible to God is possible to man [as effect] *as God's reflection*" (*Mis.* 183:13).

Mrs. Eddy understood that "when a man begins to see himself as the reflection of Infinite Good, Mind, and realizes he has within himself the capacity to act as possessing all power from the infinite good in whom we live and move and have our being, he is done with error and has reached the highest of all endowments and is fruitful of all good works" (*DCC 216*).

In explaining the Scripture: "Except the Lord build the house, they labor in vain that build it" (Ps. 127:1) Mrs. Eddy said, "Just so long as you are trying to heal the body through your own mental effort, just so long as you are trying to create health, you are laboring in vain, for you are trying to do God's work which has already been done."

Except you see, acknowledge, and practice that which you actually *are,* your labor to bring health, harmony or success to a "personality" man, a dream man, a man of dust, is in vain.

Is "the Lord" here something other than my own divine consciousness, individualized? This divine consciousness builds a house (home) in which there is integrity, honesty, infinite capacity for good, harmony, beauty, peace, "The Lord" builds the house in which the omnipresence of present perfection is realized.

"The Lord," our true consciousness, builds the house or knowledge that we live in a universe of perfect form. So when error argues, "the Lord," our divine consciousness, quickly reverses it by declaring the truth—right, left and center. In this "house" we are never in the dream where sin, sickness, and death seem so real until we wake up to *reality*. In the house which "the Lord," our true consciousness builds, we are awakened from the dream that we live in a matter body. Then nothing can alarm or "pain, fetter, and befool us."

When we fully understand the Science of being brought by "God's scribe" we will understand how our own Mind sees all that it makes, and "behold, it is very good."

BELIEF IN MESMERISM MUST BE DESTROYED

"A knowledge of error and its operations must precede that understanding of Truth which destroys error, until the entire mortal material error finally disappears, and the eternal verity, man created by and of Spirit [the substance of divine Mind], is understood and recognized as the true likeness of his Maker" (S&H 252:8). The marginal heading here is: *"Eternal man recognized."*

In *Unity of Good*, Mrs. Eddy advises us to think radically but speak wisely. Again she confided, "I have healed more patients with the spoken word than with the silent argument." So don't hesitate to voice the Truth when confronted with error.

Only Science, divine Science, will solve the problems facing the world today. When someone asked Mrs. Eddy, "Is this whole mortal life just a dream?" Mrs. Eddy answered, "No, it is hypnotism." (Another word for animal magnetism.)

In a lesson to the students in her household, Mrs. Eddy said: "You must rise to the point where you can destroy the belief in mesmerism or you will have no Cause." Mrs. Eddy teaches us how to do this rising in her Chapter, "Christian Science Practice," in our present textbook. She admonishes us to "Stand porter," and deal "with thine adversary quickly, whilst thou art in the way with him." The first five seconds is the best time.

As previously explained, she said:

[Mesmerism] tried to overcome me for forty years, and I withstood it all. Now it has gotten to the point where the students must take up this work and meet animal magnetism [hypnotism]. I cannot do it for you. You must do it for yourselves, and unless it is done, the Cause will perish and we will go along another 1900 years with the world sunk in the blackest night. Now will you rouse yourselves? You have all the power of God with you to conquer this lie of mesmerism [alias hypnotism]. . . .

Over and over she impressed on her students that they must handle animal magnetism—hypnotism, the lying pictures and evidence of the five physical senses—and "defeat the mental murderer and mental assassin who is working to defeat this Cause." ***But error is nothing.***

Through prayer and at-one-ment, Mrs. Eddy was continually demonstrating the nothingness of matter. She saw that the claim of a human body was a myth, a lie of personal sense, or hypnotism.

HOW DOES HYPNOTISM WORK—AN OFFICER'S EXPERIENCE

An English officer, upon his arrival in India to take charge of troops there, was told he must pass a test in hypnotism, for if he could be hypnotized by an opposing officer, he could not retain his position in the English army. He knew nothing about hypnotism, nor did he think anyone considered it other than charlatanism. Amused rather than anxious, he asked another experienced English officer for an opinion and was answered:

"Do I believe in hypnotism? I asked the same question of a highly educated and well-traveled East Indian on the steamer with me as we were putting into port in this same town. The day was extremely hot and sultry; the air was stifling. Before my question could be answered, there was a wild outcry from the upper deck. It was crowded with natives, naked but for the covering over their loins, who carried their weapons of war—knives and instruments that made terrific noises. All was bedlam. They were killing all their passengers with their knives and throwing the bodies on the deck below. The massacre was horrible beyond description. Battle-scarred as I am, my experience seemed as nothing compared to the wholesale slaughter. I begged the East Indian to find a way out. He led me through a passage I had not seen before, down stairs, winding and narrow, which led to a part of the ship that for a moment seemed deserted. We were at the dock and from where we stood, we could jump to the wharf, which we lost no time in doing. In less time then it takes to tell you, a storm was upon us; the wind, rain, and rush of sand were blinding. Out of it came hail— the stones sharp and heavy, cutting through my thin silk shirt and linen trousers until my flesh was cut and badly bruised. I urged my companion to leave me as I could not endure more and death would be a relief."

"At once I found myself standing quietly beside the East Indian as the steamer neared the wharf, waiting for his reply to my question. He smiled that inscrutable smile of the Oriental and said, 'Yes, I believe one can be hypnotized.'

"I, who scoffed and ridiculed the Hindu's power to hypnotize, had then, neither have I now, anything to say.

"You ask me if there is no way to withstand their boasted power. Yes, if you will mentally hold fast to a basic truth — a fact incontrovertible — without wavering, they cannot control you."

Later on, when summoned to take the test, the officer was guided to a small building consisting of only one room about ten by twenty feet with two windows and a door. It was absolutely bare — devoid of all furnishings. An East Indian whom he did not know stood silently by the door awaiting his approach. The Englishman remembered his fellow officer's rule and held to the only fact he could at the moment recall — which was that **two plus two equals four**. As long as he concentrated on that, nothing happened. Once he wondered what the Indian would do. Suddenly he saw him pick up a beautiful vase and dash it quickly to the floor, breaking it in hundreds of pieces. He realized he was being hypnotized, so he forced himself to concentrate on **two plus two equals four**. Again his thought wavered and he saw the pieces of the broken vase move, but he held fast that **two plus two equals four**, and he was safe. Finally the Hindu said, "I cannot control you — you are free."

KNOW YOU CANNOT BE MESMERIZED

This is what Christian Science teaches us to do when the five physical senses try to hypnotize us into believing in sickness and discord. We are to hold fast to Infinite Good's allness and evil's nothingness, as Mrs. Eddy tells us: 'When the illusion of sickness or sin tempts you, cling steadfastly to God and His idea. Allow nothing but [Infinite Good's] likeness to abide in your thought'" (S&H 495:14).

Once we have learned all is infinite Mind (our true Mind) manifested, we too will be free—out of the never-never land, into the land of understanding, where the illusion of sickness and sin cannot mesmerize or control us. "It is well to know, dear reader," Mrs. Eddy writes, "that our material, mortal history is but the record of dreams, not of man's real existence, and the dream [the Adam dream we seem sound asleep in] has no place in the Science of being. . . . The heavenly intent of earth's shadows is to chasten the affections, to rebuke human consciousness [engulfed in eon's old traditions and misconceptions] and turn it gladly from a material, false sense of life and happiness to spiritual joy and a true estimate of being" (*Ret.* 21:13).

The Carpenter Foundation preserved the following account: A Christian Scientist helped a boy who had been seriously injured by a train. On the way home the boy recovered miraculously—was able to walk. When Mrs. Eddy heard of the case, she asked the student how he treated the boy. A smile transfigured the student's face as he answered: ***"I did not treat him. I knew I could not be mesmerized." Mrs. Eddy answered, "That's all you ever have to do."***

Mrs. Eddy insisted that if we don't break the belief that mesmerism, animal magnetism (hypnotism) has power, Christian Science will do very little good in the world.

OBEDIENCE NECESSARY

Jesus and Mrs. Eddy gave no commands which are impossible to obey, since our ability is from the Infinite Good that is our Mind. Jesus said, "ask," "seek," "knock." By this he was teaching us by what means we attain to the Truth that makes us free—free from the many things we "know" that are **not** so.

When we indulge excuses we put ourselves on the negative side. This undermines our power to resist evil. But obedience to Infinite Good's demands supplies the strength, courage, and will to conquer. It supplies the vision to aim high to establish our authority over error, and no longer splash in shallow water. Stay in there, fighting. Said Plato, "Know that you can do anything with your thoughts if you take charge of them."

True humility gives us the vision of perfect Mind and its perfect expression. The more we courageously, unflinchingly banish error and listen to what Truth is saying, the stronger Truth's voice becomes; and evil's grim whispering disturbs us less and less. Since you have "sovereign power" within yourself, constantly affirm the fullness and nowness of your divine being; and this spiritual *fact* becomes your experience. We must begin to appreciate and realize our unlimited heavenly potential—it is to do "greater works" than Jesus did. (John 14:12).

Truth's heroic voice will rescue and regenerate us in proportion as we utilize it. We must be wide awake when we do our study. I recently heard from an insomniac patient who wrote enthusiastically: "Oh, Mrs. Wright, your books are wonderful. Everytime I start to read them I fall fast asleep." I was grateful, for we must try "to be all things to all men," and sleep at the moment seems necessary. "He giveth his beloved sleep," the Psalmist (127:2) sang. James Gordon says, "American Society is not nap-friendly, but there's an exquisite pleasure in falling asleep, particularly when you are supposed to be doing something else." Ah! "Sweet sleep that knits up the raveled sleeve of care." Perhaps helping my readers sleep is the greatest benefit my books will give!

But the ultimate goal is to awaken from the Adam dream. To do that, we must again and again prod ourselves to alertness. Mary Baker Eddy's teaching is thrilling; it includes and explains all Jesus taught. St. Peter therefore exclaims, "Rejoice with *joy unspeakable and full of glory"* (I Peter 1:8); rejoice with a joy that cannot be described! Bored? Sleepy? Are you kidding? Listen to the Psalmist: "This is the day which the Lord hath made; we will rejoice and be glad in it!" (118:24).

Men and women of the Bible became great men and women because of the spiritual power that flowed through them. When David cried unto the Lord because of the fear besetting him (Ps. 3:1 & 4) he went from fear to boldness and great power. After going to God in prayer, he became fearless, "I will not be afraid of [anything]!" he asserts. "I laid me down and slept" (Ps.3: 6, 5).

"Let us be glad and rejoice, and give honor to him [infinite Love]: for the marriage of the Lamb is come [when we have cast out of our thought all that keeps us from our "at-one-ment" with infinite Love], and his wife hath made herself ready" {Rev. 19:7). We are "full of glory" now. We must *keep awake and vigorously CLAIM IT!* Then, "when you have accomplished all that you can," wrote Victor Hugo, "lie down and go to sleep. God is awake."

HOW WE USHER IN THE MILLENNIUM

In every case when we see or hear of imperfection we are to correct our own thought. This is NOT low profile work, since if we really understood this, it would usher in the millennium. If imperfection has been banished from our thought, it can't be anywhere else. Our true identity sees only perfection. That is all that exists, since "God is All."

Let writers who defend and vindicate Mrs. Eddy comfort themselves. They need not be dismayed if people don't jump up and down while reading their books. The time will come when books that "declare what the pioneer [Mary Baker Eddy] has accomplished" (S&H vii:25), *will be* sought after, since they help us realize that because God is our true consciousness, we have all power within us. We must use it. This kingdom within is Love, which makes Love the foundation for all action. Be awake to the challenge. It beckons us on to serve in the greatest cause the world has ever known—the cause to free all mankind from the hypnotism that makes us think we are separated from Infinite Good.

The impetus of Christian Science is incorporeal and divine, as compelling as the coming of daylight in its forward march. But it is we who carry it forward as we learn there is no point of contact between our timeless, birthless Christ selfhood and the limiting sense called birth, time, age. Mrs. Eddy insists we must "discard all sense of material selfhood—all that is involved with the belief of birth, heredity, association, time, death." When this realization comes nothing can touch us.

"There is no mental, moral, or financial paralysis in God's kingdom. [But] the world is mentally and morally paralyzed to the Truth of being, and this must be handled in every case. Our treatments must be universal as well as individual. [If our prayer work is universal it leaves no one out, and therefore no one to resist the Truth, and cause us trouble.]" (DCC 224).

CHRIST JESUS AND MARY BAKER EDDY WERE DISSIDENTS

Both Christ Jesus, who founded Christianity, and Mary Baker Eddy, the Discoverer, Founder, Revelator and Leader of Christian Science, were revolutionaries, dissenters of the highest caliber. The dissenter is every human being at those moments of his life when he retires momentarily from the herd and thinks for himself.

Mrs. Eddy's revelation of Christian Science has had a tremendous impact. Since her founding of this Christ Science in human thought, millions of books have sprung from the world's presses, containing, embracing, her ideas. While few of the authors of these books have given Mrs. Eddy credit, their impact has been felt. We remember Jesus' response to St. John who reported:

"Master, we saw one casting out devils in thy name; and we forbad him, because he followeth not with us. And Jesus said unto him, Forbid him not: for he that is not AGAINST us is for us" (Luke 9:49-50).

Mrs. Eddy's revelation has deeply penetrated world thought. It will continue to do so until mankind's thinking is aligned with God's. Then all mankind will learn how completely Mrs. Eddy was governed by God in what she wrote and taught.

A century and a quarter ago when Mrs. Eddy was making her sublime discoveries, almost the entire world believed God was a man up in the sky to whom you prayed. You begged God to heal Aunt Mary, then crossed your fingers in the hope God heard your supplication. Mrs. Eddy's teachings have so educated world thought that today few are left who still pray to a man up in the sky. To a great extent Mrs. Eddy's spiritual explanations have taught individual receptive thinkers that their right Mind is God. And they can now, like Jesus, at least say, "'All power in heaven and on earth is given unto me,' since the kingdom of God is within my consciousness and matter is an illusion, merely wrong thought projected."

Five hundred years ago when a thinker first discovered that the world was round, people did not accept it. The Truth Mary Baker Eddy taught in her writings was at first accepted by only the most spiritually-minded. Today, as we keep presenting her deeper truths to mankind, the whole world is gradually accepting what for so long has eluded humanity. Though unaware of it, all are hungry for this celestial Truth.

It is marvelous how the advanced physical scientists are today grasping Mrs. Eddy's ideas, and putting them in language for the man in the street. There is a saying: **If a little science takes one away from God, a great deal of science brings one back to Him.** This certainly seems to be borne out in a trio of new books written by distinguished scientists: "*Evidence of Purpose: Scientists Discover the Creator* (by 10 physicists and biologists); *"The Faith of a Physical Scientist: Reflections of a Bottom-Up Thinker,"* by John Polkinghorne; *"The Physics of Immortality: Modern Cosmology, God and the Resurrection of the Dead"* by Frank J. Tipler.

> Barbara Dewey's *"Consciousness and Quantum Behavior"* explains: "Everything we think we can see, feel, weigh, etc., is only patterns of energy. And that energy is light. Light at a certain vibratory level feels solid; we call that mass. Light at other vibratory levels is invisible. We call that space. The universe is actually only light interacting with light. Any other reality with which we choose to endow the universe has been given it by us and our peculiar senses. In truth, we are making it all up. . . . You live within a cosmos founded and moved by a love so strong that it can will the universe into being. Hold sacred that love by "living its vision."

Gradually Mary Baker Eddy's God-revealed Truth—that in reality, we are Mind, Spirit, Soul, Principle, Life, Truth, and Love—will find its way into the textbooks of the schools, where children will begin to accept it as fact. Mrs. Eddy opened up the spiritual information super-highway, unveiling and revealing the Promised Land that is always beneath our feet. She not only had the ideas and knew the power of ideas, but she was also a genius at marketing her ideas. She knew "the education of the future will be instruction in spiritual Science, against the material symbolic counterfeit sciences" (*Mis.* 61:4). As reason triumphs, all mankind will come to know the truth about themselves and be blessed. Mortal mind's pictures will be seen as error.

ON THE THRESHOLD OF A NEW PERIOD

In the first edition Mrs. Eddy states: "Error will continue seven thousand years from the time of Adam, its origin [Adam meaning the deep sleep, the hypnotism that makes us believe matter is real, that we have corporeal bodies]. At the expiration of this period Truth will be generally comprehended, and Science [will] roll back the darkness that now hides the eternal sunshine, and lift the curtain on paradise."

Today we stand on the threshold of the seventh thousand year period since the beginning of the Adam dream. The sixth, or Truth period, is ending as the seventh or Love period enters, and there is a great over-turning. In the midst of this revolution of consciousness, sweeping global changes are taking place. While Satan seems to be in the saddle, with rampant destruction everywhere, the prophet Joel saw there are not two armies—one of destruction, the other of renewal. Both armies are "the army of the Lord" (Joel 2). When Jesus said, "Resist not evil," it didn't mean **not to be wide awake to error**—Jesus was the Christ because he loved righteousness and hated iniquity. It rather means to see the nothing-ness of evil, and forgive as ye would be forgiven. Know that only good is real. What we call animal magnetism has to be the Christ in operation, just misinterpreted, misunderstood, since *"God is All."* Seen humanly, ignorantly, the Christ-working may seem a bitter experience; and we call it animal magnetism. Seen correctly, there is only one power at work, to bring about the maximum of good. (See S&H 574:27 & Mess. 1902. 19:21).

This "army of the Lord" is ushering in the age of Love, the seventh period, ridding thought of all that would stand between us and the totality of Love that wipes all tears away and wraps us in the arms of Love—"the heaven of Love within our heart," as we, in almost everything we do, find non-verbal ways of saying, "I love you."

PART II

PREFACE TO
PART II

PART II

PREFACE TO PART II

Today many are asking what it was that spread Christian Science around the world so rapidly that by the beginning of this century "there [was] hardly a city, village, or hamlet, in which [were] not to be found living witnesses and monuments to the virtue and power of Truth, as applied through [Christian Science]" (S&H 149:31). Mr. Kimball estimated that by 1902 two million healings in Christian Science had taken place. The *Encyclopedia Americana,* in an article on Christian Science, said that no religion in modern times had such an amazing growth.

Christian Science spread because it was healing people quickly and permanently—even hopeless cases that had been given up as incurable by the medical profession. Such healing, and with it the spread of Christian Science, continued up until about the middle of this twentieth century, when it almost ceased.

To understand why this change came we need to ask two important questions:

How did practitioners, teachers and students generally regard Mrs. Eddy in those early days?

Was Mrs. Eddy regarded differently then than now?

Indeed there was a difference. Mary Baker Eddy was deeply loved and revered. She was recognized by her advanced students as representing the woman of the Apocalypse, and as the one scripturally prophesied to bring the "Comforter," the Second Coming of the Christ. This was the underlying reason for the millions of quick and permanent healings, up through the 1940's. Newspapers editorialized that Christian Science was the greatest religious phenomenon of all history.

Were there apostate students in the movement during Mrs. Eddy's time? Yes, there were. ***Disloyal students and certain sections of the press caused Mrs. Eddy many problems.*** But because of what *she was,* she gloriously triumphed over each contingency as it arose—so great was the power of her thought in its spiritual alignment with God.

Like Jesus, Mary Baker Eddy had discovered that God was her own Mind—that the kingdom of God was within her own consciousness.

Discovering and revealing all humanity's true relationship to the infinite good we call God, she fulfilled Jesus' prophecy of the "Comforter" which lifted the "mist," unveiling and revealing the "mystery hid from the beginning," namely, that we are God-beings, governed here and now by the Principle of infinite good.

She protected this great spiritual discovery by writing a *CHURCH MANUAL, which prohibited successors to her functions,* and of which she confided to Professor Hering: "The *Manual* will save the Cause."[1] The supreme tragedy in the history of mankind is the ecclesiastical hierarchy's disobedience to the **estoppels** in the *Manual,* in their endeavor to give themselves a bump-up toward absolute control. Cowering behind legalism, ecclesiasticism won out temporarily; but "eternity awaits our Church Manual" (*My.* 230:2). When the *Manual*-terminated 5-member Board of Directors told the Press, "We are Mary Baker Eddy's successor" and the field said nothing, it became the costliest error since the Friday, 2000 years ago, when Jesus was crucified.

Few realized the horrors of ecclesiasticism that lay in wait as the *Manual's* estoppels were jettisoned. Few were prepared for the breakdown and loss of world-esteem about to hit, as the Directors tried to take Mrs. Eddy's unique position. As is typical of the life cycle of those who would rule by personality—(which is the reverse of the butterfly's)—an ecclesiastical hierarchy generally starts out as a beautiful symbol to lead onward and upward, but winds up as a loathsome worm, to frustrated heaven-bent marchers. Remember, it is the **error** we condemn, **never the person.** Mrs. Eddy foresaw that her great discovery would become nothing but lifeless words if material organization continued.

Welcome to the post 1910 rule-by-personality where everything you thought and said would be held against you! Where the hierarchy, through human rules and edicts, **would suppress individual initiative and responsibility;** where, through reprimands and excommunications, those who sought to write independent of Boston's approval and blessing were silenced. **Thinkers** were either expelled or fell silent to avoid conflict. Practitioners and teachers loyal to Mrs. Eddy were kept on the hot seat, never knowing when their scalps would be called for. Need we ask why healing, with which Christian Science has always been identified, wilted and withered, and has almost been lost?

Why will the *Manual* eventually save the Cause?

---

[1]The addition of a 5th member in 1902 made it impossible for the material Mother church organization to continue when Mrs. Eddy's consent to the 5th Director's successor could not be obtained. See *If Mary Baker Eddy's Manual Were Obeyed.*

Because it contains those 29 estoppels which wrest control from the hierarchy and free Christian Science to flourish as Mrs. Eddy intended— in individual heart and mind. Obeying the estoppels will stop the spiral of decline, and end the inept reign of those in power who are "trying to build a road without knowing where it should go." It will bring the understanding of the kingdom of God within each individual consciousness.

⌐ HER IDEAS WILL BE TAUGHT IN SCHOOLS

Already many of Mrs. Eddy's ideas are being taught in schools in the name of modern science. A *Wall Street Journal* article declares: "Once, theology was the queen of the sciences. Lately it has been replaced by physics, but there are signs that the physicists want to become theologians. Books by leading physicists bearing titles like *The Mind of God, The God Particle, and Theories of Everything* now claim for physics the power to describe all of reality. Ambitions like this have important consequences." A Reading Room attendant in New York City one day exclaimed to my friend, Ruth Steiger, C.S., "I wish you had been here a little earlier. Einstein just paid us another visit; and as he left, he said to me: **"I wonder if you people know what you have in these books.""** As already noted, today physical scientists, having seen there is no matter, are spending their time explaining matter away. They are seeing there is no creator who created something. Who created 2x2=4?

The intellectual thought of the world is drawing ever closer to Mary Baker Eddy's teaching. "Weary of matter, it would catch the meaning of Spirit" (*Hea.* 11:8). Ideas that were "hopelessly original" with Mrs. Eddy over a century ago are now being openly discussed in the higher branches of learning. The vanquishing of matter has become the central point of the twentieth century. The powers of mind are everywhere ascendant. World thought is rising morally and philosophically to free itself from the canker of materialism.

The "rule of universal harmony" is Mary Baker Eddy's legacy to humanity. Disobedience to the *Manual* has today put the Christian Science movement in the **Chicken Little League.** But as the *Manual* is again obeyed, the obstacles between us and our understanding of her revelation will fall away, enabling us to find "in this present state of existence . . . a cessation of death, sorrow, and pain" (S&H 573:25). "Obey the *Manual*!" would therefore make a good bumper sticker.

Although the church hierarchy has chosen to ignore it, the *Manual* is not going to roll over and play dead. No matter where Boston's boosterism and beating the drum for rule by personality seems momentarily headed, Mary Baker Eddy's *Manual* will prevail. It has the force of divine law behind it; "eternity awaits" it. In years to come the hierarchy's Mother Goose stories declaring the "estoppels" were "consent clauses" will be seen as no more than a hiccup in a hurricane. A single truth can shatter a thousand lies.

"The time for thinkers has come" (S&H vii:13). While Mrs. Eddy was here in person, all leaned on *her* to do the mental work necessary to keep advancing the Christian Science movement. Today it is up to us—up to what Isaiah termed "the remnant [that] shall be very small and feeble." As the consciousness of this "remnant" holds "thought steadfastly to the enduring, the good, and the true," this consciousness will manifest the enduring, the good, and the true as our experience. Thoughts are the most powerful instruments in the world. "Good thoughts are an impervious armor" (S&H p. 261; and *My.* 210). As we live them, we outpicture them and help usher in the millennium. "God's thoughts are perfect and eternal, are substance and **Life**" (S&H 286:21). Since Life is God, God's thoughts have to be God. Therefore God's thoughts are law.

And our first step must be to obey the *Manual*. Its estoppels terminate priestcraft and ecclesiasticism, and establish the Church Universal and Triumphant in which we find ourselves one with God.

Mary Baker Eddy and her *Manual* are inextricably bound. Her Church was not a material structure. It is "*whatever* rests upon and proceeds from divine Principle [just as "Christian Science" is a term for all that partakes of eternal Truth]" (S&H 583:12). We lose Christian Science just to the extent the *Manual*—*especially its estoppel clauses*—is disobeyed. The history of the Christian Science movement after her departure proves this; namely, that under the repeated blows to the *Manual's* authority the healing ability of Christian Scientists drooped and shriveled.

The incredible momentum Mrs. Eddy generated caused Christian Science healing to flourish for several decades after her leaving. But Judases within the movement felt the need to rule the Christian Science movement humanly with ecclesiastical authority instead of divinely as Mrs. Eddy had always done. Gradually the subversive element, those who had tried to obtain power while Mrs. Eddy was still with us, succeeded, step by stealthy step, in usurping her God-given authority, giving them the clout to fulfill the prophesy of Rev. 13:2, "and the dragon gave him his power, and his seat, and great authority."

How did they succeed? By disobeying the *Manual*.

The *five-member* Christian Science Board of Directors treacherously remained in the saddle after Mrs. Eddy's departure, defying the *Manual's* estoppels which legally ended the five-member Board at her passing. From this position of assumed authority, with a holier than thou attitude and many evasive maneuvers, they dealt two crushing blows to the Christian Science movement:

First, they decreed that only the literature *they "authorized"* should be read by Christian Scientists. This was a dizzying blow to the movement that hadn't gotten off the mat from other punches landed since 1910. Mrs. Eddy had foreseen that such a bastion of discrimination and power (as "authorizing") would further ecclesiasticism's relentless drive for absolute control.

Second, the warning lights flashed furiously when they broke Mrs. Eddy's Trust agreement with the three Trustees of the Christian Science Publishing Society. She had legally set up the Publishing Society, as a separate entity, to promote Christian Science as taught by *her,* knowing the *written* word was absolutely essential to mankind's learning the truth about itself.

Controlled by the Board of Directors, the Publishing Society became the ecclesiastical hierarchy's vehicle for inclining the Christian Science field away from love and reverence for Mary Baker Eddy. Gradually, the wide-spread awed respect for Mary Baker Eddy's great revelation has been lost, and lost with it has been the remarkable healing ability of Christian Scientists.

Those in the "seat of great authority" have traded on people's unwillingness "to point out the evil in human thought and expose evil's hidden mental ways of accomplishing iniquity." Taking advantage of the "present apathy as to the tendency of certain active yet unseen mental agencies" (S&H 571:1 & 570:4), they traded on the general ignorance of what Christian Science is, and so tightened their grip. Bequests, such as the $1.1 billion donated by the Wrigley's, Hershey Candy, and Ralph's Grocery families, were spent—much on lawyers, no doubt—to defend their ecclesiastical authority and consolidate their power, while courageous truth-loving Jeremiahs were banished for their brave opposition.

By their apostasy the ecclesiastical authorities have so confused and divided the field that Mrs. Eddy (whose history is a holy one) is no longer loved and regarded with the veneration that formerly promoted the healing work. In 1975 the August *Journal* contained a particularly deceptive and misleading article by the Board of Directors, fallaciously stating:

"It is sometimes believed that Christian Scientists consider Mrs. Eddy to be the second witness. . . . *but this is not so.*"

This untrue statement began the shameful, cowardly public repudiation by the Directors of "Mrs. Eddy's Place." Being "Directors,"—and anointing themselves as above reproach—had evidently conferred upon them a special depth of "wisdom" that had no relation to common sense; but "a lie can travel half way around the world while the truth is still putting its shoes on."

Because of the confusion this has created in the field, loyal, hard-working Christian Science practitioners today find it difficult to heal—even if they now know more of the letter than did the practitioners who were so successful up until the late 1940's.

Those who think it wrong to expose and denounce evil can find in their Holy Bible what Jesus, John, Peter, Jude, and Paul had to say: Heb. 1:9; Jude 1; II John, 1; II Peter 2; Titus 3:10-11; II Tim. 4:3-4; II Tim. 1:15; I Tim. 4:1; Eph. 5:11; Gal. 1, 3; III John 9-11; Matt. 15:7; 23:13-39. It is error and the action it spawns which we must denounce, not individuals.

Good men, sitting in the seat of great authority—in disobedience to the estoppels in Mrs. Eddy's *Manual*—have been cruelly misled by the false belief that they can take the place of her who was scripturally prophesied to bring the Second Coming of the Christ. They have been mesmerized to think they are ahead of their Leader, instead of needing to follow her—mesmerized to think they can take the place of the woman of the Apocalypse, the "one lone, brave star" shining "o'er the grim night of chaos" *(Christ and Christmas),* the God-crowned woman whose writings are the prophesied Comforter that will set mankind free from bondage to the slavery of false beliefs.

There are Christian Scientists swept up in the belief that installing a whole new five-member Board will cure everything.

Dream on!

Mrs. Eddy's *Manual* sets every man free to be a law unto himself, as does Science and Health also. (See p. 442:30.)

Mary Baker Eddy, like Jesus, knew that "I, if I be lifted up from the earth, will draw all men unto me" (John 12:32). She knew that the "I" (see S&H 588:9) that had to be "lifted up" is the "I AM" God, her true identity, and your true identity. Half a century ago her uplifted thought was drawing all men unto her revelation of error's nothingness and Infinite Good's allness and ever-presence. Today lack of love and esteem for her whom Jesus prophesied and promised has brought the great Christian Science movement to its knees, and has all but stamped out its healing ministry.

This is indeed an emergency. Never has humanity needed healing more than at this moment. We would do well to heed a lesson from Mary Baker Eddy's own time, when healing almost ceased in a community where it had been flourishing:

> *At one point in the early years in the Chicago field, healing work suddenly stopped. This was most unusual as previously Chicago had been one of the finest fields for healing in the country. The best healers, including those having studied with Mrs. Eddy, could not heal. The situation became so alarming that a group was delegated to see Mrs. Eddy at Pleasant View. Mr. Kimball, as their spokesman, told Mrs. Eddy about their difficulties in healing. She patiently listened to their problem and then said, 'You will have to learn to love me more.' [Why? Because for healing work in Christian Science, the Christ in Mrs. Eddy must be recognized or we don't recognize it in ourselves and in our patients.] No more was said and she left the room.*
>
> *They went back to Chicago and told the Christian Scientists Mrs. Eddy's message. They took the message to heart and the healing work was again successful. (A Carpenter reminiscence.)*

Mrs. Eddy knew that a true sense of her as the Founder is the one thing necessary in order for the people to love and adopt Christian Science, and practice its healing.

History affirms what she wrote in 1899: "All the people need, in order to love and adopt Christian Science, is a true sense of its Founder. In proportion as they have it, will our Cause advance." *(We Knew Mary Baker Eddy, Vol. I, p. 40).* If we fail to love and understand her as representing the "God-crowned" woman of the Apocalypse, we fail to understand the Truth she brought concerning our divinity—your divinity and mine. Seeing Mrs. Eddy as a personality rather than the woman of the Apocalypse, chokes out gratitude and love for her.

Mrs. Eddy knew she can never be separated from what God gave humanity through her. She and Christian Science are one. "Her legacy to humanity," wrote a newspaper, was "a Christian denomination, planting itself on the written Word, and considering that written Word so alive that it is spoken of as 'pastor' and accepted as Leader."

Mrs. Eddy's work on earth is an astounding achievement. So high, so holy, so far above human comprehension was her discovery that only by small degrees does the human mind catch glimpses of its wondrous glory—like a star whose light is long in reaching this world. With every passing century a deeper sense of love and gratitude—the homage of the heart—will be felt for this woman who, alone on earth, became aware of man's true identity as generic man, God's image and likeness. Through her spiritual consciousness poured the divine revelation of man's divinity, man's present oneness with divine Principle, Love. <u>All are destined</u> to wed this divine idea—the truth that, in reality, we are one with God.

This is the theme and keynote of Mrs. Eddy's first edition's chapter, "Prayer and Atonement"—(at-one-ment). Its radical spiritual statements descended on the human mind with startling power, conferring an awesome power to heal. It clearly spelled out the momentous truth that your own real Mind is God. As in Deut. 4:35, "Unto thee [hath she] shewed . . . the Lord he is God [your own right Mind, giving you "sovereign power]; there is none else beside [this Mind]." The awareness of oneness with Infinite Good takes place gradually as we learn more of our true spiritual divine identity, and consequently lay down the mortal misconception that hides our divinity. In the measure that we learn and accept the truth about ourselves we replace the lie, the hypnotic suggestion that has chained us to the belief that we live in a mortal body.

But, "without a correct sense of [Principle's] highest visible idea we can never understand the divine Principle" (S&H 560:18). Today it is evident that only a true sense of Mary Baker Eddy—whose holy history has fulfilled prophecy—will cause people to love and adopt Christian Science. Her measureless accomplishments ushered in light where only darkness existed before. The glory of her life was molten in the furnace of affliction. Crucified over and over again by the modern method— openly reviled by the scoffers—Mrs. Eddy showed the same fortitude and forgiveness Jesus manifested.

Her love for God and man—the rule that motivated her—illumined her days on earth with increasing power and beauty as the years advanced. Her self-effacement was complete, and just as we see "the divinity of the Christ was made manifest in the humanity of Jesus" (S&H 25:31), so shall we see the divinity of humanity made manifest through a realization of the Truth brought by the Second Coming of the Christ in Mary Baker Eddy's writings. We must "not only acknowledge the incarnation,—God made manifest through man, but even the eternal unity of man and God, as the divine Principle and spiritual idea" (*Mis.* 77:9).

Mrs. Eddy's arrival on earth—in fulfillment of scriptural prophecy— was the second great turning point in human history. Posterity will recognize her as the greatest woman ever to walk on planet earth. The **human** and divine coincidence had been shown in the man Jesus, "as divinity embracing humanity in Life and its demonstration"; but with the woman, who symbolized the spiritual idea of God, we get a higher sense. "She illustrates the coincidence of **God and man, as the divine Principle and divine idea.**" (See S&H 561:16-25). Here is the demonstration of Love's generic man brought down to human perception and understanding.

Seeing in Mary Baker Eddy the human and divine coincidence we realize that her life work was such a tremendous spiritual achievement that no human pen or tongue, other than her own, can possibly honor or portray it.

I am sure all Christian Science authors sometimes ask, "Why do we write at all?" Writing means endless hours of hard work, and few make a living at the craft. There is no grinning all the way to the bank; neither does a standing ovation greet us. We are writing for an unseen audience, reaching for their eyes and ears, trying to arrest the attention and inspire readers—struggling to find a common wave length where our message may be received. Why?

A Christian Scientist writes because he feels privileged, chosen out of the nearly six billion people on our planet to know the definition of God as Mary Baker Eddy gave it—which tells us what in reality we are, as one with God. He feels he has a responsibility to share the light he sees.

Again, Mrs. Eddy has said it all; but she established the Christian Science Publishing Society because she knew "the"successive utterances of reformers are essential to its propagation" (*Mess. '01.* 30:6). So don't be afraid to write. Your book may be little noticed today. But who took notice of a babe in a manger 2000 years ago? "Be not afraid!" (See *Pul.* 4:2-6; S&H vii:25). In Christian Science conventional thinking is stood on its head, and books that explain the Science she brought to humanity help to translate thought out of the mortal, the dream, the hypnotic state, into the immortal. These books help mankind make the transition from the material to the spiritual point of view, and to establish her divine revelation securely in our consciousness.

A century ago when Judge Hanna and others wished to broadcast her sacred fulfillment of scriptural prophecy, Mrs. Eddy restrained them. She wisely saw that in her time it would be too early; the people were not ready for it even as 2000 years ago they were not ready to hear of Jesus' fulfillment of prophecy until after his crucifixion, following which "human rights were hallowed by the gallows and the cross" (S&H 134:12). Sadly Mrs. Eddy had learned "Whoever proclaims Truth loudest, becomes the mark for error's shafts. . . [but] the stake and the scaffold have never silenced the messages of the most high" (*Mis.* 277:7-14). Today, however, we *CAN* teach and proclaim her fulfillment of prophecy. We *MUST.*

It is my hope that acquainting readers with the lofty spiritual truths spontaneously set forth in the first edition of Science and Health will both aid the propagation of her revelation and hasten the needed universal appreciation of Mary Baker Eddy as the "scribe" of the divine Mind.

When Mrs. Eddy wrote the first edition she was starting where Jesus left off. This high vision was reduced to present human perception in the editions that followed. Because Mrs. Eddy totally repudiated material organization in the first edition, ecclesiasticism trumpets, through double-speak, that Mrs. Eddy said, "the first edition was spoiled . . ." This is "the enemy sowing tares among the wheat." Fortunately, anyone can read Mrs. Eddy's own assessment of the first edition (*Ret.* 37) where she calls it "The Precious Volume, . . . containing the complete statement of Christian Science." When someone mistakenly returned a copy of the first edition, Mr. Carpenter states, "Mrs. Eddy held it tenderly. With a far-off look, and with deep emotion, she said, 'No one will ever know what it cost me to write this book'"—the "little book" prophesied in Revelation 10:2.

Restoring Mrs. Eddy, God's scribe, to her rightful place in world consciousness will restore to Christian Scientists their power to heal, and bless all mankind eternally.

CHAPTER 20

PROPHECY FULFILLED

THE IMPORTANCE OF SEEING MRS. EDDY RIGHTLY

No examination of the first edition's Chapter 5 would be complete without a close look at Mary Baker Eddy herself. The *Atonement* portion of this chapter has come down to us as part of Chapter 2 in the final edition, and Mrs. Eddy has told us that while her chapter, "Atonement and Eucharist" in her 1910 edition of Science and Health is about Jesus, it is just as much about her and her life.

To write about the two greatest lives that have been manifested on earth—the two lives in which the divine glory irradiated earthly existence—is what Mrs. Eddy hoped we would do when she wrote: "Future ages must declare what the pioneer [Mary Baker Eddy compassing the teaching of Jesus] has accomplished" (S&H vii:25).

What greater or more important task is there as "the spiritual status is urging its highest demands on mortals, and material history is drawing to a close"?

Professor Hering, C.S.B. (for whom Mrs. Eddy had great love and respect) wrote to his students:

> *It is of first importance to see Mrs. Eddy rightly as the woman of prophecy referred to in the Apocalypse, as the one through whom the Comforter came, the Second Coming of the Christ. Unless we see that this revelation came through Mrs.Eddy under divine inspiration, and see it as the inspired word of God, we are not seeing Christian Science rightly. Jesus and Mrs. Eddy were the two witnesses [prophesied in the Bible] and must be seen as such. Just as Jesus* **in the flesh** *must be seen as the one who established the First Coming of the Christ, back of whom was the divinely royal man (S&H 315), so Mrs. Eddy* **in the flesh** *must be seen as the one who established the Second Coming of the Christ, back of whom was the divinely royal woman, the God-crowned woman of the 12th chapter of the Apocalypse.—Letter to his pupils, December, 1938.*

Jesus' parable of the "leaven which a woman took" foretold "the second appearing *in the flesh* of the Christ, Truth, hidden in sacred secrecy from the visible world." What is "the Word made flesh?" It is Christian Science. It is the *demonstration* we make of the Science of being. It is the life-link through which Truth destroys error. The understanding which Jesus and Mrs. Eddy had, linked subject and object. Understanding shows us there is <u>ONLY</u> God, infinite good, the Mind of man. This Mind says, <u>I AM ALL.</u> It was Mrs. Eddy's *life that was the life link (as our life also will be when we understand). Her LIFE spoke the language of Spirit. "She effaced the sense of personality so completely that she thought, spoke, and acted from the standpoint of her oneness with God."*

"THE EARTH HELPED THE WOMAN"

Mrs. Eddy was Truth and Love incarnate. Through her teaching the whole world is learning that the mind we now have, when spiritually educated and free from hypnotic suggestion, is the all-powerful, all-knowing, divine Mind. "And the earth ["the compound idea (man)," see S&H 585:5; & 591:5] helped the woman" (Rev. xii:16; S&H 570:10). This means humanity is awakening to the fact that it is "the woman." Interpreting this passage Mrs. Eddy says, "Millions of unprejudiced minds . . . are waiting and watching" for what the woman has to give—thus, a whole universe of right thinkers will "help the woman." Today we see a world of physical scientists and medical doctors are straining to become theologians. This will "help the woman."

"The world today is looking for a larger and truer version of what Christ Jesus taught. It is looking for that which will solve the basic human problems of tension, fear, worry, inferiority, loneliness. What has survived in churches as Christianity is a mere caricature of what Jesus taught and demonstrated" (*Mary Baker Eddy Reveals Your Divinity*, p. ix).

MRS. EDDY MUST BE RIGHTLY PERCEIVED

Only by understanding the divine and human coincidence can Christian Scientists rightly perceive Mrs. Eddy to be the woman of the Apocalypse. "Those who look for [her] in person, lose [her] instead of find [her]." We are given a key in the statement: "The All-wise does not bestow His highest trusts upon the unworthy. When He commissions a *MESSENGER* it is one who is spiritually near Himself" (S&H 455:24). This does not refer to just any spiritually-minded individual. It has a hidden meaning. The Concordance prepared under Mrs. Eddy's supervision lists this reference to "messenger" only under "Eddy, Mary Baker." Absolute faith in the revelation demands absolute faith in the "messenger," the revelator. This is why it is so important to keep the truth of her Christ character before the public.

"The Second appearing of Jesus [which came with Mary Baker Eddy] is, unquestionably, the spiritual advent of the advancing idea of God, as in Christian Science" (*Ret.* 70:20). But "the second appearing of Jesus (as the life work of Mary Baker Eddy) was always one with Jesus, for "in the beginning was God." What does that mean? Was the Infinite Good or God ever without Its complete reflection? No. The divinely royal man was always one in consciousness with the divinely royal woman. "The Lamb's wife presents the unity of male and female . . . as two individual natures in one" [fulfilling Jeremiah's prophecy: "a woman shall compass a man" (Jer. 31:22)]; and this compounded spiritual individuality reflects God . . ." (S&H 577:4).

Since "woman is the highest species of man" (*Un.* 51:15) isn't it evident that Christ Jesus who brought the First Coming of the Christ, and Mary Baker Eddy who brought the Second, were both predestined "before Abraham was" to be **ONE** in spiritual consciousness?—to be two individual natures in **ONE**? Could the male reflect God fully without the female when "woman [meaning God-qualities] is the highest species of man"? No. Jesus was never separated from his womanhood.

Mary Baker Eddy knew she could not be separated from her manhood. She knew she was one of the main characters of the Bible, just as Jesus was. This is the coded message she left in her last book, *Christ and Christmas,* for those students who have grown to perceive it. She explored a realm of thought where only Jesus had been before. This is why in a letter she said, "I am *alone, absolutely,* here! No one can know me really, or can see what I have to meet. . . ."

It is still too early to fully understand her great demonstration, but her explanation of the realm of the real has today begun to revolutionize the world's thinking.

PROPHECY MUST PRECEDE SPIRITUAL EVENTS

Why is it so important to recognize Mrs. Eddy's fulfillment of prophecy? Why must prophecy precede spiritual events?

Unless prophecy precedes them the human mind neither looks for, nor understands these marvelous events when they occur. Even with prophecy, recognition may take time. In the case of the Virgin Mary, and of Jesus, who were prophesied, they were looked for but were not recognized when they appeared. It is the same with Mary Baker Eddy whom Jesus and the prophets prophesied, and who was unveiled in the first edition of Science and Health. When she appeared few realized that the book of Revelation (particularly chapters 10 and 12) or the many other prophecies concerning "the woman"—the "Comforter" promised by Jesus—had been fulfilled. It is only in retrospect, and by coming to know her through her writings, that we understand **WHO AND WHAT** she was as one of the chief characters of Bible prophecy. The same was true of Jesus. Only in retrospect and in the context of prophecy could the disciples and the world really know who walked among them.

ON THE ROAD TO EMMAUS

On the walk to Emmaus (Luke 24:13) something wonderful happened—something marvelous beyond human description. An awakening took place that changed human history and laid the foundation for the advent of Mary Baker Eddy and the Second Coming of the Christ.

On the road to Emmaus, (after his crucifixion) Jesus—seeing that two of his disciples were questioning his Messiahship, and that he must defend his ministry—"drew near and went with them. . . . And beginning at Moses and all the prophets, he expounded unto them in all the scriptures the things concerning himself." He no doubt explained that when in "the ninth hour he cried with a loud voice, 'My God, my God, why hast thou forsaken me?'" he was fulfilling David's prophecy in Psalms 22:1 which reads: "My God, my God, why hast thou forsaken me?" (See Luke 24:15, 27). Jesus wanted to make sure that, at long last, they realized he had been scripturally prophesied. The enlightenment he gave them that day paved the way for Christianity and for Christian Science.

Christian Scientists understand that the "sixth seal [in Revelation], typical of six thousand years since Adam, . . . has reference to the present age." Marginal heading here is "Today's lesson." (See S&H 560:2.) Just as prophecy prepared the way for the disciples to finally see Christ Jesus as the promised Messiah, prophecy prepares the way for the entire fulfillment of Christian Science when all will recognize themselves as one with the infinite good called God.

Because Mrs. Eddy, like Jesus, fulfilled prophecy, and because her story parallels his in many ways, let us take a moment to examine Jesus in the light of scriptural prophecy.

WHY DID THE RAISING OF LAZARUS
BRING ON THE CRUCIFIXION?

Jesus' three-year ministry had passed swiftly. He now stood at the tomb of Lazarus. Here Jesus saw the "glory" where everyone else saw death. And Lazarus who "had lain in the grave four days came forth." This stirred up the high priests. Jesus had made it clear that "death would never cease until ye women cease your childbearing." He had said such awful things as "Woe unto them that be with child." And now, because of the raising of Lazarus, the people were beginning to "believe on him." Because of this it was decided that Jesus must be put to death. When there was a little wavering in the council of the Elders, Caiaphas, the high priest, held firm that Jesus must be executed. Jesus was teaching that it was a sin to create corporeally. What would happen to their nation if everyone believed Jesus' teaching? Caiaphas convinced the others "that it was expedient that one man die . . . that the whole nation perish not." (See John 11:49, 50, and 18:14.)

JESUS IN GETHSEMANE

As for Jesus, he wasn't fighting the Jewish council. For them he only asked forgiveness. ***The enemy Jesus challenged was death.*** He knew that mortal birth leads to death. As the end drew near, he prayed: "Now is my soul troubled; and what shall I say? 'Father save me from this hour? [No!] But for this cause came I unto this hour. Father, [Mind, Jesus' own true Mind], glorify Thy name." (John 12:27-28). But then again from his pale lips comes the bitter cry, "O My Father, if thou be willing, remove this cup from me." Even now, he adds, "Nevertheless, not my will but Thine be done." . . . And being in an agony he prayed more earnestly: and his sweat was as it were great drops of blood falling down to the ground" (Luke 22:42-44).

Rising with painful effort he staggered to the place where he had left his disciples, hoping for a word of love and encouragement from them; but he found them sleeping. Had they stayed awake knowing that Christ, Truth, God, could not be crucified, and had they actually worked until they saw the unreality of the crucifixion, how different history might have been!

Jesus turned away and sought again his retreat where he fell prostrate, and for the third time uttered the prayer, "O, my Father, if this cup may not pass from me except I drink it, Thy will be done." The awful moment had come. Jesus prayed for his own agonized tempted soul. He knew this moment was to decide the destiny of the world. The fate of humanity trembled in the balance. Then, having made his decision, Jesus became calm and serene, even though he again found his disciples sleeping. (See Matt. 26; Mark 14; Luke 22; John 18.)

"Thus was the devil's shuttle weaving the bride's vesture."

"The meek demonstrator of good, the highest instructor and friend of man [was about to meet] his earthly fate alone with God.. . . forsaken by all whom he had blessed, this faithful sentinel of God . . . was to prove that the Christ [our true identity] is not subject to material conditions, but is above the reach of human wrath, and is able through Truth, Life, and Love to triumph over sin, sickness, death and the grave" (S&H 49:14).

JESUS DELIVERED TO PILATE

Jesus now stood before Pilate—the unutterable burden of Gethsemane, its sadness, its agony, the betrayal," behind him.

"What hast thou done?" asked Pilate.

Jesus didn't beat around the bush. Going right to the point he told Pilate: "My kingdom is not of this world; if my kingdom were of this world, then would my servants fight, that I should not be delivered to the Jews" (John 18:36).

There was something about this prisoner that made Pilate want to go on with the questioning, and he asked Jesus of what his kingdom consisted.

Replying, Jesus gave the remarkable answer that summed up his whole ministry: "To this end was I born, and for this cause came I into the world, that I should bear witness to the truth" (John 18:37). He might have said, ". . . that I should teach you what true prayer is as it holds you in at-one-ment with Infinite good." Jesus described himself as "a man that has told you the Truth which I have heard from God [from his own Mind]."

What was this Truth?

That "the kingdom of God is within you, within your consciousness here and now." This is the great truth that the wonderful prophets who preceded Jesus had been leading up to. When Pilate asked that all-important question that has rung down the ages: *"What is Truth?" (John 18:38),* Jesus did not answer. He could have told Pilate: *"You are, if you only knew it,"* but since he knew his answer would not be understood, he remained silent.

Jesus had stated: "I am the Truth," and whatever Jesus said about himself he knew was true of everyone when correctly seen—when awakened from the Adam dream. Didn't he say, "The works that I do shall ye do also, and greater works than these shall ye do"? Jesus did not think of himself as a person, but rather as "never severed from Spirit," and as one with God, completely spiritual. He knew everyone else had the same birthright of peace and Love. He never thought of himself as different from other men except in understanding. His understanding enabled him to think and speak as the Father. However, having been "conceived by a human mother . . . . Jesus must have been tempted in all points" (S&H 315:30; 564:14).

JESUS "OPENED NOT HIS MOUTH" (Isaiah 53:7)

Ponder Jesus "opened not his mouth" at the trial. He refused to give evil a body, a mind, a mouth. (See S&H 564:18.) When he did speak it was to tell Pilate the truth, namely, "To this end was I born, and for this cause came I into the world, that I should bear witness unto the Truth." Today the whole world seems to be going through a crucifixion. Are we being called upon to prove universally what Truth is, just as Jesus proved individually what Life is? The Savior **today** is a universal Science of being, interpreting scientific Truth, bringing salvation to all—salvation from famine, crime, sin of every kind, want and woe.

Jesus knew all that **seemed** to be going on was nothing more than impersonal evil, hypnotism; and all that was **actually** going on was the action of divine Principle. Jesus was busy entertaining Love for those who were about to crucify him. He was busy being the Love that heals. The operation of Principle did not depend upon his bodily presence. As he told Pilate, "Thou couldst have no power at all against me except it were given thee from above" (John 19:11}. Jesus knew temporal power was "but the arm of flesh." When he was arrested instead of resisting he healed the soldier whose ear Peter had cut off. The operation of Principle which is *one with its idea,* has continued ever since, and through the Second Coming of the Christ we are becoming aware of it.

What does oneness with Infinite Good, with reality, mean? It can only mean that our life, like the life of Jesus and Mary Baker Eddy, is divine when we know ourselves subjectively. For example, Jesus walked on the water because to him water was subjective; but Peter sank because to him water was objective. Jesus did not see death. To him Life was subjective; he saw only Life, God, therefore he could raise the dead. To others who were burying a body life was objective. Only when we think of ourselves objectively do we appear to ourselves as human beings. Knowing ourselves subjectively, we see humanity's divinity, see the living God, omnipotent and omnipresent.

Our conscious knowing of our oneness with God will make our life a subjective experience—all within ourselves. We will know that our being is God. Like Jesus, we will know <u>we are it,</u> and <u>we do it.</u> We will then heal subjectively, within ourselves. We will see all error as our own wrong thought. Isn't this how Jesus "burst the barriers of sense . . . and the bonds of the tomb?"

When we consider how prophecy was fulfilled at the time of Jesus' crucifixion we see how Infinite Good arranged all things to further Jesus' mission.

PILATE'S DEFENSE OF JESUS

According to Roman historians, Pilate was far from a principled man; hence there was something spiritually awesome in his defending Jesus with considerable resolution, which he abandoned only when forced by the threatening of the chief priest and rulers of Israel. Pilate's defense of Jesus can only be attributed to the secret, powerful influence of Infinite Good, in order that, at the same time Jesus was condemned and executed as a malefactor, his innocence was declared in the most public manner, and with the most authentic evidence—even by the judge himself—(just as his crucifixion was the most public way for Jesus to be put to death; everyone could *see* it). "This is the Lord's doing; it is marvelous in our eyes" (Ps. 118:23).

Looking at the face of Jesus, Pilate saw not a hardened criminal but the signature of heaven. Then the question might be asked: Why did Jesus faint while bearing his cross? It must be remembered that Jesus was a human being, no different from you and me, except he knew more. Wearing a crown of thorns that caused blood to flow down his face, he had to walk on foot, bearing his cross to the place of execution. The night before had been spent without sleep; he had undergone the sufferings in the garden, he had been hurried from place to place, shuttled from Annas to Caiaphas, then to Pilate; from Pilate to Herod and back to Pilate. He had been obliged to stand during the whole time of the trial, without food or drink. He had endured the anguish of betrayal and seen his disciples forsake him and flee. Twice had he been given the merciless lashing criminals were given; stripped to the waist his back showed the long, cruel stripes of the scourging from which the blood flowed freely. He had been repeatedly spat upon—"spitting was [their] method of expressing the utmost contempt" (*Mis.* 170:26)—and laughed to scorn at the mocking, after his conviction.

Pilate must have been filled with amazement at the uncomplaining patience of Jesus, who with bleeding brow and lacerated back, had still the bearing of a king. But as the screams of the mob in derision—incited and egged on by the high priests—grew ever louder, "Crucify him! He made himself the Son of God," Pilate grew impatient and cried in despair: "Take ye him and crucify him, for I find no fault in him" (John 19:6).

As the cross—which had been prepared for Barabbas—was laid upon Jesus' bruised and bleeding shoulder, it was too heavy for his weak and suffering condition. It was the weight of all he had endured, and not any want of courage, that caused Jesus to faint under the burden of the cross. (See Matt. 27). The Christ had not failed. All through the disgraceful farce of a trial, Jesus had borne himself with dignity. He had spoken no word except to glorify God. But when after the second scourging the cross was laid upon him, he could bear no more and fell fainting beneath its burden.

The soldiers seeing he was unable to bear the weight, "laid it on one Simon." This stranger, Simon, a Cyrenian, had just come on to the scene by chance. He knew of Jesus through his two sons, but he himself was not a disciple. Hearing the taunts and cries of "crucify him!" which the high priests had stirred up the people to scream in a frenzy, he stopped in astonishment. As he expressed his compassion, the soldiers seized him and laid the cross on him. (The Jews could not carry the cross as it would "defile" them so they would not be able to keep the passover.) Tradition tells us Simon was blessed and grateful for having borne the cross, and ever after he cheerfully by choice stood under the burden of the cross.

MANY WOMEN FOLLOW ON THE WAY TO CALVARY

At this point Luke 23:27 tells us Jesus, on his way to Calvary and the crucifixion, was followed by many, particularly women who lamented the severity of his sentence. Jesus, forgetting his own distress when it lay heaviest on him, turned to the women and said: "Daughters of Jerusalem, weep not for me, but weep for yourselves, and for your children. For, behold, the days are coming in which they shall say blessed are the barren and the wombs that never bare, and the paps which never gave suck." This had been his theme during his three-year ministry; and in the Second Coming of the Christ, God's scribe, Mary Baker Eddy, would make clear that human birth is an illusion, that the real man is generic, the everywhere present image and likeness of Infinite Good of which we all must eventually become aware.

GOLGOTHA

At Golgotha, the place of execution, when Jesus was being nailed to the cross, he did not cry out in pain, but (being programmed for Love) fervently prayed for all who were responsible for his death. Even when the cross was raised and let fall with a violent and shocking jolt into the place prepared, which must have been excruciatingly painful, he did not cry out. No vengeance was invoked upon the priests and rulers, who were gloating over the accomplishment of their purpose. Jesus pitied them for their ignorance, and breathed the prayer: "Father, forgive them, for they know not what they do"—an example of forgiveness, which though it can never be equalled, should be imitated by all.

In regard to the fulfilling of the Psalmist's prophecy, Mrs. Eddy writes, "The last supreme moment of mockery, desertion, torture, added to an overwhelming sense of the magnitude of his work, wrung from Jesus' lips the awful cry, "My God, why hast Thou forsaken me?" echoing the words prophesied in Psalms 22:1. Mrs. Eddy knew "the real cross, which Jesus bore . . . was the world's hatred of Truth and Love. . . . The possible misapprehension of the sublimest influence of his career. . . This dread added the drop of gall to his cup" (S&H 50:5 & 30).

On the cross, Jesus was given a vinegar potion to drink, fulfilling Psalms 69: 20, 21. But he would take nothing that would becloud his mind. He must keep fast hold on God, be wide awake.

THE PENITENT THIEF ON THE CROSS

In his agony on the cross, a gleam of comfort came to Jesus from the penitent thief whose mind was illumined by the Holy Spirit. The thief saw, in the bruised, mocked, crucified Jesus, the "Lamb of God that taketh away the sin of the world." In hope mingled with anguish, he petitioned Jesus: "Lord, remember me when thou cometh into thy kingdom." Promptly, with love, compassion, and power, Jesus promised the penitent thief: *"Today shalt thou be with me in paradise"* (Luke 23:43). How grateful Jesus must have been to be called "Lord," when even his disciples were now doubting his divinity. Many had been ready to call him "Lord" when he was working miracles (and would again call him "Lord" after the resurrection} but only the penitent thief acknowledged Jesus' true identity as he hung dying on the cross. It is recorded that *as Jesus spoke these hallowed words of promise,* the dark cloud that had enshrouded the cross was pierced by a bright and living light.

At the direction of the priests, Jesus had been positioned between the two thieves, to indicate that he was the greatest sinner, fulfilling Isaiah

53:12: "He was numbered with the transgressors." The real meaning is that his cross was placed in the midst of a world lying in sin; and the sacred words of pardon, spoken to the penitent thief, kindled hope, lighting a lamp that would shine to the earth's remotest regions.

"IT IS FINISHED!"

As the beholders watched for the end of this dreadful scene, the sun was shining, but the cross was enveloped in darkness. Suddenly the darkness and gloom lifted from the cross. In clear resonate tones that seemed to sound throughout creation, Jesus cried: *"It is finished! Father, into Thy hands I commend my spirit."* Jesus had won! The work he had come to do, he had finished! **"His mighty, crowning, unparalleled, and triumphant exit from the flesh"** (S&H 117:21) was now assured. The light encircling the cross illumined the face of Jesus, showing forth the glory and presence of God. Jesus then bowed his head and "gave up the Ghost."

Immediately another voice was heard saying: *"TRULY, THIS WAS THE SON OF GOD."* (Matt. 27:54).

Who spoke these words?

It was the centurion, the Roman soldier, a heathen, who glimpsed the form of the Son of God disguised as the bleeding, bruised and broken body hanging on the cross.

Nothing could stop the spread of Jesus' teaching. Even on the day of his crucifixion, history records three men, widely different from one another, were converted—Simon the Cyrenian, who bore the cross; the dying thief on the cross next to Jesus; and the Roman soldier, who commanded the Roman guard, and said, "Truly, this was the Son of God."

By an unseen hand the veil of the temple was rent, tearing the coverings from bigotry and superstition. (See S&H 597:11).

Among the many other prophecies fulfilled at the time of the crucifixion was Psalms 22:18: "They parted my garments among them, and for my vesture did they cast lots." Jesus' robe, being without seam, woven from the top throughout (a symbol of the oneness of God and man) the soldiers agreed not to rend it. Instead they gambled, "cast lots," for its possession.

In fulfillment of prophecy and because of a law of Moses, it came to pass   that: "A bone of him shall not be broken," and "they shall look on him whom they have *pierced*." The soldiers thought Jesus was already dead, so they did not bother to break his legs, which would have been work. Therefore "a bone of him [was] not broken." But out of wantonness or cruelty, or at the suggestion of the high priest, they thrust a spear into his side, which if he had not already been dead would have caused instant death. This fulfillment of the prophecy of "piercing" was of the greatest importance because it demonstrated the truth of Jesus' most public death, thus preventing enemies from saying he was not dead when placed in the tomb. (See John 19:34-37).

JESUS' TOMB GUARDED BY THE MILITARY

The darkness that mantled the earth at the crucifixion was not more dense than that which enveloped the minds of the priests and rulers. The high priests, having heard Jesus' prediction of his resurrection, dreaded the "dead" Christ Jesus far more than they had ever feared the living Jesus. They therefore got permission from Pilate to place a strong military guard to watch the tomb. A great stone had been rolled in front of it, and it was sealed in such a way that the seal could not be broken. Why was this of supreme importance? Because what was designed to expose Jesus and his doctrine as rank falsehood proved in fact to be the strongest confirmation that could be given of the truth and divinity of his teaching, placing what they wanted to refute, namely, his resurrection from the dead, beyond any doubt.

Nicodemus (the Pharisee, and ruler of the Jews, who had come to Jesus by night for fear of the Jews), when he saw Jesus lifted up on the cross, remembered the words Jesus had spoken to him in the Mount of Olives: "As Moses lifted up the serpent in the wilderness, even so must the son of man be lifted up: that whosoever believeth in him should not perish, but have everlasting life" (John 3:14, 15). The events of Calvary, Jesus' prayer for his murderers, his answer to the petition of the repentant thief, these now spoke to the heart of this learned man, this counselor. Again he heard that last triumphant cry, *"IT IS FINISHED!"* Nicodemus realized it was the cry of one who has conquered. He thought of the reeling earth, darkened heavens, rent veil. *His faith was established.* What had <u>harmed</u> the faith of the disciples, <u>armed</u> both Nicodemus and Joseph of Aramathaea (another member of the Sanhedrin) with complete faith in the divinity of Jesus, and they now came to help the disciples bury Jesus.

RENDING THE VEIL OF MATTER

The hour of Jesus' release was near. Soldiers and guards placed around a *sealed* tomb were powerless to imprison Christ Jesus within a narrow crypt. Thus was fulfilled: "The Lord shall have them in derision"

(Ps. 2:3 & 4). In fact the greater the number of soldiers placed around the tomb, the stronger would be the testimony that he had *risen.*

"The cross is the central emblem of history. It is the lodestar in the demonstration of Christian healing" (S&H 238:31}. Why? "The efficacy of the crucifixion," Mrs. Eddy states "lay in the practical goodness and affection it demonstrated for mankind . . . [enabling Jesus] to triumph over the grave. . . . Jesus *'opened not his mouth.'* Until the majesty of Truth should be demonstrated in divine Science, the spiritual idea was arraigned before the tribunal of so-called mortal mind, which was unloosed in order that the false claim of *mind in matter* might uncover its own crime of defying immortal Mind" (S&H 24:27 & 564:18).

"When Jesus reproduced his body after its burial, he revealed the myth or material falsity of evil; its powerlessness to destroy good, and the omnipotence of the Mind that knows this: he also showed forth the error and nothingness of supposed life in matter, and the great something-ness of the good we possess, which is of Spirit, and immortal" (*Mis.* 201:9).

"The martyrdom of Jesus was the culminating sin of Pharisaism. It rent the veil of the temple. [Temple is defined as body—it rent the veil of belief in a corporeal body, a material creation.] It revealed the false foundations and superstructures of superficial religion [the religion referred to in St. John's Revelation as the "dragon"—the drag on of Old Theology],[1] and opened the sepulchre with divine Science, immortality and Love" (S&H 597:10). The resurrection of Jesus showed mortals what reality is.

After the crucifixion Jesus walked and talked with his disciples; he ate with them, functioning as before. The crucifixion had destroyed nothing real. Jesus proved for us that the body is entirely mental. When the body is seen as divinely mental it becomes harmonious and indestructible. Loss is gain—we need the cross to gain the crown. Every sad experience we have, actually pushes us closer to recognizing what we already are—to knowing the divinity of our being.

PENTECOST

Seven weeks after Jesus ascended, the disciples learned that they too could experience ascension—that ascension wasn't for Jesus alone. Reading Acts 2:1-4 and 17-19 we learn Pentecosting is available to all who gain the Christ consciousness. Jesus and Mary Baker Eddy were,

---

[1] "Judaism was the antithesis of Christianity" (S&H 133:19). See also (*Mis.* 162:14)

much of the time, in the transcendental state—"the fourth dimension of Spirit" (*Mis.* 22:12). This made it possible for them to be the Wayshowers to Pentacostalism, meaning Jesus' holy ascension consciousness. They showed us how we too can live as Spirit while still seeming to be in the flesh. "The fourth dimension of Spirit" is a different level of awareness (invisible to the human eye) which was Christ Jesus' and Mary Baker Eddy's dwelling place while still in the flesh. Pentecost shows us it is an awareness we all can, will, eventually, attain.

On the day of Pentecost, "They were all with <u>one accord in one place</u>"—accord means they had a shared purpose; and "place" means they had a shared state of consciousness. Verse 2: "the sound from heaven" was their understanding of the "fourth dimensional" awareness "rushing in like a mighty wind," filling the "*house*" (consciousness). "And they were all filled with the Holy Ghost: "Divine Science; the development of eternal Life, Truth, and Love" (S&H 588:7). "Speaking with other tongues," means speaking on a level others can understand, as Mrs. Eddy always tried to do.

The experience of Pentecost foreshadows our experience in the Second Coming. Here read Mrs. Eddy's Easter letter (*My. 191:15*).

PROPHECIES OF MARY BAKER EDDY
HAVE ALSO BEEN FULFILLED

Only twice in human history have the clouds of material-mindedness opened to reveal the *full* possibilities of scientific being. Both the Old and New Testaments prophesied of the "two anointed ones," the "two witnesses," to the oneness of Infinite Good reflected as man. Jesus knew the Science of existence, that he and the Father *were one.* Mrs. Eddy knew this too, and in accord with Jesus' promise and prophecy her record went much further.

Few today are aware that, like Jesus, Mrs. Eddy was one of the main characters of the Bible. Isaiah 54 is all about her just as Isaiah 53 is all about Jesus. Other Bible writers also prophesied the coming of "the woman." Concerning this, Judge Hanna wrote that it is a peculiarity of human nature to relegate prophecy and prophets to the past. This happened in the case of Jesus. His age and generation rejected him, just as Mrs. Eddy was (is) rejected in her day and today; but a <u>second</u> coming is as clearly prophesied as was the first coming. Judge Hanna asks and answers:

Must the "Spirit of Truth," or the "Comforter," that Jesus said should come, be personalized or individualized? "Yes". There could be no fulfillment of prophecy otherwise.

As astonishing as it may seem, Jesus forsaw that a simple faith in his ministry would not maintain the loyalty of his followers—that his mighty works of healing, and raising the dead, would not guarantee their loyalty to his Messiahship UNLESS that loyalty was based on *prophetic vision.* Only to the degree that his followers were willing to acknowledge HIS PLACE IN SCRIPTURAL PROPHECY would they remain loyal. The same is true concerning Mary Baker Eddy. She, like Jesus, must be seen as scripturally prophesied.

From the time that Jesus promised to "send another Comorter, . . . the Spirit of Truth, which will guide you into all Truth," Christians have been looking for this scripturally prophesied "Comforter," (See Luke 24:44–48; and S&H 118:6.)

THE TIME IS COMING WHEN EVERY PROPHECY CONCERNING THE WOMAN WILL BE UNDERSTOOD. Then "the stone," woman, Love, will no longer be rejected by "the builders." It is up to loyal Christian Scientists to defend Mrs. Eddy and herald abroad that she, like Jesus, fulfilled the many scriptural prophecies concerning her. Before Jesus walked the road to Emmaus many of his disciples had doubts. Not one had been able to stand by him the whole way.

When the disciples saw their Master's true identity in Bible prophecy, they were no longer disloyal. They were able to go forth and overcome great obstacles in his name. The same will be true of all who spiritually see Mrs. Eddy's place in Bible prophecy. They will become aware of their "sovereign power to think and act rightly," knowing their Mind is the Infinite Good called God. "Christian Scientists are fishers of men. The Bible is our sea-beaten rock. It guides the fishermen. It stands the storm. It engages the attention and enriches the being [the affections] of all men" (*My.* 295:17).

CHAPTER 21

A PROPHET AMONG US

"YOU FIND ME IN MY WRITINGS"

It is as important to know who Mary Baker Eddy is as it is to know what she taught. All Christian Scientists will become aware that Mary Baker Eddy represented the Woman of the Apocalypse and fulfilled scriptural prophecy just as the Virgin Mary and Christ Jesus fulfilled biblical prophecy. Mrs. Eddy herself made this clear numerous times in her writings. For instance, in Science and Health, page 118:6, she states: "Did not this parable point a moral with a prophecy, foretelling the second appearing *in the flesh* of the Christ, Truth, hidden in sacred secrecy from the visible world?" The Glossary's first verse of her inspired *Christ and Christmas*—her last book—makes it clear that both she and Jesus are "the root and offspring of David."

Mrs. Eddy said, "You find me in my writings," but also, "My writings are not all you know of me." Her writings inform us she knew she represented the woman of the Apocalypse.

When we look for her in her writings, who do we find?

We find: the "one God selected for the highest service"—Mary Baker Eddy.

We find: the "one God has appointed to voice His Word."

We find: "A woman clothed in light."

We find: "A woman clothed with the sun, and the moon under her feet."

We find: "an angel standing in the sun [standing in the light of Mind]," who revealed our true identity as one with God.

We find: "I [as Mary Baker Eddy] as a corporeal person, am not in your midst. But I, as the spiritual idea of God's motherhood, am in your midst."

We find: ". . . The Revelator completed [his] figure with woman, typifying the spiritual idea of God's motherhood."

We find: Mary Baker Eddy as: "God's messenger."

We find: "[Principle's] highest _visible_ idea."

We find: "A woman crowned with twelve stars."

We find: "Christian Science [with which Mary Baker Eddy is one]: "Christian Science is as old as God," and "gleams through Mind, mother [Mary Baker Eddy], man" (*Christ and Christmas*).

We find: her who, "in Spirit, . . . entered your inner sanctuary" (*My.* 188:17); who brought to view your true being "as the great I AM"; and brought to view Christian Science with which Mrs. Eddy is one.

We find her: as the "Ideal Woman"—the pure and holy God-consciousness that sees only God.

Mrs. Eddy admonished us: "Relinquish your human concept of me, or of any one, and find the divine, and you have gained the right one—and never until then" (*Mis.* 353:8). The divine concept is Mind's own concept of Itself—its full idea or manifestation, the Christ or generic man which Mrs. Eddy revealed. Only by the Christ-consciousness which beholds Infinite Good, could she bring it forth. This is what we find in her writings.

WE ALSO FIND HER IN SCRIPTURAL PROPHECY

We know, and Mrs. Eddy knew, that we also find her prophesied many times in the Scriptures. Therefore she said, "My writings are not all you know of me." Mrs. Eddy, from the mount of vision beheld the woman as symbolizing generic man, the spiritual idea of God, "the full representation of Mind" (S&H 591:6). St. John in his Revelation states: "I will give power unto my two witnesses." To her devoted students, the Millers, she wrote: **"Today, it is a marvel to me that God chose me for this mission, and that my lifework was the theme of ancient prophecy and I the scribe of His infinite way of salvation" (May 27, 1902).** The loyal students who lived with Mrs. Eddy realized how clearly she recognized her position as prophesied by St. John, the Revelator.

"Mary Baker Eddy stands for something far greater than a good personality or a great human being. When correctly estimated she stands for the complete revelation of Christ in the human consciousness. She stands for egoistic consciousness, the revealed Christ." (Martha Wilcox, Association Address, 1944).

Without doubt Mrs. Eddy embodies all the characteristics of the woman portrayed in St. John's vision. In her Glossary to *Christ and Christmas*, Mrs. Eddy quotes Jesus as saying, "Verily, verily, I say unto you, The hour is coming [*Second* Coming of the Christ with the advent of Mary Baker Eddy], and now is [*with the advent of Jesus*, the first of the two scripturally prophesied witnesses], when the dead [those 'pained, fettered and befooled' by hypnotic suggestion] shall hear the voice of the Son of God . . ." We are all, eventually, destined to hear it and live.

In her "verse 2," she describes her mission as "a loyal ray":

> In tender mercy, Spirit sped
> A loyal ray
> To rouse the living, wake the dead,
> And point the way.

The "way" is to understand that each has every God-quality, both male and female. Mrs. Eddy encompassed this "bridegroom"— she encompassed Jesus' teaching, as Jeremiah 31;22 had prophesied: "A woman shall compass a man."

Explaining, she states: "The Lamb's wife [she who brought the Second Coming of the Christ] presents the unity of male and female as no longer two wedded individuals, but as two individual natures in one; and this compounded spiritual individuality reflects God [infinite good] as Father-Mother, not as a corporeal being. In this divinely united spiritual consciousness, there is no impediment to eternal bliss,—to the perfectibility of [Infinite Good's] creation" (S&H 577:4). Eventually, through spiritual education, we shall all enter "into the infinite sense of Life and its manifestation, never more to be manifested as flesh."

She explains this in more detail in an essay entitled: "The Second Advent" *(Essays and Other Footprints*, pp. 47-49) which speaks not of the material Jesus or Mrs. Eddy, but of Christ Jesus, of Christ Mary; and that "the on-rushing centuries are declaring this idea higher and higher in the scale of being, and will erelong yield to the sense of its ascendant glory. The revelation Mary Baker Eddy brought is not something that lies in the future. It is what is happening right now in a continually unfolding way.

> *"The third appearing of the spiritual idea of the character of God will present but the disappearing of all else, and establish the supremacy of Spirit which obliterates the human sense of the divine, takes away all sense of matter and reveals the final fact that the idea, Christ, is not a materialized or finite man or woman, but is the infinite concept of infinite Mind"* (Essays and Other Footprints).

This Mind is not separate from us. It is that pure altitude of consciousness that discerns, constitutes and experiences its Self-understanding. It is as present and available to everyone as is a law of mathematics. Our

Mind, here and now, has the capacity to discern and experience generic man, which the prophesied woman in the Apocalypse symbolizes, namely, the spiritual idea of God, which "illustrates the coincidence of God and man as the divine Principle and divine idea" (S&H 561:22).

WE FIND MRS. EDDY AS GOD'S MESSENGER

It is because Mrs. Eddy was the revelator of the "Christ Science" (which she gives us as our new name [*Mis.* 167:14]) that she represents the divine idea as the woman of the Apocalypse.

Thus we find her giving her message to all mankind, as when she sent spiritual instructions to the daily newspapers of her time. When she gave vital messages on Christian Science through the secular press wasn't she embracing the whole world? Wasn't she letting the world know that she—as representing the motherhood of God—was leading all mankind out of bondage whether they called themselves Christian Scientists or not? Wasn't this also what Jesus meant when he said, "Other sheep I have that are not of this fold"?

Mrs. Eddy said of Jesus: "Not a single component part of his nature did the material world measure aright." It is equally true that "not a single component part of [Mrs. Eddy's] nature did the material world measure aright." They did not recognize her as having been predestined ("before Abraham was" to be incarnated, as was Jesus) to bring the Second Coming which shows us our divinity.

Mary Baker Eddy representing the womanhood of God saw that the Woman "has no contests," because from her divine consciousness has come the celestial message: "there is no error, no sin, sickness, nor death." Jesus rebuked the seventy when they returned boasting that "even the devils are subject unto us." Jesus knew there was no error. There was only **ONE** power, so there was no evil to be subject to them. (Luke 10:17-20). As we gain "the full recognition that being is Spirit" (S&H 29:25), belief in evil or the flesh (which is pure delusion) vanishes. We find there is no contest.

Mrs. Eddy stressed the importance of seeing her rightful place, otherwise we cannot see our own impersonal identity. Only as we see our Leader correctly from a divine standpoint can we see ourselves correctly as one with Infinite Good.

WE FIND HER AS ONE WITH INFINITE GOOD

We find Mary Baker Eddy in her writing, in her fulfillment of Scripture as God's messenger, at one with Christian Science. When we look for Mary Baker Eddy we find her also in her example as it is related to us by those who knew her.

Mrs. Eddy's holy discovery explained and made practical Jesus' teaching that "this kingdom of God 'is within you,' [that it] is *within reach of man's consciousness here, and the spiritual idea [her sacred discovery and revelation as it is lived by each of us] reveals it."* (*S&H* 576:21.)

Lulu Blackman states: "Throughout the class, Mrs. Eddy *effaced the sense of her personality apart from God so plainly that she thought, spoke, and acted from the standpoint of her oneness with the Father."* Another student, Mrs. Jennie E. Sawyer states: "There was discernible an inward light or reflection of thought that shone through her countenance. One felt drawn to a better Life just from being in her presence." Another student wrote, "At all times, she seemed conscious of a wisdom not her own." Mrs. Eddy, like Jesus, could say: "The word which ye hear is not mine, but the Father's which sent me."

Emma C. Shipman had looked forward to hearing Mrs. Eddy speak, and had pictured her in looks and manner perhaps like Julia Ward Howe and Mary Livermore, whom she had heard lecture. "Instead there was this great contrast,—one almost lost sight of Mrs. Eddy's personality in drinking in her words. The other two had big personalities, but *Mrs. Eddy was like a transparency for God to shine through."* On every visit, Miss Shipman experienced "the feeling of the greatness of the truth Mrs. Eddy taught and the self-effacement of the teacher." Mrs. Eddy knew that she, like Jesus, was "the root and offspring of David, the bright and morning star [wherein God's motherhood is never separated from God's fatherhood]." (See Rev. 22:16.) To fulfill this prophecy, Mrs. Eddy "had to get Mary out of the way" and speak from the standpoint of the Christ.

Miss Mary Brookins states that the Normal class of 1888 "was a loosening of the earth ties and a gleam of heaven, harmony, such as I had never imagined possible. One day," she said, "Mrs. Eddy had been lifting the veil of matter so that we almost felt there was none, when a student impulsively leaned forward and asked, "But Mrs. Eddy, if we had such a realization as that, wouldn't the patient disappear?" Reassuringly, with enormous directness and winning grace, Mrs. Eddy laughed, "Don't worry, my dear, when you get such a realization as you are thinking of, it will be you who will disappear, not the patient."

We find Mary Baker Eddy as the exemplification of pure Mind. Her writings replace human consciousness with the divine consciousness.

"The great miracle, to human sense, is divine Love [the divine Love which people felt in Mrs. Eddy presence]. The grand necessity of existence is to gain the true idea of what constitutes the kingdom of heaven in man" (S&H 560:11).

Being one with the Mind that is God, Mary Baker Eddy's real identity as God's messenger to this age will gradually unfold as mankind seeks an understanding of it. And with this understanding, the quick and certain healing that formerly characterized Christian Science will return.

Mrs. Eddy knew there was only one Mind. It was with this Mind, which was Love itself, that she discovered, revealed, and founded Christian Science in human consciousness. She revealed the Science that reveals. In the textbook she states many times, "Science reveals," "Christian Science reveals," "divine Science reveals." *Mrs. Eddy's Mind discovered and revealed the Science that reveals, which then teaches us how to have the Mind that reveals.* We therefore realize that everytime Mrs. Eddy refers to "Science reveals" she is referring to herself as the revelator. Christian Scientists understand divine Science to be a revelation, and Mrs. Eddy to be the revelator. This Science teaches us it is our own real Mind that reveals, since the kingdom of God is within us and we are already programmed to be all that Infinite Good is.

In a letter, Mrs. Eddy wrote: "The First Church of Christ, Scientist, our prayer in stone, will be the prophecy fulfilled . . . of Christian Science. It will speak to you of the Mother . . . [of Mary Baker Eddy] through whom was revealed to you God's all-power, all-presence, and all-Science" (*Mis.* 141:1). "I have uncovered evil [as hypnotism only], and *dis-covered* [uncovered] for you divine Science" (*Mis.* 334:28). This "true logos [communication] is demonstrably Christian Science" (S&H 134:21).

Christian Science has established the "city of our God," the "spiritual, holy habitation [that] has no boundary nor limit." An understanding of Mary Baker Eddy's revelation brings to light this spiritual, holy habitation as our true divine consciousness here and now. (See S&H 577:12-20.)

WE FIND APOCALYPTIC WOMAN
BRINGING FORTH THE MAN CHILD

In Science and Health we learn the woman in the Apocalypse is "an angel standing in the sun. . . . a woman clothed in light." This woman, "the spiritual idea, is clad with the radiance of spiritual Truth, and matter is put under her feet" (S&H 560:6).

Mrs. Eddy states: "Agassiz [whose eyes were veiled by material education], through his microscope, saw the sun in an egg at a point of so-called embryonic life" (S&H 561:5). Although Mrs. Eddy obviously had great respect for Agassiz, mentioning him six times in Science and Health, she knew that even through a microscope he could not see what was really there. Life, the Life that is God—the only Life there is—"is *not* embryonic."

Then she explains, *"Because of his more spiritual vision, St. John [the metaphysical heavyweight] saw an 'angel standing in the sun.'..."* **St. John saw what the Apocalyptic Woman would reveal, namely: what we really are as one with Infinite Good.**

Rightly seen, each individual is an angel standing in the sun. Mrs. Eddy represented the woman of the Apocalypse when she brought humanity the great Truth of the coincidence of the human and divine, which is destined to bring "harmony to earth."

"The Revelator saw also the spiritual ideal as a *WOMAN* clothed in light, a bride coming down from heaven, wedded to the Lamb of Love [wedded to the spiritualized human consciousness]. To John, 'the bride' and the 'Lamb' represent the correlation of divine Principle and spiritual idea, God and His Christ [our true being], bringing harmony to earth" (S&H 561:10). This was a prophecy of the harmony the Woman would bring to earth through an understanding of the "little book" prophesied in Revelation's Chapter 10.

We are told that the woman in the Apocalypse is the woman who "brought forth a man child to rule all nations [all states of thought, which in essence means finding the kingdom of heaven within our own consciousness]" (S&H 565:6). *HERE WE LEARN DEFINITELY THAT THE WOMAN WHO BROUGHT FORTH THE "MAN CHILD," ALIAS SCIENCE AND HEALTH, THE SECOND COMING OF THE CHRIST, IS THE WOMAN OF THE APOCALYPSE, OR MARY BAKER EDDY. It was through her beautiful spiritual teachings that Mrs. Eddy brought forth the "Man Child," your true identity.* By symbolically giving birth to the "man child," your true identity—the understanding of your at-one-ment with *Infinite Good*—she made the belief in evil obsolete. **Each one of us is that woman, symbolically giving birth to the understanding that evil is unreal**, merely a state of being hypnotized.

Mrs. Eddy's definition of God is the definition of what we are. It is also what is meant by the "man child" she brought forth. The oneness of Infinite Good, understood, brings out its own embodiment. (See S&H 216:30-1). Every individual is destined to experience the "man child"—Mrs. Eddy's seven synonyms for God as his own divine being.

Mrs. Eddy dematerialized man. The "man child"—the revelation of your true identity—was her own thought. In her chapter "Genesis" Mrs. Eddy rends the veil when she brings to human consciousness the true conception of Jesus. Because the woman's manchild, your true identity, was in Mrs. Eddy's own thought, she was therefore wedded to it. In a "wedding" that took place in heaven, Mrs. Eddy wedded the Christ idea. Looking for Mrs. Eddy in her Word, we therefore find her as the biblical "bride" and not as Mother; for "the Word is the Bride" (*My.* 125:26).

The woman crowned with twelve stars was a heavenly wonder (Rev. 12:1). Mary Baker Eddy was predestined "before Abraham was," to bring harmony to earth; and the "woman in the wilderness" was her human vehicle for "completing the work of Christ Jesus on earth."

Christian Science teaches that fatherhood and motherhood are always two individual natures *IN ONE,* for "A woman shall compass a man" (Jer. 31:22). Science and Health, p. 591, shows us our own right Mind—as a trinity: "as Life represented by the Father; as Truth, represented by the Son; as Love, represented by the Mother."

This makes it clear that Mother embraces and includes Father, "for Love alone is Life." Nothing needs to be given Life for everything eternally exists, like 2x2=4. The symbol "woman" includes the symbol, "man." This is why Mary Baker Eddy, conceiving this idea of God, could fulfill Jesus' prophecy to St. John in Revelation (12:1-5) that the "woman" would bring forth a "man child." She showed us how we too will bring forth this "man child," give birth to understanding. Mrs. Eddy's man child is Science and Health, which unveils and reveals our true identity. We will all give birth to that which we already *are.*

THE "MAN CHILD" WILL RULE

The "man child" Mrs. Eddy brought forth was her own divine thought which wrote Science and Health, which, in turn, revealed our true identity as generic man, as Christ, Science, the divine Science that is going to rule.

So, what is it that is going to rule?

"Divine Science," your real and only Mind, that is your Principle, will rule. The woman's sacred discovery, her holy revelation, and the founding of it in human consciousness, is what will rule, and is ruling now, in reality. This immaculate idea, divine Science, which according to Jesus' Revelation to St. John will be represented last by woman, will "rule" even though "the serpent pursues [it] with hatred." The spiritual idea, presented by the woman, "will burn up the chaff of error with the fervent heat of Truth and Love, melting and purifying even the gold of human character" (S&H 565:20).

THE REPRESENTATIVE OF TRUTH IN EVERY AGE MUST BEGIN BY UNCOVERING ERROR. Mrs. Eddy never hesitated to turn the class's attention to the opposite of God, not to make a reality of it, but to understand its modes and reduce it to nothingness. She knew Jesus was the Christ because "he loved righteousness and hated iniquity."

The question is sometimes asked, "Is Christian Science the same as divine Science?" The answer is yes, except that "Christian Science relates especially to Science as applied to humanity" (S&H 127;15). Mrs. Eddy states categorically, "Christian Science is absolute; it is neither behind the point of perfection nor advancing towards it; it is at this point and must be practiced therefrom" (*My.* 242:5).

Under the marginal heading, "Spiritual idea crowned" (S&H 562:11), we read that the spiritual idea is crowned with twelve stars—five more stars than Jesus held. The five extra stars stand for the motherhood of God that in the Second Coming teaches mortals how to overcome the hypnotism of the five physical senses. Mary Baker Eddy's teachings instruct us how to do that. In other words, the twelve stars represent the fact that all mortals will, step by step—led by "the bright and morning star" (alias the teaching of the Second Coming of the Christ)—"yield to the activities of the divine Principle of man in the harmony of Science."

We might say that the twelve stars represent the spiritual forward steps that all mortals must take to overcome the misconception (the hypnotism) that has bound them. Consequently, before the individual can be crowned with twelve stars there is a cross to be taken up. In the chapter, "Prayer and At-one-ment" Mrs. Eddy teaches us what this cross is through which the crown is realized, and which will lead to an understanding of the kingdom of God within our consciousness.

"THE FINAL REVELATION"

Alone, above, outside of all materiality, Mrs. Eddy stood on a height where none but Christ Jesus had stood before. "With the awful power of Truth, transfigured with eternal Love," this Leader, this woman, "clothed with the sun, clothed in light"—predestined from "before Abraham was," incarnated in the scientific age—comes to show a world awash in a sea of materiality the path to dominion and holiness.

As Copernicus correctly mapped out the stellar system, so Mary Baker Eddy correctly explored and mapped out the spiritual realm, which is dissolving the historical concept of man. So revolutionary is Mrs.

Eddy's teaching of the way Jesus marked out, that a complete mutation is necessary to handle the new spiritual consciousness this Second Coming of the Christ gives us.

The "final revelation" (S&H p. 107:5) which she brought is "without father, without mother, without descent, having neither beginning of days, nor end of life; but made like unto the Son of God" (Heb. 7:3). In a way it is like 2+2=4, it has always been; nothing can touch it, or end its life. The revelation is complete. It is our duty to walk in it.

Christian Science, understood, will bring forth a new kind of man. In a statement to the Associated Press, Mrs. Eddy said: "What remains to lead on the centuries and reveal my successor, is man in the image and likeness of the Father-Mother God, man the generic term for mankind." Through her revelation, "sooner or later the whole human race will learn that, in proportion as the spotless selfhood of [the infinite good called God] is understood, human nature will be renovated, and man will receive a higher selfhood, derived from God, and the redemption of mortals from sin, sickness, and death be established on everlasting foundations" (*Un.* 6:4).

Had Mrs. Eddy not seen this Truth about her real self, and all humanity, she could not have handled the bewildering array of problems, the multi-tentacled goliaths facing her, threatening her God-ordained appointment. Nor could she have hurdled the monumental opposition, cruel and unmerciful, attempting to thwart her every forward step.

Think of the marvel of her life! What we could learn from it if it were known in a millionth of its detail, as she overcame the world's hatred, and fulfilled the work God had given her to do! In proportion as mankind becomes aware of her holy, God-ordained mission, Christian Science healing will again flourish, because understanding and demonstration are a unit.

"FINAL IMMERSION OF HUMAN CONSCIOUSNESS IN THE INFINITE OCEAN OF LOVE"

Mrs. Eddy saw that Christian Science is destined to become the one and only religion on this planet. In bringing to view the great I AM, your real "I," it brings about "the baptism of Spirit, or final immersion of human consciousness in the infinite ocean of Love [which] is the last scene in corporeal sense. . . . Mortal man's repentance and absolute abandonment of sin finally dissolves all supposed material life or physical sensation, and the corporeal or mortal man disappears forever. The encumbering mortal molecules, called man, vanish as a dream; but man born of the great Forever, lives on, God-crowned and blessed" (*Mis.* 205:13).

Then shall the earth "be filled with the knowledge of the glory of the Lord" (Hab. 2:14). "And when this cometh to pass, (lo, it will come,) then shall they know that a prophet hath been among them" (Ezek. 33:33).

CHAPTER 22

THE GREAT REVELATION

AT THE THRESHOLD OF INFINITY 1846–1866

In 1866 Mary Baker Eddy stood at the threshold of infinity, looking out on Infinite Good. She viewed this universe, whose divine Principle is Love, not as a distant possibility, but as the only reality of being. In the hundred and thirty years since that momentous year, Christian Science has been steadily educating mankind how to rise above all material sensuousness, into spiritual consciousness—how to rise above being fooled by hypnotic pictures of matter.

Christian Science is the Christ coming the second time through the spiritualized consciousness of Mary Baker Eddy. It has come to rid the world of its present and eon's-long load of despair and misery, of its fear and dread that it is sitting on death row.

All through the ages great and wise men and women have had marvelous flashes of light, as recorded in the Bible, and in the scientific development of world thought from the time of the Greeks. Abraham had flashes of light. So did Moses and the prophets. Jesus came *giving the marvelous proof of eternal Life.* But it remained for Mary Baker Eddy to discover the Science of being. It remained for her to discover the Principle and the rule by which each one could make the same demonstration that Jesus made, and greater. *Why greater?* Because through the Second Coming of the Christ there has been a full and final revelation of evil's unreality, and man's oneness with Infinite Good. Mrs. Eddy knew "the grand necessity of existence is to gain the true idea of what constitutes the kingdom of heaven in man." Getting this straight is far and away the most important thing to become aware of practically. She showed mankind how to gain this true idea.

The writings of her who represented the woman of the Apocalypse teach us that the Christ is the activity of truth in our own consciousness as we learn the Principle and practice it. She teaches us how to stop being slaves to our own beliefs, how to turn away from believing aught but good is real, and thus, how "to turn away from the open sepulchres of sin" (*Mis.* 292:14 & 123:19).

MRS. EDDY'S 1846-66 SEARCH

Mrs. Eddy writes (Ret. 24:6): "The discovery came to pass in this way. During *twenty years prior to my discovery* I had been trying to trace all physical effects to a mental cause, and in the latter part of 1866 I gained the scientific certainty that all causation was Mind."

The work she was doing in 1846 (twenty years before the great revelation came) of "trying to trace all physical effects to a mental cause"—indeed the work she had been doing all her life—was preparing her to "launch out into the deep," as Jesus commanded Peter to do (Luke 5:4). When tempestuous waters confronted her twenty years later her ark of understanding would be ready to sail. The work Mrs. Eddy was doing in 1846 prepared her for the daring voyage that would begin in 1866 and take her into a new world of demonstrable celestial thought where only Jesus had been before.

Mrs. Eddy's labor and search, begun in 1846, would come to fruition in a time of crucial need. On her very deathbed, she would be able to recognize matter as hypnotic suggestion only, a false way of thinking, and to triumphantly repudiate, with the spiritual boldness of Christ Jesus himself, the entire evidence of the material senses.

Describing this "Emergence into light" in 1866, Mrs. Eddy writes, "The moment arrived of the heart's bridal to more spiritual existence." At this moment "a spiritual experience so deep was granted her that she realized eternity in a moment, infinitude in limitation, life in the presence of death. She could not utter words of prayer. . . . She knew God face to face. She came to 'touch and handle things unseen.' In that consciousness all pain evanesced into bliss, all discord in her physical body melted into harmony, all sorrow was translated into rapture. She recognized this state as her rightful condition as a child of God. Love invaded her, Life lifted her, Truth irradiated her. God said, "Daughter, arise!" (Sibyl Wilbur, *The Life of Mary Baker Eddy.*)

In that hour she received a revelation for which she had been preparing her heart in every event of her life. "I was waiting and watching; and lo, the bridegroom came" (*Ret.* 23:15). She defines "bridegroom" as "Spiritual understanding; the pure consciousness that God, the divine Principle, creates man as His own spiritual idea, and that God is the only creative power."

THE UNITED STATES IN 1846

Let us look back over the mist of years at what was then happening in the United States as a new nation, when in 1846, by sputtering lamp light, Mrs. Eddy began seriously the work leading to her great life-mission of discovering the Science that lay back of Jesus' mighty, unparalleled work on earth.

In 1846 the terrible Civil War to maintain the Union and free the slaves still lay ahead. This also would help prepare the way. Once the Union called America was established on a firm foundation and slavery was abolished, "the voice of the herald of this new crusade sounded the keynote of **UNIVERSAL** freedom."

"Two years before 1846," writes George Roche, the highly esteemed President of Hillsdale College, "Samuel F. B. Morse had spoken the reverential words: "What hath God wrought!" as a new strange invention translated his words into impulses over an electrical wire, and another device far away received his words instantly. The hindrances and obstructions of time and space had fallen. Immediate communication between anyone anywhere in any land would now be practical. History had changed."

This was less than one hundred and fifty years ago. During these years the world has been transformed in a way never experienced before. The steam engine, the cotton jenny, telegraph, electricity, the automobile and airplane, to mention only a few, have wrought more change for mankind than had occurred during the previous million years.

In 1846—when Mary Baker Eddy began her momentous search for the Science that lay behind Christ Jesus' "mighty, crowning, unparalleled and triumphant exit from the flesh"—many of the wonderful inventions we today take for granted did not exist. The fantastic information age of the twentieth century, and the incredible technological breakthroughs on the horizon today—rapidly spreading in this computer chip world—were undreamed of in the brave new world of 1846. The telephone, in 1846, was nearly thirty years in the future, electric power lay forty years ahead, radio and the automobile were some fifty years in the future.

In 1846 the airplane was still nearly sixty years away, jet aircraft and computers a hundred years into the future. Only steamboats and steam locomotives had been introduced by 1846. Plumbing was crude if it existed at all; glass windows a luxury.

In 1846 when Mrs. Eddy began her search to trace all physical effects to a mental cause and find all is infinite Mind infinitely manifested, life expectancy was about thirty years. Today it is about eighty years. But even the medical fraternity is saying old-age markers that we take for granted today will be nothing more than a distant memory in the next century. Indeed many people who today are reading this book will live to be 120 or more. Retirement will be a thing of the past as people harness the power of their greatest asset—their minds." We stand at the threshold of the greatest creative revolution the world has ever known. Think of the untapped genius waiting to solve every problem and realize every possibility as people who in the past would have been dead at fifty today live an extra 40 years, as our new resource.

Though life in 1846 was harder in many ways, it was a time of promise and hope. In 1846 the Republic was a new land full of robust people. It was then celebrating its seventieth anniversary of the Declaration of Independence. The number of states in the union had doubled from thirteen to twenty six. In 1846 America's western reach extended to the states along the Mississippi River: Illinois to the north; Louisiana, Arkansas, Missouri to the south. Twenty four of our present states were still to join the Union and only a few trappers and adventurers had penetrated the far west. Still ahead lay the discovery of gold in California and the great "Westward Ho!" migration it spurred, but the saga of settling America by horse power was well under way.

There, indeed, is a tale of perseverance! Grass was the gasoline of the mid-19th century; without it the horses, oxen, and mules pulling the wagons died, and usually so did the families carrying their own food. It's little more than 150 years ago that wagons and supplies gathered at Independence, Missouri, and other "jumping off" places, for the 2000 mile journey across the plains, the deserts, and mountains, to a place called Oregon. At that time, April was a good time to start. It would be late enough in the spring to get good grass for the horses, mules and oxen in Nebraska, but would allow the battered caravans to beat the snows while crossing the Cascades or the Sierra Nevada.[1]

It was the same patient perseverance and staying power that brought such inventions as Henry Ford's Model T Ford which came out in 1908 and sold for $850. Because of his persistence in perfecting a moving assembly line, the price for a Model T soon fell to $345, revolutionizing industry. Mr. Ford was fond of telling people, "Your best friend is the person who brings out the best in you." Doesn't that make Mary Baker Eddy our best friend? Mrs. Eddy saw that material evolution was just the taking away of the limitations of matter.

---

[1]What had led to all this courageous forward movement can be read in my book, *America: Cradle for the Second Coming of the Christ.* Available from Rare Book Company and Bookmark.

THE AUTOMOBILE

Henry Ford was not the first to build an automobile, but he was one who persevered. According to the *Columbia Encyclopedia,* today's ubiquitous car seems to have first been built by Cugnot of Paris in 1869. It had a maximum speed of three miles per hour. In 1881 Trevithick of England also built a three-wheeled, steam-driven vehicle. It had a maximum speed of four miles an hour. But excessive bridge and road tolls, and the "Red Flag Act" (not repealed until 1896) finally drove all mechanical vehicles off the roads. The "Red Flag Act" required that all self-propelled vehicles be preceded by a man carrying a red flag by day and a red light by night. Speed was limited to four miles an hour.

Automotive progress, however, would continue to be made in England, France, and Germany. Finally Henry Ford's gas buggy, patterned after horse-drawn vehicles, would be built in America in 1893. Similar persistence and dedication brought forth countless other inventions in the 20th century. In 1903 at Kitty Hawk the Wright Brothers flew their 750 pound gasoline-powered plane 120 feet. Sixty three years later, on July 20, 1969, Neil Armstrong flew to the moon and walked on it!

As the limitations of matter lifted, ever more wonders appeared. There is always a "**SPIRITUAL CAUSE** behind those lower things" (S&H 268:4). **Everything divinely real is already here. God's "work is done"** (S&H 3:9). The principles of every invention have **ALWAYS** existed. It only waited for a Samuel F. B. Morse, a Marconi, a Thomas A. Edison, the Wright brothers, or an Einstein to reveal the principles governing these ideas. What we are aware of is just a matter of consciousness. (See S&H 260:8 & 573:19.)

If in 1846 hard work and ingenuity were the keynote in science and industry, in politics America's watchword was liberty. In 1846 the United States was not sodden with problems as it now is. Today—when the ravening maw of big government chomps our money and our liberty— Jefferson's words to Congress: "That government is best which governs least" would be like recommending family planning to rabbits.

Our forefathers did not dance along a precipice. They knew the cost of big government could not be measured in dollars alone; it is also measured in what it does to harm the human spirit and the cause of freedom. The individual who not only is willing to live on the public treasure but demands that he be fed from it, is already dead spiritually. The necessity for struggle is one of the clever devices through which nature forces individuals to expand, develop, progress and become strong. For those on welfare, weakness replaces strength. Fear overcomes faith.

There is a price to pay for today's big government insanity. We can see some of the results in the explosion of crime and our shrinking national wealth. Let us bury our differences, come together, and overturn this Leviathan that is pushing our national debt into the stratosphere. No less than our civilization and our culture are at stake. Our forefathers knew that what we did with liberty would determine our own and our country's future. It is ordained in the eternal constitution of things, that men of intemperate minds cannot be free. Their passions forge their fetters.

Today while people around the world are looking to America for answers on how to bring political freedom to their own countries, we need to wake up again to what made America great—wake up and confront creeping socialism as it beats the drum for big government, saying: "stand still, little lambs, and be shorn [so we can have more welfare, slums, drugs, and crime]." Greatly needed today—as our country lies mired in this turmoil and moral confusion—is Mary Baker Eddy's teaching that the solution to every problem comes from within ourselves.

In 1846, when Mrs. Eddy began her search, the spirit of the Revolution was still abroad. Government was a scarcely necessary evil, the enemy of liberty, to be bound by the chains of the Constitution. "Did you know that George Washington's inaugural speech lasted only a minute and a half?" commented a friend. "I guess there's just not much to say if you are a politician who can't tell a lie." With the government having neither power nor money to buy votes, per capita taxes were limited to only a few cents a year.

1846 was a time of deep conviction in the "Great Experiment" that was America. It was a time of optimism, energy, and invention. America was still secure in its faith that "where the spirit of the Lord is, there is liberty." Born in an earthly sojourn of unbelievable hardship from the old world, America in 1846 was "a city set on a hill." A church was usually the first building in every settlement.

In this pious atmosphere of wholesome respect for religious values, in this liberty-loving environment, Mary Baker Eddy, in 1846, began her serious search for the divine Science that lay behind the "miracles" performed by Jesus during his wondrous three-year ministry on earth. Her twenty-year search culminated in the great discovery and revelation that came to her in February, 1866.

Jesus' teaching had laid the foundation for this divine event. Scriptural prophecy foretold it.

INFINITE GOOD HAD BEEN SETTING THE STAGE

INVENTION OF PRINTING

Let's take a quick look backward to other events that helped prepare the way for Mary Baker Eddy's great revelation and its founding in human consciousness.

In 1450 Johann Gutenberg's invention of printing began reshaping the world. Printing technology, in its day, spread about as fast as the microchip, and had much the same effect, say modern historians. A few decades after the invention of movable type, Luther decided to defy the Roman church with his "95 Theses." Within weeks, the printing press had spread his views all over Germany. Within months he was known throughout Europe. Before the printing press no one would have heard of Luther's ideas. He would have been silenced, perhaps executed. But instead, the new technology ushered in a new age—just as today, computers are ushering in the largest change in civilization since printing.

We know the longest cycles in history last about 500 years. Around 500 A.D. the Roman Empire collapsed. About 1000 A.D. the Dark Ages gave way to the Middle Ages. And around 1500 the Modern age began, ushered in by the printing press, Luther, and Columbus.

With the advent of Mary Baker Eddy, approximately 500 years after the invention of printing, we are assured that St. John's Revelation, Chapters XXI and XXII will be fulfilled. In 1866 Mrs. Eddy received her great revelation. Nine years later, with the publication of the first edition of Science and Health in 1875, Jesus' prophecies to St. John in Revelation X and XII, were fulfilled. The "Comforter" had come to lead humanity out of its self-imposed suffering and slavery to false beliefs.

Mary Baker Eddy stands for the complete revelation of the Christ within human consciousness—the kingdom of God within our consciousness. As the printed word enables us to learn the Christ Science, all on earth—as they understand the revelation she brought and gave example of—will be able to do what Jesus did, "and even greater works" as Jesus himself predicted.

Mrs. Eddy's spiritual stature transcends mortal measurements. She saw perfection not in the distant future but as present reality. She was as certain of ultimate harmony as she was of her own existence since the kingdom of God is within our consciousness.

Today we seem to be victims of collective belief because we are not thinking from the standpoint of Infinite Good. Mrs. Eddy's God-given job was to correct this. How? While Luther had struggled only with the church at Rome, Mrs. Eddy's struggle was **not only** against the dogmas and bitter prejudices of **many** powerful religious sects, but also against the thoroughly entrenched **sensualism** of **all** mankind. She had to change the inner attitude of men's minds, so the outer aspects of their lives could be changed.

Mrs. Eddy knew that she of herself could not have originated such a book as Science and Health. She "had to get Mary out of the way." She, like Jesus, could say: "I receive not testimony from man" (John 5:34), and like Peter and John as they stood before the tribunal (with the man they had healed at the "gate of the temple"—at the gate of their own thought—humbly stating (Acts 4:20), "We cannot but speak the things we have seen and heard."

So it was with Mrs. Eddy. She said she had to study the book herself in order to understand it. When she came to writing it each day, she did not know what to write until she picked up her pen. "It was simply divine Mind expressing Itself," she said. "God wrote the textbook. I only held the pen." The **leaven of Spirit** in that writing which God dictated, is changing "the whole of mortal thought as yeast changes the chemical properties of meal" (S&H 118:23 & see Scriptural note p. 107).

Mrs. Eddy once stated: "As Mary Baker Eddy, I am the weakest of mortals, but as the Discoverer and Founder of Christian Science, I am the bone and sinew of the world." We too become the "bone and sinew of the world" in proportion to our spiritual understanding and our grasp of reality. (Remember, Jesus also said, "Of mine own self I can do nothing.")

CHAPTER 23

THE "LITTLE BOOK" IN THE ANGEL'S HAND

First Edition Gives Highest Revelations

Why is Mrs. Eddy's first edition regarded as the highest?

It must be remembered that "Woman" is a *descending* idea. Mrs. Eddy's writings reveal the "bride," the "city foursquare" that DESCENDS from heaven. Jesus, in man's ascending role, had taken his work to the seventh rung or the seventh day of creation. And it was at this holy height that Woman had to start to bring the Christ message down to where beleaguered humanity could grasp the lowest rung of the ladder and begin the heavenly climb.

It is therefore natural that in the first edition of Science and Health—because Mrs. Eddy had to start in heaven where Jesus left off—her statements would be high, and in the main, absolute, like her statement to her first classes: "You, my students, are God." Even a **century later**, how few accepted this instruction.

Jesus' understanding and vision were so high that perhaps only St. John understood his teaching, at least sufficiently to receive Jesus' Revelation to him on the Isle of Patmos. Even two thousand years later, Mrs. Eddy spoke of the "present crude hour" (*Un.* 4:28), indicating there still was little receptivity to spiritual teaching.

Mrs. Eddy soon learned that while man's greatest height had to be Woman's divine starting point, she must bring the Christ message down to where it could be understood by humanity in a systematized way. She saw that to *teach,* you must start where people are. "Spiritual ideas unfold as we [the **readers**] advance" (S&H 361:22). This is why the first edition is very different from later ones.

WHY DID MRS. EDDY REVISE SCIENCE AND HEALTH?

The question is often asked, "Why did Mrs. Eddy revise Science and Health?" Mrs. Eddy states that her first edition contains the "complete statement of Christian Science" (*Ret.* 37). Why then did she continually revise it?

Her revisions were not metaphysical changes, but accommodations to the thought of the times in which she was writing. Remember Mary Baker Eddy began where Jesus left off. Jesus foretold she would bring the Comforter that mankind was not ready for 2000 years ago.

Mr. Carpenter, who for a year lived in Mrs. Eddy's home and was her secretary, states:

> *Mrs. Eddy revised Science and Health, not because there was anything untrue about the first edition, but because it did not present Christian Science in a form sufficiently adapted to the needs of the world. . . . No one will ever know the spiritual thought and effort Mrs. Eddy expended in order to STEP DOWN and accommodate revelation as it came to her, so that it could be comprehended by the beginner. . . . In fact she once remarked that she had brought Science and Health or Christian Science down just as far as she could, without losing it.*

The truth about Infinite Good and its creation (divine Science) had to be reduced. Human perception could take it only by degrees because man's consciousness was so deeply ingrained in the belief of matter. Man could not grasp the whole Truth, hence Mrs. Eddy "hid the leaven (divine Science) in three measures of meal."

So we can ask: Where was Mary Baker Eddy coming from when she wrote the first edition of Science and Health? Why is the first edition so different from the 431 editions that followed?

The first edition, as we have seen, was based directly on the great revelation and discovery that came to her in 1866, and on the nine years of healing and teaching work, following that glorious, tremendous and extraordinary divine revelation.

William D. McCracken was Mrs. Eddy's proofreader for the final edition. In his book, *Mary Baker Eddy and Her Book,* he writes:

> *Subsequent editions of Science and Health never changed the teaching of the first edition, but they did seek to adjust its radical statements to human comprehension; they used more of the wisdom of the serpent, understood as an adroit idea, and less of the challenge of the lion's roar."*

When Mrs. Eddy wrote the first edition there was no church and no field. The few students she garnered were, as we have seen, treated to such rare teaching as: "You, my students, are God," which, of course, was in harmony with what she was writing in the first edition. And it was perhaps only because of the spiritual impact of her teaching that some went out and healed miraculously. But in spite of the wonderful teaching and the demonstrations they performed, for the first sixteen years no student remained loyal.

After the first edition, Mrs. Eddy tried to see that everything that went into subsequent editions had been found demonstrable. And seeing how unready and unprepared people were for this great divine Truth, she began hiding it in the textbook. Even 40 years later—after finishing Science and Health in 1910—she told Laura Sargent (as recorded in Vol. II of Lida Fitzpatrick's *Association Addresses*): "There, Laura! I have hidden it, and hidden it, and hidden it. And if I hide it any more they will never find it." Find what? Find what she told the pupils in her first class, namely: "You, my students, are God."

"GOD'S LAW IS IN THREE WORDS"

Mrs. Eddy said: "God's law is in three words, 'I am All.'" But to explain these "three words" she wrote the textbook, and all that is contained in *Prose Works*,[1] besides personally teaching thousands of students, and writing thousands of letters to students explaining the meaning of those three words: "I am All." Think of the immense outpouring of divine energy this took!

"When the Science of Mind was a fresh revelation to [Mrs. Eddy] she had to impart, while teaching its grand facts, the hue of spiritual ideas from her own spiritual condition" (S&H 460:24).

In a letter to the Reverend D.A. Easton, March 10, 1893, she wrote that what was necessary to fill a need of her church was:

> *"An outpouring of love, of the Spirit that beareth witness. I found it essential, . . . to lead them by my own state of love and spirituality. By fervor in speaking the Word, by tenderness in searching into their needs—and especially by feeling myself and uttering the spirit of Christian Science—together with the letter. . . ."* (A Carpenter Foundation item).

---

[1]Science and Health and *Prose Works* are Mrs. Eddy's "two pillars." Zechariah (Chap. 6) saw **"two pillars,"** "two mountains of brass" through which the horses of revelation come. King Solomon (I Kings 7:15) had **"two pillars"** of brass in front of his temple. Mary Baker Eddy had **"two pillars"** for her heavenly temple—Science and Health, and Prose Works—pillars that here and now show us the highway to heaven.

RE: "FOUR THOUSAND STUDENTS
TAUGHT IN [HER] COLLEGE"

As students gathered around her she eventually established a college to allow her message to reach greater numbers of people. In the Preface to Science and Health she states that "during seven years over four thousand students were taught by [her] in this College." Occasionally one hears of a student questioning this statement, unaware of the history of the Christian Science movement at that point in time.

Mrs. Eddy could modestly say that "over four thousand students" had been taught by her during those seven years because Hawthorne Hall was an auxiliary to her College, and the overflow crowds that attended her teaching sessions in Hawthorne Hall, no doubt well exceeded "four thousand students."

What drew the people? The throngs may not have been well educated, but they obviously possessed that penetrating perception Infinite Good seems to give to the simple and the humble. They recognized in Mrs. Eddy's teaching an astonishing power that fascinated and lured them. They felt instinctively that her teaching had the answer to their problems, needs, and fears.

During those seven years, while Mrs. Eddy taught over four thousand students, she carried on many other activities, showing her amazing spiritual power. Only because of *WHAT SHE WAS*, namely, the fulfillment of the prophesied woman of the Apocalypse, could she accomplish such a herculean task.

How did she assess her ability to do all this—to fulfill her God-appointed mission in spite of fearful opposition? She said she could do it because: "I got Mary out of the way." She listened only for God's voice, then hastened to obey God's direction.

HER UNDERSTANDING OF GOD MADE HER
EQUAL TO THE TASK

Undaunted by the material Goliath staring her in the face and shrieking at her from every side, Mrs. Eddy worked steadily, patiently on, never shrinking from exposing the error bedeviling mankind. Because Truth and Love were plainly incarnate in the loving and pure Mary Baker Eddy—just as they were "in the good and pure Christ Jesus"—her *understanding* made her equal to the work and to the unpredictable demands that fell upon her, as they also had enabled her to write "so hopelessly original [a book] as is Science and Health" (*Mis.* 371:28).

Mrs. Eddy, like Jesus, knew without that **understanding** "the son can do nothing, . . . I can of mine own self [as a mortal without understanding] do nothing." What we need is at hand, in reality. The Mind that is Infinite Good, that is our real Mind, sees perfection everywhere, and a realization of this causes healing to take place. Mrs. Eddy made this understanding of present perfection the basis of her work.

CHAPTER 24

TEACHING AND HEALING SPREAD CHRISTIAN SCIENCE

MRS. EDDY PATIENTLY PERSISTED

When Science and Health was first published, it was forced to run the gauntlet of scorn and ridicule. In the storm of misunderstanding and criticism heaped on it—in the stress of ingratitude and betrayal—Mrs. Eddy was tried as by fire. At times, she was all but overwhelmed by the waters of malice, envy, and hate. Beset by poverty, homelessness, and loneliness, she bravely, unflinchingly, pressed on.

Like Jesus, Mrs. Eddy resolutely, patiently persisted in her work on earth to bring the Second Coming of the Christ, and fulfill Jesus' promise of the "Comforter." She knew the great divine revelation had come to her directly from God, and that she was fulfilling the scriptural prophecy concerning the woman that would bring forth the "man child," your true identity as it is unfolded in Science and Health. The textbook is the "man child" that we have always been one with, as we will realize when the veil (or the hypnotism) is lifted. Divine Love is forcing us all to purify our thought by turning away from material sense and looking toward the imperishable things of Spirit. Mrs. Eddy's perseverance prepared the way so we here and now can become aware that we *are* the presence of God, that we actually are God in action.

But all through her forty-four years of discovery and revelation, ingratitude and falsehood stalked her every forward move. When she said, "The disciples and prophets thrust disputed points on minds unprepared; this cost them their lives, and the world's temporary esteem," she was speaking from hard, cruel experience. She had learned the withering effect of words spoken too soon, and the wisdom of silence on the subject of *who she was.*

Misjudgment, the sharp return of evil for good, was her almost daily portion. It must have seemed to her that no good deed goes unpunished. The sharpest blow was the way some of her early students to whom she had revealed, unrestrained, the power of the mind to heal, perverted that power. These students, being too materially-minded, too unprepared to comprehend her instruction, used the power of the mind to harm her and her loyal students.

To mortal sense these apostate students seemed to do great harm, especially one Richard Kennedy to whom Mrs. Eddy had given much with the hope of training him to be a helper in the Cause. But as she writes, "The very circumstance which your suffering sense deems wrathful and afflictive, Love can make an angel entertained unawares" (S&H 574:27).

What was the angel "entertained unawares" in the case of this apostasy? It was her realization that she must somehow find a way to explain all error, all sin, sickness, discord, death as nothing other than hypnotic suggestion, totally unreal; she must find a way to teach that the illusions presented by the carnal mind (which are nothing claiming to be something) are only suppositional MATERIAL SENSE, alias the false belief that sensation is in matter.

Years later the harrowing "Next Friends" suit again proved that "when these things cease to bless they will cease to occur" (*My.* 143:23). The blessing in *that* particular case came after Mrs. Eddy left the earthly scene, when the faithless, disobedient five-member Board of Directors (which the *Manual* had terminated) could not persuade the Christian Science field that Mrs. Eddy was non compos mentis when she wrote the estoppels terminating the five member Board and the material Mother Church, at her passing.

In trying to persuade the field that Mrs. Eddy was off her rocker when she dissolved the material Mother Church and terminated the five-member Board, the Directors brazenly insisted the estoppels were "consent clauses"!

Why were they unable to persuade the field? Because at the time of the Next Friends suit, the attorneys *against* her had found her to be "sharper than a tack" and completely sound in mind. This attorney-verdict had come AFTER her *Manual* terminated the material Mother Church, and after she wrote the By-Law ending the five-member Board upon her departure from this mortal realm.

CLARA CHOATE'S EARLY REMINISCENCES

The attacks against Mrs. Eddy were often quite petty. Clara Choate who was active in the early days of the movement after Mrs. Eddy instantly healed her of a terrible attack of diphtheria, writes in her *Reminiscences:*

The marriage [of Dr. Eddy and Mrs. Glover] seemed to meet with the disapproval of most of the students who had been taught by Mrs. Eddy. This was nothing new, for these early students objected to nearly every move Mrs. Eddy made along progressive lines. No matter what the move was it seemed to provoke their displeasure; and dissension appeared under the least prospect of change. They did not understand Mrs. Eddy's foresight in seeing the needs of the work, and her close and entire obedience to God's leading in establishing Christian Science and the forthcoming great system into which the Cause was to develop. . . . No matter how high or wonderful were her demonstrations, the world did not then accept her personally nor her advanced revelations. [Much of this lack of love and respect could be traced to the fact that she was a woman].

Every step was cross-bearing and crucifixion. Mrs. Eddy was constantly misquoted, to the hindrance of her work. A manuscript would be mislaid, wrong dates for appointments recorded, and like troubles. . . . [In my book, "Mary Baker Eddy: A New Look," the sinister plot is covered in which Dr. Eddy was accused of murder by a jealous, disgruntled, renegade student.] Looking at the situation, it is wonderful how the work was carried to fulfillment.

However, the world's unrelenting cruelty toward Mrs. Eddy was also a blessing in disguise. It wrought out for her the law of loving her enemies. It also hastened the uncovering of evil as unreal. For the first time in human history mortals were taught that by *KNOWING THE UNREALITY OF EVIL, OF SIN, DISEASE, AND DEATH, THEY COULD NOW DEMONSTRATE THE ALLNESS OF INFINITE GOOD IN THEIR OWN LIVES, AND HAVE HEAVEN RIGHT HERE ON EARTH.*

MARY BAKER EDDY'S WORK WAS TWO-FOLD: THE EXPLANATION OF BOTH TRUTH AND ERROR

As the revelator to this age, in the Second Coming of the Christ, Mrs. Eddy's work was two-fold. She had to bring to us not only the revelation of Truth, but also the explanation of evil and error as nothing other than hypnotic suggestion, totally unreal, as the prodigal son learned when he "came to himself."

HOW TO HANDLE EVIL NOT AT FIRST CLEAR

In a poem, Mrs. Eddy writes, "'Let there be light, and there was light.' What chase[s] the clouds away?" The light is omnipresent forever; only clouds hide it. When we (the spiritual man) begin to correct our mistakes—when the hypnotism, the wrong viewpoint that has blinded us, has been corrected—the light is seen to be omnipresent. In the great revelation that came to her in 1866 it was made clear that Infinite Good was the only reality. But how to explain the nothingness of evil and error was not at first clear, and her method of handling evil evolved slowly.

At first Mrs. Eddy vigorously fought what looked like evil and error. But her final statements on evil urge us to see that the unity between man and the infinite good we call God has never been interrupted. This unity remains forever the reality.

INSTRUCTIONS ON HANDLING EVIL

One of Mrs. Eddy's last instructions to us on handling evil is found on page 210 of *Miscellany*:

"Beloved Christian Scientists [here read your own name: beloved Bill, beloved Mary; feel how Mrs. Eddy loves *you*; know that she is speaking directly to you] keep your mind so filled with Truth and Love that sin, disease and death, cannot enter."

Do we do this? Do we pay attention to this most important instruction? Do we "stand porter at the door of thought?" How faithfully do we perform our office as porter? How faithful are we about "admitting only such conclusions as [we] wish realized in bodily results"? (S&H 392:24). "If [Infinite Good] is ADMITTED to be the only Mind and Life, there ceases to be any opportunity for sin and death" (S&H 276:17).

"It is plain that nothing can be added to a mind already full." Why? In mathematics, for instance, once you have thoroughly learned that 2x2 is 4 (or any other calculation) your mind is full of that, and nothing can persuade you that 2x2 is 5 or 6. This is how Jesus and his disciples, and Mrs. Eddy and her students did their seemingly miraculous healing.

"Good thoughts [God's thoughts, Truth,] are an impervious armor; clad therewith you are completely shielded from the attacks of error of every sort." It's the right understanding of God—of the infinite good that is our own Mind—that will shield us from "the attacks of error of every sort."

"Christian Science and the senses are at war. It is a revolutionary struggle" (*Mis.* 101:8). Mortals do not attain the realization of their present divinity without a mighty effort. There will be many battles and the constant crossing of swords with the temptation to believe the testimony of the five physical senses. We will prosper in proportion to the spirit of Love that nerves the endeavor to forsake error of every kind.

GREAT CAUSES INVOLVE CONFLICT AND PERSECUTION

"Conflict and persecution are the surest signs that can be given of the greatness of a cause or of an individual, provided this warfare is honest and a world imposed struggle. Such conflict never ends till unconquerable right is begun anew, and hath gained fresh energy and final victory" (*Mess.* '00. 10:5).

> *Self-renunciation of all that constitutes a so-called material man, and the acknowledgment and achievement of his spiritual identity as the child of God, is Science that opens the very flood-gates of heaven; whence good flows into every avenue of being, cleansing mortals of all uncleanness, destroying all suffering, and demonstrating the true image and likeness. There is no other way under heaven whereby we can be saved, and man be clothed with might, majesty, and immortality.* (*Mis.* 185:7).

As the pioneer of Christian Science, Mrs. Eddy, **"trusting in Truth and having no other trusts,"** stood absolutely alone in this conflict, this "world-imposed struggle." Energetically, vigorously, she smote error with the sword of Truth.

It was this aloneness with the reality of things that enabled her to experience "infinite progression [as] concrete being" when she discovered new truths about her own revelation right up to her final year.

THE MIGHTY UNPARALLELED CHALLENGE

The mighty, unparalleled challenge that faced Mrs. Eddy was how to find ways to share her revelation with the world. It required awakening mortals to the *opposite of their deepest convictions,* the unsealing of the world's frozen resistance to Truth, the melting of the hardened concepts of the carnal mind's unbelief and skepticism, in order to reveal the man of Infinite Good's creating. She must communicate totally new spiritual truths in a language formed chiefly, primarily, to serve mankind's *material* needs and wants.

HEALING WAS THE ANSWER

Healing was the answer! Healing was the smallest part of Christian Science, but in this hour of millennial anticipation and awakening it would be the "bugle call to thought and action" (*Rud.* 2:24). Healing was what people needed and wanted, therefore HEALING would be the bugle call!

Mary Baker Eddy's advent on earth—her God-appointed mission to bring the scripturally prophesied Second Coming of the Christ—was ushered in with her performance of wonderful healings, only a few of which have been recorded. Fortunately some, including a few early ones, are buried in the Archives of the Mother Church. For example, one night while living at No. 8 Broad Street, Mrs. Eddy had supper with her tenants and met a Mrs. Godfrey who was visiting them. Mrs. Godfrey had a badly damaged finger that had become so swollen the doctors said she might lose her arm if she did not have the finger amputated.

At one point Mrs. Eddy reached over and touched Mrs. Godfrey's hand, asking what was wrong with her finger; then the conversation turned to other things. That night Mrs. Godfrey slept peacefully. When she woke in the morning her finger was almost normal. Years later her daughter described how her mother gave a little scream, jumped out of bed, and ran into the next room in her nightgown, calling to her nephew, "William, look at my hand!" The nephew's laconic response was: "Guess Mrs. Glover has been trying her works on it." Within a few days the healing was complete.

Later there was another healing for the Godfreys. Little Mary Godfrey had suffered all through childhood from alarming attacks of membranous croup. On the occasion of the next severe attack Mrs. Godfrey wrapped Mary in a blanket and set off for Lynn in a blinding snowstorm, "for healing."

Arriving at 8 Broad Street the two Godfreys were met at the door by Mrs. Glover "who took in the situation at a glance. Cheerfully she told the little girl to run upstairs to the Nashes' apartment and play. That was the end of the trouble. An instant certainty had communicated itself to both mother and daughter, and before the latter had even reached the next floor she was healed." —A Mary Godfrey *Reminiscence*. (*WKMBE Series*)

MORE REMINISCENCES

A Duff *reminiscence* relates another healing that occurred at 8 Broad Street.

> *I was sick, and my mother called a medical doctor. The physician gave my father a prescription to fill at a drugstore. While he was gone Mrs. Glover came in. She stopped at the door and listened to my mother's fears about me. Mrs. Glover said, "Put away the medicine. Flora is allright." When my father came with the medicine, I was*

playing on the floor perfectly well....I have been well all my life. I have nursed all kinds of contagious cases without fear. [Flora became a medical nurse].

None of the people Mrs. Eddy healed in the early days became Christian Scientists. Most were comfortable with their own church, and thought of Mrs. Eddy as just having a special gift for healing. Many, of course, denounced Mrs. Glover's works as witchcraft. Yet she pressed on. How fortunate we are that Mrs. Eddy did not let personal setbacks discourage her.

Another of "Mary Godfrey's *Reminiscences*" states:

"A carpenter came to our house . . . who had his arm in a sling. Father asked him what the trouble was and he said he had strained the ligaments and paralysis had set in. The arm was partly withered and all the physicians said that it would continue to wither. . . . Father told him about [Mrs. Glover] and asked him if he went to her to come and tell him the result. About a week later the carpenter came to the house to tell father that he was completely healed. . . .

"I might add when this man came to see Mrs. Glover she was too busy to come down to talk with him and just opened a window in her parlor room on the second floor and called down to him. . . ."

Not understanding the truth behind such "miracles" many confused Mrs. Eddy with mediums, in spite of her vocal opposition to spiritualism.

Mrs. Alice Swasey in her *Reminiscences* tells of suffering severe abdominal pains which doctors had been unable to relieve. A friend proposed she go to Lynn to consult "the 'medium' who healed without medicine." She says that on her arrival,

"Mrs. [Glover] talked with me a few minutes and then said, 'Now we won't talk any more.' She closed her eyes and sat with her hands in her lap for about ten minutes and then she said. 'You will not have that trouble any more.' And I said: aren't you going to rub me—or do anything—and she said, 'you are healed' and I was."

Hundreds of Mrs. Eddy's spontaneous healings took place in the early days of Christian Science, and continued to take place all through her forty-four-year ministry on earth, but only a few have been recorded. Mrs. Eddy once told a student to record her healings, and said she regretted that the rush of events had prevented her from doing so.

In former books, I have related other healings, such as the teamster that was thrown to the ground in such a way that a heavily loaded wagon ran over him, crushing his body. Thinking he was dead, some men carried him into Mrs. Eddy's house. Hearing the commotion Mrs. Eddy went downstairs to where the body was laid. In half an hour the man became conscious, stood up declaring he was not hurt, and walked back to his team.

Another healing at Lynn was that of a man escaped from an asylum. His appearance was frightful, clothes tattered. The mother and daughter in the house fled, and asked Mrs. Eddy to come. When he saw her he raised a chair as if to strike her. Mrs. Eddy faced him without fear and felt a great love and compassion for him. He dropped the chair, fell on his knees before her and began to sob. Sixteen years later this man called on Mrs. Eddy in Boston to express his gratitude. He said when he returned to the asylum that day, he was quickly discharged as well, and had never again been insane.

Mrs. Eddy, through her compassionate and loving thought was always breaking mesmerism. Her healings of severely crippled people on the street were well known. Such a healing in Lynn was witnessed by Mrs. Lucy Allen from her window. Mrs. Eddy saw a cripple with one knee drawn up to his chin; the other limb was drawn the other way. A Piece of paper pinned to his shoulder said: "Help this poor cripple." Her heart gushed with unspeakable pity as she went to God in fervent prayer. Leaning over him, so that her face was close to his, she said, "God loves you," and went on. Almost immediately the man arose and walked.

A letter in the Mother Church files states that the writer had come at last as one of the lepers to give thanks for healing. "You, Mrs. Eddy, healed me many years ago of a loathsome disease with just a word. The trouble has never returned. Words fail to express my gratitude for that healing."

Over and over again we hear the same familiar story. Hanover P. Smith, born deaf and dumb, was quickly healed, at the age of nineteen, when his mother took him to Mrs. Eddy.

Janet T. Coleman was expected to die in childbirth. When Mrs. Eddy heard of it, she healed her instantly.

Mary H. Crosby suffered severely when the lining of her stomach was destroyed. Doctors told her she had but a short time to live. A friend told her to see Mrs. Eddy. She did. Mrs. Eddy listened to her story but did not promise to treat her. That same evening, however, the trouble forever disappeared.

John Scott, a farmer, had a bad case of enteritis. He had no bowel movement for two weeks and suffered terribly. The medical could not help. Mrs. Eddy healed him in one hour and he became a changed man. His wife wrote Mrs. Eddy of her gratitude for John's healing, "but more than all else I am grateful for what you have done for him morally and spiritually."

Mrs. Eddy knew healing, alone, would ensure the prosperity of Christian Science because it was *healing the people wanted.* So she healed—with a word, a touch, a gaze, a thought, demonstrating the infinite Love of the Mind that is the true Mind of us all. And she taught her students to heal.

HER EARLY STUDENTS

Interestingly, during Mrs. Eddy's first sixteen years of teaching and healing, many students became successful healers for a time, but not a single student remained loyal; the evidence of the physical senses held them captive. Her experience in this regard was similar to that of Jesus. Of the seventy he sent forth (and who reported wonderful healings) only twelve stayed with him, one of whom betrayed him. Of the 70 Jesus alone knew there never was any error to heal, but only hypnotism to remove.

When students finally came to Mrs. Eddy, who *did* remain loyal, they struggled mightily to heal in a Christ-like manner.

A daughter of Mrs. McDonald, one of these early practitioners, wrote of the days when more than half of Mrs. Eddy's students came from rural districts and small towns. Visits to lonely farms were a prominent part of the Christian Science picture in those days.

> *"I remember many times when my mother received calls from different places in the country, eight or ten miles out of Green Bay, which was a long way in the day of horses. My father would have to walk about five blocks to where the horse was stabled, harness the horse and take mother where she was called. Often they would be gone the rest of the night. Sometimes she would get a dollar for a week's treatment, sometimes five dollars, but more frequently nothing. Often she had to go to homes and stay overnight. Many times she would have to sleep in the spare-room that had been closed all winter and had no heat in it; it would be so cold that she would have to go to bed with all her clothes on, and even then not be warm."*—A Marian McDonald Reminiscence.

MRS. EDDY INSTILLED UNBOUNDED CONFIDENCE

Seeing our Leader rightly, we will be able to partake of the great confidence she instilled in the workers who had the privilege of instruction from her. Bicknell Young stated that as a beginner in Christian Science and for a number of years thereafter, he was quite intimately acquainted with many of Mrs. Eddy's students. He states:

> *"They were a devoted body of men and women, mostly women. Some of them had healings to their credit that were not less remarkable than those recorded in the New Testament. Scarcely any of them were what we would call highly educated, but they were naturally clear thinkers and Mrs. Eddy's instructions had given them something absolutely invaluable. I do not know how to describe it by a better word than confidence, and their confidence in their work, according to what they had grasped of Mrs. Eddy's instructions, was unbounded."*

Mrs. Eddy declares, "The confidence inspired by Science lies in the fact that Truth is real and error is unreal." Therefore, "when an accident happens, declare you are not hurt and understand the reason why, and you will find the ensuing good effect to be in exact proportion to your disbelief in physics, and your fidelity to divine metaphysics, confidence in God as All" (S&H 368:2; 397:17).

By the time Mrs. Eddy left the human scene there were thousands of working practitioners who had this confidence in their work. I grew up with some of them, for which I feel greatly blessed. In Sunday School I had a practitioner as teacher. Once a child my age was crying. Her dog was expected to die that day. But when the child got home after Sunday School, the dog ran to meet her, healed. This was everyday fare. I could relate many such healings. They made a great impression on me. Imagine the impact Mrs. Eddy's healings must have had on her students.

The following healings by our Leader were recorded by Arthur Fosbury:

Mrs. Eddy called at a house looking for a room to rent. The wife said they could not rent her a room because they had a sick daughter, dying of consumption. Mrs. Eddy went upstairs and the girl was immediately healed. There were many such instantaneous healings. Consumption (tuberculosis) was the "No. 1 killer" in Mrs. Eddy's day, but as Christian Science routinely healed case after case, all fear of this disease began to leave.

Still people seldom asked for Christian Science in those days till all other hope was exhausted. Another time a mother brought her four-year old child who had died to Mrs. Eddy. Mrs. Eddy stood at the foot of the bed and did her work. The boy sat up and said: "I *is* sick." Mrs. Eddy talked to him and then took him out of bed and stood him on his feet, but he was still so rebellious that he foamed at the mouth. Our Leader went on with her work and continued talking to him. Presently he hung his head and leaned against Mrs. Eddy's knee; then she took him on her lap and he was completely healed. When the mother came in she nearly collapsed. What astonished her was not that he was alive, but that he walked. He had never done so before, having been paralyzed from birth.

A student tells of Mrs. Eddy healing a baby that had passed on. Cradling the baby in her arms, the mother brought it to Mrs. Eddy, and she restored it to life. How such healings must have strengthened the confidence of those who witnessed them.

The world was not always so receptive. Irving Tomlinson, on hearing of the above healing, said that Mrs. Eddy, when living on Columbus Avenue, enjoyed seeing a baby who lived on the street opposite. Not seeing the little one for several days, and noticing the doctor's carriage at their door, Mrs. Eddy called at the house and learned from the mother that the child had passed on. Mrs. Eddy sat beside the child, realizing the truth as no one had done since the time of Jesus. The child was healed. Instead of gratitude being expressed by the mother, she took the child and expressed ugliness toward our beloved Leader."

We all know the oft-told healing of the daughter of Mrs. Eddy's eldest sister, Abigail Tilton, who was opposed to Christian Science, terribly embarrassed by what her sister was doing, but when her little daughter lay dying, she permitted Mrs. Eddy to see the child. Mrs. Eddy quickly healed the little girl. When the mother came in and saw them playing together on the floor, she exclaimed: "It is the work of the devil." This shows how ignorant the thought was at the time Mrs. Eddy began her great God-sent work on earth, and also how she was shunned and alienated from her family because of the divine Truth she had discovered. "When my father told me if I disgraced the family with Christian Science I should never darken his door again, and my sister would not speak to me, I gave them all up; [then she added:] I am now being punished [her grown-up son was then suing her for money, circa 1907] for the fruits of my first marriage" (*DCC* 32).

Yet despite the obstacles of ignorance and hatred she kept on, determined to bring her revelation to awaken the human consciousness.
Though Mrs. Eddy found "the descent and ascent . . . beset with peril,
privation, [homelessness], temptation, toil, suffering, found venomous
serpents hiding among the rocks, beasts of prey prowling in her path,
wolves in sheep's clothing [her own students in high places] ready to
devour" (*Mis.* 323:10), she pressed on, with a transcendent heroism born
of trust in Good.

CHAPTER 25

PRAYER AND ATONEMENT AT WORK

WINNING THE LICENSE TO HEAL

Mrs. Eddy knew that establishing Christian Science would require hard work as well as revelation. Almost up until the year she left us she persevered in perfecting Science and Health—the "little book open in the hand of the angel"—and in spreading Christian Science through teaching and healing.

History in the Christian Science movement tells of patient perseverance, persistence—a saga of long hard consecrated effort (which is prayer and at-one-ment with Infinite Good, at work). In field after field it won for Christian Scientists the same license to practice Christian Science treatment that medical doctors had, to practice their healing art.

New Hampshire was the first state to legalize Christian Science treatment. This came about through an interesting *Court* battle. It was explained to me that in New Hampshire the attorneys for the monolithic medical fraternity argued that "If we don't stop these Christian Scientists, inside a year half the people in New Hampshire will be wiped out."

Whereupon, the attorney for Christian Science said, "Now that is a very good argument! Let's agree to stop the trial, and if a year from now one person has died because of Christian Science treatment, we will say you are right." The judge agreed to this. During that year no case was lost by Christian Scientists, so their practice was legalized in the courts of New Hampshire.

In North Carolina Christian Science treatment was legalized through the *legislature,* rather than the courts. Here the behemoth medical establishment had since 1901 been preparing a high-profile campaign. It was to be a high-wire legislative act—introducing a bill to prohibit Christian Science practice. The Christian Science practitioners there had also worked diligently preparing a safety net. In 1903 this bill came up before the legislature to compel "all who practice the art of healing for fee or reward to pass an examination before the Medical Board of North Carolina." (Imagine Jesus and the disciples having to get a license from the medical faculty before they could practice healing.)

Mrs. Eddy had asked to be informed of the day and hour of the hearing of this bill in the Legislature before the Joint Medical Committee, so that she could work for its defeat.

The epic victory for Christian Science was so complete that not one enemy was left on the field.

THE PERSECUTION OF JAMES NEAL

Christian Science was also advanced by the staunch and unwavering persistence of individual practitioners, often in the face of great adversity. James Neal, like many others, was no shrinking violet when it came to dealing with error—sin, sickness, death. His healing practice was so successful, and drew so much attention, that the medical faculty lay in wait for something to pin on him. At last their chance came—a case of a child that the doctors had been treating for months was given to James Neal for one *day*; then the frightened mother returned the child to the hospital where it soon died.

So powerful was the medical faculty that every local newspaper printed the medical notice: "Child dies under Christian Science treatment." A shameless trial ensued, but the charge could not be upheld. Neal was vindicated; and some who had been the most vicious and cruel in prosecuting him came to him for treatment and help.

DOCTORS AND DRUGGISTS ALSO FAIL IN MASSACHUSETTS

In many places the battle to outlaw Christian Science actually brought it to public attention, and helped it advance. Joseph G. Mann's healing from what doctors considered a fatal gunshot wound became widely known at the time it occurred because it had been presented at a hearing of a committee of doctors and druggists. They were attempting, through legislation, to prevent the practice of Christian Science healing in Massachusetts. The opposition of this committee was savage, relentless, and determined, just as it had been in the case of James Neal. But in the end, Joseph Mann was vindicated. Again, as in the case of Neal, some who had been the bitterest in persecuting him came to him for help. And once more, Christian Science spread.

It was spread in many other ways. In the World's Fair in 1893 when the Fair's officers declined to give space in which to exhibit Christian Science publications thinking that the subject was not of sufficient importance, Edward Kimball said, "If it could be authentically established that one single case of cancer had been cured by a physician using material remedies, you would be willing to grant space on which to erect a monument to that man a mile high, and yet the Christian Scientists who have healed hundreds of cancers, are obliged to entreat you for a place in which to exhibit the books that show how it is done." In the course of time the World's Fair officers provided ample space, and did more than they were asked to do. In this way again Christian Science spread.

As Christian Science grew in stature and public recognition, we see the power of our Leader's thought as she worked for the world's freedom from self-imposed bondage.

Step by patient step Mrs. Eddy's supernal courage led the Christian Science movement forward. Its healing practice was made respectable in the courts and legislatures of the land. Even the prestigious Mayo Foundation sent their incurable patients to Christian Science practitioners for healing, and they were *healed*!

THE REVOLUTIONARY IMPACT OF HER TEACHING

The uncompromising metaphysical truth of Mrs. Eddy's teachings came with revolutionary impact to her students. They felt they were stepping into a new universe fresh from Infinite Good. It was not a new theory but a new life they were encountering. Evils seemed to be slipping away. Why? Because Mrs. Eddy's teaching left no place for evils to operate in a perfectly ordered universe of Spirit. (Spirit, in Mrs. Eddy's writings, always denotes good, order, and that the divine Mind is the only substance and reality.) The false evidence had to go as the true logic gained acceptance.

Mrs. Eddy showed her students they did not have to go to the slums of Boston to look for evil. Old habits of thought in ourselves—the hostility and obstinacy of the human mind that is committed to its own world of material appearances, in other words, the anti-Christ—is enough to reveal Armageddon right at hand.

She showed them that *they never had to deal with anything except their own thoughts, their material sense of things.* **The important thing was to learn the nature of God, then they would realize what their own real nature was, since God and man are one.**

She reminded them they could control their thinking; they had the power to select and decide what they would think; their destiny was never in the hands of other people. On the human plane we often meet our destiny on the road we took to avoid it. But knowing spiritually that our destiny is in our own hands will free us from bondage and bring to view our present divinity. All that hinders healing is the reality we make of matter. "This Science," she taught, "has nothing to do with matter, except to say and to *establish in the back of our mind that there is no matter.*"

TEACHING AND HEALING

As Mrs. Eddy struggled to awaken the sleeping consciousness of mankind, teaching and healing often went hand in hand. Many healings took place in response to lectures.

Julia Bartlett once saw a cripple on two crutches helped into Hawthorne Hall by two women. After Mrs. Eddy's service he walked out with his crutches on his shoulder. Miss Bartlett also tells of the healing of a girl who could scarcely speak a word, healed at a service at Hawthorne Hall.

At other times a demonstration taught a lesson—for instance that Infinite Good is not limited to a particular time or place: One day Mrs. Eddy, leaving her house to call on a patient, was met on the steps by a woman and her blind daughter. They wanted Mrs. Eddy to go back in the house and treat the daughter. Mrs. Eddy maintained God could heal right there. The girl's eyeballs were white. As Mrs. Eddy watched she saw the eyeballs begin to clear up a little on the right side. The free part gradually enlarged until the eyes were completely cleared and the girl could see perfectly.

Mrs. Eddy showed us that no need is too humble to warrant our compassion. She once asked the driver of her carriage: "What is that bit of black fur under the pony's collar?" The driver explained the horse had a sore spot on his neck. When the pony was unharnessed that afternoon the sore spot was gone.

Time and again Mrs. Eddy gently pointed her students to the right path. A woman who had a strong resentment against her immoral husband was told by Mrs. Eddy that Jesus healed the Magdalene by condemning the sin, not the woman. Said the wife: "Yes, but I have not the consciousness Jesus had." Our Leader instantly rebuked this, insisting she should **claim** the Christ-consciousness, otherwise she could not heal a single case. The student's consciousness was so illumined and uplifted by what Mrs. Eddy said that her state of mind changed towards her husband. When she returned home she found him healed.

Mrs. Eddy once wrote:

We then gained the proof that the Principle or Life of man is a divine intelligence and power which when understood can heal all diseases and reveals the basis of immortality.

When students were able to understand, they healed. When understanding faltered they could turn to Mrs. Eddy. Mr. Tomlinson tells of sending his patients to watch Mrs. Eddy pass by in her carriage, and when Mrs. Eddy saw this or that patient they were healed. With engaging charm, Tomlinson declared: "This is the way I lose my patients."

We too can always turn to Mrs. Eddy, finding her in her writings, as she promised. And sometimes we will find, as Mrs. Eddy did, that there is something else we need to know in back of an accident or illness, as when Mrs. Sweet was badly hurt when she fell while inspecting the church in Concord. The students tried to help her by knowing there was no accident, no broken bones, in Mind. When Mrs. Eddy heard of it she told the woman why that would not heal her: "Because you were brought here to help me; you are one of my best workers." The trouble was only an argument to interfere with her usefulness to Mrs. Eddy. When that fact was recognized she was healed immediately.

Animal magnetism several times tried to rob Mrs. Eddy of her faithful secretary, Calvin Frye. In previous books I have told of several instances where Mrs. Eddy restored Mr. Frye after he had passed on. Henrietta Chanfrau on another occasion states, "One morning Mr. Frye was taken seriously ill, and apparently was passing on. Mrs. Eddy was told, and immediately came to his room where several of us were gathered. With calm confidence she walked straight up to where he was lying on his bed, and firmly called out, 'Calvin, rise up! They are trying to kill your Leader!" [She knew this death threat was a lethal strike aimed at her. She really depended on Mr. Frye. He was her loyal helper who for thirty years gave his all as he shielded her from annoyance and discomfort, serving her in countless ways.] Resolutely, stoutly, she repeated her command two or three times. Suddenly he sat up, looked about him and was restored immediately to health."

THE HEALING OF GEORGE KINTNER'S PATIENT

While George Kinter was a member of Mrs. Eddy's household he had as a patient a woman who drove out on several occasions for treatment of rheumatism of the knee. One day Mrs. Eddy said, "George, what is this carriage I've seen here for several days?" He answered, "That's a patient, Mother, who has been coming to see me." Mrs. Eddy asked about the case and then, impressively striking her own knee with a sharp slap with her hand, said: "George, what is this?" "That's your knee, Mother." She struck her knee again and repeated the question. He said, "That's your leg, Mother." Finally she said, "George, wake up! It's mortal mind. Now take care of that case." The patient was healed that same day.

Mrs. Eddy was here demonstrating what she wrote (S&H 397:23-28): "Mortals are no more material in their waking hours than when they act, walk, see, hear, enjoy, or suffer in dreams. We can never treat mortal mind and matter [the leg, the knee] separately, because they combine as one." Only mortal mind can see a fleshly or matter leg or knee. "Into the real and ideal man the fleshly element cannot enter" (ibid. 332:31). This is the great verity of being that we need to know in order to heal the sick.

Mrs. Eddy was knowing as Mind knows. She was being the healing Christ, the "I Am that I Am." She knew nothing was going on outside of her own being—"the Christian Scientist is alone with his own being and the reality of things." The Christ Mind she was demonstrating is the divinely subjective state of Mind that knows there is no material personality. You need facts for solid conviction. Solid conviction is the true Spirit. "Demonstration is the whole of Christian Science, nothing else proves it, or will save it or continue it with us" (*C.S. Journal*, Vol, 54, p. 156).

MRS. EDDY CONFRONTED TOTAL MATERIALISM

Why did Mrs. Eddy face so much mulish as well as venomous opposition? In teaching and demonstrating this radical new doctrine she confronted not only the establishment of her day but the whole current of modern history as it rushed toward complete materialism.

God, however, had been "graciously preparing" Mary Baker Eddy for this great and final revelation of the omnipresence of present perfection. In this "final" revelation, Mrs. Eddy—the highest visible idea in our age, "the second appearing in the flesh of the Christ"—saw "the human and divine coincidence shown in the man Jesus, as divinity embracing humanity in Life and its demonstration—reducing to human perception and understanding the Life which is God" (S&H 561:16).

Whose Life is God?

Your Life!

In this divine revelation material and corporeal selfhood disappeared, and the spiritual idea was understood.

Mrs. Eddy's energetic and masterful teaching of this divine revelation spread Christian Science around the world during her time with us. It spread because of her spontaneous demonstrations of her divine teaching, and because of the millions of seemingly miraculous healings, by her and by thousands of her students.

THE HEALING OF THE WITHERED LIMBS

The following letter from Mrs. Charlotte F. Lyon to Mrs. Eddy recounts another typical healing.

I had an uncle by marriage who was a helpless cripple and who was deformed. All his limbs were withered. On very pleasant mornings a policeman would wheel him out on Boston Commons in his wheelchair. One morning a number of years ago, he sat there in his wheel chair as you were passing through the Common, and you stopped and spoke to him, telling him that man is God's perfect child, and a few other words. Later, after you had left him, he declared you had helped him.

The next morning he looked and looked for you in the same place, and morning after morning continued to do so, until one day you came. Again you repeated to him what you had said before, and this time he was healed and made perfect,—every whit whole; and after that he was able to go into business for himself and provide his own living. No doubt you will remember the whole circumstance. His bones had hardened so that when sitting or lying down his knees were drawn up and rigid, his brother having to feed and care for him all the time; but after he was healed through your spoken word, he was able to be as active as other men and earned his own living; and whereas before he could not even brush a fly from his face, he regained the use of his hands, and became more than an ordinary penman.

It was you, dear Leader, who spoke to him of the healing Christ and set him free, when you met him so long ago on Boston Common, and many times I have desired to tell you about it, and to express to you my gratitude for the many benefits I also have received from Christian Science. Words can never express it.

With deepest love, in which my husband joins me,
Your loving student, Mrs. Charlotte F. Lyon

Although Mrs. Eddy brought to pass hundreds of such beautiful healings with the spoken word, few of those healed seem to have written her a letter of thanks. Countless healings such as this one (by her and her students) whether acknowledged or not, however, were responsible for establishing Christian Science, and spreading its message around the world in her day. When I (the author of this book) was six years old, it was healings similar to this, experienced by my parents, that instilled such a sense of gratitude in my heart that all my life I have wanted in some way to show my gratitude to Mary Baker Eddy.[1]

The spiritual idea has its visible expression. Mrs. Eddy gave us a visible demonstration of the spiritual idea, which we will one day learn to see manifest in everything about us. Under the marginal heading, "Millennial glory," Mrs. Eddy encourages:

As material knowledge diminishes [as the consciousness of corporeality is outgrown], and spiritual understanding increases, real objects will be apprehended mentally instead of materially. (*S&H* 96:27).

But "the individuality of man is no less tangible because it is spiritual and because his life is not at the mercy of matter" (*ibid.* 317:16). *The spiritual idea must have its visible expression, its incarnation, or else Christian Science is only abstraction.* **In Mrs. Eddy we see the full visible expression of the spiritual idea.** What a never-ending debt of gratitude we owe this God-like selfless woman who struggled valiantly for so long to bring us the ultimate blessing—the Second Coming of the Christ by which we finally learn **I AM ALL.** Love's kingdom is within me. Our prayer should be: **Teach me to love, to be Love.**

---

[1]This healing of my parents is told on page 112 of *Mary Baker Eddy: A New Look.* Obtainable from Bookmark or Rare Book Company.

CHAPTER 26

DEFENDING THE TRUTH
ABOUT OUR LEADER

"THE HOLY GHOST SHALL COME UPON THEE"

Mrs. Eddy's loyal students knew that the first requirement of scientific integrity was a willingness to put the demands of fact before any other convenience or commitment. Mrs. Eddy had to know the fact of present perfection in order to write the textbook. She states: "It was not myself, but the divine power of Truth and Love, infinitely above me, which dictated 'Science and Health with Key to the Scriptures'" (*My.* 114:23). It can't be stressed too much that, like Jesus, Mary Baker Eddy was predestined from all eternity to be incarnated for the purpose of fulfilling all the many scriptural prophecies concerning her advent. She would have labored in vain if, of her human self, she had tried to write the "little book" prophesied in Revelation 10:1 & 2.

Some of the students had their severest struggles from the necessity of surrendering their most deeply entrenched personal inclinations, which were at odds with divine logic, and which are the anti-Christ. "Beware of self-love," which Mrs. Eddy named as a form of the anti-Christ. "Beware of acknowledging [Infinite Good] and Its Science but all the while loving yourselves more." Mrs. Eddy healed because she got "Mary out of the way." Her dominion over the anti-Christ was fully revealed when she left Pleasant View, even though she knew moving to Boston would mean "being delivered up to her enemies," as she told Henrietta Chanfrau. She willingly laid down her life in order to share with others the Truth that had been revealed to her.

In Luke 1:35 the angel foretells: "The Holy Ghost shall come upon thee." The Holy Ghost or Divine Science comes upon each receptive heart that "studies thoroughly the letter and imbibes the spirit" of this divine Science that is "the development of eternal Life, Truth, and Love."

The angel continues:

> *And the power of the Highest shall overshadow thee; therefore also that holy thing [the Christ consciousness] which shall be born of*

thee [through the development of eternal Life, Truth, and Love] shall be called the Son of God.

The angel is talking to the Virgin Mary, but the message is also true for you and me and all humanity.

The birth of "the Son of God" in our consciousness takes place as we "ponder in thought our infinite harmonious, Christ-expressing selfhood, and claim it as true of us now—as we drink in its [present] perfection, its moral beauty, its integrity, its worth, its unspeakable safety [it's as safe as 2x2=4]. All the truth and beauty of Infinite Good's creation is yours and you [here and now]." (Substance of a letter Mrs. Eddy wrote Judge Hanna].

WHY THE TRUTH ABOUT OUR LEADER IS IMPORTANT

Naturally, you only experience your Christ Selfhood as you accept the teaching of the Second Coming of the Christ. Christian Science is founded upon perfection, upon perfect *manifested* being. It was because Jesus and Mrs. Eddy understood themselves to be the Principle that expresses itself as Life, Truth, and Love—and thus understood themselves to be the concrete manifestation of God—that they were able to demonstrate this fact, able to give proof of it.

This is the Truth about us, but if we don't see the divine Love and intelligence that animated Mrs. Eddy as the highest visible idea in our age, we can't see our own divinity, our own divine identity correctly. We must see "the second appearing in the flesh of the Christ . . ." (S&H 118:7) as a reflection of the Mind that is God, the Mind that is our Mind too.

That is why the truth about Mary Baker Eddy is so important to each one of us. Without a correct sense of its highest visible idea (the Discoverer and Founder of Christian Science) we can never understand the divine Principle (our true Mind, the divine **fact.)**

Neither Jesus nor Mrs. Eddy longed for recognition from their followers for any personal reason. No one ever lived who sought personal homage less. Their great yearning for recognition was born of their *desire that humanity might see God as Love reflected through them*—through God incarnated. They desired to show you and me that the same Love that animated them, animates us too.

DO WE LOVE GOD'S SECOND "WITNESS"?

When Judge Hanna asked Mrs. Eddy why the students weren't more grateful to her, Mrs. Eddy replied, "Because they have not grown to it." The question is: "Do we love that which represents God most, His highest idea as seen today?" (*Mis.* 336:8).

> *When Ira Knapp recognized Mrs. Eddy as God's "witness," she found in that recognition a consciousness which could be helpful to her. . . . This acknowledgment in the hearts of Christian Scientists was the foundation upon which the [true] Church must be built. Only then the gates of hell can not prevail against it. —The Destiny of the Mother Church.*

"All the people need in order to love and adopt Christian Science is a right sense of its [Discoverer, Revelator, and Founder]. It seems such a simple thing, yet today we can clearly see the harm that a *wrong* sense of its Founder has done to the prosperity of the Christian Science movement.

Mr. Wiggin once explained to a critic of Christian Science that Mrs. Eddy found a "parallelism" between herself and the woman clothed with the sun who was persecuted by the great red dragon; but he added, "it is not her personality that she supposes to be persecuted but the Truth that speaks through her."—Phare Pleigh, *Christian Science and the Bible.*

THE DRAGON PERSECUTED THE WOMAN

In Revelation 12:13-17 we read that the dragon persecuted the woman which brought forth the man child (your true divine identity). This prophecy has been abundantly fulfilled. Mortal mind's vitriolic resistance has flooded the field with false teachings—not about Christian Science or the "man child"—but about Mary Baker Eddy, that she did not represent the woman of the Apocalypse, did not fulfill scriptural prophecy, was not the "second witness," etc. Why?

Because nothing like what Mrs. Eddy was doing had ever before been done in the history of the human race. Therefore she, like Jesus before her, must be stopped. The "higher Truth [lifted] her voice, the louder error screamed," just as today, often those who don't have the facts on their side, just scream!

Sin rejects Love. Because woman was the one to see the beguiling nature of the serpent, she had to destroy it, thus incurring the enmity of the serpent. God sent her to be "an helpmeet" to Adam, to awaken him from his deep sleep, and to overcome the claims of the serpent, the hypnotism of the physical senses. Instead of supporting her, Adam was used by the serpent to oppress the helpmeet God gave him. Thus he lost her revelation; and the Judaizers of St. Paul's divine message made certain that women would be kept in bondage. When woman, "God's scribe," brought the Second Coming of the Christ, unveiling and revealing man's oneness with God, the red dragon lay in wait to attack with the lies of the serpent.

Then, as says the Bible, the dragon "went to make war with the remnant of her seed," those who love their Leader, see her place in scriptural prophecy, are obedient, and refuse to be corrupted by false teachings about her. Against these the dragon employs character assassination, secret counsel, jealousy, intimidation, ridicule, and ostracism. Mrs. Eddy said no one will ever drink the cup she drank, but that neither will anyone get to heaven without tasting the cup. We should remember this when those we trust betray that trust. "Friends will betray, and enemies will slander, until the lesson is sufficient to exalt you" (S&H 266:13).

It is against the spirituality of Mary Baker Eddy's revelation that the carnal mind directs its antagonism. One of the most vicious lies the dragon spreads about our Leader is that anyone reasonably prepared in 1866 could have been the one to discover Christian Science. This is no more true than that anyone reasonably prepared two thousand years ago could have done what Jesus did. That Mrs. Eddy's work is indeed the Second Coming of the Christ and the Wayshower is shown by the fact that the serpent began to persecute the woman when it was found impossible to destroy the Christ by crucifying the human Jesus.

From the earliest days Mrs. Eddy was maligned, scorned, attacked, and dumped on by the ecclesiastical and medical professions, as well as by faithless students. Nothing less than total selfless devotion to the cause of humanity could have sustained her as she unremittingly labored to bring scientific Christianity with its unlimited possibilities of healing and regeneration to all seekers for help and light. Unflinchingly Mrs. Eddy faced and overcame the ridicule and every form of opposition which obstructs the path and defies the purpose of the pioneer of Truth.

MRS. EDDY'S ARTICLE ON WAR AGAINST THE WOMAN

It is obvious that much of the cruelty dealt Mrs. Eddy was due to her being a woman. After all it is not so long ago that men were debating whether women had souls. Christendom has acknowledged God's manhood, but even Christian Scientists often do not acknowledge God's womanhood. In the following article in Mrs. Eddy's own handwriting, entitled "Catholicism, Protestantism, Christian Science," the warfare against womanhood is graphically depicted. (Preserved by the Carpenter

Foundation; see also *Essays & Other Footprints, p. 54)*. This handwritten article was included in my free pamphlet, *Mary Baker Eddy, Leader Forever*,[1] but because of its importance it is repeated here:

> *Each religion defined by what the words include is right; but fatally wrong and wronged in its interpretation by the world, the flesh, and the devil . . .*
>
> *The woman has cast into these three measures of iniquity, the leaven that is fermenting them. Therefore they, inherent in mortal mind, take vengeance on their destroyer . . . Not one of these three religions—misused—is the rock on which Christ, Truth, builds the church against which the gates of hell cannot prevail. And the last one, Christian Science, is named the final one; therefore it holds the MOST RELENTLESS WAR AGAINST THE WOMAN.*

✓Even in the earliest days, all but one or two forsook, scorned her in her darkest hour. "Even those I raised instantly from the dream of death would shun me in the street . . ." she states.

Mrs. Eddy had to teach her students how necessary it was to defend her. In *Precepts* IV. p. 117, she asks her workers to "Take up at once the so-called Christian Science Lecturers that they do their duty to their God and their poor unworthy Leader and friend. A city that is set on a hill cannot be hid, and the life of their Leader must be shown as it IS. Never did I neglect Jesus in my sermons in the first days of Christian Science; now they must not forget me."

Think of it, Reader. One can scarcely hold back the tears as one reads the pitiful pleas of our God-sent Leader who for forty-four years hung on a cruel cross in order to give us the truth about ourselves. Think of the tragedy—that she had to beg her students to answer vicious attacks on her, had to beg them to stand up for her and tell the world the truth about her.

Mrs. Eddy knew Christian Science would suffer if she was not defended and upheld by the students. She asked her students:

> *"Are you a Christian Scientist or not? Then take up the work and put an end to these scandalous attacks on your Leader and best earthly friend. . . . When will blind eyes see their Leader as she is?"* (DCC. 52).

---

[1]Obtainable from Mary Baker Eddy Institute, 2100 3rd Ave., #2601, Seattle, WA 98121

MRS. EDDY'S PLEA FOR OBEDIENCE TO THE MANUAL

In 1905 Mrs. Eddy sternly, with unsparing insistence, wrote the Directors:

> *If the Publication Committees neglect their duties, so plainly stated in the By-Laws of the Mother Church, they alone must be responsible for it, or our Cause at the very hour of its triumph will go down. I say this prophetically. The Manual of our Church requires the Publication Committees to defend Christian Science AND ITS LEADER. I have laid myself on the Altar for you and all, for almost forty years! I can no longer bear the strain. The officers who are salaried and responsible to God for performing their offices must do it. I can no longer do it for them.—(Seventh Day, p. 313).*

This doesn't mean that only the Committee on Publication can defend Mrs. Eddy, it means <u>all</u> Christian Scientists should energetically, vigorously, intelligently defend their Leader as St. Paul steadily, unwaveringly defended Jesus. But today many in high places in the Christian Science movement are both subtly and openly leading the sheep away from the truth about our Leader, and failing utterly to defend her, even though they sometimes prate effusively with forked tongue, **about** defending her.

WHY SHOULD WE DEFEND OUR LEADER?

Why should we defend our Leader? Because she is one with what she revealed. We find her only in her writings. Her life was the life-link to reality. It spoke the language of Spirit. It gave her mission spiritual sense. Through her the Word became flesh—i.e. was made understandable to us. This is why we can never love her enough. We could start by obeying *the estoppels in her Manual*. They were written out of her love for us. Continuing disobedience to these estoppels shows a total lack of love for our Leader.[2]

To terminate material organization was Mrs. Eddy's only reason for writing the *Manual*. She knew continued material organization would be the death-blow to spiritual growth—would make everything she wrote "nothing but lifeless words." When the Directors disobeyed the *Manual* it became a serpent, evil. We should obey the *Manual, as she wrote it,* and should expose those who paid lawyers to interpret the sacred *Manual,* according to human law, thus waiving all conditions requiring her con-

---

[2]The subject of obedience to Mrs. Eddy's *Manual* has been covered in my two books on the Manual. Obtainable from Rare Book Company or The Bookmark.

sent and approval. Abandoning Mrs. Eddy's estoppels has brought the great Christian Science movement to its knees, and all but stopped its healing ministry.

We need to be active in defending our Leader. Explaining to a promising student that he could not in reality suffer for defending her, but only rise higher, she said:

> *Everyone that stands by me and is governed by God [infinite good], the divine Principle of his work, will experience from the influence of Satan trying him just what you are experiencing. It is only the influence of malicious mesmerism, the influence of a lie. Now remember, dear, your cardinal points in Science: viz., a lie is never true; that Truth and Love are your only Life, substance and intelligence, or Mind, and you cannot lose your true Mind any more than God can. You cannot suffer for defending me, which is acceptable in God's sight.* (DCC 89).

We know that Love exists, so hatred and injustice do not exist except as illusions or as hypnotic suggestion.

> *"In warfare with error, you attack with intent to kill, and the wounded or cornered beast bites you if he can; the sin you assail turns on you and succeeds in getting the world to condemn you that it may justify itself"* (First ed. p. 368).

Be bold in what we stand for but careful in what we fall for. Telling right from wrong is not all that hard. The hard part is overcoming laziness and cowardice to do what one perfectly well knows one should. Let us, as the proverbial "remnant," (though now "small and very feeble," as Isaiah prophesied) continue to do the best we can to uphold the hands of her who represented the Woman of the Apocalypse, and was the Revelator to this age.

Mrs. Eddy has shown us how to surmount every attack. During her lifetime with us, the attacks on her (which time and again looked as though they would destroy Christian Science or her Cause), were always dissipated, completely overcome, and each time served to prove that Christian Science is the Christ in its full and final appearing through her who represented the woman of the Apocalypse. Through **living** Love she vaulted and vanquished scorn and persecution, triumphantly overpowering each obstacle that beset her forward steps. Following her we shall do the same.

STUDENTS' LACK OF LOVE FOR MRS. EDDY
GREATLY HARMS CHRISTIAN SCIENCE HEALING

"Why is there so little healing in the Christian Science movement today?" students ask. Mrs. Eddy reminded us that "the truth in regard to your Leader heals the sick and saves the sinner." It is obvious, from the lack of healing, that "the truth in regard to [our] Leader" is not reaching mankind.[3]

While Mrs. Eddy was with us, and incessantly dogged by evil adversaries, she consistently pulled victory from the jaws of defeat—always coming from behind as the victorious underdog in every battle. She was well aware that the Number One priority of the anti-Christ would be to bury her. As the Discoverer, Revelator, Founder, demonstrator and Leader of Christian Science, she became the main target in her lifetime; and she knew that after she was no longer personally present to do the required spiritual realization, the enemy's campaign to destroy all memory of her would be stepped up.

She saw exactly what St. Paul "with tears" warned of in Acts 20:28-31 when he said:

> *Take heed therefore unto yourselves, and to all the flock, over the which the Holy Ghost [the development of Life, Truth, and Love] hath made you overseers, to feed the church of God . . . For I know this, that after my departing shall grievous wolves enter in among you, not sparing the flock.*
>
> *Also of YOUR OWN SELVES shall men arise, speaking perverse things, to draw away disciples after them. Therefore watch, and remember. . . I cease not to warn every one night and day with tears.*

This is exactly what happened in the Christian Science movement, as St. Paul says: "of your own selves" meaning apostate students among you, the harm would be done. Perverse speaking, disloyal students would "draw away disciples after them." No attacks from outside the Christian Science movement could hurt it. But as Mrs. Eddy realized and said, "My own students have done the most good and the MOST HARM." The harm was done by those who failed to see that she had fulfilled Jesus' prophecy of the Comforter, and St. John's prophecy of the Woman of the Apocalypse.

---

[3]To counter this, I recently sent out a ninety-page booklet, entitled: "Mary Baker Eddy, Leader Forever," in a strong defense of our Leader. This booklet was later reduced to 44 pages for much wider distribution. Booklet and pamphlet are still available, free, from the Mary Baker Eddy Institute.

WHAT INJURES OUR CAUSE MOST?

Mrs. Eddy's *Manual* plainly states that members of the church should defend themselves against aggressive mental suggestion and NOT BE MADE TO FORGET NOR TO NEGLECT THEIR DUTY TO GOD, TO THEIR LEADER, and to mankind."

On Jan. 25, 1902, Mrs. Eddy wrote her Board of Directors:

> *Nothing could injure our Cause more than the general silence that prevails on the topic of your Leader's character. [When the most vicious lies were published about Mrs. Eddy, her Board, the Lecturers and others responsible issued only the mildest of protests and reproaches, if any.] This silence is causing the press to publish Peabody's lies, for it looks as if the Board of Lectureship is ashamed to speak in defense of your Leader, or has nothing to say in her behalf! Pass this By-Law and publish it in the next Sentinel, and I will write to the members of the Board to do their duty.*

The By-Law stated:

"It is the duty of the Board of Lectureship to include in each lecture a true and just reply to public topics condemning Christian Science and bear true testimony to the facts pertaining to the life and character of our Pastor Emeritus."

One can hardly hold back the tears when one reads the shabby treatment accorded Mrs. Eddy by even some of her best students in high places, as she heart-renderingly implored them to defend her. For instance, she found it necessary to write Kimball, "For the world to understand me in my true light and life, would do more for our Cause than aught else could. This I learn from the fact that the enemy tries harder to hide these two things from the world than to win any other points. Also Jesus' life and character in their first appearing were treated in like manner. And I regret to see loyal students are not more awake to this great demand in their measures to meet the enemy's [ruthless and sinister] tactics."

Mrs. Eddy knew that if Jesus had not been remembered in honor, the great glorious work he did and is still doing for mankind would have been lost and forgotten long ago.

Even the super-loyal Judge Hanna had to be reminded that "Keeping the truth of her character before the public will help the students, and do more than all else for the Cause." Today, as the Christian Science movement lies almost in ruins, we can see what NOT keeping the truth of her character before the public has done to the movement and its healing mission. "Christianity in its purity was lost by defaming and killing its defenders. Do not let this period repeat that mistake. THE TRUTH IN REGARD TO YOUR LEADER HEALS THE SICK AND SAVES THE SINNER. The lie has just the opposite effect. [As loyal Christian Scientists have learned] the evil one that leads all evil in this matter knows this more clearly than do the Christian Scientists in general."

WHAT THE UNITED PLAN OF THE EVIL DOERS IS

Further she wrote Judge Hanna: "The united plan of the evil doers is to cause the beginners either in lecturing or teaching or in our periodicals to keep Mrs. Eddy as she IS (what [Infinite Good] knows about her and revealed to Christ Jesus [concerning her], out of sight." She warned against keeping her "as she is NOT (just another white-haired old lady) constantly before the public. This darkens the spiritual sense of students and misleads the public. It misstates the ideas of the divine Principle that you are trying to demonstrate and hides it from the sense of the people."

Today we don't hesitate to defend Jesus. Mrs. Eddy made it clear that it was just malpractice that made Christian Scientists think they did not need to defend their Leader. Malpractice of this sort dominates today as Mrs. Eddy warned.

"If Christian Scientists are not awake and alert to the necessity of defending their Leader, it will hold back Christian Science for centuries."

We can see how this failure to defend Mary Baker Eddy has held back Christian Science in the latter half of this century, and almost wiped out the wonderful healing that was done in Mrs. Eddy's time and for several decades following her sojourn with us as it was swept along on the momentum she had generated.

Every genuine self-respecting Christian Scientist will defend Mary Baker Eddy, our Leader, just as St. Paul defended Jesus in the synagogues and everywhere, preaching his place in prophecy, well-knowing it might cost him his life, as it finally did. In a wonderful lesson to her household Mrs. Eddy explained that "our whole salvation rests upon the manner in which we treat her, since the way comes to us through her" (*DCC p. 100:14*).

As she stood alone, with an utterly sublime courage resting on God, it was Mrs. Eddy's Christ character that enabled her to complete her God-appointed mission. Her humanity, honesty, affection, compassion, hope, faith, her absolute trust in Truth, her meekness, brought understanding, expressed in "wisdom, purity, spiritual understanding, spiritual power, love [that alone is Life], health, holiness" (S&H 115:26-116:3).

As the second of "two anointed ones" she was destined to "compass" and bring forth the stone (the womanhood of Christ Jesus) that had been rejected. Science and Health teaches us that Woman—the stone which the builders rejected (Psalms 118:22 & Matt. 21:42-45) is generic. Generic here means that Infinite Good is everywhere present and embraces the whole world. This is what Mrs. Eddy's thought did—it embraced the whole world when, for instance, she sent spiritual instructions to the daily newspapers. **"The foundation stone, even the stone rejected, is Love. We can build on none other"** (Mary Baker Eddy, *Misc. Doc. 205*).

"Though error hides behind a lie and excuses guilt, error cannot forever be concealed. **Truth, through her eternal laws, unveils error"** (S&H 542:5). The womanhood of Christ Jesus, "the stone which the builders rejected," was compassed by Mary Baker Eddy in the Second Coming of the Christ. Then "Truth, through her eternal laws [unveiled] error." When it is seen that Mrs. Eddy stands for the complete revelation of the Christ, **Truth,** within human consciousness—when it is seen that she made practical the kingdom of **Truth** within our consciousness— healing in the Christian Science movement will again flourish. "The promises will be fulfilled."

The enemies' tactics are to confuse the issue regarding the human person and the divine idea. Recently the main attack on Christian Science, directed as usual against Mary Baker Eddy, has been disguised as an attack on the Bliss Knapp book. This story with its enormous legacy, suddenly filling the airwaves with rumors and causing T.V. camera crews to lurch into action, has had legs. It has served a useful purpose in giving world-wide publicity to Mary Baker Eddy's holy mission, alerting loyal Christian Scientists to be ever more watchful concerning "the jaws of hate," as they go "out through the door of Love, on to the blest above" marching with "the one hundred" (*Mis.* 106:11).[4]

SHAMEFUL ATTACKS ON MRS. EDDY CONTINUE

"Throughout history, the most common debilitating ailment has been cold feet." But genuine Christian Scientists are not afraid to defend their Leader.

Each day the issue of Mrs. Eddy's place in Bible prophecy becomes more important as the Second Witness—the "Comforter" promised by

---

[4]*The Student's Reference Dictionary* defines "one hundred" as a complete circuit or series.

Jesus to bring the Second Coming of the Christ—is realized as having been fulfilled. It was fulfilled when Mrs. Eddy brought the "little book" revealing our true identity as one with Infinite Good. Mrs. Eddy knew healing in the Christian Science movement would flourish only in proportion as "the world understood her in her true light and life." She explained: "The truth in regard to your Leader heals the sick and saves the sinner."

Today the main attack on Christian Science is still against our Leader, and it is coming from those in high positions within the Christian Science movement. They refuse to admit Mary Baker Eddy brought the Second Coming of the Christ, and so fulfilled the many scriptural prophecies concerning "the woman," just as the Virgin Mary, in the flesh, fulfilled the prophecy concerning her; and Jesus, in the flesh, fulfilled the prophecies of his coming.

As we march forward to confront error, the truth about our Leader is our surest weapon. Remember: "It is only by laying bare the atrocities and malicious mental malpractice, that the human race can be saved from bondage . . ." (MBE to Clara Shannon}.

Listen to her plea: "This evil is here. It is being practiced now. What shall we do about it? Shall it be ignored? Or shall it be exposed and destroyed? Meet it! Expose it! No matter what it may cost you. . . . My students have not had the moral courage to meet these malicious thoughts and expose them, but have allowed me to be the only mouthpiece against them. Through the consciousness of the Allness of [Infinite Good] you must see the nothingness of this claim of error" (*Documents,* p. 96).

Why did Mrs. Eddy for forty-four years hang on the cross of the world's hostility and ingratitude?

She did it out of love for you and me and for all humanity. She did it in order that we might awaken from the hypnotism that has since time began held us in bondage to a matter body. She patiently persevered so that you and I might gain our birthright of freedom from enslavement to the testimony of the five physical senses, and learn of our present perfection. Christian Scientists love her because she first loved them.

No person can take the individual place of the Virgin Mary. No person can fulfill the individual mission of Jesus of Nazareth. No person can take the place of the author of Science and Health, who demonstrated the human and divine coincidence, and whose writings—in the Second Coming of the Christ—will bring about the realization of the divinity of humanity.

Mrs. Eddy *lived and proved* what she wrote. She *wrote what she lived and proved.* She and her words are inseparable, and therefore we find her in her writings. It is up to us to acknowledge her.

Science and Health tells us that "without a correct sense of its highest visible idea [Mary Baker Eddy] we can never understand the divine Principle." Her life of Love was the life-link to our understanding of our divine Principle, Love. Who illustrated the divine Principle? Mary Baker Eddy. Who made you aware that you and the divine Principle are one? Mrs. Eddy. Mary Baker Eddy demonstrated that she and the divine Principle were one, else how could she have written Science and Health? Remember she spoke of: the "little Book that our heavenly Father has written through me for you and for all mankind." How could she have fulfilled scriptural prophecy by bringing the Second Coming of the Christ, the Comforter promised by Jesus unless she and the divine Principle were one? Demonstrating that she and the divine Mind, the divine Principle, were one, she showed us **we** could demonstrate it too. We only have to *learn* our Principle, Love; but to do this we must have an unclouded view of our life-link, the Mind of Mary Baker Eddy.

We can see that attacks on the Discoverer, Founder, Revelator, and Leader of Christian Science are not only attacks on the Cause itself, but are also attacks on each individual Christian Scientist. The only attacks that harm the Cause of Christian Science are the attacks that come from inside the movement, from so-called students of Christian Science, especially those in high places who fail to see Mrs. Eddy's place in scriptural prophecy, and so fail to obey her *Manual estoppels.*

How many occupying higher positions in the movement today see that healing will continue to diminish until a true sense of its Founder is gained? Mrs. Eddy knew the only way Christian Science healing would prosper was for the world to understand her in her true light and life. That is why we must defend her.

CHAPTER 27

WHY MRS. EDDY HID HER TRUE IDENTITY

A TIME TO KEEP SILENT

The question is asked: Why didn't Mrs. Eddy come out more openly in her classes, in the periodicals, and with the students in her home, with regard to her fulfillment of scriptural prophecy?

She had two important reasons; both concerned with protecting Christian Science.

Her first reason was to avoid a cult of personality which would derail Christian Science. When Mrs. Eddy was asked "to answer for [herself], 'Am I a Second Christ?'" she immediately saw it as an attempt to deify a mortal personality as some religions have deified the human Jesus. She would have none of it! She said even the question shocked her. "I always explain Christ as the invisible and never corporeal. Jesus was a man corporeal. Christ was, is, and forever will be . . . the spiritual idea of God. I am corporeal to the senses, even as Paul was. But God has anointed me to do His work, to reveal His Word, to lead His people" (Letter to Stetson, dated Dec. 17, '00).

Her enemies, however, would twist Mrs. Eddy's Art. VIII, Sect. 3 of the *Manual* (which said "Careless or irreverent reference to Christ Jesus is abnormal in a Christian Scientist") to prevent any equating of Mrs. Eddy's work on earth with that of Jesus, when actually the *Manual* article referred to the poor judgment of a C.S. Lecturer. (See Vol. 17, p. 77 of *The Christian Science Journal*).

Her second reason was to shield Christian Science in its infancy, from the merciless attacks of an antagonistic world. Mrs. Eddy knew what had happened to Jesus when he openly proclaimed his true identity as one of the two witnesses, when he acknowledged that he and God were one and the same, that his own Mind was God.

When Jesus stood before Pilate and "answered [him] nothing" he demonstrated for all Christendom that there were times when silence has the loudest voice. "And Pilate marveled" (Mark 15:4 & 5). Mrs. Eddy knew the scorn and ridicule that would be heaped upon her, to the harm of Christian Science, if she openly proclaimed that she represented the God-crowned woman in the Apocalypse, and that she was one of the two witnesses prophesied in the Bible. ***Still she made it clear in the 16th to the 50th editions of Science and Health, that she fulfilled St. John's prophecy of the Woman in the Apocalypse.*** In these early editions she speaks of the "bride coming down from heaven, grown impersonal and wedded to <u>Wisdom</u>," with a capital W, signifying God. Wisdom means unfoldment from within her own (and your own) consciousness. "Bride: Purity and innocence, conceiving man in the idea of God"—Mrs. Eddy's God-Mind conceived man in the idea of God. In these editions she makes it clear that she is fulfilling Revelation XII, and bringing the "little book" prophesied in Revelation X.

But when hatred became intense concerning the issue of Mrs. Eddy's place, Wisdom told her to hide the truth about herself. So in later editions she veiled this fact. Even so, in the end, Mrs. Eddy paid with her life for her spiritual teaching, when her own students in high places were responsible for her "mental murder."

Mrs. Eddy wrote: "Science and Health makes it plain to all Christian Scientists that the manhood and womanhood of God have already been revealed in a degree through Christ Jesus and Christian Science, His two witnesses" (*My.* 346:29). **In giving this statement to the Associated Press (May 16, 1901), Mrs. Eddy wisely avoided revealing that *both Christ Jesus and Mary Baker Eddy are God's two witnesses. The truth about the woman was kept "secret from the foundation of the world." Mrs. Eddy knew this "secret" must be told at the right time, but while she was still with us was <u>not</u> the right time for this fact to be published openly, as we can, must, do today. Mrs. Eddy, as the Revelator to this age, cannot be divorced from scriptural prophecy, or we reduce her celestial Discovery to just another of the many forms of Protestantism of the last several hundred years.***

Today we find no difficulty in connecting Jesus with Christianity. There had to be a person to symbolize the living truths of Christianity. And the time will come when there will be no opposition to connecting Mrs. Eddy with Christian Science. Her demonstration of generic man— the everywhere present image and likeness of God—"the coincidence of God and man as the divine Principle and divine idea" (S&H 561:23) will be understood. She will be recognized as the symbol of Christ, Science.

Mrs. Eddy is the highest symbol of Christian Science. In mathematics we do not keep the symbol hidden. **To separate the symbol and the ideal concept in the human realm is to destroy the bridge to the acceptance and understanding of Christian Science.**

THE WOODBURY TRIAL

The Woodbury Trial in 1899 has been used to challenge Mary Baker Eddy's identity as the woman of prophecy.

Christian Scientists familiar with the Woodbury trial know that Mrs. Eddy considered the trial a cosmic struggle. Mrs. Woodbury, jealous of Mrs. Eddy, coveting her place, schemed to bring about her downfall. She instituted a lawsuit hoping it would cause Mrs. Eddy to admit at the wrong time, in the wrong way, and before the wrong court of law, that she fulfilled the prophecy of the woman in the Apocalypse, God's "second witness."

Our Leader saw Mrs. Woodbury "as both the instrument and the symbol of entrenched materialism. She saw the suit as a test case. It involved: Did Mrs. Eddy mean that Mrs. Woodbury personally was the Babylonish woman? This, of course, brought up the question of Mrs. Eddy's being the Woman of the Apocalypse.

Because of all that was involved at that time, Mrs. Eddy discouraged her students from admitting they knew she represented the Woman of the Apocalypse. Even Kimball, who certainly realized Mrs. Eddy represented the Woman, skirted the question when asked by the press concerning it, because he sensed the evil afoot to ensnare him and harm Mrs. Eddy.

Kimball was seeking to protect Mrs. Eddy at a crucial time in Christian Science history. He was well aware of Mrs. Eddy's warning that "in metaphysics we learn that the majority of mortal opinions outweigh the minority, therefore a wise, honest, and skillful metaphysician casts not pearls before those who trample upon them. . . . This illustrates that saying of our great Exemplar, to war not with ten thousand against twenty thousand (Luke 14:31)."

To shield and defend Mrs. Eddy and the cause of Christian Science, Kimball simply stated that Mrs. Eddy did not "teach" she was the woman of the Apocalypse. He was speaking the literal truth. She didn't teach it because it was not the right time for that truth to be taught.

Though the court ruled in favor of Mrs. Eddy on all points, the case left confusion and doubts in its wake. Unfortunately those Christian Scientists who have been led astray to believe Mrs. Eddy does not represent the woman of the Apocalypse are using the press interview with

Kimball as proof of their position. They are wrong. Mrs. Eddy's reluctance to pronounce herself the woman of the Apocalypse was based on other factors than the truth of that claim.

In the following notice which appeared In The Christian Science Journal of August, 1890 (Vol. VIII, p. 193), Mrs. Eddy protests articles that had been proclaiming that she represented the woman of the Apocalypse and that she was fulfilling scriptural prophecy. Note that her disclaimer says nothing about the truth of the assertions, rather it questions **THE APPROPRIATENESS OF BRINGING THEM FORTH AT THAT TIME:**

> *Mr. Editor:- The late articles referring to me in the July issue of the* **Journal***, contain presentiments that I object to having uttered or written* **NOW** *in regard to myself. God alone appoints the befitting path and place for each of His children; and mankind should wait on Him, and* **let the ages declare judgment. It is my impression that at least a half century will pass away before man is permitted to render his public verdict** *on some of the momentous questions that are now agitating the world.*

JUDGE HANNA'S ARTICLE

A communication between Mary Baker Eddy and Judge Hanna in 1898 clearly shows her understanding of her identity and of the issues involved in revealing it.

Judge Hanna had seen that Isaiah 53 was a prophecy of Jesus and the First Coming, and that Isaiah 54 was a prophecy of the Second Advent, and had written an article, *"A Prophetic Vision,"* concerning it.

Mrs. Eddy recognized it at once as "wonderful." She knew that infinite Love had inspired him to say what was in the article, but that it would be animal magnetism to shout it abroad at THAT time. Apparently she would have liked to have had it as the lead article and wrote him: "Your vision article is too grand, TRUE, to be tampered with. . . . I want it where all will catch sight of it."

But she also wisely cautioned against casting pearls before the unprepared thought, writing him: "The time has not yet come in which to say the wonderful things you have written . . . unless you qualify them." "Now you may hold your ground as therein, but do not say blandly that I represent the SECOND APPEARING of the Christ [even though she knew she did], because that assertion will array mortal mind against us, and malicious animal magnetism has put it into your mind to say it." Mrs. Eddy knew who she was and what God had dictated. She knew that INFI-

NITE LOVE [HAD] INSPIRED HIS VISION, though not his choice of words. "Now, be wiser than a serpent. Throw out your truths not as affirmations or protestation, but as suggestions. Then you catch your fish, and make the wrath of man praise Him."

With such sage advice it might have been possible to reword the article so its inspired perception could begin to open people's eyes. However, the cruel Woodbury suit arose about this time. It was therefore deemed wisdom not to publish Hanna's "grand" article.

In the face of the merciless virulence of this trial it is easy to see Mrs. Eddy's wisdom in evading the question concerning her place in prophecy—in always gracefully side-stepping the issue. She knew the storm of antagonism, of envy, jealousy, and hatred it would generate, and the harm to herself and to the cause of Christian Science if she boldly proclaimed *what she knew she was*. But hidden away in her last book, *Christ and Christmas*, in a coded message, she tells future generations— those who today have eyes to see—who she is, as metaphysically and spiritually one with Jesus. She knew she was fulfilling Jeremiah's prophecy that "a woman shall compass a man [compass the teachings of Christ Jesus]."

Mrs. Eddy understood what Samuel Greenwood relates in *Footsteps of Israel:*

> *It soon became apparent that the spirituality of the new religion [Christian Science] came too strongly in conflict with the passions and appetites of men, to find a smooth and unobstructed course. History records that every effort to exalt the spiritual above the material has been viciously opposed by the animal nature of mortals. The natural outcome of practicing Jesus' teaching [as in Christian Science] would be the subjugation of sensuality, and mankind generally have not yet found themselves ready to undertake this; hence the resistance which every spiritual movement has encountered not only from its open antagonists, but from the materiality of its own professed adherents.*

Again: *"It is clear that a proper resolution of the present situation in Boston is wholly dependent upon the attitude of Christian Scientists to their Leader and her provision for the evolution and government of the Christian Science movement under its divine Principle, Love."* —A COMPENDIUM, published by Trustees of Christian Science Foundation, Cambridge, England. (*A free copy may be obtained by writing to:* **Christian Science Foundation, P.O. Box 440, Cambridge CB4 3BH, England, U.K.**)

Mrs. Eddy knew that she need not, indeed should not be proclaimed and exalted in her own lifetime. Foreseeing that all would one day be made plain, she wrote: "When Christian Science and animal magnetism are both comprehended, as they will be at no distant date, it will be seen why the author of this book has been so unjustly persecuted and belied by **wolves in sheep's clothing**" (S&H 104:3).

Writing this, she had to know that it was those she trusted who would turn against her. Looking back today we see that it was indeed so. It would be "wolves in sheep's clothing" in high office in the Mother Church—hypocrites, panting for power and craving authority, determined to disobey the *Manual's estoppels*—whose disobedience would bring the end of her sojourn with us and the decline of the Christian Science healing mission. Mrs. Eddy foresaw that it would be her own students— those who *failed to see her as the woman of scriptural prophecy, who would wage "the most relentless war against the woman."*

OLD THEOLOGY THE MOST BITTER ENEMY

From dire experience Mrs. Eddy had learned, and firmly declared:

"Old theology was the most bitter enemy of all the schools Truth had to fight. It crucified the hardest—worse than medicine. Christian Science had to be revealed by a woman [by patience and unquenchable Love]. If it had been revealed by a man it would have been lost."—Mary Baker Eddy *(A Carpenter Foundation item).*

In order to teach mortals that their real being is God, infinite good, Mrs. Eddy stood alone. Her divine discovery cut sharply across many accepted standards of thought and conduct, and challenged mankind to higher issues. With sublime and unmatched courage she faced the entire world's antagonism and ignorance. Heroically, with incredible fortitude, she met the whole entrenched belief of life in matter that seemed to concentrate itself in opposition to her discovery when she began communicating to the world what the light of revelation had poured into her searching heart. Two thousand years ago the Pharisees had warned the people to beware of Jesus, contemptuously calling him "this fellow." In the harsh, cruel treatment Mrs. Eddy received, we see history repeating itself.

When Judge Hanna first came to Christian Science he was like a kid who has just been given the keys to a video-game store. Enthusiastically he wrote Mrs. Eddy: "My cross is light!" She took him a step further to prepare him for the way that lay ahead:

You will find the cross is light—and sometimes heavy. Both condi-tions are the weight we, not God, give it. Jesus said, 'My burden is light,' yet he fainted under it."

How many times did Mrs. Eddy faint under the weight of the cross she bore for forty-four years? We glimpse her struggle in her description: "Physical torture affords but a slight illustration of the pangs which come to one upon whom the world of sense falls with its leaden weight in the endeavor to crush out of a career its divine destiny. [Here again we see Mrs. Eddy was well aware that, like Jesus, she had been predestined to bring salvation to the world] . . . Love bruised and bleeding, yet mounting to the throne of glory in purity and peace, over the steps of uplifted humanity—this is the deep significance of the blood of Christ. Nameless woe, everlasting victories, are the blood, the vital currents of Christ Jesus' [and of Mary Baker Eddy's] life, purchasing the freedom of mortals from sin and death" (*No.* 34:14).

DR. EDDY'S DEATH, THE PRICE SHE PAID

For the price Mrs. Eddy paid we need only look at the sorrow that engulfed her when malicious animal magnetism took Dr. Eddy from her, as related in Hugh Studdert Kennedy's *Mrs. Eddy:*

"Funeral services were held in the house on Columbus Avenue. . . . But Mrs. Eddy did not go. Neither did she go to the memorial services, . . . She almost sank under the load. Her students rallied as well as they could, but they were badly shaken, and only the most faithful really stood by her in her hour of trial. One of these was Arthur Buswell. . . . who, in response to a call from Mrs. Eddy, hurried to Boston. . . . He took charge of things and brought some semblance of order and calmness out of the chaos which followed Mrs. Eddy's withdrawal. He saw at once that the first thing to do was to get her away from it all as completely as possible. He finally persuaded her to accept an invitation for herself and a com-panion, Miss Alice Sibley, to spend the next few weeks or months at his old homestead in the small country town of Barton, Vermont.

"And so they set out, leaving the faithful Julia Barlett and Mrs. Abbie Whiting to care for what was left to care for in the big house on Columbus Avenue.

[But was this bitter experience in our Leader's life animal magnetism, or was it Love, wounding to heal? Was it Infinite Good decreeing it was time for her to lean on Infinite Good alone however painful it seemed? Only someone who has lost the one nearest and dearest can in a measure feel the grief, the ache, the longing, she experienced in this "greatest of all earthly bereavements." And yet it was not animal magnetism, but divine Love saying, "Ye have need of all these things" (*Mess. '02.* 19:21)].

"The road back was a long one and the way dark enough: 'Oh, I have nothing left me of earth or on it to love, as I do love, satisfied to have solitude and toil if only I had one to call my own! I cannot feel much interest in anything of earth. Long after I shall smile and appear happy shall I have to struggle alone with my great grief.' So she wrote to two of her students in Boston, even though she found solace in the conviction, Yes, we shall know each other there; we shall love and be loved; we shall never lose our identity; we shall find it more and more in its order, beauty, and goodness.

"But it was a fight to the finish, and she never really gave in for a moment. . . . After a night of agony, she would emerge from her struggle with a radiant face and luminous eyes, and they would hesitate to speak to her for fear of disturbing the peace that enveloped her.

"It was her last great struggle with threatened failure and defeat before turning into the road which was to lead on to continuous success. In the summer of 1882 she descended into the depths, but before the summer was over she had planted her feet firmly on the ascending path. From there, and then on, she moved in only one direction and that was upward."

Mrs. Eddy knew it was maliciously directed animal magnetism—by the mesmerists that aimed to overthrow her divine system—that caused Dr. Eddy's death. She states: "The loss of our husband was the resurrection morn over [this] night of silent crime. It rent the veil of sin, and we saw for the first time the full remedy for even this directed envenomed barb of sin, and it fell from the quiver of malice powerless before us. We can now teach every Christian student the practical power of divine Science over all mesmerism . . ." (*Items* p. liii-liv). Mrs. Eddy had seen that all death is mental murder. Even when one dies under medical law, it is mental suicide, mental murder. Disease never kills anyone. It is fear that kills him. Mesmeric poison mentally administered killed Dr. Eddy.

HOW MRS. EDDY WORKED THROUGH DIFFICULTIES

In a beautiful example of "Prayer and At-one-ment," Mrs. Eddy described how she worked through difficulties:

"There have been times in working out a problem when I have

not known just what step to take and finding it necessary to make a move of some sort, I have taken a step as nearly as I could in the right direction. Perhaps I would find out shortly that it was wrong, but this step gave me a new point of view that I would not have had, had I not taken it as I did though it seemed to be a mistake. I would not condemn myself therefore, but would include it as part of the working out of the problem.

This should encourage us not to let what we can't yet do interfere with what we can do.

Mind, Spirit, Soul, our Principle, is always there—like the sun behind the clouds—expressing, manifesting Itself. Illusion, hypnotism, alone hides Truth and Love from us. But "reason, the most active human faculty," informs the sentiments and awakens our dormant sense so that we "learn the nothingness of the pleasures of human sense and the grandeur and bliss of spiritual sense which silences the material or corporeal" thus enrichening us immeasurably. (See S&H 327:29).

HANDWRITTEN NOTE TO ADAM DICKEY

In a handwritten note to Adam Dickey, Mrs. Eddy instructed:

"Remember that the so-called human mind is expected to increase in wisdom until it disappears, and divine Mind is seen to be the only Mind" (*Memoirs of Mary Baker Eddy, by Adam H. Dickey, CSD, p. 84-a*).

Another true lesson in "Prayer and At-one-ment" was given to Mr. Dickey when one afternoon Mrs. Eddy rang his bell. He writes:

I responded immediately to find her seated in a chair, dressed for her drive, painfully drawing on her gloves. She said to me, "Mr. Dickey, I want you to know that it does me good to go on this drive." Instantly she felt my questioning thought and replied, "I do not mean that the physical going for a drive does me good, but the enemy have made a law that it hurts me to go on this drive, and they are trying to enforce it, while I want you to take the opposite stand with God [infinite good] and know that every act I perform in His service does me good. I do not take this drive for recreation, but because I want to establish my dominion over mortal mind's antagonistic beliefs."

A daily drive was not a pleasure for Mrs. Eddy. She took it to refute the constant charges that she was dead or incapacitated. She knew that as long as she appeared in public every day it would satisfy mortal mind. Mr. Dickey saw the point she was making, and knowing that pessimism never wins a battle "replied to her with encouraging statements of Truth from her own book, and in a few moments every trace of the attack had disappeared."

Then Mrs. Eddy said,

> "Mr. Dickey, I want you to see what we have done. We have routed the enemy and broken the belief that it injured me to go on this drive. Now take this lesson to yourself, and whenever anything happens to you of an unfortunate nature, do not admit anything on the wrong side, but instantly declare that the experience does you good. Even if you should fall down and break your leg, get up and say, 'I am the better for this experience.' This is the Truth as God would declare it, for every attempt of evil, when surmounted and destroyed, helps the one who is attacked, and your quick and right declaration to the effect that instead of harming you it has done you good, breaks the claim of evil, and you become a law to yourself that evil cannot harm you" (*ibid.* p.86).

CHAPTER 28

MRS. EDDY BETRAYED BY HER OWN TRUSTED STUDENTS

THE HISTORY OF HER FINAL DAYS

Many have for years wondered what caused Mrs. Eddy to dictate and sign the message for every student of Christian Science to see, namely, that **"it took a combination of sinners that was fast to harm me."** What was about to unfold was a repetition of Jesus' experience. In 1903, Mrs. Eddy had told students, "It was not the material cross that killed Jesus. It was the desertion of his students." Why did "she murmur, as though lost in thought: 'If my students had obeyed me, I might have lived and carried the Cause'"? (Today you and I know—since we find her in her writings—she has "lived and [has] carried the Cause.")

Why did she insist that those nearest her tell the world she was **"mentally murdered"?** What did she mean? Why was she so anxious to have the world know this?

Like Jesus, Mrs. Eddy was betrayed by her own students—not only in 1910 _but today as well_—betrayed by those students in high places who coveted her spiritual power and questioned many of the progressive spiritual steps she took. They constantly tried to have her make the revelations and directions she got from God conform to the opinions and usages of men.

Revelation 12:12; 13; & 17 had prophesied that "when the dragon saw that he was cast unto the earth, he would persecute the woman which brought forth the man child," our true, divine identity as one with God. This prophecy was, and today still is being fulfilled in a world that is little aware of Mary Baker Eddy's divine revelation.

MRS. EDDY NOT DISTURBED BY THE ENEMY OUTSIDE

The enemy from _OUTSIDE_ did not disturb Mrs. Eddy. For instance, at the time of the "Next Friend's" suit, in a letter to McLellan, George Kinter wrote:

> I wish that you and every worker in the field of Christian Science, and indeed the whole world, might have [the] opportunity . . . of

passing through what to almost anybody else would be a great and trying ordeal; whereas she, on this very eve of the trial, is as sweetly content to let God rule as if there were nothing to disturb the water, as in reality there is not. But one needs to be at her side to realize how great is her spiritual understanding, for <u>she literally trusts God, and this is the secret of her wonderful career</u>. [It explains why she dared courageously and ventured fearlessly to challenged the whole world's wrong thinking. Awed and solemnized by the presence of a serene and beautiful spirit, redeemed by the Lord from all selfishness, she could maintain: "God is All; there is no other mind."]

For forty-four years Mrs. Eddy had met every cruel design of evil—from *outside* of her movement—to overcome her and obliterate her great revelation of man's present oneness with Infinite Good. From outside her movement no plan of the destroyer was able to overwhelm or bring an end to her God-ordained mission.

The quick, sharp and merciless stroke that led to her death had to come from within. Only from within the fold could evil strike a lethal blow at the heart of the woman sent by God to free all mankind from the slavery of their own beliefs.

BEWARE THE ENEMY WITHIN

From Mrs. Eddy Mr. Kimball learned that "the chief menace to the cause of Christian Science is to be found among Christian Scientists, and that if the movement should ever pause, it will be because of the questionable mental condition, attitude, and conduct of Christian Scientists themselves. . . . Let us not felicitate ourselves upon the supposition that it will stand and endure unless we stand and endure temptation. . . ."

Our beloved St. Paul foresaw the same problem and warned his little flock that they should "watch [for the enemy within]. By the space of three years I ceased not to warn every one night and day with tears" (Acts 20:31). Dear loyal, staunch, steadfast St. Paul. He fought the good fight and kept the faith! Despite some of his beautiful letters being spoiled by the traitorous editing of Judaizers regarding women, his own sacred teaching comes through clearly as the true, resolute, consecrated warrior for Truth that he steadfastly remained in spite of torture and imprisonment.

Mrs. Eddy was not so fortunate in some of her most eminent students. She loved Mr. Kimball dearly. He was of tremendous help in launching the movement. She corrected many of his talks, so that they became "clear, correct, teaching." His depth of character had a certain majestic kindliness, which together with his brilliant intellectual capacity and rare winning charm, drew many to him. But there was a certain flaw that caused him, on occasions, to bitterly disappoint Mrs. Eddy, as when he disobeyed her command not to cooperate with Newspapers after the 1892 World's Parliament of Religions. Later, to her great distress, he called on the Pope in Rome, presumably to talk about Mrs. Eddy and her work. An Alice Orgain letter states that when he returned from his Pope visit, Mrs. Eddy refused to see him.

We have seen how Mrs. Eddy continually struggled to keep her students on the right path. Think of the heavenly progress she could have made if she had not had a single student! To quote a gifted writer: "To envision a subject in all its scope and variety, its possibilities and urgencies, its depth and implications, and then to see all this cut down by the exigencies of classroom instruction and the limits of student comprehension—this is to long for a new language of communication, immediate, irresistible, suprapersonal." Mrs. Eddy is recorded as having said: "Oh, if only I didn't have a single student!" (Oakes, *Seventh Day, p. 94*).

THE MERCILESS STROKE FROM WITHIN

In the end Mary Baker Eddy, like Jesus—having fulfilled the scriptural prophecies concerning herself—was betrayed by her own highly-placed students. This betrayal was destined to cause a radical decline in the church. The decline was not due to circumstances or world resistance, but almost entirely to the despotic control wielded by Boston, and slavishly accepted by the field.

Having brought the Second Coming of the Christ in books where man's living unity with Infinite Good shines from every page, she could in ringing words proclaim, "I am thy deliverer." In talking with Mr. Gilbert Carpenter, Sr. he said Mrs. Eddy stressed, "The revelator and the revelation are one and cannot be separated." But her true identity was little realized by those she walked among, and to whom she made clear that as we assimilate and demonstrate the truth of her writings, this truth shows us our present divinity—shows us our oneness with Infinite Good as it awakens us from the Adam dream which since time immemorial has imprisoned us in a matter body.

Mrs. Eddy never sought Leadership. In the face of the great problems given to her, she felt herself nothing. There was always a voice telling her: "Mary, take yourself out of the way and let God act through you." She knew that "to carry out [her] holy purpose [she] must be oblivious of human self" (*Mis.* 162:28).

Mrs. Eddy saw her role and its consequences. In Science and Health she had written, "If a career so great and good as that of Jesus could not avert a felon's fate, lesser apostles of Truth may endure human brutality without murmuring" (p. 40:19). Again, she wrote "I was a scribe under orders: and who can refrain from transcribing what God indites, and ought not *that one to take the cup, drink all of it, and give thanks?"*

For forty-four years Mrs. Eddy had laid her all upon the altar. With love, and a great longing to show mankind reality, she had taken "the cup," willing to drink all of it, and give thanks. Only the vision of the inexhaustible and irresistible power of good sustained her as she endured the world's venom and the human hatred of Truth. **Even today loyal students cannot come to Mrs. Eddy's defense without being shamelessly pilloried as advocates of "deification," etc.**

Speechless and alone, Mrs. Eddy had born all burdens, suffered all inflictions, endured all piercing for the sake of others. By her holy example she taught us never "to draw back from our duty of exposing error and thus causing it to be destroyed . . . whether it appears likely to harm us or the Cause of Truth." (Tomlinson, *Twelve Years,* p. 76). ". . . When my students become blinded to me as the one through whom Truth has come to this age, *they go straight down" (Sue Harper Mimms' Memoirs).* We, today, have seen this happen as the death throes stalk the once mighty Boston colossus of the Christian Science hierarchy.

MENTALLY MURDERED

A student in Mrs. Eddy's home records that she found Mrs. Eddy on her knees, praying aloud, over and over, in heart-wrenching tones: "Lord, dear Lord, keep my students straight!" Mrs. Eddy, like Jesus, knew she would be "harmed," mentally murdered, by her own students.

Statements recorded by the Carpenter Foundation, as well as in Adam Dickey's book and in other reminiscences indicate Mrs. Eddy knew the betrayal she faced.   When she was informed by a trusted student that a triumvirate consisting of Archibald McLellan, William Rathvon, and Clifford P. Smith had hatched a plot to disregard her *Manual with its By-Law estoppels* she, on November 28, 1910 (five days before she passed from our sight) dictated the following signed statement to Laura Sargent: *"It took a combination of sinners that was fast to harm me."* What is the story behind this note? Why did Mrs. Eddy instruct members of her household that, if she should die, they should tell the world that she had been mentally murdered?

Why did she, on her last carriage ride with Laura Sargent, murmur, as though lost in thought, "If my students had obeyed me, I might have lived and carried the cause?—I might have made it"? (We know she *did* make it.) Why did she tell Dr. Baker that "All the trouble I have has been with my students"?

A STUDENT'S RECORD OF THE PLOT
"The Hall of Shame"

A loyal student's record of his talks with the Board of Directors tells the sad story behind the treacherous betrayal of Mrs. Eddy by the three conspirators, William Rathvon, Clifford P. Smith, and Archibald McLellan.

The three conspirators, who all held important positions in the church, saw from *the Manual's estoppels* that they were standing on a slippery pinnacle. Their positions of great authority were threatened. The estoppels—which stated no officer of the church could be elected without Mrs. Eddy's consent—terminated the material Mother church and ended the five-member ecclesiastical Board of Directors. Why? Because the legal four-member Board (which the five-member Board would have become had they obeyed the Manual) had no power over anything except the Boston church and its property. According to the estoppels in the *Manual*, upon Mrs. Eddy's leaving, **power passed totally to the individual Christian Scientist.** There was no longer a Mother Church *organization*.

The triumvirate's plot to overthrow the estoppels, and put mankind's freedom through the shredder, thus fossilizing Christian Science, is a sordid tale that, to paraphrase Shakespeare, tells us "something is rotten in Boston." The triumvirate cast a long shadow, acting as if darkness was a blank canvas on which they could paint anything they wanted to see—not aware that something was crumbling, "leaving to rot...ruin [and rubble]" (*Peo.* 7:4) that from which something indistinct but magnificently transcendent would arise, namely a higher understanding of humanity's divinity.

THE TRIUMVIRATE'S SECRET PLAN

The record, as preserved in a trusted student's papers states that "in 1910, motivated by the false belief that Mrs. Eddy must die or be decrepit, William R. Rathvon, Mrs. Eddy's Assistant Secretary at that time, composed a secret plan to depose Mrs. Eddy and replace her with an executive committee. He recruited two other students, namely, Clifford P. Smith, First Reader of The Mother Church, and Archibald McLellan, then Chairman of the Christian Science Board of Directors."

This was not the first attempt to usurp Mrs. Eddy's position. The Board of Directors had several times petitioned her to remove the estoppels that terminated the powerful ecclesiastical five-member Board and also terminated the material Mother Church at her leaving (as no officer of the church could be elected without Mrs. Eddy's consent). But each time the Directors petitioned her to remove the estoppels, she refused. She "considered the estoppels sacred. They were dictated by God."

Those high in the movement then repeatedly **asked Mrs. Eddy to step down.** Calvin Frye's diary notes: "Judge Clarkson dined with Mrs. Eddy today and after dinner tried *AGAIN* to convince her she was mistaken and the cause was going to ruin, and men were essential to take the lead of the cause of Christian Science and assert their rights without her dictation." Just as in the early days of Christian Science, the men were attempting to kidnap her discovery so they could promote it by the world's method for their own self-advantage. The belief of male superiority was very strong in Mrs. Eddy's day. The notion that she should retire and let the men rule the Christian Science movement was most prevalent among those in high office. But as long as Mrs. Eddy was here, whenever they tried to put her out of business, she had news for them.

In answer to Judge Clarkson's urging, Mrs. Eddy, with a ring of triumph, wrote and copyrighted the famous, spirited article: "Man and Woman," which every Christian Scientist should read and study. (It is recorded in *Essays & Other Footprints, p.44*). A few months after Judge Clarkson failed to persuade Mrs. Eddy regarding male superiority, he left the movement.

Disgruntled and disillusioned at Mrs. Eddy's absolute refusal to change her *Manual* or to step aside, these men felt they now must take the power into their own hands. They decided to use Mrs. Eddy's age (approaching 90) as their weapon against her. They would tell her they would commit her to an asylum if she did not sign their proposed By-Law which would give an executive committee of three power to lead, power to supervise the Board of Directors, and power to make or change any *Manual* By-Laws as they saw fit.

Their plot to displace Mary Baker Eddy and take over was extensive and thorough. A censored 89th *Manual* had been secretly printed and made ready to ship to Reading Rooms as soon as Mrs. Eddy was no longer here to supervise. It eliminated Mrs. Eddy as Pastor Emeritus, and ominously gave the Boston Board of Directors control over branch churches, totally defeating Mrs. Eddy's plan of government by the infinite good called God.

TRIUMVIRATE REMOVES MRS. EDDY'S PICTURE FROM SCIENCE & HEALTH

Evidently their plan also, even then, included erasing all memory of Mrs. Eddy from the minds of her followers.

As detailed in my previous books, a letter by Alice Orgain states that Mrs. Eddy's picture appears as the frontispiece in all her 1910 editions of Science and Health. Why was it removed? The *Christian Science Sentinel* issued a week before Mrs. Eddy's passing on December 3, 1910, contained the following notice which is positive, irrefutable proof that Mrs. Eddy herself did not remove her picture as the frontispiece in her 1910 last edition:

> *The Christian Science textbook, "Science and Health with Key to the Scriptures." This work contains important changes and additions by the author, also a PHOTOGRAVURE PORTRAIT OF MRS. EDDY . . .*

Mrs. Orgain states she had someone ask the Boston Board of Directors if Mrs. Eddy had it removed. They answered that they did not know why or when it was removed. . . . that Mrs. Eddy must have instructed orally that it should be dropped but that they had never found anyone so instructed and no record whatsoever of its authorization for removal. . ."[1] Imagine, Reader! SUCH AN IMPORTANT MATTER! Can anyone sympathetic to Mrs. Eddy, and the Second Coming of the Christ, doubt that the removal of her picture was anything but part of the plan for her effacement at the time the Directors were ignominiously planning to be her successor?

Consider also the following: Not only was Mrs. Eddy's picture removed but all 1910 editions of Science and Health containing her picture were called in and burned, making *her* 1910 edition extremely scarce. Subsequent editions contained subtle, yet major changes stealthily obscured by illegal copyright extensions in 1934 and 1971. Had Boston's copyright not been annulled it would have imprisoned Science and Health for another 75 years. Mrs. Eddy wrote, "Christian Science is not copyrighted" (*Ret.* 76:2). The final edition contained vital, far-reaching changes, but Mrs. Eddy did not copyright it.

Among the immediate changes made in Science and Health after 1910, besides removing Mrs. Eddy's picture, was the removal of two inspiring testimonies, especially selected by Mrs. Eddy to meet specific claims of fear and sin, on pages 604 and 698. This left a blank space on

---

[1]Shortly after Alice Orgain's passing, the author purchased Mrs. Orgain's extensive Christian Science library from the Rare Book Company, and her personal and private letters.

the last page of the textbook. Late in 1911 "A Grateful Testimony" was moved to page 698; it had closed the Second Coming of the Christ with the profound words, **"from darkness into LIGHT."** Shamefully, since late in 1911, Mary Baker Eddy's great lifework was concluded on an incomplete page, with the negative sentiment: "Thus I have progressed *a little way . . .*" Revelation 22:19 warns of the "taking away" and "adding to" God's Word.

MRS. EDDY LOST HER BUFFER ON THE BOARD

Returning to the loyal student's account, the three traitors tried to enlist Judge Hanna in their plan. He promptly retorted, "If you do not immediately go to Mother and confess this plot, I will!" They refused, saying the execution of their plan was too advanced to stop.

Judge Hanna told Mrs. Eddy of the traitorous plot. Shortly after Ira Knapp heard of the traitorous scheme he passed on, and Mrs. Eddy then said, "I have lost my buffer on the Board." This statement by Mrs. Eddy gives the reader some conception of how powerful the Board of Directors had become. For approximately the last 18 years the Board alone had dealt with the field.

MRS. EDDY FOILS THE PLOT

Of course, Mrs. Eddy refused to assent to this diabolic conspiracy against her. Being put away so that the Christian Science church could be molded into a permanent tool of tyranny did not fit her or Infinite Good's plan. Trusting in divine good to guide her in taking the right steps, she took various actions to end her service on earth. On December 3, 1910, after dictating the fore-mentioned note to Laura Sargent disclosing that it had taken "a combination of sinners that was fast to harm [her]," she purposely succumbed to malicious animal magnetism.

She thus prevented herself from being forced to give power to a traitorous triumvirate to change the *Manual* or any of its By-Laws. Ultimately the *Manual* would stand. Today the world knows the 88th *Manual* is Mrs. Eddy's final one.

The traitorous plot from *inside* the movement failed to accomplish its ultimate objective to take Mrs. Eddy's place as the head of the Christian Science movement. However, the triumvirate had managed to incorporate changes in the 89th *Manual—shamefully, passing them off as Mrs. Eddy's.* These dishonest changes gave the ecclesiastical hierarchy a grim and ominous control over the branch churches.[2]

---

[2]These changes have all been listed in my two books on the *Manual*, as well as in my other books.

Their *Manual* eliminated Mrs. Eddy as Pastor Emeritus until the mid 1920's when pressure from the field restored it. *This bogus Manual has been the only one for sale since Mrs. Eddy's passing*, and has proved disastrous for the prosperity of our movement. But "this too shall pass." Today the Boston pillars, shaking in the high winds, find themselves in dire straits as more and more are **not** falling prey to their wiles and wonkish ways. However, since "a lie left to itself is not so soon destroyed as it is with the help of truth-telling" (*My.* 130:18), the all-out effort of the "remnant" is needed to do some "truth-telling."

"Why did Mrs. Eddy write the *Manual?* Perhaps Thomas Jefferson's analysis explains:

> *Many voices at the Constitutional convention in 1787 advocated leaving a great deal of "flexibility" with the central government, because after all, it would be run by decent, good people. Jefferson listened to that, and then made a statement that contains the wisdom of the ages. He understood the frail nature of man and the seductiveness of power, and said, "Let us hear no more about the goodness of man, but bind him down with the chains of the Constitution."*

Mrs. Eddy too knew that power corrupts, and said,

> *There was never a religion or philosophy lost to the centuries except by sinking its divine Principle in personality* (*My.* 117:22).

The cruel and dishonest act of putting out an altered *Manual*—this act of betrayal—temporarily defeated what Mrs. Eddy hoped to accomplish with the *Church Manual*. But we know she was correct when she wrote: "Notwithstanding the sacrilegious moth of time, eternity awaits our Church Manual, which will maintain its rank as in the past [in her time] amid ministries aggressive and active, and will stand when those have passed to rest" (*My.* 230:1). As Mrs. Eddy had told Professor Hering, "The *Manual* will save the Cause."

MRS. EDDY WAS YOUTHFUL AND VIGOROUS AT 89

We cannot doubt that Mrs. Eddy's apparent passing was intentional, and that her actions preceding it were likewise deliberate and well thought out. She gave solid evidence of being free of the claim of senility, a claim which those who wanted her out of the picture tried to lay on her. She knew she was being "mentally murdered" by the serpents and Judases she had trusted and placed in high positions. The greatest examples of victims of human resistance to Truth and the overcoming of this supreme resistance, are found in the lives of Christ Jesus and Mary Baker Eddy—the two most ardent Exemplars of living Love the world has ever known. Jesus was nailed to a cross because of what he taught, and Mary Baker Eddy was mentally murdered by those who coveted her position and authority.

The faithful student's record states Mrs. Eddy told Calvin Frye to tell the students after she was gone that her problem was not old age but a peculiar attack of malicious animal magnetism she could not defeat other than by passing on and leaving a body.

That her problem was not "old age" was testified to by the fact that she was in excellent health at the time of her death. Both the doctor and the undertaker testified to the perfect physical condition of Mrs. Eddy's earthly body. She did not die of any physical cause. The cause was mental—mental murder, which Mrs. Eddy embraced, in all its pain, for our sakes, just as Jesus embraced the crucifixion.

By passing on and departing in 1910 Mrs. Eddy accomplished her goals. She froze the *Manual* as a rod of iron. And she prevented any legal basis for taking over the Christian Science church.

With a dead body evident in 1910, a court could not make Mrs. Eddy a ward; neither could it declare her—as it certainly would have if she had ascended—a missing person, and thus give itself or others the power to lead for seven years, until she be declared dead or found. **By passing on, Mrs. Eddy had foiled a demon scheme.**

She also plainly labeled the conspirators. In speaking with Judge Hanna, she called them a "cabal." To Ira Knapp she wrote that they were a "triumvirate." The last sentence she wrote was: "God is my Life." But the second to the last words were: "It took a combination of sinners that was fast to harm me." Why was she so anxious to have the world know this? She insisted those nearest her tell the world she was "mentally murdered" to make sure the plot against her and her *Manual* would one day be uncovered so that the 88th *Manual* would be recognized as the true one and obeyed as she intended. Her *Manual* made every follower her successor. And Christian Science Societies could continue as long as needed.

Since according to the *Manual* no officer could be elected without Mrs. Eddy's consent, the material Mother Church would cease to exist. The First Church of Christ Scientist must, then for all time, be administered exactly as she had outlined, with no changes, or nullification. By making this outcome ultimately unavoidable Mrs. Eddy had triumphed.

CHAPTER 29

"WHO WAS SHE?"

WHO WAS THE WOMAN AT THE FUNERAL?

Though the body of Mary Baker Eddy would lie in state in a great funeral in the street of the great city, reminding us of God's "Two Witnesses" (Rev. 11), she would not be dead. Note:

> At the permanent burial at Mt. Auburn Cemetery, Jan. 26, 1911, newsmen looked a last time on her face. It was unchanged though seven weeks had passed since the funeral. Now the open view plate was closed forever and the casket loaded onto a hearse. Loving students, some elderly, white haired, some in the prime of stalwart manhood, walked proudly with their burden, tears unheeded streaming down their faces. Horses and men began drawing it the quarter mile to the waiting tomb. But suddenly there appeared with the procession an unidentifiable woman.
>
> Who was she?
>
> Everyone had been admitted to the high-fence-enclosed cemetery by ticket only. All identifications had been verified. And all other people had been removed by caretakers before the Eddy procession had arrived. Only men had been invited. The day was cold, not fit for a woman to be there. Newspapers finally presumed the woman was the funeral director's assistant who had seven weeks before prepared the body for burial. But the director adamantly denied that _she_ was at Mt. Auburn! The woman at the funeral was as unrecognized to all in that final cemetery procession of Mary Baker Eddy as was Jesus to Mary Magdalene when she met him, risen, beside the sepulcher of the Arimathean.

> Many witnesses attest to the fact that Mary Baker Eddy is not dead. As she says in Science and Health, p. 464:9, "Others could not take her place, even if willing so to do. She therefore remains unseen at her post, seeking no self-aggrandizement, but praying, watching, and working for the redemption of mankind."

Many earnest students of Christian Science have felt Mrs. Eddy's help and direction. Mrs. Eddy makes it clear (S&H 72:23) that good may flow from the departed to mortals. This author, in writing books on Mary Baker Eddy, has also felt our Leader's presence, guidance, and help— often in astonishing ways. Many persons have found that when they surrender themselves completely to a goal beyond themselves, **something, Someone, seems to show them the way to reach it.**

As we feel her support and guidance and meet her face to face in her writings, you and I today know she has "lived and carried the cause."

THE FIELD ALLOWS THE BOARD TO SEIZE CONTROL

The treacherous triumvirate, however, were glad enough to imagine Mrs. Eddy dead and themselves in charge. On December 4, 1910, the Christian Science Board of Directors announced to the world that Mary Baker Eddy was dead. Alfred Farlow, spokesman for the Directors, told reporters brusquely: "She just got sick and died." Then the Clerk, Dittemore, was asked what this would mean to Christian Science.

"Well," he said, adjusting his coke bottle glasses, "this is a business. The death of Mrs. Eddy means little or nothing to us, it is as though anyone of us had passed away."

From that moment an unrelenting war has been waged to discredit the woman of the Apocalypse. Need we look further for the cause of the Christian Science movement's steady decline?

When the Directors, ignoring the *Manual's* estoppels, seized control of the Christian Science movement, the field made little protest. For eighteen years while Mrs. Eddy was in "retirement"—**working night and day for the entire world's salvation**—they had looked to the Directors for leadership. The field did not realize that while they dealt solely with the Directors, Mrs. Eddy had always held a tight rein on the Board of Directors.

How tight she actually held the reins can be inferred from Frederick Dixon's account of his talk with Board member McLellan when Dixon chided Director McLellan for disobeying the *Manual's* estoppels. "McLellan answered fiercely with uncompromising candor—in unprintable language—that he had enough of obeying Mrs. Eddy while she was here, and he felt "no obligation to obey her when she [was] no longer here." He further stated, "If we had obeyed Mrs. Eddy's *Church Manual* and dissolved the church organization, we men would have been left **obeying a woman—a DEAD WOMAN! [Unthinkable!]** We could never do that."

McLellan and those who wished to rule by personality gagged at the estoppels, seeing them more as a "mandate from hell" than as the most inspired edicts since the Sermon on the Mount. McLellan, like Mrs. Eddy's publisher, William Nixon, felt it beneath him to obey a woman. He failed to see Mrs. Eddy as "Christ Mary," but he was well aware that one of the obstructions to universal acceptance of the Second Coming of the Christ was the fact that **a woman** received it and gave it to the world.

When the Ohio publisher of the *Columbus News* asked McLellan how the Board could continue in view of the *Manual's* estoppels it is not hard to image McLellan, wearing the steely grimace of a besieged general, again answering defensively: "How can we get the consent of a dead woman?" [In this he was soundly backed by the revolting insouciance of Clifford P. Smith, another of the infamous triumvirate, who was also adept at putting the best spin on their announcements]. (See Oakes: *Mary Baker Eddy's Lesson's of the Seventh Day, p. 285*).

McLellan knew he had the unthinking masses in the field behind him. It could be said of him that "he kept his heart in the drawer among the collar studs and his mind under the mattress all night long so it would have a nice smart crease in the morning, to make his position clear." Unfortunately he was not just another windbag with a voice like rolling thunder who would slink silently into history, and so **prevent** a meltdown of the field's love for their God-sent Leader.

Could anything be further from what was needed to steer our movement through the perils of the post Eddy world.

THE TRIUMVIRATE'S PLOT & THE C.S. PUBLISHING SOCIETY

A decade after Mrs. Eddy's passing, we see the further unfolding of the triumvirates's diabolical scheme: Seeking control over what would be written about Mary Baker Eddy, the Board of Directors mounted a hostile take-over of her Publishing Society, and a **great litigation** ensued. Taken to court by the Publishing Trustees, the Directors busied themselves weaving a web of innuendo and misinformation that slithered to new depths, as emissaries of the Board fanned out over the country urging the sheep in the field to write letters to the court in favor of the Directors.

Why could the Directors enlist the field to support them?

It was because during Mrs. Eddy's "retirement" to Pleasant View she had stayed in the back ground, and the field dealt solely with the Board of Directors whom Mrs. Eddy **publicly** praised. To the field the Directors were without sin and could with impunity cast stones as they saw fit. The field's loyalty to the Board was unquestioned. In supporting the self-seeking Directors they were not aware they teetered precariously over the brink of the great abyss of ecclesiastical tyranny that has always "muzzled the mouth lisping God's praise; and instead of healing, it palsied the weak hand outstretched to God" (*No.* 44:16).

At the same time the field had no contact with the Publishing Society Trustees. This explains why the field, in their letters to the Court, overwhelmingly supported the Board of Directors.

CHARLES EVANS HUGHS' STATEMENT ON HARMONY

In the Board's statement to the court against the Publishing Society Trustees, the Board fallaciously argued that harmony in the field was the overriding consideration. Charles Evans Hughs (who later became Chief Justice of the United States Supreme Court) was the attorney for the Publishing Trustees. He responded faultlessly that "there are **two conceptions of harmony.**"

A strange and solemn hush fell over the crowded courtroom as he spoke words bound to become a landmark in religious history:

> *A GOOD DEAL HAS BEEN SAID WITH RESPECT TO THE IMPORTANCE OF HARMONY. . . . BUT THERE ARE TWO CONCEPTIONS OF HARMONY. ONE IS THE HARMONY PRODUCED BY DESPOTIC POWER; THE OTHER IS THE HARMONY THAT RESULTS FROM A UNITY OF IDEAS AND COMMON VIEWS OF RELIGIOUS TRUTH. IT SEEMS TO US MOST UNJUST TO MRS. EDDY, MOST CONTRARY TO HER TEACHING, TO ASSUME FOR A MOMENT THAT SHE RELIED UPON THE EXERCISE OF THE DESPOTIC POWER [THE DIRECTORS ARE SEEKING]. . . .*

Unfortunately the outpouring support of the field for the Directors caused the court to cast their verdict for the Board, against Mrs. Eddy's Publishing Trustees, even though the court recognized the righteousness of the Christian Science Publishing Society's cause and claim, and specifically so noted. This court battle was a powerful God-sent signal alerting the field to the treachery lurking in ecclesiastical control. (See Rev. 12:12).

RULE BY PERSONALITY

Mrs. Eddy had seen that once she was gone ecclesiasticism would operate as despotic control over spiritual individuality. Therefore she had taken care to frame By-Laws so the church would be a self-dissolving symbol at her passing. But in the scramble for power after Mrs. Eddy's leaving, all principles went out the window. Ecclesiasticism's only goal now was to cobble together whatever would assure their dominance, as they saw themselves hurtling ever-closer to the cliff.

Encumbered with this ball and chain, afflicted with this baneful attitude at the helm, the Christian Science movement, after Mrs. Eddy's passing, lurched forward for several decades on the marvelous momentum she had generated. But heavily burdened with its unenviable cargo of "rule by personality" and "who shall be greatest?" the momentum could not be sustained.

Today with the benefit of hindsight and nearly a century of disastrous disobedience to the freedom-bringing estoppels, let's turn our attention to obedience, and to becoming better healers. Mrs. Eddy warned: "Concealed crimes, the wrongs done to others, are millstones hung around the necks of the wicked [of those who deprive humanity of what the Second Coming of the Christ brought, and of what the Christian Science Publishing Society was set up to do]" (*My.* 160:32).

While McLellan was editor Mrs. Eddy had deftly praised him **publicly,** but privately, she kept him on track with such periodic broadsides as: ". . . there must be better literature and more interesting, in the *Sentinel* . . . The last two issues' articles on the first pages are shockingly wanting in quality." Today she might refer to them as epochally dreary. After eighty years of ecclesiastical government by personality, Mrs. Eddy, if she were here, might well refer to the Christian Science Publishing Society as a basket case. It has not kept "abreast of the times" as she insistently admonished.

Mrs. Eddy knew the propagating of Christian Science would depend largely on the *WRITTEN WORD*. It was for this reason that she provided a Christian Science Publishing Society to facilitate the embellishing, elaborating, and treating in more "detail so infinite a theme" (S&H x:14). At the same time her *Manual* abolished—explicitly terminated—the material Mother Church organization. This cleared the way for the Church Universal and Triumphant—the "structure of Truth and Love" in our consciousness. Here Infinite Good knows itself as you and me, knows itself as the only "I," the I that I am here and now.

WHY DID MRS. EDDY CHOOSE McLELLAN?

At this point, the question might be asked, "Why did Mrs. Eddy choose McLellan when Christian Science demands "thou shalt be cleaner than Caesar's wife"? Why did Jesus choose Judas? No doubt because McLellan as well as Judas had a God-given job to do. Without McLellan's betrayal Christian Scientists might have gone on much longer without realizing their complete freedom from ecclesiastical domination.

Did Mrs. Eddy have a premonition when naming McLellan editor-in-chief of the Periodicals? She wrote him (in part):

> *. . . You are aware that an editor should be reliable in word and deed, adroit, wise, apt in discerning the public need, in rebuking the private evil and unselfish in doing it.*
>
> *Cowardice, deceit, and will without wisdom, have imposed on me tasks incredible. It is wise to protect as far as possible a Leader, instead of putting her to the front in every battle, laying her on the altar and saving themselves. I have now no relatives to defend me and my age requires some consideration after thirty-six years of constant conflict. (Oakes, Lessons of The Seventh Day, p. 32).* [McLellan's later actions show he took cruel advantage of her last sentence.]

His attitude and deeds quickly brought the abomination, the unmercifulness and oppressiveness of priestcraft, to the surface just as ten years later the Board's breaking of Mrs. Eddy's Publishing Deed of Trust alerted thousands to the evils of rule by personality. Evidently each generation must learn for itself that the stove is hot. Episodes like this may be necessary to show us that ecclesiasticism and priestcraft have no relation to Christian Science, and to think they have is to manacle oneself to a corpse.

Ecclesiasticism (priestcraft) is malpractice. Mrs. Eddy wrote:

> **God has bidden me to uncover . . . wickedness and I follow His voice. Let all Scientists aid in this work . . . I have put on paper enough to reveal criminal magnetism [which is what disobedience to her estoppel By-Laws is], and to meet its developments for time to come, when my voice will be no longer heard** (*Christian Science Journal*, Vol. VI, No. 11).

Mrs. Eddy knew that "unless malpractice is exposed by Christian Scientists, the world will be little benefited by Christian Science." **The most harmful malpractice the world has ever known has been the disobedience to Mrs. Eddy's *Manual estoppel* By-Laws. This disobedience has deprived the world in general of the teaching of the "Comforter," the Second Coming of the Christ.**

TRUTH WILL TRIUMPH

Following its take-over of the Publishing Society, the Boston hierarchy systematically used its new power to undermine Mary Baker Eddy's position. By controlling what can be written and read concerning

Mrs. Eddy it has attempted to destroy the love and veneration for her that alone enable us to rise to follow her example and to grasp the full import of her teaching.

In 1890, as before noted, Mrs. Eddy wrote: "God alone appoints the befitting path and place for each of His children; and mankind should wait on Him, and let the ages declare judgment. **It is my impression that at least a half century will pass away before man is permitted to render his public verdict on some of the momentous questions that are now agitating the world."**

In 1938 the "half century" period was up, and the archives, *Journals, Sentinels, etc.* were searched for clues to what Mrs. Eddy herself *knew she was,* to answer the question: "Whom did Mrs. Eddy consider herself to be?"[1] In 1943 the whole world was informed of what the committee of six—three incumbent editors and three retired editors of the Periodicals—had uncovered regarding Mrs. Eddy's place in scriptural prophecy. Their 57 typewritten pages recorded literally and textually "whom Mrs. Eddy *KNEW* herself to be."[2] Even the unbelievers on the panel of six were convinced.

In "the fullness of time," the irrevocable, irrefutable, and unalterable 1943 position of the church was proclaimed in the Christian Science periodicals, that Mrs. Eddy did indeed represent the woman of the Apocalypse.

Other great discoveries regarding the pure Science of Christian Science, showing our true God-nature, also came to light at that time, and these discoveries have continued to unfold.

Because the 1943 verdict regarding Mrs. Eddy, as published in the periodicals, **had always been the feeling of all loyal Christian Scientists** it was immediately and generally accepted by the church membership. But there were those "in high places" in the movement, who had the "flesh and blood" view. They could not afford this state of affairs, and perceived the "Six Points" only intellectually, not as something revealed by God. They were understandably alarmed at the grim prospects these six points posed for their continued power and authority. Being shrewd and charming performers on the stump, they cunningly seized on Mrs.

---

[1]Many readers of this book have received a letter from me detailing how in 1938, Mr. Richard C. Shoup, Sr. was God-prompted to go to Boston, and while there was able to persuade the Board of Directors to appoint a committee of six to search the archives, resulting in all six becoming convinced that Mrs. Eddy did, indeed, consider herself to be "The Woman" prophesied in the twelfth chapter of Revelation.

[2]For *Mrs. Eddy's Place* and this segment of Christian Science history please write to the author for free pamphlet, *Mary Baker Eddy, Leader Forever.*

Eddy's refusal to *publicly* proclaim herself as the Second Witness and as representing the Woman of the Apocalypse. They interpreted it to be a denial, and again used it to erode her position.

As they succeeded in modifying the official view regarding Mrs. Eddy, the Boston hierarchy prevailed upon Robert Peel, the church's official and authorized biographer of Mary Baker Eddy, to begin turning the tide of trust and reverence away from our Leader.

Peel began his trilogy in 1966. I remember reading his books with great interest, and with admiration for his writing skill. Being an excellent writer, he was able to build up confidence in his correctness and precision. But once he had gained the confidence of his readers, a not so subtle change began taking place. His last book, entitled *The Years of Authority*, was published late in 1977. The careful reader sadly notices how he has begun to negate the place of Mary Baker Eddy in Bible prophecy, and his subsequent humanizing of her life.

Tragically, this Peel book, authorized and promoted by the Boston hierarchy, remains in the Christian Science Reading Rooms, while the wonderful positive books by Sibyl Wilbur, Lyman Powell, Irving Tomlinson and others were gradually removed. Yet, because of the Bliss Knapp controversy they may soon be available again.

Today, unparalleled in Christian Science history, and often masked as an assault on Bliss Knapp's book, the stepped-up Eddy-bashing is culminating in fierce attacks on *her*. Even so-called "loyal" Christian Scientists have been misled to join in this "relentless war against the woman," and those defending her are labelled advocates of deification. So the saga rolls on.

But though the process seems slow, we will all eventually rise above the views that presently shackle mankind. However Mrs. Eddy wrote, **". . . If those calling themselves loyal do not meet the attacks from the disloyal students, with truth relative to the lies told, they will fall and go down taking the Cause with them." Isn't this what has happened? Aren't those who defied the *Manual's* estoppels today mounting a last attempt to pull their tottering hierarchical empire back from the brink? Mrs. Eddy continues, "For I have done my life work [meeting the attacks, the lies]. Now it is you whom God calls to do yours and unless you do it, you will betray this glorious work into the hands of the enemy [the ecclesiastical Goliath], crucify anew the Christ—and kill yourselves because of this"** *(Stetson Letters, p. 5)*.

Mrs. Eddy made it clear that lack of love for her who brought the Second Coming of the Christ would hide her life-demonstration, the human and divine coincidence. Those who lack love for Mrs. Eddy cannot perceive her spiritual individuality, her at-one-ment with God. The arguments of the red dragon keep the truth about Mrs. Eddy hidden. But our love for our Leader will reveal ways we can help the world see her as she is, as God knows her. Our work is to learn to love all mankind as she loved us.

CHAPTER 30

THE FINAL RELEASE

DIVINE LOVE TRANSCENDS DEATH

Those who have not read *Mary Baker Eddy: A New Look*, published in 1980, may find the following account of Mrs. Eddy's last day with us interesting. It relates that **after her passing** she was seen by Adelaide Still, Laura Sargent, and Calvin Frye:

> *As summer gave place to autumn, Mrs. Eddy moved quietly into the closing weeks of her earthly career. On the first of December she went for her usual drive. It was a bright frosty day. Silently she rode through the beautiful winter scene with Laura Sargent at her side. To Mrs. Sargent, Mrs. Eddy seemed intent, perhaps far away, deep in prayer. It was to be her last drive.*
>
> *When she arrived home she asked for her writing tablet and wrote her last message to the world she loved so much: "God is my Life."*
>
> *It was a message that summed up the "Life in and of Spirit" that for forty-four years she had patiently tried to make clear to humanity.*
>
> *The next day she spent in prayer and deep thought, as she sat at her desk. She talked at times to those about her with her usual calm and serenity, but those accustomed to her ways were aware of a change. In the evening she went to bed at her usual time. In the morning she did not get up. It was to be her final day.*

It is reported that she sent messages to the "watchers"—Frye, Adelaide Still, Laura Sargent—and for several hours prayed silently for herself, at the end of which, says Adelaide Still, she was very much improved and asked the watchers to drop the argument. "Just leave me with divine Love. That is all I need."

Battle-scarred and battle-hardened, inured and disciplined by half a century of warfare, this faithful sentinel of God set her face for the last watch in this mental and spiritual Armageddon. The life-and-death struggle between her realization and conviction that Spirit is the only reality, and the "combination of sinners that was fast," must have called up Jesus' lonely fight of which she had written many years earlier:

> *In the garden night-walk, that hour of gloom and glory, the utter error of supposed life in matter, its pain, ignorance, superstition, malice, and hate reached him in their fullest sense. His students slept. "Can you not watch with me one hour?" was the supplication of their great spiritual Teacher, but receiving no response to this last human yearning, he turned forever away from earth to heaven, from sense to Soul, and from man to God. . . .The weight of mind bearing on him at that hour, from the throng of disbelievers in the great Principle for which he was to be crucified, weighed heavily . . . (S&H, Early Edition).*

Mrs. Eddy was speaking for herself as well as for Jesus when she wrote that the real cross Jesus bore up the hill of grief was "the world's hatred of Truth and Love" (S&H 50:30). In the forty-four years since her great revelation of Life in and of Spirit she had done all she could to show that Truth (God) is the actual Life of man, and that Love decrees man's eternal perfection, therefore man is not subject to human birth resulting in death.

Now she must leave the world and commit her writing to honest seekers for Truth. That night at 10:45 (Saturday, December 3, 1910) Mary Baker Eddy—the most spiritually-minded woman in human history, one of the chief characters in the Bible, whom the first edition of Science and Health had unveiled—quietly passed to a higher state of divine consciousness.

ADELAIDE STILL'S ACCOUNT

Carl Lundstrom, for many years a Journal-listed practitioner, had the privilege of interviewing the sister of Adelaide Still, Mrs. Eddy's loyal companion. Her account, given Mrs. Eddy's holy history and her immaculate spiritual understanding that there is no death, carries the ring of truth. Her account of Mrs. Eddy's final hour was known to such stalwarts as Peter V. Ross and Paul Stark Seely, as well as others.

The sister's recital states that only Adelaide Still, Laura Sargent, and Calvin Frye were present with Mrs. Eddy during her last hours. The sister further stated that on that night, Dec. 3rd, the furnace in Mrs. Eddy's Chestnut Hill residence broke down. A repairman was called immediately as it was extremely cold. When the repairman arrived Laura Sargent went downstairs to admit him. Mr. Frye then went down to show the repairman where the furnace was. He quickly returned to the first floor where Mrs.

Sargent waited for him, and together they went to the second floor to rejoin Adelaide Still who had remained with Mrs. Eddy.

When they reached the second floor they noticed Adelaide standing in the doorway leading into Mrs. Eddy's room. Mrs. Sargent called out to Adelaide but she did not answer. Laura and Calvin approached the doorway and stood slightly behind Adelaide. The three, looking into the room, saw Mrs. Eddy standing near the foot of the bed, smiling.

Mrs. Eddy acknowledged their presence and stood silently nodding her head as she smiled at them. She raised her left hand in a sweeping gesture towards the bed *where her lifeless body lay*, and turned her head from side to side, indicating, "No! That lifeless form is not me. 'I am alive for evermore.'"

As they returned their gaze to Mrs. Eddy they witnessed the vision of their beloved Leader slowly fading before their comprehending eyes.

NO WORD UTTERED FOR AN HOUR
(THERE IS NO DEATH)

What an insight into the magnitude of Mrs. Eddy's mission this gave the three faithful watchers.

They must have been overwhelmed with the same feeling the disciples experienced when they beheld their beloved Master being parted from them while he blessed them. (Luke 24:51)

No audible word was spoken. Mrs. Eddy silently communicated the great message that all mankind eagerly awaits to hear, and which all mankind must grow to understand: *there is no death*. Jesus had proved this in the "transfiguration scene" (Matt. 17:1-9) when "his face did shine as the sun, and his raiment was white as light." He showed Peter, James, and John that he and Moses and Elias were forms of light. Dr. Moody, who wrote on life after life, tells us a witness testified to the "indescribably beautiful luminescence of beings in the hereafter who, like Jesus, appear in the "most exquisite light . . . drenching the one in contact with, with a beatific, overflowing, spiritual Love. The love we have on earth for family and friends pales in comparison with the blissful, ineffable, rapturous Love expressed by beings in the hereafter who have grown in nobleness of character and spiritual understanding.

Dr. Moody tells of another witness who saw people standing on a hill, dressed in beautiful robes of magnificent colors. To talk with them she "just thought herself up there" and by desiring to be there, she was there. They spoke to her telepathically. "The ear does not really hear" (S&H 213:17 & 84:19).

Another witness related that "for a brief moment she knew all the secrets of the ages, all the meaning of the universe . . . There was nothing that was not known . . . There are not words in any language to describe it." Mrs. Eddy states: "Human language can repeat only an infinitesimal part of what exists" (S&H 520:5) Here the limitations of time and space do not exist. In a sermon on Life, Mrs. Eddy said, "The side of nature which seems to the senses as matter is but the veil that hides the [glorious] reality of being." (See Mrs. Eddy's references to "translates.") This almost unimaginable splendor is already within us here and now. It only awaits our growth in spiritual understanding.

Returning to Adelaide Still's account, her sister further relates that the three watchers, Calvin Frye, Laura Sargent, and Adelaide, experienced no grief after that moment. However, they each related that for an hour after the vision they could not utter a word.

END OF AN ERA

A booklet, published 1895, *The Latter Days, With Evidence from The Great Pyramid,* stated December 3, 1910 would be the end of the present era. This book (now in the Mother Church Archives) was on Mrs. Eddy's desk (with that statement marked in pencil) on December 3, 1910, the night she passed from human sight. The booklet foresaw a period of great tribulation, following 1910. The past eighty years have borne this out. (See S&H 96 & 97 for Mrs. Eddy's prediction of these times.)

McLELLAN URGES SILENCE REGARDING THE VISION

When Archibald McLellan and Alfred Farlow, representing the Board of Directors, arrived, they advised the members of Mrs. Eddy's household to keep silent about their wonderful experience of seeing Mrs. Eddy alive and smiling after what mortal mind calls death. Mr. McLellan was able to convince the three witnesses that the world would criticize and ridicule Christian Science if they published the facts of what really occurred on the night of December 3.

Thus through fear of ridicule, a blanket of silence descended on the beautiful experience of the three witnesses—only an inner circle of teachers and lecturers became aware of it.

Adelaide Still, Laura Sargent, and Calvin Frye no doubt interpreted what they had witnessed—in the vision of Mary Baker Eddy alive and smiling and then gradually fading from sight—as her *ascension.* If they did communicate this reverent feeling and interpretation to the "practically-minded" McLellan, it no doubt caused alarm bells to ring furiously in his mentality. [Her death, of course, had foiled the triumvirate's plot to take over, Now his concern was **how to cling to power.**] This, along with his fear of ridicule instantly wiped out any desire to participate in their spiritual interpretation.

WHAT JESUS AND MRS EDDY ACCOMPLISHED

The Directors saw Mrs. Eddy as dead, and were intent on burying their concept of her, in accordance with Jesus' teaching, "Let the dead bury their dead." They did not realize "ascension" has nothing to do with taking away a material body, but instead demonstrates there never was life in matter in the first place. Mrs. Eddy had proved beyond cavil that matter is nothing but an image in mortal mind. She had demonstrated to humanity that man is a *calculus* of divine ideas that doesn't come and go, *is not born and cannot die,* but is ever-present as the perfect reflection of living Love, your true identity. We have Mrs. Eddy's promise: "The impersonation of the spiritual idea had a brief history in the earthly life of our Master; but 'of his kingdom there shall be no end,' for Christ, God's idea, will eventually rule all nations and peoples—imperatively, absolutely, finally—with [the] divine Science [she founded in human consciousness]" (S&H 565:13).

Mary Baker Eddy, like Jesus, was well acquainted with the Scriptures. She, like Jesus, knew prophecy cannot be broken. Jesus and Mary Baker Eddy both taught the allness of Spirit and the non-existence of matter. She, like Jesus, sought solitude in hours of communion with God. Like Jesus, she demonstrated her oneness with God by healing the sick, reforming the sinner, and teaching thousands to do likewise. Both Jesus and Mary Baker Eddy knew their own right Mind had sovereign power to think and act rightly. Jesus said, "Heaven and earth shall pass away: but my words shall not pass away" and they have not, and never will. His "words," his promise regarding the "Comforter," his prophecy to St. John on the Isle of Patmos regarding the "little book," and the God-crowned woman of the Apocalypse were fulfilled by Mary Baker Eddy.

As the "Comforter," she explained how Jesus did his healing work. She revealed to us our oneness with Infinite Good and so became the life-link to our divine being. She is thus the greatest, most Christ-like woman planet earth has ever known. Her career is without parallel in human history. As Jesus is loved and honored today, time will love and honor her.

Today we can look back through a mist of tears to the ceaseless toil, the indomitable persistence, self-renunciation and love that cleared the pathway for us. No one else can drain the cup she drank to the dregs as the Discoverer and teacher of Christian Science. But sooner or later we will find that its inspiration cannot be gained without tasting this cup.

Both Jesus and Mary Baker Eddy, "God's two witnesses," fulfilled, without faltering, their separate missions to bring the First and Second Coming of the Christ—to heal and save all that needs healing and saving in a world filled with darkness. Their work on earth will stand forever, revealing to us that God is our own Mind. Their work fulfills Jesus' prophecy to St. John, that "God himself shall be with them and be their God."

As we rise to At-one-ment on wings of Prayer, upheld by love for Mary Baker Eddy, the veil will drop from our eyes. All bondage cease, all fetters fall when we our scepter claim. Touched by the loadstone of Love we learn that "Love alone is Life." We will find God to be with us, to be our God, our own Mind. In Rev. 21: 4 & 5 & 11:17 we read: "And God shall wipe away all tears from [our] eyes; and there shall be no more death, neither sorrow, nor crying, neither shall there be any more pain; for the former things are passed away. And he that sat upon the throne [our own real Mind], said, Behold, I make all things new . . . Thou [meaning you] hast taken to [thyself] thy great power and hast reigned."

ADDENDUM

TODAY'S ATMOSPHERE CAUSES HEALING WORK TO SUFFER

It is imperative that we lift our Leader up before the world. She knew the warfare of Christian Science is never with people but with **mortal sense.** This must be seen so the healing work of Christian Science will not continue to suffer   in today's atmosphere, especially in the United States which presently seems overrun with creeps and criminals; where the ferocity of violent crime has reached truly frightening levels as whole neighborhoods are mired in violence—violence that turns poor neighborhoods into hellholes of fear, decay and human suffering; where guns and drugs are staples of existence, and cops cope with a level of crime that seems to have everyone but the bad guys afraid to walk the streets. Who can concentrate on getting to work on time if it requires an act of courage just to step outside onto the streets?

In Science we are learning there is no danger or calamity at all for right in the place where such conditions are supposed to exist is the presence and power of God.

Never was this healing Truth more needed. Our textbook has forty-five references to "crime," showing crime can only appear where there is ignorance of reality, and where the "dream" is given identity. As all this sin, eroding values, and transgression runs alongside a legal and social culture that is more than a little loosed from its former moorings, we see Jesus's prophecy to St.John (Rev. 12:12, 13, 17) being fulfilled. Jesus said, "Scripture cannot be broken" (John 10:35).

Mrs. Eddy saw this time coming: "Marvels, calamities, and sin will much more abound as truth urges upon mortals its resisted claims" (S&H 223:28), because the "higher Truth lifts its voice, the louder will error scream," but the eternal laws of Truth will continue to unveil error. (S&H 97:23; 542:7).

The rising tide of mediocrity in our schools is alarming. Even more alarming is the radical religious right's (Vatican-aided) full-scale assault on the American public education system. In its wake, as it oozes from coast to coast, this assault would break down our Constitutional church-state separation.

Error, pulling unconscionable lies out of its hat of horrors, seems today determined to stem the tide of Truth. Those back of this frantic, ingrained paranoia, working through the media colossus—film, print, and electronic press—know what Alexander Pope knew when he wrote: "Vice is a monster of so frightful mein, as to be hated, only needed to be seen. Yet seen too oft, familiar with its face, we first endure, then pity, then embrace."

This knowledge on the part of wicked individuals fosters crime and is surely the fulfilling of Revelation 12:12, ". . . the devil is come down unto you, having great wrath, because he knoweth he hath but a short time." Error knows it can't get out from in front of the blade of Truth. It knows it has humanity by the neck only until humanity has a change of consciousness and realizes its freedom through an understanding of the "Comforter," divine Science. Surely the real solution to crime lies in changing the hearts and minds of so-called criminals. This solution is nearing.

One of the biggest news stories, though unreported by the media, is the return to traditional values. Millions have had enough of the rebellious, "anything goes:" sexual "liberation," abandonment of individual responsibility, and the denial of virtue. Now they are participating in a grassroots movement to change this.

IT IS TIME FOR "WOMAN'S HOUR"

Domestic violence, presently an epidemic, has been called "the dirty little secret of America." It too is being given wide attention. The sad historical anachronism that men **own** their wives, that they **possess** them, that wives are just a piece of property—is reinforced today when politicians of the radical "religious" right craftily depict women as chattel, and shamelessly keep their notions right out front. The radical right is **not** a religious movement. It is being exposed as a highly organized, lavishly financed political movement. Venomously "choked with ambition of the meaner sort" (Shakespeare, Henry VI), it is determined to disempower women.

To invoke God's name on behalf of depriving women of equal rights is blasphemy. Our "Bill of Rights" is today under attack. It's time to open our eyes to this monolithic "far right" propaganda machine in its stealthy pursuit of political power that would rob Americans of their constitutional rights. It is releasing its heaviest barrage against women's rights in its spreading coup. Through trust and faith in divine good we must hold these zealots at bay; and prevent their juggernaut—that is working for the steady erosion of constitutional values and individual rights—from turning young minds against our nation's heritage of religious freedom and tolerance. There is much to stand up for. Many wonderful **men** are helping in this struggle, and here and there one finds women who are a disgrace to their sex.

This view against women was imposed on the western world by the Judaizers of St. Paul's writings, with such appalling advice as: "Wives submit yourselves to your husbands, **as unto the Lord!** Here's another one: **"For the husband is the head of the wife even as Christ is the head of the church"!** There are many more such whoppers. For offensively blatant Judaizing, read I Tim. 2:8-15!

Women—Priscilla, Phoebe, Persis, and many more, were leaders in churches St. Paul founded. D ummelow tells us Nymphas was a **woman** and the church was at *her* house. But the Judaizers from the Mother Church in Jerusalem—whom Mrs. Eddy called "dull disciples," and Paul called "dogs" to "beware of" (Phil. 3:2)—doctored Colossians 4:15 to make it sound as though Nymphas was a man, and the church was in *his* house. The Judaizers were always busy behind Paul's back, attempting to undo his inspired teaching which **gives perfect equality to both husband and wife.** Historians tell us the church in Rome contributed greatly to this vendetta against women. "Wife beating, at the church's instigation, had become so popular by the fifteenth century [that even a priest was once moved to protest.] . . . Provided a husband did not kill or cripple his wife, he was free to exercise punishment without the law interfering if she contradicted him or refused to obey his commands" (Women's Roots, p. 179). In the Middle Ages, when the priest "consecrated the bread and wine with "Hoc est corpus meum," Protestants of the Middle Ages contracted it into "Hocus Pocus."

In the battle raging today—as the anti-woman view is crashing on the shores of reality—we see women finally gaining equality with men. We need to stand firm against the serpent. Let's have no more psychobabble about perpetrators as victims—"she provoked it," etc. Glorification of this violence in the movies, T.V., rap music—all peddling violence, much of it against women—contributes to this violence. But "Woman's hour" has come. Relief for the terrible magnitude of violence against women is today beginning to see the light of day, as spiritual wisdom imparts the quantum jump that we are divine beings.

HEAVEN. . . . OR HELL?

"How long [we] will suffer the pangs of destruction [brought by clinging to shattered shibboleths, dogmas, debunked bromides, and rejecting the Truth brought by the Second Coming of the Christ] depends upon the tenacity of these errors." (S&H 296:20.)

Mrs. Eddy, in Prose Works, has a number of references to hell. For the past 20 years hell seems to have been mislaid. It just disappeared and no one noticed. In an update on "Whatever happened to hell?" a *Wall Street Journal* article states, "Hell went into eclipse in the late '60's during the 'Is God Dead?' period. But today it's a burning question on college campuses, cafes, and wherever people meet; even 300-page books on the subject are selling like hotcakes. In a new edition of the catechism of the Catholic Church, the fiery furnace stuff is back."

While at present the scale of the government's incompetence is staggering, the good news is that if enough individuals take responsible action to see that error does not continue to get its way, then, once more the American system will be able to make a mid-course correction before the train goes over the cliff. There can be no doubt America **will** surmount its present difficulties. (See Rev. 21 & 22.) We are heartened by the unparalleled phenomenon of freedom resurging in ancient countries, indicating the twentieth century will close in glory. A great shift in human consciousness toward spiritual awareness is taking place, worldwide, as it moves into a higher dimension of thought. We bless the world when we highlight the positive and recognize what is right with ourselves and others. Looking within, to the kingdom of God within us, we are releasing the imprisoned splendor as we learn to *BE* the glory of God.

"Each successive period of progress is a period more humane *and spiritual*" (*Mis.* 26:4). Today spiritually-minded movers and shakers are redoubling their dedication to see the omnipresence of present perfection everywhere. Like Jesus, who "hated iniquity," they are working to "hold crime [hell, creeping socialism and moral decay] in check. Mrs. Eddy saw the unabashed arrogance of the promoters of socialism masquerading as the stalwarts of the poor while acting as their tormentors. She saw the evil in a government that, like modern day Lilliputians, tied down the mighty engine of capitalism that made this country an economic powerhouse supplying work and salaries to the needy. Democratic capitalism has been history's sharpest weapon against poverty, oppression, and tyranny. She said, "You are master of the bad tendencies of Socialism and not at all at their cruel mercies" *(DCC 108).*

Benevolent agencies are today developing a real blueprint for social betterment, one that will restore the once-reliable sense of civic and moral outrage so needed today. Great credit is due these many philanthropic actors addressing themselves to caring for the destitute, those "who have fallen among thieves" (Luke 10:30); lost in the misery of the streets, their only home the cold, lonely sidewalks. Unshaved, street-beaten and homeless, their clothes stiff with filth, these hurting men, women, and children—broken and weary, alone, lost in addiction and despair—are still good people who often, when given food, will see that the faithful dog sitting beside them is fed first. Wonderful caring agencies are making practical Jesus' parable, Matt. 18:12, 13, enabling many to leave their missions clean, sober and employed.

Amazing and incredible work is also being done in prisons. Prison Fellowship, alone, has more than 90,000 volunteers who invade these fortresses of despair with the hope of the Gospel, causing it to grow exponentially in the most unlikely places: behind prison walls.

Because of this bastion of tolerance, this epochal love in action—the divinely good in human nature—and the many selfless Christian Science prayers, "dogma and creed will pass off in scum, leaving a solid Christianity at the bottom—a foundation for the builders" (*My.* 301:7). The breaking up of material beliefs is forcing error to come to the surface and be corrected. The understanding of our true identity which Mrs. Eddy brought is "propelling the greatest moral, physical, civil, and religious reform ever known on earth" (*Pul.* 20:17). Today, because women have fewer children and live forty years longer than they did a century ago, we stand at the threshold of the greatest creative revolution the world has ever known. As men and women give up the whole level of objective thought and gain the vision given us in Mary Baker Eddy's writings, Revelation XXI with its "new heaven and new earth" will be fulfilled. The time has come to experience what we are as God being.

Great and good goals require great and good people to accomplish them, people who are willing to "work, watch, and pray" for that in which they believe, people who with long-suffering persist until every difficulty is overcome. Eventually all the world will look up to those grand and noble people who patiently persevered to help humanity in its forward march.

AS THE SIXTH-THOUSAND-YEAR PERIOD DRAWS TO A CLOSE

A sense of history suggests we have already turned a page and are in a new era. We must choose optimism, not pessimism. There will be new problems, but the new century will be resplendent with new opportunities to seize as it creates new jobs and wealth for all, at all levels of society.

"The economic advance, of course," says Robert Bartley, "will not necessarily buy happiness. For that we will need a spiritual rebirth, and there are many signs that this is at hand."

Yes, the sixth thousand-year period (from Adam) with its "marvelous good and mysterious evil" (*Mis.* 237:20) is drawing to a close. This sixth period is called the Truth period in which materiality and all ignorance of the infinite good, called God, is being uncovered and is fading, as mankind awakens from the Adam dream of life, substance and intelligence in matter.

Mary Baker Eddy's writings have brought to mankind the truth that exposes the error and rids us of the lie, the hypnotism, which so long has held mankind in bondage.

CHEER UP, TROUBLED WORLD

A recent article by Ann Beals of Bookmark, states, "Above and beyond the discord within the Church a Spiritual Age is dawning. At the heart of this divine event is the light of Christian Science. As this new age unfolds, Christian Science will be recognized as the promised Comforter, and also as a scientific discovery of the first magnitude. Then it will be seen that the challenges we now face are really a growing time in which the present structure of the movement is being forced to change in order for Christian Science to go forward and fulfill its mission of spiritualizing world consciousness."

First and foremost this entails restoring Mary Baker Eddy to her rightful status in world consciousness, which seems at present to be the burr under the saddle of ecclesiasticism intent on disobeying the *Manual's* estoppels.

THE RISING TIDE

Spurred on by empty churches and the loss of healing ability, many are joining the "remnant," the dissidents, insisting on obedience to Mary Baker Eddy's estoppels. They are becoming aware **"Thou shalt obey the Manual"** has been carved on tablets of stone, and we will not be out of the woods and in the Promised Land until it is obeyed. All signs today point to a spiritual renaissance, indicating Babylon-Boston's paralyzing days are numbered. An estoppel-friendly Boston waits in the wings— eager to free the Christian Science Publishing Society to carry out the mission Mrs. Eddy intended, and established it to do. That this will ultimately come to pass there can be no doubt.

As the sixth-thousand-year-period of uncovering evil's nothingness comes to an end, the seventh-thousand-year period of Love is rushing toward us at an ever-quickening rate, and humanity is poised on the edge of a great awakening. Let the little book **sound the trumpet call! Let Mrs. Eddy's Manual be obeyed. Let the Church Universal and Triumphant shake off its chains and rise to lead us forward!**

The moment is coming, as today we see signs of the Boston ecclesiasticism's decay and collapse as the inexorable tide of progress pushes onward the "remnant's" movement to dismantle the rigid authoritarian structure that has been in place since shortly after Mrs. Eddy left.

The freedom movement—demanding obedience to her *Manual* estoppels—is growing in numbers and urgency as it presses to the "possession of unburdened bliss . . . [and] casts out fashionable lunacy" (*My.* 192:4). "Through great tribulation"—as we ride the crest of an immense wave of historical change—a new era of enlightenment is being ushered in, in which "Love fulfils the law of Christian Science, and nothing short of this divine Principle, understood and demonstrated, can ever furnish the vision of the Apocalypse, open the seven seals of error with Truth, or uncover the myriad illusions of sin, sickness, and death. Under the supremacy of Spirit, it will be seen and acknowledged that matter must disappear" (S&H 572:12).

In the first edition we read, "Error will continue seven thousand years from the time of Adam, its origin." In less than a thousand years, looking back on today, we will see it as like the stone age or the cave man days.

Year 2994

"Just think, less than a thousand years ago people thought they had matter bodies— born of a woman—that could sin, get sick, and die!

OUR ancester

Year 1994

"The time will [have] come when the **spiritual origin of man, the divine Science which ushered Jesus into human presence, [IS] understood and demonstrated**" (S&H 325:26).

Then it will be seen that "the depth, breadth, height, might, majesty, and glory of infinite Love fill all space. . . . and thought [will have accepted] the divine infinite calculus" (S&H 520:3) through having learned how the seven synonyms for God (your true divine being) operate through the four divine modes of Word, Christ, Christianity, and Science—the "four sides of the city foursquare" (our true consciousness)—on the four levels of our spiritual thought, namely, Science itself, divine Science, absolute Christian Science, and Christian Science. "The numerals of infinity [our 7 synonyms - timeless eternal values that operate in fixed relations] can never be reckoned according to the calendar of time. [They] appear as mortality disappears, [revealing *humanity's divinity*] eternity, newness of Life, in which [Love and man coexist as Principle and its idea] and all sense of error [has] forever disappeared." We have learned that "Love alone is [our] Life."